THE ECONOMIC DIPLOMACY OF THE SUEZ CRISIS

Diane B. Kunz

~

THE ECONOMIC DIPLOMACY OF THE SUEZ CRISIS

~

The University of North Carolina Press ~ *Chapel Hill and London*

© 1991 The University of North Carolina Press

Library of Congress Cataloging-in-Publication Data

Kunz, Diane B., 1952–

The economic diplomacy of the Suez crisis / Diane B. Kunz.

p.   cm.

Includes bibliographical references and index.

ISBN 0-8078-1967-0 (cloth : alk. paper)

1. United States—Foreign economic relations—Europe—
History—20th century. 2. Europe—Foreign economic relations—
United States—History—20th century. 3. United States—Foreign
economic relations—Egypt—History—20th century. 4. Egypt—Foreign
economic relations—United States—History—20th century. 5. United
States—Foreign economic relations—Israel—History—20th century.
6. Israel—Foreign economic relations—United States—History—20th
century. 7. Egypt—History—Intervention, 1956. 8. Suez Canal
(Egypt)—History—20th century. I. Title.

HF1456.5.Z4E855   1991

327.73'009045—dc20   90-24882

CIP

*The paper in this book meets the guidelines for
permanence and durability of the Committee on
Production Guidelines for Book Longevity of the
Council on Library Resources.*

Manufactured in the United States of America

95 94 93 92 91   5 4 3 2 1

To the memory of my father,
who first introduced me to history books

CONTENTS

~

Acknowledgments   xi

Introduction: The Sinews of War?   1

ONE

Special Relationships   6

TWO

Playing the Game   36

THREE

The Stick, Not the Carrot   58

FOUR

Saving the Nation   73

FIVE

A Fatal Mistake   95

SIX

Using Force   116

SEVEN

The American Way   153

EIGHT

Conclusion: The Importance
of Having Money   186

APPENDIX A

The Anglo-American Financial Agreement   195

APPENDIX B

The Tripartite Declaration   197

APPENDIX C

Information Concerning the Supply
of Middle Eastern Oil in 1956   199

APPENDIX D

Principal Aspects of the Anglo-American
Offers to Fund the Aswan High Dam   202

APPENDIX E

Sterling Assets   204

Notes   207

Select Bibliography   281

Index   289

ILLUSTRATIONS

~

Eisenhower and Dulles meet with
Churchill and Eden   26

Eisenhower and Dulles greet Eden,
Lloyd, and Makins   61

Eisenhower meets with his senior advisors   144

Eisenhower and Dulles confer with
Mollet and Pineau   175

Eisenhower greets Macmillan   184

Eisenhower and Dulles greet
Macmillan and Lloyd   190

ACKNOWLEDGMENTS

~

This book grew out of my continuing fascination with the uses and limitations of economic power in international relations. When I left the world of corporate law in 1983, after seven years on Wall Street, I decided that I would attempt to use my legal and financial training in my historical writing. In an earlier book I examined the actions of American bankers during the British financial crisis of 1931. Now I have sought to illuminate the way in which the American government, after 1945 the financial master of the Western world, used its economic clout during a major turning point in twentieth-century history.

I started this study as a doctoral dissertation at Yale University under the direction of Gaddis Smith. No student could ask for a finer supervisor: as teacher, dissertation director, and colleague he sets a standard I can only hope to emulate. I also benefited from the generosity and guidance of my Yale colleagues John Morton Blum, Peter Gay, Paul Kennedy, and Cynthia Russett.

I also thank for their unstinting assistance Harold James, Fumiko Nishizaki, William McNeil, Joanne Parnes Shawhan, and Marc Trachtenberg.

For my research I relied mainly on archival sources. In this connection I received assistance from the knowledge and expertise of Carl Backlund of the Federal Reserve Bank of New York; Nancy Bressler and Jean Holliday of the Seeley Mudd Manuscript Library, Princeton University, Princeton, New Jersey; the staffs of the Eisenhower Library and the National Archives; Henry Gillett of the Bank of England; Helen Langley of the Bodleian Library; the archivists of Churchill College, Cambridge, and Trinity College, Cambridge; and the gracious staff of the Public Record Office. Crown Copyright documents are quoted by permission of the controller of Her Majesty's Stationery Office.

As a neophyte in the study of Middle Eastern history, I benefited greatly from the advice and encouragement of Wm. Roger Louis, who has done so much to explain the course of Western relations with the developing world. I also received generous assistance from men who participated in the Suez crisis or its aftermath: Raymond Bonham Carter, Lord Caccia, Douglas Dillon, Lord Sherfield, Adam Watson, and Sir Denis Wright.

For the past four years my family has patiently put up with my absorption in the events of 1956–57. I am grateful to my husband, Tom, for his support of this project and his willingness to watch our children on weekends, which gave me extra time to write. I am also indebted to my son Charles whose daily question, "How many chapters did you write today?" spurred me on when I most needed encouragement.

Diane B. Kunz
New Haven
July 1990

THE ECONOMIC DIPLOMACY OF THE SUEZ CRISIS

INTRODUCTION

THE SINEWS OF WAR?

In Washington Lord Halifax
Whispered to Lord Keynes
It's true they have the moneybags
But we have all the brains
—Anonymous

The Suez crisis of 1956–57 remains one of the most interesting episodes in twentieth-century history. When President Gamal Abdel Nasser of Egypt nationalized the Suez Canal on July 26, 1956, he kindled a crisis that exposed the new realities of the postwar world. No longer could imperial powers such as Britain and France force a Middle Eastern nation to do their bidding through force of arms. The British government and people reluctantly confronted the fact that Britain had slipped from the first rank of powers. In the wake of the Suez crisis the United States, which had been using Britain as its surrogate in the Middle East for over a decade, decided that Pax Americana required open American leadership in the region. The Soviet arms deal with Egypt, announced on September 27, 1955, had been one of the factors that had contributed to the crisis; the intermittent Soviet diplomatic initiatives during the fall of 1956 signaled that Moscow would no longer be content to leave the Middle East as a Western sphere of influence. Finally, the emergence of another stage of the Arab-Israeli conflict, which was the trigger event for the military invasion of Egypt, on the one hand illustrated that Israel dominated the region militarily but also demonstrated the implacable nature of the confrontation between Arab and Jew.

Much has been written about various aspects of the Suez crisis and the men who determined its course. Yet the economic diplomacy of the conflict has been neglected. To be sure, authors who cover the topic feel obliged to incorporate certain myths concerning American use of its financial power that have achieved the standing of fact.[1] But nobody has undertaken a systematic treatment of how the American government, with varying degrees of success, used its economic power against Britain, France, Egypt, and Israel. Economic diplomacy defined the course of the Suez crisis from beginning to end.

In 1956 the United States stood at the apogee of influence, among other things, controlling all sources of economic power in the "free world." Ten years after the end of the Second World War, which had devastated the world economy, Western Europe remained heavily dependent on the United States. Britain, in particular, found itself facing a perpetual crisis as it sought to retain sterling's role as an international reserve and trading currency. No other country possessed resources sufficient to compete with or to provide an alternative to American economic power. Accordingly, during the Suez crisis the American government had great latitude to use its financial muscle for political purposes.

The administration of Dwight D. Eisenhower, who held office from 1953 to 1961, looked both to the past and to the future. Many senior Republicans, shut out of office for two decades, retained ideas formed before the depression. Despite America's superpower status, they still feared that crafty, sophisticated Europeans would take advantage of their naive American country cousins. By contrast the president and most of his senior colleagues were men of vision who perceived the massive changes that had occurred during the previous twenty years and tried, with varying degrees of success, to steer the right course. The Suez crisis presented them with a dilemma. While Eisenhower recognized that the British and French governments believed that Nasser had thrown down an unavoidable gauntlet, the president perceived that the time for gunboat diplomacy had long passed. This realization influenced both the administration's decision not to take a confrontational stance against Nasser and its dependence on economic weapons that appeared to offer a way of ending the crisis without resort to military means.[2]

Indeed an act of economic diplomacy, the decision by Secretary of State John Foster Dulles to withdraw precipitately the American offer to fund the Aswan High Dam on July 19, 1956, triggered the Suez crisis. One week later

Nasser proclaimed the nationalization of the shares of the Suez Canal Company and ordered Egyptians to take control of the canal. As soon as the British and French governments discovered Nasser's revenge, they began planning a military response. The American government, increasingly convinced that armed intervention would lead to the wrong war in the wrong place, laid its emphasis on international conferences and multilateral negotiations. In the interim both Britain, to a greater extent, and the United States, to a lesser one, froze Egyptian assets in their countries.

Their economic weapons proved to be ineffective against Egypt, which benefited both from its lack of economic pretensions and from alternative sources of financial sustenance. Furthermore, the American government never utilized all its economic might against Egypt, preferring instead to keep a bridge open to Nasser. After three months of frustrating diplomatic and economic initiatives, Israeli troops, with the cooperation of the British and French governments, invaded Egypt on October 29. Kept in the dark about the Anglo-French demarche, the American government responded by focusing all its economic power on its errant allies. France, having providently borrowed from the International Monetary Fund (IMF) on October 17, proved relatively resistant to American economic power. In contrast Britain remained extremely vulnerable to American financial tactics. British leaders believed the strength of sterling to be both a key indicator as well as an indispensable component of Britain's postwar strength, already seriously eroded. They also remained wedded to retaining financial hegemony over the "sterling area," the group of countries that after 1931 had linked their currency to sterling rather than gold. Prime Minister Anthony Eden and his colleagues had assumed that the United States (albeit perhaps grudgingly) would support any policy choice Britain made. During November the British government struggled against the double-barreled American blows of no aid for the pound, no oil for Western Europe. The battle was uneven, the outcome certain. At the end of the month, the British government agreed to withdraw ignominiously from Egypt, trailing its French ally in its wake.

At this point the Eisenhower administration trained its sights on Israel. While the American government's economic aid to Israel had been stopped on November 1, no action on the much larger American private donations to Israel had been taken. In January the stalemate over Israeli withdrawal from Gaza and the Gulf of Aqaba worsened. During February the administration signaled its willingness to use economic sanctions against Israel. This step proved unnecessary; on March 1 Israeli Foreign Minister Golda Meir announced at the United Nations that Israel would fully withdraw all its forces from occupied Egyptian territory. In this case, the administration used economic sanctions to remind the Israeli government that Israel's national security depended on the United States.

This summary illustrates that the American use of economic pressure produced mixed results: it was effective against Britain, ineffectual against Egypt, with the cases of France and Israel falling into the middle. Economic pressure worked best against Britain because its leaders had created their own vulnerability by placing so much reliance on the importance of sterling. In each of the other cases, the American government found its financial power far less potent. The economic diplomacy of the Suez crisis therefore provides an excellent (and neglected) case study of the use of economic sanctions in international relations. Given the relative decline in American economic potency during the three and a half decades succeeding the Suez crisis, this study also provides instructive lessons for a country that might someday be on the receiving end of economic pressure.

The economic diplomacy of the Suez crisis also presents an enlightening tale of governmental errors. From beginning to end, statesmen miscalculated the course of events and misjudged each other. The process began with the Anglo-American offer to fund the Aswan High Dam. Western leaders believed that because the project was very important to Nasser, donating the money for the dam would win over Nasser for the free world. Yet when he withdrew the American offer, Dulles assumed Nasser would pacifically accept the slight, never imagining that the Egyptian leader would respond by nationalizing the Canal Company.

The chain of miscalculation continued to determine the course of events. As soon as they heard about Nasser's action, British leaders decided upon a military response. As Sir Ivone Kirkpatrick, permanent under secretary of the Foreign Office, said, Her Majesty's Government refused to "perish gracefully."[3] French officials leapt to the same ill-founded decision. They defended their rush to arms on the grounds that one blow against Nasser would be worth a thousand in North Africa. In the aftermath neither justification for military measures could be considered meritorious.

The British government's perceptions about the response of its American counterpart to an Egyptian invasion proved equally faulty. While Eden and his colleagues assumed that the Eisenhower administration would be un-enthusiastic about Operation Musketeer, British ministers believed that they had boxed the American government into a corner where it would have no choice but to support its closest ally. The British government never dreamed that Washington, far from supporting its decision, would actually take the lead in opposing its actions, at the United Nations and elsewhere.

The American government made its share of important miscalculations. Fearing that a direct approach would needlessly alienate its allies, the Eisenhower administration avoided a forceful enunciation of its stand against the Anglo-French military plan, instead placing its faith in oblique pressure. This course backfired, causing far more European hostility than a direct warning could ever have done.

Egyptian and Israeli leaders made their share of misjudgments. Nasser expected neither a world crisis nor a military response to the nationalization of the canal, while the Israeli leaders never realized that their nation, together with its European allies, would be faced with American economic pressure far in excess of that levied against Egypt. All in all the Suez crisis vindicates Dr. Johnson's observation that "every age and every condition indulges some darling fallacy; every man amuses himself with projects which he knows to be improbable, and which, therefore, he resolves to pursue without daring to examine them."[4]

ONE

SPECIAL RELATIONSHIPS

1945–1954

The certainties of one age are the
problems of the next.
—R. H. Tawney

T wo special relationships influenced the course of American economic diplomacy during the Suez crisis. The effect of Britain's declining financial position and its increasing economic dependence on the United States cast the mold in which Anglo-American policy during the crisis would be made. The record of Middle Eastern diplomacy established by Britain, long the dominant colonial power in the region, and the United States, now the leader of the free world, proved equally important. As George Kennan has said, "Every mistake is in a sense the product of all the mistakes that have gone before it."[1]

POSTWAR ANGLO-AMERICAN FINANCIAL RELATIONS

The 1950s represented the apogee of American power. Simultaneously, British strength, seriously ravaged during World War II, continued to decline. This decrease was particularly true in the economic sphere. The United States had emerged from the war as the world's largest creditor; Britain had the dubious distinction of being the world's largest debtor. Of the major powers, only the United States escaped the war and war-related destruction that had decimated the productive capacity of virtually the entire industrialized world.

Becoming the "arsenal of democracy" had turned out to be very good for American business, yet neither the American people nor their government appeared ready to play the part of world economic colossus. Partly responsible for this attitude were the scarring effects of the Great Depression. It had taken the Second World War to lift the nation out of its profound economic slump, and many feared that the war's end would precipitate another financial crisis. Also important were the fiascos of interwar reparations and war debts that stimulated a popular American conviction that Europeans always tried to take financial advantage of the United States. Therefore, the American government often acted the part of a worried and competitive number two, not a country that produced over half of the world's economic goods.

That British leaders failed to comprehend their nation's impoverished state was far more dangerous than American flights of fancy because Britain's financial plight at the end of the war was so desperate. Instead of using American loans to pay for the Second World War, as Britain had done to a substantial degree in the First World War, the mother country had subsisted on American lend-lease aid and had drained the foreign exchange resources of the empire and Commonwealth.[2] By the war's end Britain had accumulated sterling debts of £3.355 billion.[3] These were in the form of sterling balances, blocked bank accounts held in London, three-quarters of which were owed to members of the sterling area, that group of nations that conducted their trade in sterling and allowed Britain to hold their foreign currency and gold reserves.[4] As John Maynard Keynes had warned in 1944, "It seems . . . that the time and energy and thought which we are all giving to the Brave New World is wildly disproportionate to what is being given to the Cruel Real World."[5] Yet the postwar period brought a further expansion of British financial responsibilities with the Exchequer funding the cost of the British occupation forces in Germany and the supply of foodstuffs to the German civilian population in the British occupation zone.

By July 1945, it had become clear to British policymakers that, in Keynes's phrase, Britain was facing a "financial Dunkirk."[6] After President Harry Truman abruptly terminated lend-lease on August 21, Prime Minister Clement Attlee responded by sending a high-level delegation headed by 'Keynes to Washington in the autumn of 1945 to solicit financial assistance. Badly miscalculating the American attitude, Keynes had been relatively sanguine about the chances of a large grant in aid, but he was quickly disabused of this notion. From the British point of view the American picture had changed for the worse. Truman lacked the relatively sentimental Anglophilia of his predecessor; his views reflected the anti-British attitudes of the midwest and of the United States Senate in which Truman had served for over a decade. Sentiment in Congress and in the public at large was running strongly against American aid for postwar reconstruction, as much for economic as political reasons.[7]

Complicating the British position was the fact that even diplomats who liked and admired the British, such as Harry Dexter White, believed that Britain would come out of the war stronger than it had been during the previous decade. White feared that Britain, using the sterling monetary and tariff areas as a base, would develop a network of trade throughout the world from which the United States would be excluded.[8] It would take a further two years for Washington to understand Britain's financial plight, in part because Whitehall's emissaries, still clinging to their nation's prewar status, failed to explain their predicament to their American counterparts.[9]

Despite these and other problems, the American and British governments realized their basic community of interest. After two months of intensive and sometimes painful negotiations the Anglo-American Financial Agreement (U.S. Agreement) was signed on December 6, 1945. Although brief, it did not omit any of the points important to American negotiators. White was not alone in fearing the effect of the Ottawa system of tariffs and exchange controls on American trade;[10] the American business community was well aware that both imperial preference and inconvertible sterling greatly limited the amount of goods which United States companies could sell to the sterling area.[11] The American answer was to insist on including in the U.S. Agreement provisions concerning trade discrimination and currency convertibility. In exchange for accepting these clauses, the British government received a loan of $3.75 billion, together with a generous settlement of Britain's outstanding lend-lease debts.[12] The loan bore interest at the rate of 2 percent per annum, and repayments were not scheduled to begin until five years after the loan agreement was ratified by Congress and Parliament. The British government's default on its World War I war debts to the United States had made both sides sensitive to the difficulty of making repayments during bad years. Accordingly, the agreement included provisions for a waiver giving the British government the unqualified right to postpone an installment of interest (although not of the principal) under certain specified circumstances. Unfortunately, these clauses were ambiguous and never worked as intended.[13]

Rather than receiving plaudits, the British delegation met sharp criticism for signing the U.S. Agreement. As Keynes wrote to an American colleague, "You will easily see how deep is the disappointment and anxiety here."[14] British officials failed to understand that the agreement represented an enormous evolution from the previous American "business as usual" attitude. Instead both Labour and Conservative members of Parliament attacked the American government's lack of generosity and the administration's meddling in Britain's sovereign affairs. To many British officials and to the general public as well, the United States, having so obviously prospered during the war, owed Britain a large grant. Robert Boothby, a prominent Conservative backbencher and close friend of Winston Churchill, expressed the sentiments of many when he labeled the negotiations an "economic Munich."[15]

Notwithstanding the objections, the U.S. Agreement was approved by Parliament, although in the House of Commons the entire Conservative front bench, including Churchill and Anthony Eden, former and future foreign secretary, abstained. During the debate in the House of Lords, Keynes, in one of his last speeches, gave an elegant address mocking an opponent's suggestion that the British opt out of the global economy and set up their own separate, sterling-based system. It would, he said, consist only of countries "to which we already owe more than we can pay, on the basis of their agreeing to lend us money they have not got and buy only from us and one another goods we are unable to supply."[16] Keynes correctly perceived that the British government had no choice but to play the financial game by American rules. This sober fact of life would circumscribe British policy during the next decade. Furthermore, both British policymakers and the public at large failed to come to terms with the reality that from this point on, the American taxpayer would be partially funding both British military might and civilian benefits. Even the most generous benefactor expects to have his opinion taken into account.

Congressional hearings on the U.S. Agreement held in the spring of 1946 revealed that opposition to its terms was not confined to one side of the Atlantic. Where the British saw the return of "Uncle Shylock," many Americans remembered Franklin Roosevelt's observation that the United

States always emerged the loser from any international economic confrontation.[17] The administration was forced to lobby hard to obtain legislative approval of the loan, in a battle that presented a paradigm of the domestic American opposition foreign assistance proposals engender. More than most aspects of diplomacy, positive economic action, especially the granting of foreign aid, remains subject to legislative scrutiny and whim. As with any question of foreign policy, opinions are based on political or diplomatic considerations. Americans of Irish and Jewish descent wished to register their disapproval of specific British colonial policies. The fact of continued British imperialism also raised the hackles of American idealists; the New World's resistance to the British Empire had a long pedigree.[18]

Economic questions, however, contain an extra dimension: individual legislators are influenced by the views of their constituents who often take a dim view of assistance that might jeopardize their own financial well-being. In this case many American companies did not support aid to Britain, which had been their most significant prewar rival.[19] Bankers, eager to expand American financial networks, also opposed such aid. Prewar isolationists and fiscal conservatives also joined the fray, making the battle for legislative approval a close one.[20] The Truman administration achieved success partly because of its willingness to expend the political capital necessary to overcome congressional and public opposition. Equally important was the intensification of the Cold War. The Soviet-American confrontation over Iran helped convince reluctant legislators that the United States could not afford to let Britain plunge into bankruptcy.[21]

The American loan did not end Britain's economic crisis. After a breathing space in 1946, the following year again proved disastrous. By June 1947 the Treasury had spent over half the American loan, and with sterling convertibility under the U.S. Agreement's terms due to begin on July 1, British officials realized that the available dollars would be exhausted well before year's end.[22]

The Cabinet prepared a two-tiered response to Britain's worsening financial plight. The first line of attack was to reduce the scope and cost of British overseas commitments. In February 1947 the British government delivered its famous letter to the American government concerning Greece and Turkey that triggered the Truman Doctrine. Nineteen forty-seven also saw Britain's abandonment of the Palestine Mandate and the decision to accelerate the process of Indian independence. Second, on August 15 the Cabinet decided to suspend sterling convertibility indefinitely. While important, these steps signaled neither the end of the British Empire nor Britain's acceptance of its decline into the second rank of world powers. On the contrary, these and other actions were taken in order to concentrate British strength and maintain that part of the empire deemed salvageable.

Increasingly aware of the financial distress gripping Britain and the rest of Europe, the American government took several important steps. While the administration froze the $400 million balance of the U.S. Agreement upon learning of the British suspension of convertibility in violation of the agreement's terms, Washington did not publicly brand Britain a defaulter. Furthermore, when Britain found itself in dire need of money in December, the administration relented and allowed it to withdraw the final $400 million of the American loan although the Attlee government had not pledged to return sterling to convertibility.[23] More importantly, the American government created the Marshall Plan, which ultimately transferred $13.5 billion to sixteen countries. Motivated by a fear of Communist expansion and a recognition of the dire European economic predicament, the Marshall Plan resurrected the economies of Western Europe. It also represented an American recognition of the United States' responsibilities as a creditor nation. Even so, this realization remained a partial and intermittent one.

Marshall aid, which started flowing in 1948, did not allow the Attlee Cabinet to escape a one-third devaluation of the pound in the autumn of 1949, from £1=$4.03 to £1=$2.80, where it stood until 1967. It had long been apparent that the pound remained overvalued and that, consequently, British exports suffered. But the British government resisted devaluation as long as possible. Opposition from Commonwealth and empire governments, loath to see the value of their frozen sterling balances drastically reduced, partly determined this reluctance. But at least as important was the belief, which grew stronger with every passing year, that the existence of the sterling area and a high exchange rate for the pound remained important both symbolically and actually to Britain's continued status as a global power. That the burdens of the pound's position as an overvalued trading and reserve currency far outweighed the benefits would not be clear for another twenty years.[24]

The British financial position continued to deteriorate during the 1950s.

When, in 1951, the first repayment of the American loan was due, the British government debated whether to try and claim the waiver. Notwithstanding a budget crunch, the Attlee Cabinet decided that it would make the required payments because to do otherwise might jeopardize Anglo-American relations. The following year the Conservative government of Winston Churchill, returned to office in October 1951, came to the same conclusion.[25]

The American government's attitude about its world economic responsibilities in general and toward Britain's financial situation in particular changed surprisingly little during the Eisenhower years. Administration officials, unenthusiastic about foreign assistance, advocated trade, not aid.[26] This approach required congressional backing for the extension of the Reciprocal Trade Agreements Acts (RTAA), which provided a mechanism for reducing American tariffs in exchange for comparable reductions by other countries. Unfortunately many Conservative Republicans adhered to their party's traditional high tariff position. Since 1952, when he received the Republican nomination, Eisenhower had attempted to placate Old Guard Republicans.[27] Once president, the immature behavior of Senate Republicans and the death of Senator Robert A. Taft exacerbated the difficulties of his job.[28] Although the latter had been Eisenhower's bitter opponent until the Republican presidential convention, the Ohio senator had closed ranks with the new president and, as Senate majority leader, lent his considerable conservative credibility to most White House proposals. His death in the summer of 1953 left senators more unruly than ever. Preoccupied with fighting ridiculous notions such as the Bricker amendment, the administration generally took a hands-off approach to questions of economic diplomacy.[29] Unless the point was a major one, the administration conceded and compromised.[30] But because the extension of the RTAA was basic to a trade-focused approach, Eisenhower and his officials used their powers of persuasion on fellow Republicans. Even then the president had first to settle for a one-year extension in 1954, which was followed by a three-year extension the following year.[31]

Increased free trade also required the resurrection of general monetary convertibility. Making dollars freely exchangeable for other currencies, according to free trade apostles, was the only way to increase international trade, which would then extend world prosperity (and American profits).[32] Because they wanted sterling to remain a major trading and reserve currency, British officials were also anxious to return the pound to convertible status. Unfortunately such a step would diminish British reserves of dollars and gold because convertibility means that holders of a currency can exchange it for another currency at will. The need to accumulate reserves haunted every British government from 1945 until the era of fixed exchange rates ended in 1971. But Britain found it difficult to amass new reserves because its financial base was greatly overextended. Three factors caused the Exchequer's plight: first, the cost of social programs that had been implemented by the Attlee government and that, in this era of "Butskellite" consensus, were deemed sacred by both parties; second, the military and related costs involved in the attempt to remain a great power; and third, the costs of maintaining the sterling area.[33] Since British leaders viewed the latter two demands as the pillars on which their greatness rested, they were willing to sacrifice domestic prosperity in order to retain them. Actually, Britain's economic and military "overstretch" proved the ever more significant cause of its economic weakness. Given the unwillingness of government and people to endure wartime controls, Britain simply did not have the resources to match the outlays of the United States or the Soviet Union.

The sterling area represented a continuous problem for Britain after 1945. The contribution of the rest of the sterling area to the sterling area's balance of payments, which had benefited Britain during the war years, reversed direction thereafter, and countries such as Australia now drained dollars from Britain. Furthermore, to the extent that other nations become major holders of a country's currency, the reserve currency country is at their mercy. But, for several reasons, retaining the sterling area remained British policy throughout this period. First, British officials believed that the continuance of the sterling area encouraged the growth of the empire and the Commonwealth trade upon which Britain increasingly depended.[34] Second, the reality of the sterling area seemed to give a tangible substance to the inchoate Commonwealth. Finally, British leaders viewed the sterling area as a substitute both in terms of prestige and power for the greater resources and strength of the superpowers.

Unfortunately part of the price necessary to keep the sterling area alive was the retention of a fixed and overvalued parity for the pound. Indeed the only original British monetary concept of this period, the ROBOT scheme of 1952, which provided for a freely floating pound, was shot down largely by Commonwealth governments; they realized that under the circumstances an unpegged pound would rapidly move in one direction—down. Having lost a third of the value of their sterling reserves consequent to the

1949 devaluation, they warned Chancellor of the Exchequer R. A. Butler and Treasury officials that jettisoning a fixed rate would mean the end of the sterling area. This argument ended the discussion as far as the Churchill Cabinet was concerned, and the British government dropped the concept of a freely floating pound for almost thirty years.[35]

Britain continued to sacrifice to retain the sterling area. After 1954 the Treasury and the Bank of England relied on monetary policy to control British reserves. In other words, interest rates would be raised when the Bank of England's stocks of dollars and/or gold dropped in order to attract foreign investors' deposits to London. As in the late 1920s, internal investment was again dampened by the process now called "stop-go" or "zig-zag" economics.[36] Yet British government officials accepted the price because they never questioned whether the game was worth the candle. At a time when obvious portents pointed to the decline of Britain, they clung with ever greater tenacity to what was left. Unfortunately, by doing so British officials provided the American government with the perfect weapon to use against them. Trying to run a financial system with insufficient reserves meant that the British government was exceedingly vulnerable to financial pressure. That so much had been sacrificed to retain the dollar value of the pound further intensified the British devotion to the rate of £1=$2.80. Consequently, when a choice had to be made, British policymakers could be counted upon to make great concessions in order to save the sterling area and keep the value of sterling high.

The Churchill government similarly clung to military commitments that increased its dependence on the United States. Britain still had the army and the obligations of a great power, but the American government paid many of the bills. The British military received the highest allocation of American mutual security assistance of any country, and as late as 1956, Britain received surplus American food.[37] Such was the price of overextension. The British government clearly had the resources to conduct the foreign policy that Germany, for example, then pursued.[38] It could even afford to be a European power. But London did not want to settle for second rank status. For that, Britain needed American assistance.[39]

BRITAIN, AMERICA, AND THE MIDDLE EAST

That postwar Anglo-American relations reached their nadir over an issue of Middle Eastern policy is not surprising: British governments displayed the

most independence in the Middle East, a region in which Britain traditionally had a significant interest as yet unmatched by a corresponding
American commitment. Yet even there, Britain found it necessary to seek
American intervention at moments of crisis. Such is the price of a declining
empire. But the British government refused to see that asking for assistance
means surrendering autonomy. Until 1956 it suited both countries to present an image of two equal allies jointly formulating policy. The Suez crisis
indelibly altered the picture. Thereafter American dominance was clear for
all to see.

More than any other individual, Ernest Bevin, foreign secretary from
1945 to 1950, molded the shape of British postwar foreign policy.[40] In
company with most of his British contemporaries, Bevin believed that save
for Europe, the Middle East remained the area of greatest importance to
Britain.[41] British interest in the region partly resulted from a sentimental
attachment, similar to what Americans felt for China. Furthermore, pragmatic reasons dictated increased British attention to the Middle East; not
only was it the route of empire and Commonwealth, but this region
provided more and more of the oil on which Britain increasingly depended.

Bevin's policy differed, however, from his Conservative predecessors' in
its emphasis on nonintervention. As Wm. Roger Louis states, "What
distinguished the postwar Labour government was the conscious affirma-
tion of the belief that intervention would ultimately undermine rather than
sustain British influence in the Middle East."[42] The converse was also
believed to be true. Given skillful diplomacy it would be possible for the
British government to retain significant influence in the Middle East, if not
regional hegemony.

The case of Syria presents an instructive example of postwar British
policy. In 1920 the French government received the League of Nations
mandate over Syria. Frequent anticolonialist agitation had led the French
government in 1939 to promise independence to Syria. The war provided a
reason to abrogate its promise. In 1941 Free French forces, aided by British
troops, invaded the country in order to forestall its use as a German base.
While Syrian independence was proclaimed on January 1, 1944, French
officials became increasingly reluctant to cede control, something that
British diplomats found very worrisome. The showdown came in May
1945. With French-Syrian fighting raging in Damascus, British troops
landed in Beirut and marched to the Syrian capital in a decisive intervention
that forced the French troops to agree to a total evacuation.[43] This defeat

marked the end of French control in the Levant. While France retained an interest in Middle Eastern affairs, it became an increasingly tangential one, motivated more by European or North African events than by Middle Eastern developments.[44]

At the cost of placing a great strain on Anglo-French relations, Britain had improved its standing in the Middle East. Foreign Office officials drew the lesson that the demise of the French Empire resulted from injudicious, outmoded operational methods. They responded by placing ever greater confidence in a policy of conciliation. Yet the British government could not see that the Middle East was increasingly being swept by nationalistic forces adamantly opposed to any kind of Western control, whether of the iron fist or the velvet glove variety.

When the Second World War ended, the future of Palestine dominated Middle Eastern relations and also proved the biggest stumbling block for Anglo-American relations. Britain had ruled the area since 1917 but never could reconcile its contradictory commitments to a Jewish homeland in Palestine and the accommodation of Arab rights. The holocaust intensified the question of Jewish immigration to Palestine that Britain had attempted to settle to the Arabs' satisfaction in 1939.[45] President Truman's advocacy of immediate entry permits for survivors of Nazi death camps began two years of Anglo-American disputes over the form and content of Palestine policy. The British government resented the administration's desire for power without responsibility. For its part the Truman administration saw the British government's ostensible evenhandedness as inadequate to the needs and aspirations of the surviving remnant of European Jewry and the Zionist vision. Finally, as the British Palestine garrison grew until there was one soldier for every square block in the country, the Attlee Cabinet, with relief tempered by bitterness at American meddling and Jewish ingratitude, in February 1947 dumped the intractable problem into the lap of the United Nations.[46]

Three months later the General Assembly created the United Nations Special Committee on Palestine (UNSCOP) and charged it with determining the fate of the Palestine Mandate. Unable to achieve unanimity, the committee submitted two reports. The majority advocated partitioning Palestine into separate Jewish and Arab states with Jerusalem to be placed under international control. The minority report, based on an earlier British proposal, called for a single binational state. A rare moment of superpower consensus allowed the partition plan to be approved by the General Assembly on November 29, 1947. That the independent Muslim states unanimously voted against partition prefigured the implacable opposition the Jewish state would meet. Indeed, skirmishing between indigenous Arab and Jewish forces began in the autumn of 1947; the British government's announcement that all its troops would be withdrawn on May 14, 1948, accelerated both sides' preparation for total war.

While Arab forces won the early battles, by April 1948 Jewish troops began to gain the upper hand. On May 14, as the mandate expired, David Ben-Gurion proclaimed a Jewish state and was elected its first prime minister.[47] Both the United States and the Soviet Union immediately recognized the new state. Within hours Egypt, Syria, Iraq, Lebanon, and Jordan declared war on Israel and sent armies to invade the new nation. Again the initial Arab advantage proved ephemeral, and Jewish forces triumphed, aided by inter-Arab rivalries and a divergence of goals among the Muslim nations. Recognition by Arab leaders of their defeat prompted the combatants to enter into a series of cease-fires with Israel in early 1949. However, the Arab League maintained its state of war against Israel, attempting to use economic means to do what military force could not.[48]

The British government not only opposed partition but, once it was a reality, inclined strongly toward the Arab side. Yet, in order to explain their defeat, Arab rulers quickly seized on the explanation that Israel had been aided by Western powers seeking to foist a new colonial foothold on the Middle East. As a result, the creation and continued existence of the state of Israel damaged the standing in the Arab world of the Jewish state's most ardent Western opponent.

The interim settlement of the Palestine problem following the Israeli War of Independence removed the Jewish state from a high place on the current American agenda. However, one significant step was taken in May 1950 when Britain, France, and the United States entered into the Tripartite Declaration, which pledged their governments both to limit the sale of war material to the Arabs and Israelis and to take action should either side be guilty of aggression.[49] The Tripartite Declaration had two purposes. Its immediate aim was to lessen the chances of a second Israeli-Arab confrontation. But it had a more wide-ranging goal: to pave the way for a regional settlement permitting the accommodation of both Israeli and Arab interests in an overall pro-Western framework. Unfortunately for British and

American interests, this quest, which also envisioned a combined Middle East command force discussed below, proved to be not only futile but counterproductive.

Events in Iran and Egypt now shaped Middle Eastern developments. British ties with both remained far stronger than American connections. For this reason and because of the American preoccupation with the Far East, British governments continued to take the initiative in formulating Western policy toward the Middle East during the first decade of the postwar era. Circumstances, however, were not in Britain's favor. In 1948 the Iraqi government, arguably Britain's closest Middle Eastern ally, found it politically impossible to enter into the Treaty of Portsmouth, which would have extended British base rights. As an American intelligence study concluded, for British Middle Eastern policy to succeed would "require a major feat of political juggling because it still involved several contradictory elements and the British are uncertain whether they have found the formula to do so."[50]

Largely because of their realization that the Persian Gulf region was the world's richest source of oil, American officials now began to take an increasing interest in Middle Eastern affairs. What coal was to the nineteenth century, oil became to twentieth-century America—the predominant energy source. While the United States retained significant domestic supplies, in 1948 it became a net importer of oil; by 1953 the American market accounted for over 60 percent of world petroleum consumption.[51] The American government had traditionally left petroleum policy to the oil companies, an approach that did not alter in the postwar years.

The world created by the seven major and various minor (or independent) oil companies was arcane, to say the least.[52] During the early part of the twentieth century, when the importance of petroleum deposits became clear, the seven sisters (as the majors were called) started dividing up rights to oil deposits among themselves; by 1950 this process was virtually complete. Neither supply nor demand influenced the production or price of oil. Given that oil is a fungible commodity the supply of which until recently far exceeded demand, the oil companies realized that unless they rigorously controlled production and price, their profits would be eaten up in price and supply wars. The solution was a series of agreements among the majors and their various joint-venture subsidiary companies, the most famous being the Achnacarry Agreement of 1928.[53] Also known as the As Is

Agreement, the heart of this contract consisted of seven "principles" that provided for the friendly carve-up of world petroleum deposits and markets, to the lasting benefit of the companies but to the detriment of both customers and oil-rich countries.[54]

Among other things, the As Is and other agreements illustrated that the seven sisters believed that antitrust legislation stopped at the water's edge. Yet a symbiotic relationship between Washington and American oil companies serving the needs of both parties had developed by mid-century. Officials acquiesced in demands made by the companies because they believed that the United States was getting an assured supply of a necessary raw material while simultaneously accomplishing various foreign policy goals on the cheap. For their part, the companies wanted government aid without any corresponding responsibility. The evolution of the 50-50 royalty split on oil provides an archetypical illustration of the interrelationship of oil companies and the American government.

Traditionally oil companies paid the host government a royalty determined by the number of barrels produced. In 1948, Venezuela passed a law mandating a 50 percent tax on each barrel of oil extracted. Led by Standard Oil of New Jersey, the various oil companies relatively cheerfully acquiesced because in return they received forty-year contracts and assured government cooperation. Almost immediately King Ibn Saud of Saudi Arabia began agitating for an increase from his royalty payments of 12 percent per barrel. Aramco men in the field and American government officials both sought to placate the Saudi government. As George McGhee, at the time assistant secretary for Near East, South Asia, and African Affairs (and a former vice-president of Mobil), later explained to a Senate committee: "The Arab States were very hostile to us because of our involvement in the Israeli affair[s], as we know. Saudi Arabia . . . was more tolerant than the others. . . . There was, however, threats of strikes against us in Saudi Arabia. Always in the background there was the possibility of some nationalist leader, particularly in the countries where there were kings and sheiks, who might seize power as Nasser did later."[55] Unfortunately, Aramco's parent companies were less than enthusiastic about paying increased royalties. Apparently a Treasury official deserves the credit for the solution: using the tax code, the United States government would foot the bill for increased royalty payments to Saudi Arabia. Royalty payments are generally treated as business expenses which, given a 50 percent corporate tax rate, means that they were worth fifty cents on the dollar. The State and Treasury departments, in collusion with the oil companies, now proposed to treat these royalties for tax purposes as foreign income taxes, which would be granted a dollar for dollar credit against American taxes. The fact that Saudi Arabia had neither many corporations nor a corporate income tax was remedied by dispatching a team of Treasury and industry lawyers to Riyad to draft a corporate tax code for Ibn Saud.

The resulting transfer of dollars from the American Treasury to the Saudi one was clear. In 1950 Aramco paid the U.S. government $50 million in income tax, and the Saudi government received $66 million. The following year Aramco paid only $6 million to the American Treasury while Ibn Saud received $110 million from the company. In 1952 Aramco paid only $1 million in United States taxes and thereafter, due to the foreign tax credit, paid no American income tax.[56] But because they credited these increased revenues with keeping Saudi Arabia on the American side, both the Truman and Eisenhower administrations approved. Even better, this subsidy was not subject to congressional scrutiny or veto. The American oil companies were delighted, for they had further entrenched their positions in the Middle East at no cost to themselves.

For their part, neither British businessmen nor government officials shared this enthusiasm because the American action negatively affected Britain. It increased the prestige and power of the Saudis, who were not British clients and in fact would soon begin feuding with the British protectorates later known as Oman and the United Arab Emirates over the oasis of Buraimi. More serious was how knowledge of Saudi Arabia's increased oil revenues exacerbated the tensions between the Anglo-Iranian Oil Company (AIOC) and the Iranian government. Britain had long controlled the oil of Iran; drilling rights had been granted to what was then known as the Anglo-Persian Oil Company in 1901.[57] Fifty-one percent of the shares of AIOC had been purchased by the British government at the instigation of Winston Churchill to ensure an adequate supply of oil for the Royal Navy. British dependence on Iranian oil grew in tandem with AIOC's expanding production: in 1945 oil pumped from four Iranian fields exceeded the combined production of all Arab states.[58] The refinery at Abadan, the world's largest, was a gigantic installation whose British employees and their dependents lived a sheltered, truly British life.

Production consistently increased during the postwar period. In 1952 world oil production was 637 million tons, of which 30 million came from Iran.[59] Such high production benefited Britain because it allowed Britain to pay for oil in sterling, thus obviating the need to spend still precious dollars. During the postwar period British domestic use of oil increased rapidly, and unlike the United States, which possessed significant domestic reserves, the British relied wholly on Middle Eastern imports. Furthermore, AIOC's production earned for the British Treasury, $400 million per annum in foreign exchange.[60] But this bounty came at a price. The British government found its policy put into jeopardy by a company whose shares it controlled but whose policies were autonomous. Indeed AIOC was rivaled only by the Suez Canal Company in its ability to learn nothing and forget everything.

The Aramco agreement with Saudi Arabia began a period of increasing tension in Anglo-Iranian relations. In early 1951 AIOC offered a contract similar to the Aramco agreement to the Iranian government. This gesture came too late and promised too little. The British government's concurrent announcement that it would help AIOC resist nationalization then escalated the conflict. Pro-Western Prime Minister Ali Razmara's attempt to avoid a confrontation ended in his assassination by an Islamic fundamentalist on March 7, the day before the oil committee of the Majlis (the Iranian Parliament) voted to nationalize the oil concession; the full Parliament approved the measure on March 15.

The nationalization laws and accompanying implementation decrees received the assent of the shah of Iran and went into effect on May 1, just two days after the appointment as prime minister of Mohammed Mussadiq, the man who deserved the bulk of the credit for the expropriation.[61] While to the Iranians Mussadiq was a hero, the British government, regarding him as a demagogic fakir, intended to resist the new order in Iran.[62] Secretary of State Dean Acheson responded to the Iranian nationalization of the AIOC facilities in May 1951 by declaring that "we recognize the right of sovereign states to nationalize provided that there is just compensation."[63] Although the British government recognized this right for itself (during the preceding six years the Labour government had nationalized major segments of British industry and services), its tolerance of such things did not extend to underdeveloped nations. Fundamentally, Britain, retaining its imperialist mentality, regarded Middle Eastern nations as less sovereign than itself. However, the British government worried that the

Iranian action would trigger a domino effect that could imperil all their foreign investments if a strong stand were not taken over Iran.[64] The Truman administration was much more aware of nationalism's growing importance and, so long as the issue was not obfuscated by anticommunism, sympathized with peoples who were in its eyes emulating the American example in liberating themselves from the British.

As the Anglo-Iranian crisis worsened, the United States walked a fine line. While the Truman administration strongly cautioned the British against the use of force, officials also took a tough stance against nationalization. On May 18 the State Department issued a statement deploring unilateral cancellation of contractual commitments.[65] Unsatisfactory negotiations in May and June brought an end to Iranian oil production, the departure of the manager of the Abadan refinery, and an AIOC threat to pull out all personnel. As British warships assumed a threatening stance Truman proposed that veteran American diplomat Averill Harriman serve as mediator and try to reopen negotiations. The Iranian government quickly accepted the offer, and while British officials remained unenthusiastic, Harriman journeyed to Teheran in July 1951.

By the end of the month Harriman had devised a proposal that led to Anglo-American negotiations. When they foundered, at the end of August, the British government declared the talks irrevocably broken off and withdrew all British personnel from the oil fields. Rejecting Harriman's advice to let the situation simmer, the British government opted for a show of force, sending four destroyers to join the ten British naval ships already in the Persian Gulf. In early September, attempting to tighten the economic noose, the Bank of England removed Iran from the transferable account area, thereby denying it the use of dollar reserves. Iranian forces then occupied the Abadan refinery and demanded that all British employees of AIOC leave the country by October 4. The British government considered invading Abadan Island, but as Prime Minister Attlee informed his Cabinet on October 4, it did not seem expedient to use force "in view of the attitude of the United States government."[66] Instead both the Iranian and British governments waited for economic pressure to take its toll.[67]

Contemporaneous events in Egypt helped convince the British government not to take military action against Iran. Since 1882, when British forces entered Cairo, Egyptians had attempted to expunge the British presence from Egypt. The high-handed actions of British officials during the Second

World War, combined with the Indian and Palestinian examples, gave new momentum to the nationalist movement. The postwar atmosphere was evocatively described by Anwar Sadat: "Egypt lived in terror, with the severest restrictions of the freedoms of meeting, speech and the press. She was in a pre-revolutionary state."[68]

During the two years immediately preceding the Egyptian revolution of 1952, Anglo-Egyptian relations steadily deteriorated. Whitehall miscalculated by sending Field Marshall Sir William Slim in June 1950 to discuss security questions. The hero of the British campaign in Burma conveyed to the Egyptians the impression that the British government intended to perpetuate the old imperial order. Strained Anglo-Egyptian negotiations stalled during 1951 over the issue of the Sudan. Since 1899, Britain had ruled what was theoretically a joint Anglo-Egyptian condominium. While British diplomats envisioned that the Sudan would become an independent nation, their Egyptian counterparts sought to incorporate it into Egypt.

Exacerbating tensions further was the future of the huge British base at the Suez Canal to which British military forces were guaranteed access by the Anglo-Egyptian Treaty of 1936. This enclave extended from the Mediterranean to the Red Sea and westward almost to Cairo, including the depot at Tel-el Kebir, the site of the Egyptian defeat in 1882 that signaled the British triumph. The base covered 9,714 square miles and was built at a cost to the British government of £500 million. During the war there were over 200,000 troops stationed there; by the beginning of the next decade close to 50,000 men remained.[69]

The loss of India and Palestine, which British military men had coveted as a perfect Middle Eastern base, increased the importance of the Egyptian location. Although Egyptians had conducted a campaign of harassment against British soldiers since the war's end, the Churchill government clung to the base. American officials, increasingly concerned at the negative effect of the base issue on Anglo-Egyptian relations, devised, with their British counterparts, the Middle East Defense Organization. Cast in the mold of the North Atlantic Treaty Organization (NATO), it was designed to enclose British retention of the base in a multilateral package. Western officials hoped this wrapping would make the perpetuation of British control more acceptable to Egyptian opinion.[70]

Yet the future of the Suez Canal constituted the most important component of Anglo-Egyptian relations. The Suez Canal Company (officially the

Compagnie Universelle du Canal Maritime Suez) was an Egyptian-chartered company, owned by British and French investors, with the British government holding 44 percent of the voting shares. To the British, the canal was, in the oft-quoted phrase, the "lifeline of Empire." Originally India had been the chief motivation for the British purchase of the Canal Company shares and subsequent control over Egypt. After the Indian subcontinent's independence, British officials supplied new reasons to retain possession of the canal: to maintain as close contact as possible with the empire and Commonwealth, which in the postwar years became ever more important to Britain, both symbolically and economically; and to ensure Britain and Western Europe a reliable source of oil. Unlike the United States, which at mid-century utilized significant domestic petroleum deposits, Britain relied on Middle Eastern oil shipped through the Suez Canal.

Egyptians of all political persuasions took an opposing view. The Canal Company ranked as the richest corporation in Egypt, with a market worth in the mid-1950s exceeding £70 million. Profits paid to foreign shareholders stayed high in part because monies paid to the Egyptian government remained low. Furthermore, the Canal Company remained an unreconstructed imperial venture. Egyptians were hired only for menial positions and then often grudgingly. Consequently, pride and profit both dictated that repossessing the canal become a central Egyptian aspiration.

In October 1951 Egyptian Prime Minister Nahas Pasha announced the abrogation of the Anglo-Egyptian Treaty, which still had five years to run. The atmosphere in Egypt grew increasingly tense. In January 1952 a small incident ignited the Cairo riots that left the famous Shepheard's Hotel in flames and nine British subjects dead at the Turf Club, the bastion of British privilege. This explosion signaled the start of the Egyptian revolution. King Farouk dismissed Nahas and during the next six months four prime ministers attempted to form a government. Martial law was declared as a sense of impending radical change grew. Increasingly the future seemed to belong to a group of military men, which included Gamal Abdel Nasser and Anwar Sadat, known as the Free Officers. The king, doubting the army's loyalty, decided to arrest some of the dissident officers on July 20. The Free Officers answered with a flawlessly executed coup, and by July 23, 1952, they controlled both the army and the nation. On July 26 King Farouk left for exile. Most of his countrymen shared the feelings of Jehan Sadat, who rejoiced that "for the first time since the Persians invaded Egypt in 522 B.C., Egypt would be governed by an Egyptian."[71]

Initial Western reactions to the Egyptian revolution were favorable. Mohammed Neguib, the most respected general in the Egyptian army, received the titles of commander-in-chief and president of the Revolutionary Command Council. He presented a liberal but not unduly threatening image; outsiders as yet did not realize that Neguib was a figurehead for younger and more radical men such as Nasser and Sadat. British officials expressed satisfaction that the new government was willing to take a conciliatory position on the Sudan. American diplomats approved of the regime's assertion that it would concentrate on domestic reform rather than on a "second round" against Israel. On September 3 Truman, at Acheson's suggestion, made a favorable statement on the Neguib regime and hinted at possible American aid.[72]

Prime Minister Churchill never understood the unshakeable grip of nationalism on the Arabs. Nor could he accept that the British government might have to alter how it ran the empire. Yet Churchill, far better than Foreign Secretary Anthony Eden, accepted that British power now depended on the United States for its basic sustenance. As he had written to Lord Cranborne in 1945: "Always remember that there are various large matters in which we cannot go further than the United States are [sic] willing to go."[73]

American policymakers took British dependence for granted. As a State Department intelligence report on the British position in the Middle East concluded, "A major factor of strength in the present British position is that the United States has supported the basic assumption that the United Kingdom is the predominant power in the Middle East." Yet, as this report recognized, American support of the British position ran the risk of identifying the United States with British imperialism, to the detriment of American goals.[74] The Eisenhower administration would be forced to try to reconcile the irreconcilable—to continue to support Britain, fellow Anglo-Saxon and ally in the fight against communism, while also encouraging the growth of a benign form of nationalism in the Arab world.

EISENHOWER'S AMERICA

Winston Churchill welcomed the prospect of Dwight D. Eisenhower as president of the United States. Having cooperated successfully during the Second World War, Churchill hoped to resurrect what Eisenhower termed "the special place of partnership they [the British] occupied with us during

Eisenhower and Dulles meet with British Prime Minister Winston Churchill and Foreign Secretary Anthony Eden at the White House, June 1954. (Courtesy Dwight D. Eisenhower Library/National Park Service)

World War II." The president-elect, for his part, rejected the idea of a special relationship. While there might be occasions when prior Anglo-American discussions would be desirable, Eisenhower intended "to treat, publicly, every country as a sovereign equal."[75] Even without other problems, such divergent views of their relationship would lead to friction between the two allies.[76] Another complicating factor was that the British, in common with most Europeans and many Americans, underestimated the new president.

Having spent a quintessentially American boyhood in Abilene, Kansas, he had attended West Point. Thereafter Eisenhower had made a career for himself in the peacetime American army, serving as an aide to General Douglas MacArthur, first in Washington and then in the Philippines.[77] The imperious MacArthur no doubt provided a perfect illustration of how a military man should not conduct himself. This lesson served Eisenhower well during the Second World War when he demonstrated an uncanny ability to get along with Roosevelt and Churchill as well as difficult fellow officers such as George Patton and Bernard Montgomery. After the war Eisenhower served first as president of Columbia University and then as supreme allied commander in Europe. Both political parties tried to capture him; the Republicans' victory over the general prefigured their first presidential success in twenty years.

The newly elected president was a strange blend of the provincial and the sophisticated. He certainly did not have the elegant breeding or the cosmopolitan interests of a Roosevelt or a Harriman. Yet in 1953 he was no political neophyte; he already had a decade of experience dealing with European allies. Furthermore, it is clear that to the extent he wished it, which varied depending on the subject, Eisenhower made the decisions in the White House. The allies' failure to perceive his power led them to assume that the secretary of state orchestrated foreign policy. This mistake would cost them severely.[78]

Various high-level appointments also increased the tension between Washington and London. The first was the selection of John Foster Dulles as secretary of state.[79] Both his grandfather, John Foster, and his uncle, Robert Lansing, had been secretary of state. Dulles attended his first international conference at The Hague in 1907 and in his early thirties joined his uncle's team at Versailles.[80] It was already obvious that he shared with Woodrow Wilson a principled, moralistic conception of international relations, strengthened by a strong Christian faith. It was equally apparent that Dulles, like Wilson, had the faults of his virtues. The same belief in the rightness of his cause often turned to self-righteousness and could become an impediment to understanding the merits of the other side's position, especially since this belief coexisted with Dulles's driving ambition to succeed.

During the 1920s Dulles, now a partner at the New York law firm of Sullivan & Cromwell, became known as an expert on German debt in general and reparations in particular. The advent of Adolf Hitler and the National Socialist dictatorship did not unduly trouble Dulles. As head of his law firm, he allowed it to maintain a Berlin presence long after other American law firms had left.

Not previously identified with any party, Dulles spent the war years as foreign policy advisor to Republican presidential contender Thomas E. Dewey. Mindful of the partisan fiasco at the end of the First World War, both Roosevelt and Truman consciously appointed Republicans to foreign policy-making positions. Appropriately, Dulles served as a member of the American delegation to the United Nations from 1945 to 1949. Appointed to fill an interim term as senator from New York in 1949, the next year he ran for a full term. After an unpleasant campaign that included anti-Semitic slurs against his opponent, Herbert Lehman, Dulles was defeated by a narrow margin. Restless in the practice of law, he approached the Truman administration for another assignment. Although Dulles had run on an anti-Truman platform, the administration opted for pragmatism over pique, and Acheson appointed him chief negotiator for the Japanese peace treaty in May 1950.[81]

These negotiations, which were concluded in September 1951, marked the beginning of Dulles's discordant relationship with Anthony Eden. The so-called Yoshida Letter concerning the question of Japanese recognition of the People's Republic of China provided the igniting spark. The United States did not maintain diplomatic ties with the Communist government and only reluctantly accepted the British decision to recognize the Communist regime. The British government remained under the impression that the question of Japanese recognition of the People's Republic was still unresolved when, in the summer of 1951, it became public knowledge that Japanese Prime Minister Shigeru Yoshida had secretly agreed in writing with the United States not to establish relations with Beijing. The Cabinet responded in anger, Eden believing that American officials had deliberately misled him. For their part Dulles and Acheson maintained that the slip was inadvertent. In any case, this incident proved prophetic.[82] Furthermore, the Yoshida Letter imbroglio led Eden in the spring of 1952 to advise Eisenhower not to nominate Dulles as secretary of state should Eisenhower be elected president.[83] As can be imagined, this meddling did not endear Eden to Dulles.

Another incident that prefigured the problems that would plague Anglo-American relations during the Eisenhower years occurred during the interregnum prior to the former general's inauguration. The imbroglio centered around Dulles's precipitate announcement that Winthrop Aldrich would replace Walter Gifford as ambassador to Britain. As Dulles had not previously informed either Gifford or the British government that the statement would be made, both were justly angry. Dulles acted with undue haste because he had learned that the change was about to be leaked to the press.

In a demonstration of the same need for control that would be evident throughout his term in office, Dulles quickly announced the news himself.[84] As Eisenhower reflected in his diary, Dulles "seems to have a curious lack of understanding as to how his words and manner may affect another personality."[85] The appositeness of the president's observation would be proved again and again in the years that followed.

The selection of George Humphrey as secretary of the Treasury would also have major ramifications on British affairs.[86] Back in the days when the American steel industry played a dominant role in the nation's economy, Humphrey, as head of the Mark A. Hanna Company of Cleveland, Ohio, more than fulfilled the expectations placed on him, actually running his company at a profit and expanding its operations during the depression. His chief experience in public service was as head of the Reparations Survey Committee, which studied postwar industrial conditions in Germany. Eisenhower esteemed him highly, writing that Humphrey was "possessed of a splendid personality" and noting that he always added something to any conference he attended.[87] Sharing Humphrey's passion for economy in government, the president often deferred to his treasury secretary. As Eisenhower's first term progressed, the intimacy between the two men increased, and the president began vacationing at Humphrey's Thomasville, Georgia, plantation.

Humphrey tirelessly spread the gospel of a balanced budget. Building on the precedents set by Henry Morganthau and Harry Dexter White, he involved the Treasury in international relations to an unprecedented degree. To Humphrey foreign aid usually fell into two categories: either it consisted of unproductive loans that would threaten to unbalance the American budget, or the money would be used to create successful businesses that would then compete with American companies. In either case, Humphrey generally opposed Treasury subsidies.[88]

Because of the saliency of economic issues, Humphrey played a prominent role in Anglo-American relations. His influence was increased further because Dulles, despite the fact that he had made his reputation in the field of international finance, proved surprisingly uninterested in economic diplomacy once he became secretary of state.[89] Instead Dulles delegated foreign economic questions to a succession of subordinates; from 1954 to 1957 Under Secretary of State Herbert Hoover, Jr., had this responsibility.[90] That Hoover relied heavily on the advice of his close friend George

Humphrey again multiplied the treasury secretary's leverage.[91] For their part, British officials found Humphrey puzzling. He established warm relationships with British Ambassador Sir Roger Makins and Economic Secretary Lord Harcourt.[92] Yet British diplomats remained perplexed by this man who did not share the Anglophilia of most American financiers and viewed European countries as a "gang of spenders."[93]

Eisenhower's selection of Henry Cabot Lodge, Jr., to be the American ambassador to the United Nations also significantly affected Anglo-American relations. The president continued to be grateful to the Massachusetts man who had run the successful Eisenhower-for-president drive, in the process sacrificing his own Senate seat. Eisenhower promised his new ambassador Cabinet rank, which gave Lodge reason to believe that he would have ample authority to implement his plans to cement an alliance between the United States and the independent nations of Asia and Africa. Lodge's almost messianic antiimperialism, as well as the anti-British bias Walter Lippmann had rebuked him for ten years earlier, would have major consequences in the years ahead.[94]

MAKING MIDDLE EASTERN POLICY

A State Department assessment prepared in December 1953 revealed the new administration's view of the Middle East. The report concluded that due to Britain's overall loss of power, its declining role in the region had to be assumed. Arab countries would thus "naturally turn to the United States as the stronger power (and whose traditions are intended to be sympathetic to nationalism and colonialism) to help solve their problems with the British." Officials worried that this area could be "lost," not as a result of direct Russian aggression, but rather if the Middle Eastern nations began "to look upon the West with greater fear and suspicion than they do their northern neighbor, the Soviet Union." Therefore, the State Department's goal was "neither the removal or the replacement of British influence but rather its strengthening and effective readjustment to present day realities."[95]

The particulars contained in this memorandum formed the basic principles that governed the Eisenhower administration's Middle Eastern policy. That the president and his officials viewed Middle Eastern questions with more urgency than had their predecessors was immediately clear: Abba Eban, Israeli ambassador in Washington during the Eisenhower years, ascribed this change to the fact that "Dulles, unlike Acheson before him, found intellectual fascination in issues that seemed to bore his predecessor to death."[96] The administration's Manichaean worldview, featuring a constant struggle between the free world's light and the darkness of the Communist side, also contributed to Washington's intensified interest in Middle Eastern problems. In the contest between the Soviet Union and the United States for the hearts and minds of the underdeveloped world, every country counted. The Arab world was a valuable prize for several reasons: its proximity to the Soviet Union, the presence of oil deposits, and its size.

Where Dulles saw the Communist nexus when he thought about the Arab world, State Department officials were influenced by their dislike of Zionism. Indeed Eliahu Elath, Israel's first ambassador to the United States, wrote that he never met a State Department official who was sympathetic to Zionism.[97] While during the Truman administration there were countervailing pressures to the view from State, in the Eisenhower years, the Bureau of Near Eastern Affairs occupied the middle ground and consequently proved more influential. The president believed that if he had been in Truman's shoes, he might not have recognized Israel. Dulles maintained that the Truman administration had "gone overboard in favor of Israel." Officials therefore intended to replace this perceived tilt toward Israel with a policy of evenhandedness between the Arabs and the Israelis that boded ill for Israel.[98] Not surprisingly, Abba Eban would later recall the "extraordinary gravity" of Israel's position during 1953–56.[99]

Yet, for all the administration's rhetoric, it must be emphasized that to the president and his colleagues this area of the world still ranked in importance well below Europe, Latin America, and the Far East. Indeed the administration paid significant although still intermittent attention to the Middle East only when Moscow began to show interest in the region. It took the Suez crisis to make Middle Eastern policy, at least temporarily, a matter of first importance.[100]

Iran was the major issue dominating Anglo-American discussions about the Middle East during the first year of the Eisenhower presidency. Britain and Iran had continued their confrontation throughout 1952. With American help, AIOC shut out the National Iranian Oil Company from the international oil market. As revenues from petroleum production dwindled, the Iranian government, which depended on oil for most of its foreign exchange, was left in a precarious position.

The noose tightening, Mussadiq, on May 28, 1953, again appealed to the United States for economic aid. After a month Eisenhower denied the request. The American refusal intensified the pressure on Mussadiq, losing support from the army and the mullahs, to take drastic action. In response, he announced his plan to dissolve the Majlis, although under the Iranian constitution this step was the prerogative of the shah. The shah in turn dismissed Mussadiq as prime minister on August 12. Mussadiq refused to leave, and the shah, fearing for his safety, fled the country. But Mussadiq had not sufficiently protected his position, and as Tudeh (Communist) party mobs rioted and attacked mosques, resistance to the prime minister spread. On August 19, gigantic pro-shah demonstrations, aided by the Central Intelligence Agency (CIA) and British intelligence, took place in major cities. The armed forces, religious leaders, and pro-royalty factions, also backed by the CIA and British intelligence, united against Mussadiq, who was subjected to house arrest. The shah returned, and his retainer Ahmed Zahedi was installed as prime minister. The United States now quickly moved to support the new government, sending a $45 million emergency grant on September 5.[101]

Although the AIOC concession was not reinstated, and the National Iranian Oil Company remained the owner of the Iranian oil fields, a consortium of foreign oil companies was given the right to control and market the oil.[102] That AIOC's share was cut to 40 percent did not embitter British officials as much as might be expected. Rather, many in the government and Foreign Office took the view that without the American action, AIOC would not have retained any oil rights at all.[103] As with the Palestine issue, the outcome of the Iranian dispute should have put the British government on notice that a heavy price had to be paid for American assistance. Furthermore, the reduction of Britain's ownership interest in Iranian oil from 100 percent to 54 percent increased Britain's vulnerability to Arab pressure and also lowered the Exchequer's hard currency earnings from oil payments.

What shifted American policy from nonintervention to active plotting? Although Mussadiq had first solicited the American government for financial assistance, his announcement of negotiations with the Soviet Union provoked the administration. The increasing importance of oil played a key part. Indeed reexamining the Iranian confrontation, the president wrote his brother: "A year ago last January we were in imminent danger of losing

Iran, and sixty percent of the known oil reserves of the world. . . . There has been no greater threat that has in recent years overhung the free world."[104] Too, it must be said that the Eisenhower administration justified covert operations as qualitatively different from overt military action, particularly if there was an anti-Communist nexus. Understandably but unfortunately, British and French statesmen never comprehended this distinction.

With Iran, Korea, and the death of Josef Stalin preoccupying the administration, other diplomatic questions received little White House attention during 1953. This approach was in keeping with Eisenhower's management style. Trained by years of army experience to delegate, the president appointed men whom he trusted and, except in times of crisis, left them alone to run their departments. While Dulles was not originally an Eisenhower man, their relationship evolved into one of mutual respect and loyalty during seven years of collaboration. In large measure their relationship proved successful because the secretary cultivated his chief; Dulles made it clear that he would never attempt his own foreign policy. In return Eisenhower gave his subordinate wide latitude to implement policies jointly agreed upon. But many observers, in the 1950s and thereafter, misunderstood their partnership. In fact, Eden, writing to Churchill on Easter Sunday, 1957, said: "Ike may protest that he means well, may be he does, but he don't [sic] count much more than Petain did. Laval did the work."[105] That Dulles accepted blame as well as credit for actions mutually agreed upon further increased the president's affection for him.

For Churchill and his colleagues, Egypt remained a major problem during 1953 and 1954. At the personal urging of the prime minister, Eisenhower to a lesser extent and the State Department to a greater extent became involved in the emotional issue of the future of the Suez Canal base.[106] American officials realized, as their British counterparts could not, the depth of the Egyptian resentment toward Britain. However, although anxious to cultivate the Free Officers' regime, the administration held up American aid pending resolution of the base's future.[107]

As the Anglo-Egyptian negotiations on the future of the Suez Canal base continued, it became clear that the two sides held irreconcilable positions.[108] The Egyptian government found the Churchill Cabinet's desire to retain an ongoing presence in Egypt totally unacceptable. Furthermore, the successful American detonation of a thermonuclear device and related technological advances made far-flung bases, including the Suez location, less necessary in any conflict with the Soviet Union. Slowly the British negotiators gave way, eventually agreeing to the total withdrawal of both British troops and technicians. American officials, particularly Ambassador to Egypt Jefferson Caffrey, took a major role in the discussions, Caffrey later saying that the part he played in the Anglo-Egyptian negotiations "was the most complicated in his forty year career in the Foreign Service."[109]

Yet administration pressure was not solely responsible for the seemingly felicitous conclusion to the Anglo-Egyptian discussions. Just as important was the entrance onto center stage of Anthony Eden, who took the leading role in the negotiations after Churchill suffered a stroke in June 1953. Eden's career is one of the most interesting in twentieth-century history.[110] After studying Persian and Arabic at Oxford University, Eden chose to enter politics rather than join the diplomatic service. His rise was swift, in part due to his extraordinary good looks and the patronage of Stanley Baldwin. When Baldwin became prime minister in 1935, Eden entered the Cabinet as minister without portfolio for League of Nations affairs. There his idealistic attitude toward the world organization served as an inspiration for younger colleagues and the general public.[111] Six months later, when Samuel Hoare resigned over the issue of Abyssinia, Eden, only thirty-six, replaced him as foreign secretary.

Just over two years later, it was Eden's turn to resign. Notwithstanding the popular image, Eden and Prime Minister Neville Chamberlain did not come to a parting of the ways, as it were, over the appeasement of Adolf Hitler. In fact, before the war Eden took a fairly muted view of the Nazis. Rather, Chamberlain's insistence on conducting personal diplomacy with Benito Mussolini drove Eden out of the Cabinet. Thereafter, although he had not completely thrown in his lot with the Churchillian dissidents, once Churchill became prime minister in May 1940, Eden again became foreign secretary. He regained this position and that of heir apparent to the elderly prime minister when the Conservatives returned to office in 1951.

Given what was to follow, it is ironic that Eden could claim not one but two Egyptian feathers in his cap. As foreign secretary he had been responsible for the Anglo-Egyptian Treaty of 1936, which in its time had been a forward-looking document. Now, having embraced Bevin's belief that the best offense is sometimes a strategic withdrawal, he fought in the Cabinet for the Suez base accord. Eden was also helped by the fact that, as he recovered, Churchill began to accept the notion of British departure from the Suez base, both out of his pragmatic understanding of political and financial realities and because he comprehended the lessened need for such an expensive and awkward base in the thermonuclear age.[112] Against the opposition of the right-wing Conservative "Suez Group," Eden prevailed. British and Egyptian negotiators initialed an outline of agreement on July 28, 1954, and executed the accord itself on October 19, 1954. It provided for total evacuation of all British troops over the next two years but allowed British civilian workers to remain for another seven years. British armed forces were permitted to reactivate the base under emergency conditions, and the Egyptian government endorsed the Constantinople Convention on the Suez Canal. In a statement released to the press Dulles said, "I believe that the removal of this deterrent to closer cooperation will open a new approach to peaceful relations between the Near Eastern States and other nations of the free world."[113] It seemed as if a more optimistic era in Western relations with the Middle East could now begin. Actually, the clash between residual British (and French) imperialism and increasingly strident Egyptian nationalism had merely been postponed. It would take the Suez crisis to end forever the old order in the Middle East.

TWO

PLAYING THE GAME
NOVEMBER 1954–DECEMBER 17, 1955

*This High Dam project is one which the
Prime Minister and I, after much thought,
regard as an essential move in the game. We
must get it one way or another.*
—Foreign Secretary Harold Macmillan,
October 20, 1955

During 1955 the British government, eager to improve its relations with Egypt, increasingly focused on the financing of the Aswan High Dam as an important weapon in its battle to win Egypt's President Gamal Abdel Nasser. Unable to afford such a massive expenditure alone, the British government importuned the United States to provide the lion's share of the funds. The Eisenhower administration was willing to consider the project because it agreed with the British government that Nasser was important to the Middle Eastern balance of power and central to the achievement of an Arab-Israeli settlement. The allies moved slowly, but their pace quickened after Nasser's announcement on September 27, 1955, that he had agreed to purchase arms from the Communist bloc; the news that Moscow had established a foothold in the Middle East drove the British and American governments to enter a bidding war for Nasser's allegiance. During the autumn, officials in Washington and London hurriedly put together a financing package for the Aswan High Dam. The success of this initiative in December 1955 augured well for the Anglo-American diplomatic efforts.

THE NEW EGYPT

Gamal Abdel Nasser dominated Egypt from July 1952, when the Free Officers' revolt overthrew King Farouk, until his death in September 1970.

Born in 1918 to a village postal clerk and his wife, he had grown up in interwar Egypt absorbing the anti-British currents so prevalent in his society. After being identified as an agitator by police for demonstrating against British rule, Nasser was expelled from school. At the age of nineteen, taking advantage of recent reforms that allowed those from poorer families to join the Egyptian army, he became a professional soldier. Becoming a career officer not only radically improved his social standing but contributed to Nasser's lifelong belief in the virtues of military rule. He was quickly promoted, and during the war he remained in Egypt, serving as an instructor at the Military Academy. This vantage point permitted Nasser to observe the humiliation of King Farouk by British Ambassador Miles Lampson and also allowed him to make contact with other young officers, such as Anwar Sadat, who were eager to rid Egypt of the British.[1] Seven years later their efforts were successful.[2]

General Mohammed Neguib, who headed the first postrevolutionary government in Egypt, had been a last-minute draftee of the Free Officers, not a core member like Nasser or Sadat. Not surprisingly, after the revolution a struggle began for control of the Egyptian government. While Neguib remained the head of state, perceptive observers such as Kermit Roosevelt, a top operative of the CIA, struck up firm ties with Nasser, whose popularity and power base were continually widening.[3] This uncertainty was settled in 1954, to Nasser's satisfaction. By October 1954, at the age of thirty-six, he was the undisputed leader of Egypt.

The new Egyptian leader captured the imagination of much of the underdeveloped world. Clearly Nasser possessed intelligence and charisma. Furthermore, as someone not part of the traditional ruling elite, he inspired great loyalty in the impoverished peasants of the Middle East. That Nasser never lost his commitment to helping the fellahin remained one of his most attractive attributes. Raymond Hare, American ambassador to Egypt from September 25, 1956 to March 29, 1958, painted this portrait: "Nasser . . . had never outgrown his youth actually, and he had this feeling of Egyptians being exploited, losing their dignity and that sort of thing. . . . There's a second thing. He was very much a man, an Egyptian, interested in the Egyptian people, and this was that way right to the end, right to the end." Yet Nasser's swift rise had its price. Jehan Sadat, whose husband, Anwar, was one of Nasser's intimates, recounted that Nasser's suspicious nature made him a very difficult person to get along with—he "was almost paranoid about the loyalty and intentions of others."[4] Both aspects of the man would be apparent in the years to come.

Three issues dominated Middle Eastern developments during the months prior to the Suez crisis: the Baghdad Pact, the Arab-Israeli imbroglio, and the Aswan High Dam. The Baghdad Pact, the first Western demarche after Nasser's full assumption of power, proved disastrous for Anglo-Egyptian relations. Originally called the Turco-Iraqi Pact after its initial signatories, the pact stemmed from the American "pactomania" of the early 1950s, which also saw the creation of NATO, ANZUS, and SEATO. The first parties signed the treaty on February 24, 1955, and Iran, Pakistan, and Britain affirmed their agreement within the year. The Foreign Office welcomed this initiative, for it exemplified the Bevinite policy Whitehall had advocated for a decade: using an international umbrella to shield a continued British presence in the Middle East.[5]

Although Secretary of State John Foster Dulles could well have claimed to be its spiritual father, immediately after the pact was announced, he began to distance the United States from the idea. Indeed, while the administration granted the signatories military aid and American observers attended meetings, the United States never joined the Baghdad Pact—the administration realized that the disadvantages to American membership far outweighed the advantages. Turkey and Pakistan, both members of the organization, had deadly antagonists outside the pact, Greece and India, respectively. Joining the pact might seem to indicate an American preference for one set of regional foes over another. Israel, too, viewed the possibility of American membership in the pact with alarm. Surrounded by hostile states and feeling increasingly abandoned by the Eisenhower administration's avowed policy of evenhandedness in the Arab-Israeli conflict, which seemed anything but, the Israeli government urged that if the United States joined the pact, Israel should as well. Iraq obviously would have found such a suggestion totally unacceptable, but the Eisenhower administration found the Israeli alternative, a separate American security guarantee to Israel, inimical to American interests in the Arab world.

Finally, American membership in the Baghdad Pact would have offended Nasser. The Nile has competed with the Tigres-Euphrates Valley for Middle Eastern hegemony for several millennia, and the Egyptian president saw the Baghdad Pact as a vehicle for Iraq to gain the upper hand in the struggle. American policymakers failed to understand why Nasser took the

Baghdad Pact so much to heart, for they believed that it threatened neither his country nor his rule. But Nasser abhorred the pact, seeing it as a disguised form of British imperialism and believing that it was directed against him. In response he struck out against the idea, particularly using the Cairo controlled "Voice of the Arabs" radio station, which constantly and persuasively attacked Britain and its Arab allies.[6]

American knowledge of Nasser's increasing disaffection partly motivated the second prong of Western Middle Eastern diplomacy at this time: the attempt to find a solution to the Arab-Israeli conflict. The question of oil and the threat of communism had raised the Eisenhower administration's estimate of the importance of the Middle East. As they sought to improve the standing of the United States in the region, Dulles and his colleagues came to view the Arab-Israeli conflict as their chief stumbling block. In the administration's opinion, the Arabs disliked the United States because they viewed it as Israel's chief protector. The answer, then, was to find a solution to this imbroglio that would remove it from the current agenda.

The first move in this direction came in the autumn of 1953 when Eisenhower sent a personal representative, industrialist Eric Johnston, to the Middle East. For the next two years Johnston sought a solution to the Israeli-Jordan dispute over the Jordan River waters. Johnston also hoped to make more irrigated land available for the resettlement of Arab refugees, as Palestinians were referred to during the 1950s. Indeed the refugee problem remained an important component of all administration planning for the region; officials placed a priority on this issue that would not reemerge until the middle 1970s. The Johnston approach was very American in its emphasis on technical problem solving and money to overcome intractable political and religious differences. While Israel cautiously accepted the plan, the Arab League rejected it.[7]

The following year British and American diplomats began working on Project Alpha, the centerpiece of Anglo-American peace efforts during the 1950s. This venture in Anglo-American cooperation was launched at a December 1954 meeting between Dulles, Eden, and their aides. The basic plan was finished the following month, although continual emendations were made until the plan's demise in 1956. The scheme envisioned an Arab-Israeli settlement that would include a Western guarantee of Israel's borders if Israel made territorial concessions and reached an agreement on the repatriation of Palestine refugees. In exchange for publicly renouncing any aggressive aims toward Israel, Egypt would gain Israeli territory and American military assistance.

As had been previously agreed, the Egyptian government was the first to be approached. In March 1955, the new American ambassador to Egypt, Henry Byroade, submitted the plan, first to Foreign Minister Mohammed Fawzi and then to Nasser himself.[8] A former military man, Byroade had instantly liked Nasser, and his esteem for the Egyptian leader remained high.[9] Negotiations with Egyptian leaders over Alpha's terms continued while the British worked on the third leg of Western efforts in the Middle East at this time: the funding of the Aswan High Dam.

Creating a high dam at Aswan had first been discussed during the 1930s.[10] Immediately upon taking power in 1952, the Free Officers' government began planning the dam, formally known as the Sud al Ali project. It was to be located above the existing Aswan dam and would hold each year's entire surplus Nile waters, which would be used for irrigation and to supply power for rural and increased urban electrification.[11] During the preceding decades the large population increase unmatched by corresponding increases in cultivatable land had lowered Egyptian per capita income. The dam would improve Egypt's per capita income by adding new acreage under irrigation. Given the place of the Nile in Egyptian culture, the project also had great symbolic value to Nasser and his people.

In 1953–54 a group of German companies led by the Hochtief engineering firm prepared preliminary feasibility studies. During early 1955 several British firms, notably the English Electric Company, joined the venture. Immediately, the British companies began to pressure their government to aid the project. The dam's cost was very high—the original estimate for the first and major section was E £210 million, of which E £102 million would require foreign exchange, and the rest Egyptian pounds.[12] The foreign companies, now known as the Consortium, tried to help the Egyptian government find the necessary foreign exchange. One obvious source stood out. During the Second World War, the Egyptians had accumulated sterling balances amounting to more than £400 million, a total second only to that of India.[13] In 1951, pursuant to an unsigned, de facto agreement, the Bank of England began releasing some convertible sterling to the Egyptian government.[14] As of January 1, 1955, the Egyptian balance remained £150 million, or enough to pay all the foreign exchange costs of the dam and have a bit left over to fund other schemes.[15]

Egyptian officials began pressuring the British government to release the balances. On the surface their case appeared unassailable: the sterling balances were Egypt's money to which the Egyptian government was legally entitled. However, the British government refused to return the blocked funds. In the days when the pound was the most frequently used currency, accounting for over 40 percent of the world's trade, British reserves fluctuated between $2,000 million (£700 million) and $2,400 million (£800 million), with the former amount being considered the bare minimum necessary for the smooth functioning of the British and sterling area economies.[16] Consequently, the Egyptian balances represented about one-fifth of the British total. Given that the British government was trying to ensure the continued existence of sterling as a reserve currency, the Bank of England would not consider distributing so high a percentage of its reserves at one time to one creditor. Furthermore, in this case the bulk of any such transfers would flow to non-British participants in the Consortium. Why should the British government pay for foreigners' lucrative contracts?

But in order to better woo Egypt, and for the economic objective of winning contracts for British companies, the British government in the spring of 1955 made the dam a high priority. A working group consisting of officials from the Treasury, the Board of Trade, the Export Credits Guarantee Department, and the Bank of England began to meet on a regular basis, on their own and also with members of the English Electric organization. Two questions particularly interested the group. The first was the distribution of Nile water between Egypt and the Sudan. The existing Nile Waters agreement of 1929 allocated the flow between the two countries. Now the Nasser government was contemplating a project that would convert part of the Sudan into a lake and also decrease its portion of the river flow. But before the Sudanese government agreed to anything, officials wanted firm assurances that their country would share proportionately in the benefits from the dam.[17]

The matter of Egypt's creditworthiness posed another problem. As one Bank of England official stated: "With her growing population Egypt has little alternative but to embark on a large scale development programme. . . . But it is clear that this will, even in its initial stages, strain her resources and may well call for outside assistance from friendly governments acting on purely political motives, over and above the credit which Egypt could hope to receive."[18] Hence the British conclusion that under the best of circumstances the Egyptian government would find it difficult to fund the dam.[19] Any new major financial commitment, such as arms purchases, would make it impossible for Egypt, even with the best will in the world, to live up to its financial obligations.

Notwithstanding these concerns, the British government became increasingly determined to push ahead and use the dam to win Nasser's support. The World Bank, formally known as the International Bank for Reconstruction and Development (IBRD), seemed to be a feasible alternative. Two years earlier, its head, Eugene Black, had suggested the possibility of an Aswan High Dam to Eisenhower, and by 1954 World Bank officials had visited Egypt.[20] Now the British emissaries urged Egyptian officials to seek World Bank funding for the dam.[21] But while they talked with IBRD officials, the Egyptians were apparently unenthusiastic about borrowing from the World Bank partly because they saw the World Bank as an American institution and apparently they did not wish American companies to participate in the project.[22]

The British pressed on. In May 1955, British representatives in Washington began discussing the feasibility of IBRD funding with Black. Two critical points emerged. First was the issue of how to finance that part of the cost of the dam not covered by a World Bank loan. Black apparently contemplated a donation from the United States and special British sterling releases. Thus having gone to the World Bank to avoid using British funds in order to finance the Aswan Dam, the British government was now facing the possibility of having to release blocked sterling anyway.[23] The second point concerned World Bank procedures. Out of necessity and inclination the World Bank intended to follow commercial banking construction lending practices, which mandated close supervision of both the economic state of the borrower (i.e., Egypt) as well as the progress of construction. While these clauses met bankers' standards, they were repugnant to a country sensitive about its sovereign rights.

At this point a third problem emerged: the rules and regulations governing World Bank assistance required competitive bidding. Since the British government was partly encouraging this project to aid the British companies in the Consortium, the last thing it wanted was to see the contracts go to different companies. After some negotiation the World Bank said that while it could not abandon the principle of competitive bidding, it might be possible to restrict its application.[24]

Working with the World Bank proved frustrating for the British. Borrowers and their advisors often say that finding a bank means acquiring a partner: once a bank decides to make a loan, it starts directing and supervising a borrower's business and making financial decisions as well. Thus Martin Flett, a British Treasury representative in Washington, warned senior officials that Black had involved himself in the issue of the renegotiation of the Anglo-Egyptian agreement on sterling balances and that he would disapprove of any attempt to link their release to the funding of British contracts for the dam.[25] For months the British government had been under pressure from both Egyptian officials and the Consortium to reach an agreement on this question. During the summer of 1955, the Bank of England and the Treasury assiduously negotiated with Egyptian representatives. The new agreement, signed on August 30, 1955, provided for the release of £15 million in 1955 and £20 million each year until 1963, when Egypt would receive the remaining balance.[26] British and Egyptian negotiators, on this issue at least, had found a fair compromise. At the price of returning a minimum of the sterling balances, the Bank of England was able to retain the bulk of the accounts for several years. While the sums released would not pay for the Aswan Dam, they increased Egypt's foreign currency reserves and reassured potential creditors such as the World Bank. Each side, then, had benefited financially and, equally important, a long-standing issue between the two nations had been resolved.

At the same time the Egyptian government pushed forward with plans for the dam. In the middle of September members of the Egyptian High Dam Authority came to London and met with the British firm of consulting engineers of Sir Alexander Gibb & Partners to discuss its serving as principal consultants.[27] However, intensifying Egyptian negotiations with the United States on the one hand, and the Soviet Union on the other, on the question of Egyptian purchases of armaments during the summer of 1955, had overshadowed discussions concerning the dam. The Egyptian government's announcement on September 27, 1955 of an agreement with Czechoslovakia for the purchase of Soviet made arms significantly altered the environment of the Middle East. Among other things, the dam now was transformed from an important to an urgent priority.

WOOING NASSER

The Soviet diplomatic coup came as a shock to both the United States and Britain. Western leaders both feared its implications for the Arab-Israeli conflict and worried about a possible overall Soviet strategic advantage. The train of events that brought about the Soviet-Egyptian arms deal had begun in early 1955. The Israeli raid on the Gaza Strip staged on February 28, 1955, proved to be of key importance.

The six years since the signing of the Arab-Israeli armistice accords in 1949 had been marked by continual Arab incursions on Israeli border settlements. In reaction Prime Minister Moshe Sharrett authorized a raid on Arab refugee camps in the Gaza Strip. An infelicitous area located between Egypt and Israel, the Gaza Strip was given to the Arabs by the 1947 Palestine partition plan and seized by Egypt during the 1948 Arab-Israeli war. Thereafter, Egyptian officials administered the area but refused Gaza residents either citizenship in Egypt or integration into Egyptian society. Not surprisingly the area became a center of anti-Israeli sentiment.

This particular reprisal raid (it was not the first) was notable for its violence—thirty-eight Arabs and eight Israelis died. To Nasser the raid emphasized his potentially tenuous position in Egypt. The Israeli humiliation of Arab armies in the 1948 war had provided a vital impetus to the Egyptian revolution. The army's support was crucial to Nasser's victory over Neguib and the Muslim Brotherhood. If the president could not protect Egypt from Israeli incursions, would not Nasser himself become vulnerable to the army's wrath?[28]

In order to protect his country and prevent his political demise, with increasing urgency Nasser sought equipment for the Egyptian army. When the Eisenhower administration decided to tie any arms aid to Egyptian cooperation with Project Alpha, Nasser began to weigh the possibility of obtaining Soviet arms. Fortuitously for Nasser, a reorientation in Soviet foreign policy was simultaneously occurring. Instead of the contempt for bourgeois revolutions that had earlier dominated Kremlin thinking, the new Soviet leadership consisting of First Secretary of the Communist Party Nikita Khrushchev and Premier Nicolai Bulganin now advocated a more expansive policy toward the third world. En route to the Bandung Conference of Non-Aligned Nations in April 1955 Nasser met with Zhou En-lai, who intimated the possibility of Soviet arms; on his return home Nasser told Soviet officials that he was seriously interested in a deal. Specific Egyptian-Soviet discussions commenced shortly.

In June 1955 Nasser told Byroade of his conversations with Soviet officials, hoping to launch a bidding war. An agreement in principle on

Egyptian arms purchases in the United States was quickly reached, and during the summer Egyptian representatives compiled lists of their require-ments.[29] While CIA operative Kermit Roosevelt took the Soviet threat seriously, the State Department did not, particularly after Khrushchev told Dulles during the July 1955 summit that he would not authorize the sale of arms to Egypt. During August, as Russo-Egyptian talks progressed, Dulles concentrated on Project Alpha, unveiling it before the Council on Foreign Relations. Finally, in mid-September the secretary of state acted on By-roade's advice and attempted to counter the Soviet arms offer. But the dispatch of Roosevelt to Cairo proved futile, and on September 27 Nasser dramatically announced his agreement to trade Egyptian cotton for Czech arms.

With this one declaration Nasser had transformed the Middle Eastern situation. Dulles's policy of using the Northern Tier countries of Turkey and Iraq to wall off a Communist threat to the area had been dealt a severe blow—the Soviets had simply leapt over the barrier. Israeli officials, who previously perceived themselves threatened by developments in the Middle East, now felt positively besieged. Most importantly, Nasser's prestige in the Arab world skyrocketed. In retrospect 1955 would appear to have been his annus mirabilis. Earlier in the year he had scored a huge success at the Bandung Conference. There this ill-educated neophyte, making his first trip outside the Arab world, received the welcome due a major world figure. Now the arms coup brought him huge tangible and intangible rewards.[30]

Although he never claimed to be a great partisan of Israel, Dulles appre-ciated the threat to the Middle East balance of power from 150 Russian built planes, 300 tanks, and miscellaneous other equipment.[31] The secretary particularly feared that Israel might launch a preemptive strike, while the thought of Soviet technicians sitting on British built Egyptian airfields was "too much" for Foreign Secretary Harold Macmillan.[32] Normally Dulles would have leapt at the opportunity to arm a nation apparently threatened by Communists. But to side openly with Israel could jeopardize the stand-ing of the United States with the Arabs. The choices were clear, if difficult. The West could punish Egypt directly by arming Israel or use economic aid to induce Nasser to stay in the Western camp. Eden thought that the question of the dam was crucial; he told Sir Evelyn Schuckburgh, the Foreign Office official in charge of the Middle East, that the threat of

Russian economic aid to Egypt was far more serious than the supply of arms.[33]

During the month after the arms deal was announced, the American and British governments debated their alternatives both separately and together. Dulles told Eisenhower in mid-October that the weapons deal "was creating widespread repercussions, which could not yet be fully appraised and it might at a later date require considered attention by the two of us." Dulles already had written to Nasser that the United States viewed the Egyptian acquisition of Communist arms with extreme distaste and that it would have a negative effect on American-Egyptian relations.[34] But even while showing the stick, the administration began to accept the British proposal to offer an economic carrot to Nasser rather than use the withholding of aid to punish him for cooperating with the Communists.

Eisenhower now wrote to Bulganin expressing his concern, and British and American officials began regularly discussing Egypt.[35] During early October Dulles held a series of meetings in Washington with Foreign Secretary Harold Macmillan. During a meeting with Dulles, the secretary made a comment that prefigured what would happen during the Suez crisis: "It seems to me that you [the British] should try very hard to avoid being sucked into a course of action with the Soviets which we could not or would not share."[36] The problem was that while the two nations had many common interests, their policies periodically diverged. At such times Britain always found itself in a very difficult position because it could not afford to conduct foreign relations on its own.[37]

THE ROLE OF ANTHONY EDEN

Anthony Eden never realized the extent to which financial realities constricted Britain's freedom of action. In April 1955 he had finally succeeded Churchill as prime minister, after having been kept waiting for almost two years after Churchill's stroke. During this period Eden also had been seriously ill, and he never fully recovered his strength.[38] Not only did he suffer periodic relapses, but he was often physically not at his best. In any event the Conservative party and the British public had their doubts about him, for separate reasons. To the die-hard, right-wing, Tory Suez Group, Eden was the traitor who had sold out the nation by the Suez Canal base accord.[39] Eden also faced the problem of never having held any domestic ministry; while few doubted his competence to handle foreign policy, many questioned his ability to deal with domestic affairs.

Eden's ability to govern was hampered by other problems as well. A Churchill manqué, he had his predecessor's romantic view of Britannia without Churchill's tempering realism. Like Churchill, Eden demanded a great deal from colleagues and subordinates. However, as Eden lacked his predecessor's compensating charm and good humor, he increasingly incurred the dislike of those around him.[40] Foreign Office officials particularly resented Eden's extensive and intrusive attention to minutiae. Eden proved no better at getting along with other statesmen. His relationship with Dulles, which had begun badly, worsened during 1954, first because of Guatemala. The United States opposed any discussion before the United States Security Council of the CIA sponsored coup that led to the overthrow of Jacobo Arbenz Guzman. Eden, however, believed that "Western nations will surely wreck the moral authority of the United Nations if from motives of expediency they refuse any investigation." By contrast, Churchill considered his foreign secretary's position to be foolish; he thought that Central American issues, in which Britain had no interest, should be left to the American government.[41]

Eden's masterminding of the Geneva accords on Indo-China and the Anglo-American misunderstanding about United Action, Dulles's last-minute attempt to shore up the French effort in Indo-China, provoked an even more important disagreement.[42] Eden viewed the Geneva agreements as his greatest success. Indeed his handling of the various parties at the negotiations had been impressive. Unfortunately Eden concluded from the American acceptance of the Geneva accords that the administration would always accept an independent British policy.

The Middle East occupied much of Eden's time during the autumn of 1955. As he sought to rescue his policy of moderation toward Nasser, the prime minister found himself under increased pressure, particularly from the right wing of his own party, which continued to excoriate Eden for his role in negotiating the Suez Canal base agreement. The American government supported Eden's conciliatory approach. Moreover, in October 1955 Dulles told Attorney General Herbert Brownell that unless a bipartisan Middle Eastern policy was created, "We may lose the whole Arab world and maybe Africa. It could be a major disaster comparable to the loss of China."[43] For all this note of imminent peril, until the denouement of the

Suez crisis the administration never lost its sense of complacency about the
Middle East.

WINNING THE DAM

As the British and American governments attempted to develop a policy to
counter Soviet moves in the Middle East, completing the financing package
for the Aswan Dam emerged as the most likely alternative. Pressure on the
United States to go this route came from three directions. The Egyptian
ambassador to the United States listed help for Aswan as the first priority in
improving American-Egyptian relations. Reports circulated in Cairo that
the Soviet Union had already offered to lend money for the project in
exchange for Egyptian cotton added additional pressure.[44] Finally, British
officials urged their American counterparts to involve themselves directly
in the issue, something the Eisenhower administration had heretofore
avoided. Nasser's gamble had apparently worked: his turn to Moscow had
not only produced arms but had pushed the West into contemplating the
offer of an immense financing package for the dam.

Foreign Secretary Harold Macmillan took the lead in tackling the Egyptian problem. Macmillan, half American like Churchill, during the 1930s
had entered the House of Commons, where he made a name for himself
with *The Middle Way*, a book that advocated a more caring brand of
Toryism. After serving as minister resident in North Africa during the
Second World War, where he worked closely with Eisenhower, Macmillan
reentered politics. While he did not attain his first Cabinet office until he
became minister of housing in 1951 at age fifty-seven, thereafter his star rose
rapidly. In April 1955 when Eden became prime minister, Macmillan succeeded him as foreign secretary. The two men were never very comfortable
with each other (Eden knew a rival when he saw one), but this appointment
made tactical sense. Eden was weakest with his party's jingoist Suez Group.
By appointing Macmillan, who was known to be a hardliner on colonial
issues, foreign secretary, Eden both assuaged right-wing fears and coopted
a major rival. However, the choice had an important disadvantage: Eden
wanted to be his own foreign secretary, and Macmillan was not easily
ignored.[45]

During the fall Macmillan focused on Aswan. He exhorted the British
ambassador to Washington, Sir Roger Makins, to concentrate on the dam,

saying it was "an essential move in the game."[46] Makins was instructed to find out if the American government would be willing to supply sufficient economic aid to Egypt to make the project feasible and whether the Aswan Dam would enjoy the support of both the administration and the World Bank. Further, the foreign secretary wanted Makins to tell Dulles that he desired to discuss the issue of the dam "at the highest possible level as soon as possible," and therefore Macmillan would personally raise it with Dulles at their meeting scheduled for the end of October.[47]

In its quest for American assistance, the British government continued to face many problems. Chief among them at this stage was the question of a negotiated contract. The Egyptian government wanted to give the work to the Consortium because it thought that this choice would provide quickest results. Such a route obviously had the support of the British government because of the participation of the English Electric group.[48] But the possibility of American financing complicated matters. United States regulations explicitly required competitive bidding for governmental work. For domestic political reasons the administration could not circumvent this requirement; congressional and public opinion, lukewarm at best toward foreign aid, would not accept an American financial contribution without the participation of American companies. Furthermore, the World Bank remained convinced that a negotiated contract would greatly increase the project's cost. Yet Macmillan cabled Makins to remind him that "it would be very unpopular with the British element in the consortium and no doubt with others if the result of your approach to the United States government were to be pressure to admit U.S. firms into partnership with the consortium."[49]

Such sentiments prompted Eisenhower to comment to his good friend, General Al Gruenther, supreme commander of Allied troops in Europe, that the British and French wanted commitments from the United States without giving anything in return.[50] Makins understood that it was both logical and politically necessary for the administration to expect American participation in exchange for American money. Accordingly he told the Foreign Office that the association of American firms with the Consortium was a sine qua non for American funding. London's response showed an utter blindness to the financial realities of mid-century life. Makins and his economic minister, Lord Harcourt, were instructed to see Black and urge him to go ahead with the project while waiving the requirement of international competitive bidding.[51] Then the Egyptians could sign a contract with the Consortium (which now also included French firms) with full confidence that the necessary foreign exchange would be there to pay the bills.[52]

The Foreign Office told Makins the only reason they did not wish to include American firms was the need for extreme speed.[53] At best the response from the Foreign Office only provided part of the reason for the Consortium's reluctance to include new companies in what promised to be the largest construction financing ever attempted; neither the Consortium nor the British government wanted to share these lucrative contracts. But London had no choice. What the British would not or could not face was that during the 1950s the United States funded and controlled the IMF and World Bank. As Secretary of the Treasury George Humphrey said to Dulles, a loan from the IMF (and by extension from the World Bank) was the same as a loan from the American government.[54] It was therefore ludicrous to think that Black would help British officials circumvent American objections, especially given his close relationship to the administration.

The British ambassador's position remained unenviable. Subjected to a continual barrage of cables, he found himself negotiating with both Washington and London. After again informing Sir Ivone Kirkpatrick, permanent under secretary at the Foreign Office, that American and World Bank aid without American participation was "a political impossibility," Makins, together with Harcourt, continued discussing the dam with Humphrey and Under Secretary of State Herbert Hoover, Jr.[55] During these discussions British representatives gained a clear sense of American priorities. As Hoover pointed out, if the Soviets had promised arms to a country in Latin America, the matter would probably have a much higher priority than a similar Middle Eastern transaction. This hierarchy remained a constant during the Suez crisis, something that the British, who saw Egypt (in Makins's words) as a "no. 1 priority in view of its strategic importance and as the gateway to Africa," never understood.[56]

Yet American officials found themselves paying increasing attention to the Aswan project. State Department officers in April had judged that an endeavor along the lines of the dam was essential for Egypt to cope with the population pressure it faced and that, moreover, the United States had a direct interest in such a plan because Egypt's stability would be undermined if its standard of living declined any further.[57] Now, as diplomats continued to assess the impact of the Soviet arms deal, George Allen, assistant secretary of state for Near Eastern Affairs, concluded that "the U.S. should recognize the political and economic importance of this project to the Government of Egypt and the political gains which will accrue to countries participating in its financing and construction." But Hoover preferred that the World Bank proffer all the financing required for the dam; he feared that direct United States government funding would bring a deluge of similar requests from other underdeveloped countries.[58]

Discussions continued on the Aswan project during November as the Egyptians signed a contract with engineers Gibb and Co., and the Consortium assembled its own financing package. These developments increased the pressure on the British government to obtain foreign financing for the dam lest it be forced to use Exchequer funds. Already the government had succumbed to the lobbying of the Edison Electric group and agreed to provide foreign currency cover for the British portion of any Consortium contract.[59] Pressure on the administration also increased. The Soviet-Egyptian arms deal was publicly viewed as a defeat for the West. No less a personage than Walter Lippmann wrote that "if the Russians secure the High Dam project, there will be no doubt at all that Egypt has been drawn into the Soviet orbit," and then, echoing Dulles's comment of several months earlier, he added that this might "prove to be a setback for the influence of the West second only to what happened on the mainland of China." Indeed Black now told Harcourt that the administration had asked him privately to help them reappraise American policies "now that the cold war had shifted to the economic front."[60] Arranging funding for the Aswan Dam presented an obvious first step in this campaign.

Before a Western offer could be made, the local and foreign currency cost of the project had to be estimated.[61] Previous projections had varied widely both because of the nature of the project and because the Egyptians had a vested interest in keeping them as low as possible. Now World Bank estimates surpassed $1 billion, making the Aswan project the most expensive venture ever attempted.[62] While World Bank officials believed that Egypt could afford the dam with just IBRD assistance, they based their conclusion on the assumption that the government would be willing to undertake a program of internal austerity and sacrifice. But Humphrey and Hoover pointed out two major flaws in the project estimates. First, they presumed the accuracy of the estimated cost of construction, a highly unlikely eventuality. Moreover, the Americans pointed out that "no Egyptian government would dare to impose upon the country the standards of austerity implied in the [World] Bank report."[63]

New problems surfaced as the administration seriously considered using foreign aid for the project. Washington officials had already suggested that, given the Anglo-American nature of this scheme, perhaps the British government should match any appropriation that the American government might choose to make.[64] Because of the British government's deteriorating financial position during 1955, any contribution would present a major problem. Following upon a 1954 decision to return the pound to quasi-convertibility, Chancellor of the Exchequer R. A. Butler[65] had announced in February 1955 that the Bank of England would support the official rate of transferable sterling within 1 percent of parity ($2.80).[66] The result was that British reserves, as of December 31, 1955, stood at $2,120 million, having declined $642 million during the year.[67] While the amount of money in circulation during the 1950s was far less than it is today, this reserve base represented a ludicrously small balance on which to support the viability of an international currency. Not surprisingly, Butler, at the annual IMF meeting in September 1955, felt compelled to reassure Humphrey that the pound would not be devalued.[68]

The British financial plight prompted Whitehall officials in November to consider applying for a waiver under the U.S. Agreement. This clause had been designed to allow the British government to postpone making interest payments in a year when Britain's external financial position made such a payment an undue hardship.[69] Even George Humphrey, that most conservative of financiers, thought that the British should consider requesting a waiver. However, as Makins pointed out, "In the public mind it would be difficult for us to be known to be making a loan or granting a credit for the building of the High Aswan Dam whilst simultaneously appearing to default on our debt to the United States."[70] Once again the British dilemma was apparent. Ministers sought to keep the role of great power but could not afford to do so without American assistance. But taking American assistance heightened the dependency that increasingly disqualified the British government from the game it sought to play.

Hoover spelled out the price of dependency when he informed Makins that by signing a contract with the Consortium, Egyptian officials would foreclose the possibility of American financing. For commercial reasons the

British Cabinet still hoped to get the contract for the Consortium and, at the same time, obtain World Bank funding. Furthermore, some ministers, such as President of the Board of Trade Peter Thorneycroft, feared that including the Americans might "seriously disturb our present happy relations with the Egyptians on this matter."[71]

However, the ever-realistic Makins and Harcourt urged ministers to reexamine their position. As Makins put it: "If we try to finesse this . . . we shall, whether successful or not, earn the resentment, and ill-will of the State Department, Treasury and Black. With the waiver coming up and convertibility perhaps in the offing, is this a risk which you feel you must run for the sake of an exclusive contract?" The Washington embassy prevailed, and Makins was told that there was no thought of attempting to strike a deal with the Egyptians behind the administration's back. Moreover, the Foreign Office assured Makins that he could freely discuss any contacts with German and French officials with the State Department. There matters stood as the diplomats prepared for the visit of Egyptian Finance Minister Dr. Abdul Kaisouni to Washington, scheduled for the end of November.[72]

When Dr. Kaisouni arrived in London en route to the United States, he seemed convinced of the need to work with the World Bank.[73] The foreign secretary cabled Makins that because the Cabinet had decided "to pursue urgently the question of obtaining a loan for the project from the International [World] Bank," he should continue trying to persuade the American government of the need for its assistance. But on the subject of a British contribution, the ambassador was told, "You should make it clear that we consider we have already made a generous and substantial contribution toward the financing of the High Dam by agreeing to an increase in the rate at which Egypt's blocked sterling is released."

A Treasury memorandum prepared at this time presents a further example of the British condescending and unrealistic approach toward the United States. A. K. Potter, a senior Treasury official, wrote that "the Ambassador will have to resist any pressure from the Americans that in return for their aid the participation of American firms should exceed 25%." This statement came at a time when the British envisioned that the administration would pay at least 80 percent of the cost over and above the World Bank contribution.[74] One can only pity Makins, who was apparently expected to advertise as a major example of British generosity an acceleration in the release of sterling balances that, after all, represented Egyptian money that the British had refused to return for over a decade.

The British ambassador did his duty. Stressing to Hoover the importance of speed (for otherwise "we might lose the game"), Makins organized and attended tripartite meetings with Black and Hoover and their respective aides designed to have an offer ready when the Egyptians arrived in Washington. Egypt's ability to finance that portion of the costs not forthcoming from outside sources remained the major problem. The British government recognized the validity of this concern that had originally motivated Whitehall's quest for IBRD financing. However, officials worried that the World Bank's intrusive and insensitive manner would infuriate the Egyptian representatives so much that they would walk out of the meetings, return to Cairo, and then ask the Consortium to proceed independently, leaving the British government in the same awkward position from which it had been trying to escape for the previous three months.[75] From Cairo came further pressure as British Ambassador Sir Humphrey Trevelyan reported rumors of a Polish offer to finance the dam and cabled that the Egyptian finance minister was waiting until the outcome of the Washington talks to decide Egyptian tactics.[76]

The Washington negotiations stretched over almost four weeks, from November 21 through December 17, with the participation of the American State and Treasury departments, three Egyptian delegates, the British embassy, and the World Bank. The first week's meetings did not go smoothly. The question of a negotiated versus a competitive contract proved to be the chief stumbling block. With the projected World Bank loan estimated at $200 million (by far the largest the World Bank had contemplated granting), the bank stood firm on its objection against the idea of using the Consortium on the grounds that it would lead to needless expense. As Egyptian officials felt that competitive tendering would lead to unnecessary delay, British negotiators were caught in the middle.[77]

Still hoping that the World Bank could carry the ball, the administration initially kept aloof from these negotiations. American tactics changed after Eden sent a personal plea to Eisenhower. Eden first reminded the president of the likelihood of a Russian offer, stating that if the Soviet Union had access to the Nile, "the outlook for Africa then would be grim indeed." He then asked Eisenhower to intervene in the Consortium contract dispute.[78] But the administration was not united. While the British government viewed the dam as a question of "the greatest national importance" requiring regular discussion in Cabinet, the administration had not yet paid extensive high-level attention to the issue, in part because officials hoped to avoid direct American government participation.[79] Now that a United States contribution appeared inevitable, Hoover, Humphrey, and John Hollister, the director of the International Cooperation Administration (ICA), the current vehicle for foreign aid distribution, debated various alternatives.[80] Concurrently, Egyptian negotiators met with the World Bank. Makins, in the meantime, attempted to "lose no opportunity of trying to urge on the Americans the need to make up their minds quickly."[81] The Egyptians had been scheduled to depart on December 8, but when Hoover asked them for more time to allow the administration to study the various aspects of the project, they agreed to stay another week.[82]

Humphrey's opposition to the project provided a major explanation for the delay. He was concerned about the project's feasibility and worried over possible increased competition for American producers, principally cotton farmers. Although Humphrey usually won any arguments in the field of foreign economic diplomacy, this time he lost to Hoover. The under secretary maintained that the project was feasible; that it provided a better use of aid funds to Egypt than small, piecemeal projects; that there was no proof that increased competition would result; and that ample evidence indicated that if the United States did not proceed, the Soviets would.[83]

On December 12, American officials announced their "bottom line" to British negotiators. It was not what the Cabinet had hoped. The United States declared it would be necessary for the two countries to finance the entire amount of foreign exchange costs for the first phase of the project. An expenditure of Exchequer moneys was precisely what the British government had hoped to avoid by involving the World Bank and the United States in the project. Now American administrators informed their British counterparts that British money was a prerequisite to any American funding.

Not surprisingly, once the two delegations began to discuss specific amounts, they found themselves far apart. While the British Treasury had assumed that the Egyptians would also be required to contribute foreign exchange to the first phase of the project, the State Department plan envisioned only Anglo-American contributions. However, the Cabinet had, after great agonizing, authorized a contribution of $10 million, 25 percent of the original estimate of a foreign exchange shortfall of $40 million. According to Makins both Humphrey and Hoover "expressed grave disappointment" at this number. As the ambassador pointed out, the Americans knew the British balance of payments problems as well as he did, but they still pressed for a larger contribution—at the least $15 million or 20 percent of Phase I's foreign exchange cost now estimated at $70 million. During that week, Makins was also forced to ask London for authority to agree to make the British contribution in freely convertible dollars. This step would further increase the cost of the contribution.[84]

The American government had failed to take cognizance of the strained British financial position. Washington officials professed not to understand why the British government, getting 80 percent of the grant it had wanted from United States, could possibly object to paying the remaining 20 percent. Interestingly, during the same week, Sir Leslie Rowan, a senior British Treasury official, had been in Washington discussing Britain's financial plight and the possibility of a waiver.[85] Rowan had observed that there seemed to be poor liaison among the various departments in Washington.[86] More importantly, the administration was willing to accept the British illusion of great power status, so long as the British government did not do anything that violated American wishes. However, this fiction contributed to the failure of both governments to assimilate the reality of Britain's difficult financial position.

The administration also insisted upon competitive bidding. Eden again wrote Eisenhower to plead the Egyptians' case for a negotiated contract, thereby confirming Hoover's belief that the British officials were encouraging the Egyptians' obstinacy on this point.[87] Hoover stood firm on the point while, on Dulles's advice, the president did not reply directly to Eden. The prime minister never established his own special relationship with Eisenhower, in part because the secretary of state resented Eden's attempt to conduct foreign relations directly with the president. Dulles said that "this would throw an intolerable burden upon the President and I don't think we should encourage it."[88] While Dulles's stewardship undoubtedly reduced the president's work and pleased Dulles, the secretary's seemingly firm control over American foreign policy confused British leaders about the extent of Dulles's power and allowed them to believe that Eisenhower might support an alternative policy, if only they could approach him directly.

Egyptian attempts to find a compromise on the bidding question were ended only by Hoover's announcement on December 15 that Eisenhower had decided that the United States could not participate in the project without competitive tenders. Notwithstanding their defeat on both the question of Anglo-American contributions to the project and the issue of competitive bidding, the realization that all their hard work had paid off delighted Makins and Harcourt. The next day Hoover and Makins presented the Egyptians aide-mémoire detailing their offers.[89] The Egyptian delegation stated that the proposals were "most satisfactory" and that they would recommend that Nasser accept them.[90] Having determined that the still-unsettled Nile waters question could be postponed, Black handed Kaisouni the bank's offer letter on December 17. The World Bank's president told Harcourt that the Egyptians "had left him in good spirits and that his impression was that the combined offers would be accepted."[91] It seemed as if the promise presented by the Suez Canal base accord might be fulfilled.

THREE

~

THE STICK, NOT THE CARROT

DECEMBER 17, 1955–JULY 26, 1956

*Colonel Nasser . . . cannot cooperate as he is
doing with the Soviet Union and at the
same time enjoy most favored nation
treatment from the United States.*
—John Foster Dulles,
March 28, 1956

The promise presented by the successful December 1955 negotiations for the Aswan High Dam financing soon evaporated. In March 1956 Britain and the United States decided to substitute the stick for the carrot in their dealings with Egypt. Thereafter, relations deteriorated until the British and American governments decided not to fund the Aswan Dam. No announcement was made until Nasser brought matters to a head by sending his ambassador to Washington to sign the loan documentation. For a combination of domestic and foreign policy motives, Dulles, with British acquiescence, decided not to "play it long" and bluntly told Ambassador Ahmed Hussein that the American offer was withdrawn. No one envisioned that this determination would lead to a turning point in postwar history.

COMPLETING THE ASWAN OFFERS

The Aswan Dam financing was not yet, in business parlance, a "done deal." While the IBRD and Anglo-American offers had been made, Nasser had not accepted them. Restrictive provisions contained in the World Bank offer letter presented the largest stumbling block. These provisions, designed to insure that the bank remained satisfied with Egypt's financial condition, troubled the Egyptians for two reasons.[1] Finance Minister Dr. Abdul Kaisouni feared that they would allow the bank to back out of the loan at will.[2] In particular, they would give the IBRD the right to withdraw from the project if Nasser again purchased Communist arms. Furthermore, such financial monitoring clauses rubbed Egyptian nerves raw because similar provisions had forced the Khedive to accept the domination of a European Debt Commission in 1876, a capitulation that ultimately led to the British occupation of Egypt six years later. The Americans might not have heard of this event; the British relished it; but to Nasser and his countrymen, the occupation of Egypt was one of the most inglorious moments in their history. Consequently, the Cairo government firmly resisted similar restrictions.

Nasser reiterated Kaisouni's reservations, telling American Ambassador to Egypt Henry Byroade at the end of December 1955 that he resented the constricting nature of the bank's conditions. Dulles viewed Nasser's reaction to the offers as "not very encouraging."[3] Yet to a certain extent the American and British governments had only themselves to blame for Nasser's truculent attitude. Rather than punish him for his Communist arms deal, the West had rewarded him by offering him an enormous financing package. Why then should Nasser not conclude that a continued hard-line stance would bring better terms?[4]

Both the British and American ambassadors to Cairo believed that the Egyptian leader wanted Western financing but genuinely feared these clauses.[5] During January, as other Egyptian officials again complained to British Ambassador to Egypt Sir Humphrey Trevelyan about the competitive bidding problem, it became clear to Western observers that the Aswan deal could unravel.[6] Yet Nasser's personal role in the negotiations raised the stakes higher than ever.[7] Therefore, World Bank President Eugene Black departed for Cairo to discuss these issues directly with the Egyptian leader.

Foreign policy imperatives and financial prudence again collided. Although Egyptian fears about the financial clauses were legitimate, these provisions were standard ones that any lender would include. The suspicious attitude of the New York financial community (the source of the World Bank's funds) exacerbated Black's dilemma. Determined to avoid Wall Street accusations that he was sacrificing proper standards, Black had to resolve the financial doubts without jeopardizing the political gains represented by the Aswan offers.[8]

For two weeks after his arrival in Cairo on January 27, Black attended meetings—with Nasser, with his aides, with the American and British ambassadors. Trevelyan and Byroade did their part, reminding Nasser of the importance with which their governments viewed the dam. Black presented a new draft memorandum that watered down the objectionable provisions but also diluted the bank's commitment to lend. The Egyptians replied with a redraft that omitted almost all Egyptian covenants while adding a firm IBRD commitment not just to Phase I but to the entire project.[9] At the same time Kaisouni and his colleagues proposed that in lieu of the aide-mémoire, the British and American governments furnish to Egypt firm funding commitments for the entire project. Hoover immediately rejected this idea; among other objections, congressional restrictions on foreign aid precluded any such long-range commitment.[10] Hoover also now worried about another problem that had surfaced: the possibility that after accepting Anglo-American funding for the dam, the Egyptians could simultaneously obtain Communist aid as well.[11] Such an eventuality would be anathema to the administration, which had no desire to share any of the credit for funding the project with the Soviet Union.

With so many subjects unresolved, not surprisingly Black left Cairo without signed documentation. Yet his mission appeared to have convinced the Nasser government of the World Bank's sincerity. On February 9, Black and Kaisouni issued a joint statement that lauded the negotiations as "very fruitful" and stated that "substantial agreement has been reached concerning the basis of the Bank's participation."[12] Black took home with him contracts containing weaker financial restrictions that made them more satisfactory to the Egyptians. These could now be presented to the IBRD's board of directors for approval. In the interim the other open issues could be discussed by the concerned parties.

Concurrently with Black's mission, British and American diplomats in Washington negotiated a secret memorandum embodying the Anglo-American understandings on funding for Phases I and II of the dam.[13] They had just completed this task when, on January 30, Eden, together with his new foreign minister, Selwyn Lloyd, arrived in Washington for meetings with the administration.[14] The two days of wide-ranging discussions were cordial; in his diary Eisenhower recorded that he had "never before attended any international talks of an official character where the spirit of friendship was more noticeable than in this one."[15] Eden was now benefit-

Eisenhower and Dulles greet Eden, Foreign Secretary Selwyn Lloyd (left), and British Ambassador to the United States Roger Makins in the White House during Eisenhower's only meeting with Eden as prime minister, January 30–February 2, 1956. (Courtesy Dwight D. Eisenhower Library/National Park Service)

ing from the Cabinet reshuffle he had ordained in December. Foreign Secretary Harold Macmillan had been sent to the Treasury, where he could cope with the economy, which was the government's weakest spot, and in Lloyd, Eden had the perfect number two who would always be willing to defer to the prime minister. However, in retrospect Eden's changes would prove to have been a major error.[16]

Anglo-American discussions about the West's relationship with Nasser now sounded distinctly pessimistic.[17] Eden labeled the Egyptian "a man of limitless ambition" and opined that it was difficult to know whether he could be trusted. Secretary of State John Foster Dulles replied that he "did not mind ambition" but feared that Nasser might become a "tool of the Russians." In that case, the secretary of state agreed, a revision of policy might be called for.[18] Dulles speculated that Black's meetings might provide Nasser's litmus test.

In the event, other factors led to a decision by both the British and American governments to change their Egyptian policies. It was the British government that initiated this shift; by the end of March a significant alteration had occurred in London and Washington. Ironically, the British government never perceived the danger in which it had placed itself. In fact Eden and his colleagues, pushed on the one hand by the Suez group and by Nasser's seeming arrogance on the other, now set in motion a chain of events that would have the most negative effects on Britain itself.

Nasser's continued diplomatic offensive against the Baghdad Pact played a major role in antagonizing Britain. During December 1955, apparently violating its previous undertaking to Nasser, the British government began to pressure Jordan to join the pact in exchange for munificent military assistance. In response, Cairo's Voice of the Arabs radio station broadcast Nasser's attacks against Britain, pro-British Middle Eastern governments, and the Baghdad Pact itself. Three successive Jordanian Cabinets collapsed until King Hussein restored order by announcing in January 1956 that Jordan would not join the pact.[19]

King Hussein's decision to dismiss General Sir John Glubb ("Glubb Pasha") from his position as head of Jordan's army, known as the Arab Legion, on March 1 further inflamed British opinion. As Voice of the Arabs often targeted Glubb personally, the British government took his dismissal as proof of an ominous growth of Nasser's influence in the Middle East. As Schuckburgh said, Eden "wants to strike some blow, somewhere to counterbalance."[20] Therefore, the prime minister, determined to take a strong line, wrote to Eisenhower on March 5: "There is no doubt that the Russians are resolved to liquidate [the] Baghdad Pact. In this undertaking Nasser is supporting them and I suspect his relations with the Soviets are much closer than he admits to us. Recent events in Jordan are part of this pattern. . . . I feel myself that we can no longer safely wait on Nasser."[21]

Eden's personality and political experience now began to play a decisive role. Eight months after attaining his long-held goal of becoming prime minister, Eden found himself under bitter attack. His December 1955 Cabinet reshuffle had been poorly received, and during February, continued financial problems forced the government to make unusual budget adjustments, including cuts in the bread and milk subsidies. Rumors began to circulate that the prime minister might resign. Eden made the mistake of publicly denying the stories. More press speculation then followed, and when Eden responded with an intemperate denunciation of the press, many in Britain questioned his stability and leadership.[22]

Facing a hostile media, the prime minister's resolution to stand up to Nasser, a leader who seemingly echoed Hitler and Mussolini, increased.[23] Making matters worse, Eden stumbled his way through the most disastrous parliamentary appearance of his career during the Commons debate on Jordan.[24] Further, the prime minister took personally both Nasser's lack of gratitude for the base accord and the Aswan offer, and his anti-British statements. Having made his reputation for sacrificing his career to the principle of standing up to dictators, at this time of personal and political turmoil, Eden reenacted the psychological high point of his life by over-emphasizing the threat posed by Nasser and by becoming increasingly obsessed with the Egyptian president.[25]

During the first week of March, Lloyd and Dulles had met in Karachi, where they discussed Egypt. The foreign secretary had come from Cairo, where he had met twice with Nasser. The issue of Egyptian propaganda broadcasts had placed high on Lloyd's agenda. The British government particularly resented Voice of the Arabs' new Swahili programs that urged Africans to revolt against British rule. Yet Nasser had refused to pledge himself to ending the radio programs.

The Baghdad Pact had remained equally problematic. Nasser went so far as to state that the pact had dissipated any good will Britain might have earned from the Suez Canal base accord.[26] Not surprisingly then, Lloyd subscribed to the Cabinet's new and harder line, which he now urged Dulles to follow. The secretary responded that while the administration had not yet decided upon a new Egyptian policy, the turning point was fast approaching. "Unless Nasser did something soon," said Dulles, "we would have to ditch him."[27]

The American decision to "ditch" Nasser, as it were, came quite soon, triggered by Nasser's lack of receptiveness to the administration's latest attempt at Arab-Israeli shuttle diplomacy. Code named Project Gamma, it featured Robert Anderson, who was appointed the president's special emissary to the Middle East in November 1955.[28] His mission: to arrange a meeting between Nasser and Ben-Gurion as a first step in the quest for an Arab-Israeli settlement. The choice of Anderson signified a high-level White House commitment to the project. The president had great faith in the Texas businessman, believing that Anderson was "just about the ablest man that I know everywhere."[29] Between January and March 1956, Anderson conducted three rounds of talks in Cairo and Tel Aviv. Returning in early March he met Eisenhower and Hoover at the White House and reported that he had made no progress in arranging an Arab-Israeli meeting because "Nasser proved to be a complete stumbling block. He is apparently seeking to be acknowledged as the political leader of the Arab world." Anderson's account carried great weight, all the more so since his opinion coincided with the president's perception of events. One week earlier Ike had reflected that "the Arabs, absorbing major consignments of arms from the Soviets, are daily growing more arrogant and disregarding the interests of Western Europe and of the United States in the Middle East region."[30]

After Dulles returned to Washington, he also advocated a tougher line against Egypt.[31] On March 24, he posed a series of questions: Could Nasser rally the Arab world behind him? Could the administration obtain the support of the Saudis and Iraq? What precisely was the oil situation and how vulnerable would the West be if oil shipments through pipelines or the Suez Canal were disrupted?[32] Nothing on his list deterred Dulles from taking an anti-Nasser line because none of these items directly affected the United States. Consequently the administration now embarked upon a course with deep and unforeseen consequences.

When the secretary of state met with the president on March 28, he brought a memorandum on Middle East policies that embodied the line the administration would pursue through July. The key paragraph stated: "The primary purpose would be to let Colonel Nasser realize that he cannot cooperate as he is doing with the Soviet Union and at the same time enjoy most favored nation treatment from the United States. We would want for the time being to avoid any open break which would throw Nasser irrevocably into a Soviet satellite status and we would want to leave Nasser a bridge back to good relations with the west if he so desires."

Dulles gave the president a three-part plan. The first listed possible anti-Egyptian actions such as denying arms export licenses, delaying PL 480 grain and oil assistance, holding up the 1956 CARE program, and postponing the conclusion of negotiations for the Aswan Dam financing. Then came actions involving other countries such as shoring up the Libyan government and increasing aid to the Baghdad Pact. Finally, there were more drastic steps to be taken if other measures failed to persuade Nasser to change his attitude and policies. Their nature cannot be ascertained because the paragraph enumerating them has been censored.[33] It is conceivable that they included the covert overthrow of the Nasser regime. If so, it would help explain the British government's miscalculation of the American position. In any case the administration's main priority was to try to walk a fine line, punishing Nasser for his transgressions without alienating him completely. While the administration had decided to substitute the stick for the carrot in its treatment of Nasser, the American government wanted neither a definitive break with Nasser nor active hostilities. However, the American government's diplomacy was not up to this task. Having first given Nasser the signal that his anti-Western actions would be rewarded, American diplomats never effectively communicated the administration's changed position that from now on, the United States expected a quid pro quo.

A POLICY IN FLUX

Eisenhower insisted on the importance of coordinating American policy with Eden and Lloyd, and notwithstanding later British allegations, administration officials consulted frequently with their British counterparts during the next three months.[34] The stalling of the Aswan negotiations represented the first manifestation of the new Anglo-American policy. Egyptian actions considerably eased this process. At the end of February, Egyptian Vice-Premier Gamal Salem informed Trevelyan that Cairo wanted further changes in the aide-mémoire. Most important, while the Egyptian government had decided not to proceed with Phase I until a Nile waters agreement had been reached with the Sudan, it expected that the American and British governments would immediately disburse their grants. Further, Salem sought to modify the documents in order to make it more difficult for the Western powers to stop their funding should Egypt purchase more arms. He also sought wording changes so that the documents would better serve Egyptian propaganda purposes.

These Egyptian demands gave the West a justification for delay. For Eden they served as additional provocation; the prime minister said, "We could never agree to these greedy demands."[35] In Washington, the administration faced the fact that the monies previously allocated for the dam would not be expended during the three remaining months of fiscal year 1956. Therefore, without any public announcement, Hoover now began quiet negotiations with congressional leaders concerning other uses for the $54.6 million. If the Egyptians inquired, they would be told that the Americans awaited Egyptian comments on the offer and that Nasser's decision to proceed first with the Sudanese discussions had lowered the temperature on the Aswan question.[36]

The administration was now actively pursuing a double balancing act, on the one hand trying to nudge Nasser to a more pro-Western line without totally alienating him and on the other trying to stake out a position independent of both Egypt and Britain. Therefore, on April 4, Dulles drafted a message to Eden from Eisenhower that stated, "I fully agree with you that we should not be acquiescent in any measure which would give the Bear's claws a vital grip on the production or transportation of the oil which is so vital to the defense and economy of the western world." However, publicly the secretary of state took a very mild position against Nasser, refusing to associate him definitively with the Soviet Union.[37] As Trevelyan observed from Cairo, this American policy created the impression in Egypt that the hard-line approach was solely British and British interests could suffer accordingly. Trevelyan advocated full, public Anglo-American cooperation.[38] But as Dulles told congressional leaders on April 10, the administration was "most reluctant publicly to identify ourselves in the [Middle East] area with the U.K."[39]

During this period the British government became increasingly aware of its vulnerability should there be a confrontation with Egypt; several departments studied, in the words of a Foreign Office official, "what we can do to Egypt and what Egypt can do to us."[40] The reports, which covered exchange control, oil supplies, the efficacy of sanctions, and other economic questions, deduced that because of the nature of its economy and its ties to the Communist bloc, Egypt was not very vulnerable to British pressure. By contrast, Britain would suffer if Middle Eastern conditions deteriorated, because of its reliance on Middle Eastern oil, British use of the Suez Canal, and the extensive Anglo-Egyptian financial ties. These exhaustive reports were circulated to all major British government departments. But the Eden Cabinet chose to ignore the possible consequences of its harder line. Furthermore, it embarked on a policy it could not afford without first ensuring American support.[41]

For the present, American and British policy coincided, both sides attempting, in Foreign Office official Sir Evelyn Schuckburgh's phrase, "not to show Nasser our hand too early."[42] The two Western nations continued to appear willing to negotiate about the dam. Eisenhower and Dulles even refrained from taking a harsh attitude toward Nasser in the wake of the announcement on May 16 that Egypt had recognized the People's Republic of China.[43] But under the outward calm, both the American and British governments became increasingly reluctant to fund the dam.[44]

The future of the Aswan project now presented the administration with a dilemma. While officials shied away from delivering to Egypt a final rejection, by the end of May, Dulles had no intention of proceeding with the offer. Not surprisingly the secretary now gratefully seized upon a rather disreputable solution suggested by the State Department. Egypt had not yet settled the Nile waters question with the Sudan. If the administration could encourage the Sudan and other riparian states, such as Ethiopia and the nations of equatorial Africa, to demand that Egypt convene a conference of riparian states in order to discuss fully the allocation of Nile waters, a lengthy delay in the Aswan project would be inevitable. During this time Britain and the United States could continue to keep the offers open, knowing full well they would not be called upon to make good on their promises.

Once Dulles approved this stratagem, the State Department sent cables to American ambassadors in Khartoum, Addis Ababa, London, and Cairo. Only Byroade dissented. He told Dulles that "the scheme is so transparently a subterfuge that it would be promptly recognized as such by all concerned." However, Byroade's blatant partisanship on Nasser's behalf had destroyed his credibility in Washington, and his words were discounted. While the British government welcomed any plan that would postpone the inevitable, the implausibility of this scheme was immediately obvious. As the British and American governments previously had been willing to proceed solely with Egypt, the sudden need for an international conference would obviously appear suspect. Furthermore, as one Treasury official observed, when Nasser woke up, the British risked being the ones "left holding the baby." In other words, having discovered that the Western governments had not been negotiating in good faith, Nasser might retaliate. And, as the official presciently concluded, "There is not much he can do against the United States but a lot he can do against us."[45]

Trevelyan had pointed out to the Foreign Office in early April that the policy of letting the dam question "languish" could not work indefinitely; by the end of June the moment of decision was fast approaching.[46] Moreover, another factor made an explosion far more likely. Until June 18, British troops still remained at the Suez base. Although only a token contingent lingered, its presence no doubt exercised a restraining influence on Nasser. But on June 18 the last troops departed.[47] Almost as soon as the celebrations were over, rumors spread that Nasser was sending Egyptian Ambassador Ahmed Hussein back to Washington to conclude the dam negotiations.[48]

Unfortunately Dulles was at this point overburdened because of Eisenhower's ileitis attack on June 8. The president did not return to Washington until July 16. In Eisenhower's absence the secretary gave top priority to the fight over foreign (mutual security) aid. The reception of Eisenhower's January 1956 budget message had revealed that several influential members of Congress opposed the request of $4.5 billion for foreign aid (both civilian and military) for fiscal 1957.[49] During the spring, as the administration pushed for passage of the required legislation, opposition from both parties intensified.[50] The fall presidential and congressional elections magnified the attention normally paid by legislators to foreign aid packages. The need for unity for the autumn contest made it harder for the Democratic party leadership, which tended to accept administration guidance on foreign affairs, to control its infantry. Further, election year politics intensified Dulles's reluctance to antagonize the Old Guard on economic issues.

By its decision to spend the 1956 money earmarked for Aswan, the administration had limited its alternatives. Congressional hearings made it clear that the administration's lengthy campaign on behalf of the dam had been less than a rousing success and also revealed the extent of the opposition to the project, especially from cotton state senators concerned that the Aswan Dam would increase Egyptian production.[51] Exacerbating the situation, the Senate Appropriations Committee threatened to include an amendment to the foreign aid bill prohibiting funds from going to the Aswan project. Had the administration confronted the Senate on this addition, it might well have won.[52] But with Eisenhower ill, Dulles, himself unenthusiastic about the dam project, instead wrote a letter to the committee promising to discuss any funding for the dam with senators prior to reaching any decision.[53]

During the first two weeks of July both the British and American statesmen decided not to go ahead with the Aswan Dam. Britain's shaky financial position played a major role in bringing about this change of heart. Under the circumstances, the meager return in Egyptian goodwill did not warrant the enormous expenditure required. Furthermore, it seemed senseless for Britain to do more for a government seemingly so opposed to British interests than it was doing for its friends. The American administration resented Nasser's apparent lack of interest in its Middle Eastern peace initiatives and his recognition of the People's Republic of China. The significant congressional opposition was also important. Finally, personal animosity toward Nasser, particularly in Britain, played a part in the mutual Anglo-American decision not to support his pet project. What remains surprising is the blitheness with which this decision was taken. In December the British government had regarded the dam as a question of vital national interest, while the administration had come to the conclusion that its foreign policy goals mandated Western financing of the project. The refusal to fund the dam six months later made the British and American governments look worse than had no offer ever been made at all. This decision reflected an Anglo-American colonialist mentality that refused to consider the obvious retaliatory measure available to Nasser. Both Dulles and State Department professionals could only envision one significant avenging action that Nasser might take: accepting a Soviet offer to finance the dam.[54] While the British worried about being blamed for the turn-around, the Foreign Office never predicted that Nasser would seize the Suez Canal, although, as shall be seen, his government had been putting increased pressure on the Suez Canal Company throughout the first half of 1956 and, with the removal of the final contingent of British troops, the last armed deterrent to such a seizure was now gone.[55]

On July 11 Byroade informed Washington that Hussein would leave for Washington on July 13 with orders from Nasser to accept the Western offer more or less as it had been left in February.[56] Nasser's motivation deserves reflection. As late as June 20, when Black had met with him in Cairo, Nasser had raised substantive objections to the offers.[57] Nasser was probably aware both of the Anglo-American change of heart and of Dulles's domestic problems. Accordingly the possibility that he deliberately forced the issue cannot be excluded. If so, it was a brilliant move. If Dulles agreed to fund the dam, the Egyptian leader would have financing in hand that he could also use to get more money out of the Soviet Union when he went to Moscow in August. If the American government refused, Nasser would have the excuse he may have been seeking to remove the most glaring symbol of Anglo-French colonialism.

Hussein having departed on schedule, Byroade, who was increasingly upset at Washington's hard line, cabled Dulles on July 13. The ambassador first urged Dulles to reexamine his hard-line policy. Byroade pointed out again that Washington erred when it viewed the Middle East through the prism of the conflict between the Communist and the free worlds. He believed that Nasser was seeking closer cooperation with the Soviet Union, not out of pro-Communist sympathies, but because of Middle Eastern imperatives, namely the Egyptian president's need to obtain arms. Then Byroade observed that "while economic assistance provides a very useful lubricator for foreign policy operations which become closely intermeshed with those of other countries as a result of joint approaches to common objectives, economic assistance does not (rpt not) in itself establish basic common bonds between us and recipients and does not (rpt not) coincide with our programs and policies for containing [the] Soviet threat."[58]

While the secretary completely ignored Byroade's plea, as of July 13 Dulles had not decided what to do. While he was inclined to tell Hussein bluntly that the American offer was withdrawn, he had not yet shut his mind to the British preference, shared by the State Department's Near Eastern desk, to try to "play things long" for awhile longer.[59] But the report of the Senate Appropriations Committee precipitated a final decision. Instead of requesting the administration to consult with the committee prior to making any appropriation for the Aswan project, the report mandated prior Senate approval for any such appropriation.[60] Dulles was very angry; having sent his letter to the committee, he felt that he had kept his part of the bargain but the committee had reneged on its agreement. Moreover, he believed that such a clause was unconstitutional. But the administration found its hands tied. Senate Minority Leader William Knowland informed Dulles that if the administration announced its intention not to be bound by the report, the senators would simply write the prohibition against funding the Aswan project into the bill itself. The president did not want to veto the bill and could not veto the report.[61]

Dulles, therefore, told British Ambassador to Washington Sir Roger Makins on the morning of July 19 that while he would have preferred to postpone the Aswan question, in consultation with the president, he had concluded that the Senate's action made this impossible. In order to render unnecessary the committee's obnoxious rider, Dulles would tell Hussein during the afternoon that the administration would not fund the dam. Makins commented that while his government would have preferred a chance for a further exchange of views with the administration, "the general view in London was the same." Dulles said any delay was impossible because he "was not prepared to let the control of foreign policy pass to Congress and he would rather the Executive Department made the decision."[62] Yet the congressional opposition provided Dulles with the perfect excuse to avoid funding the dam without offending Nasser. If Dulles had chosen to place the blame for withdrawing the offer squarely on congressional shoulders, he could have achieved his desired result while simultaneously minimizing the offense to Nasser. One would have thought that a diplomat of Dulles's caliber would have seized this opportunity. Indeed the administration generally used congressional opposition in just this manner, for example, telling the British government each year that legislative doubts made amendment of the U.S. Agreement impossible.

Certainly Dulles was faced with a difficult political problem. However, the secretary's need for public control over foreign policy apparently overrode a considered response. Instead, exhibiting the same impulse that had led him three years earlier to announce precipitately the replacement of Walter Gifford as American ambassador to Britain, Dulles took full responsibility for the Aswan decision. For the second time, personalities decisively affected the Aswan project. The March 1956 Anglo-American volte-face on Egyptian policy had been triggered because of Eden's psychological and political needs. Now, because Dulles insisted on preserving the image of his domination over foreign policy, the administration would take the worst possible approach toward Nasser.[63]

As Makins had indicated, British officials had not yet decided to inform the Egyptian government about the Aswan decision.[64] However, their objections were a matter of form rather than substance, and they recognized that given American domestic circumstances and the fact that this was mainly American money, Dulles had the right to make the decision. Furthermore, British officials betrayed a sense of relief that the irksome dam problem was solved.

Accordingly, when Hussein arrived at the State Department late in the afternoon, Dulles immediately informed him that the United States had decided not to fund the dam. In defending his decision Dulles invoked not only the Nile waters' question but two other issues. The first was the long range impact of the project on Egyptian-American relations. The secretary acknowledged that the project was now popular in Egypt. But he feared that its enormous costs would lead the Egyptian people to blame the American government for any resulting economic stringency. Second, Dulles stressed the domestic American opposition to the dam, which came largely from a "feeling that the Egyptian government was working closely with those hostile to us who sought to injure us where ever they could." Hussein attempted to change the secretary's mind, but Dulles reiterated that the matter was closed, although he said that the American government would consider other riparian projects.[65] Again the secretary made a tactical blunder. It would have made far more sense for him to tell Hussein that the administration was fed up with Nasser's arrogant attitude rather than to attribute partly his decision to Egypt's penurious economic position. Even a less proud man than Nasser would have retaliated.[66]

Dulles was impressed with the manner in which Hussein had taken this news, telling his brother Allen that the Egyptian had "handled himself surprisingly well and with dignity."[67] A relaxed Dulles left for Peru, while Eisenhower was in Panama. The British government announced on July 20 that it concurred in the American decision not to fund the dam.[68] Since the American government had taken public responsibility for the decision, the British government believed that it would not have to pay the price for Dulles's action. One week later it would find out otherwise.

FOUR

SAVING THE NATION

JULY 26–SEPTEMBER 5, 1956

I feel that the situation created by the
Egyptian Government imperils the survival of the
U.K. and the Commonwealth, and represents
a very great danger to sterling.
—Sir George Bolton, Executive Director,
The Bank of England,
August 1, 1956

asser's surprise nationalization of the shares of the Suez Canal Company on July 26, 1956, exactly one week after Dulles's announcement that the United States would not fund the Aswan High Dam, struck Britain and France with the impact of an armed attack. The next day the British government, joined by the French, which had its own reasons for taking a truculent position, began planning military and other measures against Nasser. Simultaneously the Eisenhower administration started a three-month campaign to restrain its European allies from using force against Egypt. As its vehicle the American government used the London Conference of August 1956, whose deliberations resulted in a proposal to internationalize the Suez Canal.

BACKGROUND TO THE NATIONALIZATION

Nasser's nationalizing of the shares of the Suez Canal Company should not have come as a shock to Western observers. Both the Egyptian government and people abhorred the Canal Company for symbolic reasons and because its management treated Egyptians with imperial arrogance. Pursuant to a 1949 convention signed with the Egyptian government, the company had grudgingly begun to appoint some natives as pilots and clerks. However,

Egyptian officials resented the fact that the company only complied with the letter, not with the spirit, of the agreement.[1] During the autumn of 1955, the Egyptian government demanded that the company, which was chartered in Egypt, sell its foreign exchange reserves to the government. Egyptian Law No. 80 required Egyptian companies to do so, but the Canal Company had heretofore been exempted. With foreign exchange scarce, largely because of payments made to Communist bloc nations in connection with arms purchases, Egyptian officials could not pass up the company's rich hoard of reserves.[2]

In the new year the company and the Egyptian government held a series of difficult negotiations. Four issues were involved: Egyptian Law No. 80, the reappointment of Egyptian directors, the hiring of more Egyptian pilots, and the Egyptian government's desire to be represented on the comité de direction that ran the company.[3] The Canal Company had not only dragged its feet on the hiring of the Egyptian pilots while continuing to recruit foreign pilots but also begrudged giving Egyptian personnel the same subsidized loans for housing that foreign pilots received. These actions prompted the British representative on the comité de direction to observe that the company was providing excellent ammunition for its Egyptian critics.[4]

In March British officials in Cairo and in London warned that "Egyptian pressure on the Company has increased and shows every sign of increasing."[5] The Canal Company's concession expired in 1968, and the British government wanted to retain a role in the operation of the canal thereafter. To this end Whitehall's policy was to try to appease the Egyptian officials concerned with the canal. The Canal Company officers did not make this easy. Ignoring London's advice, they made no concessions to Egyptian sensibilities.[6] Managing Director Jacques Georges-Picot became the symbol of company arrogance: he was thoroughly disliked by Egyptian officials as well as resented by Whitehall.[7]

Negotiations on the company's foreign exchange reserves continued without resolution during the spring of 1956. While an agreement seemed in the offing in early April, at the end of the same month, Nasser apparently set aside Egyptian Finance Minister Abdul Kaisouni's recommendations. This development led Adam Watson, head of the Foreign Office's African Desk, to write on April 24, "It looks as though power is going increasingly to Nasser's head and that he finds it harder to tolerate the trammels of international agreement." Evelyn Schuckburgh responded, "This is a new field for Nasser's nationalistic excesses."[8] Watson four days later observed, "At present the Egyptian government are becoming increasingly short of money. The negotiations for a loan agreement for the Aswan High Dam are not complete and Egyptian pressure on the Suez Canal Company has increased in the last week or so."[9]

These perceptive statements raise the question, Why did British officials fail to foresee the possibility of Nasser nationalizing the canal? Partly the explanation lies in the propensity of British officials to take at face value the company's statements that Egyptians lacked the technical ability to run the canal. Also, Watson and others assumed that Nasser's need for money would prevent him from risking the canal revenues by nationalizing the canal and killing the golden goose.[10] Most important, British officials retained imperial prejudices about the incapacity of third world peoples and governments, which prevented them from foreseeing the possibility of nationalization.[11]

Reports from the company grew more ominous in May. The agent supérieur, the company's chief operating officer in Egypt, believed that the Egyptian government would make some move against the canal during the next month or two, perhaps linked to the final base evacuations and the Egyptian National Day celebrations on June 18.[12] No one thought in terms of nationalization; speculation focused on greater Egyptian pressure to join the management board.[13] Furthermore, at the end of May, one difficult issue was removed when the company and the Egyptian government reached a compromise on the foreign exchange issue: the company agreed to invest significantly in various Egyptian improvement plans.[14]

Nothing untoward disturbed Egyptian festivities on June 18. One month later, while Nasser was in Yugoslavia, Dulles announced the withdrawal of the American offer to fund the dam. When Nasser returned to Cairo on July 19, he saw the text of the American announcement for the first time. According to his close friend Mohammed Heikal, it was on that day that Nasser decided to nationalize the Canal Company. In one stroke he would be able to redress his wounded prestige and also procure financial assets that would make possible the building of the Aswan Dam. (Nasser took the additional precaution of insuring that he would also receive Soviet assistance for the Aswan project.)[15] To increase the symbolic effect of the nationalization, Nasser chose July 26, which was the fourth anniversary of King Farouk's post-coup departure.

As they awaited Nasser's response to the withdrawal of the Aswan offer,

Western diplomats concentrated on the possibility that Nasser might expel the American Point Four economic aid mission from Egypt. Lest the United States be caught unaware, on July 25 William Rountree, who would be promoted from deputy assistant secretary for Near Eastern Affairs (NEA) to assistant secretary the next day, drafted a press release dealing with such an expulsion. On the same day, George Allen, who was leaving NEA to become ambassador to Greece, agreed with French Ambassador Maurice Couve de Murville that the best tack Nasser could take the next day would be to announce to the world that "Egypt will go ahead with the Dam even if we must build it alone, and we will begin when we can see it through."[16]

Nasser had a more dramatic response in mind. Appearing in Alexandria on the night of July 26, in an open car, lit by a spotlight from behind, Nasser made his way to a hastily built speakers' platform. He launched into an outline of Egyptian history and then discussed Black and the World Bank loan. When Nasser shouted, "But de Lesseps imposed conditions on the Khedive. I am not the Khedive," the Egyptian team led by Mohamoud Younis began the nationalization of the company offices. Nasser then informed the crowd that "Compagnie Universelle du Maritime de Suez shall be nationalized as an Egyptian Company and transferred to the state with all its assets." The crowd of a quarter of a million apparently stood silent for a moment. Then pandemonium erupted.[17]

WESTERN REACTION TO NASSER'S COUP

If the Egyptian crowd was surprised at Nasser's coup, the reaction in the West was one of complete astonishment. The news reached Eden in the evening of July 26 during a dinner for King Feisel of Iraq at 10 Downing Street. Iraqi Prime Minister Nuri Pasha shared Eden's view that Nasser should be hit hard and soon. After his guests departed, Eden called in the three chiefs of staff and found to his dismay that while the services could immediately respond to a nuclear attack they were not in a position to retaliate rapidly against Nasser.[18]

Eden also spoke that evening with the French ambassador and the American chargé d'affaires Andrew Foster, telling them that the British government took a very serious view of the situation and that any failure to regain Western control over the canal would have "disastrous consequences for the economic life of the Western powers and for their standing in the Middle East."[19] Foster attended an emergency Cabinet meeting after midnight, in the company of the chiefs of staff and the French ambassador. Eden advocated a militant stance, suggesting that Canal Company employees should quit work, although, under the terms of the Egyptian nationalization decree, such a step would mean their imprisonment. The Cabinet ordered the military men to prepare immediately a study of the requirements and goals of a possible retaliatory strike. But Foster noted that the Cabinet saw the attitude of the United States government as the most important issue.[20]

In order to encourage Eisenhower to take the "right approach," Eden wrote the president the next day. Brushing aside as a legal quibble the Egyptian government's right to nationalize an Egyptian company, Eden stressed the need for international control over the canal and stated that, in his view, economic sanctions would not suffice. Eden continued: "My colleagues are convinced that we must be ready, in the last resort, to use force to bring Nasser to his senses. For our part we are prepared to do so. I have this morning instructed our Chiefs of Staff to prepare a military plan accordingly." Eden concluded this letter by stressing the need for tripartite cooperation and asked Eisenhower to send an American representative to London, where Christian Pineau, French foreign minister, honoring a long-standing commitment, was due to arrive on July 29.[21]

The French government fully supported Eden's belligerent attitude toward Nasser. On July 27 Pineau had told American Ambassador to France C. Douglas Dillon that Nasser's action was equivalent to Hitler's seizure of the Rhineland. Were it not stopped, the inevitable result would be the complete seizure of Middle Eastern oil pipelines by Arab countries and the end of Western influence in the region.[22] However, Algeria provided the central motivation behind the incessant pressure exerted by the French prime minister Guy Mollet and his colleagues on their British counterparts to take firm action against Nasser.[23] The Algerian civil war became the crucible for France during the 1950s. Driven out of Indo-China, the French government intended to hold on to Algeria, which, unlike other African territories, had been integrated into metropolitan France. Nasser openly supported the Arab *front de libération nationale* (FLN), the spearhead of the Algerian revolt, thereby earning the almost irrational enmity of many French leaders. Striking at Nasser would deny the FLN material support and would help assuage the growing feeling of impotence engendered by the peculiarly destructive nature of guerrilla war. Not to take action against the Egyptian leader would enhance his prestige at the West's expense and improve the morale of Algerian rebels.[24]

On July 27, the Treasury implemented economic sanctions against Egypt both to coerce Nasser and to defend the British pound. Although this was an offensive action, defensive concerns motivated it. By the afternoon of July 27, official sterling was under such strong pressure that the Bank of England could not determine the rate for transferable sterling.[25] Officials believed that the Egyptian government was dumping all its free sterling on the market.[26] To counter this threat, the Treasury regulations removed Egypt from the transferable account area and mandated that no payments could be made to or from Egyptian accounts without the permission of the Bank of England. In addition, all Egyptian private and government accounts were blocked, as were those of the Suez Canal Company. Only limited exceptions were made.[27]

Throwing this financial strike against Nasser heartened British officials although they did not believe that it would be decisive in the crisis. As the prime minister commented during the Cabinet meeting of July 27, the blocking of Egypt's sterling assets, amounting to £14 million, would not seriously inconvenience Egypt.[28] More troubling, it was a double-edged sword. By blocking accounts, the British government halted the extensive Anglo-Egyptian trade, thereby diminishing British exports that the government had fought to increase in order to improve the balance of payments and strengthen sterling. Furthermore, sterling purported to be an international currency. A key attribute of a reserve currency is its availability in international trade. Now the British government had undermined the viability of sterling's international status. In response, other nations, particularly in the Middle East, might withdraw their sterling and convert it into dollars. This dilemma was the first of many the British government would face during the next five months.

American reaction to Nasser's action was far more muted. Eisenhower met with Allen Dulles, Colonel Andrew Goodpaster, and Under Secretary of State Herbert Hoover, Jr., on July 27 to discuss possible American responses and to draft a State Department statement.[29] After consulting by telephone Foster Dulles, who was in Lima, Peru, the White House issued a statement emphasizing the gravity of the situation and the need for consultations.[30] The American government's reluctance to use force and its determination to keep free of any precipitate entanglement with the British and French governments clearly emerged from these meetings. In fact, the administration was unenthusiastic even about tripartite planning.[31] Adamantly opposed to Eden's idea of a joint meeting in Washington, Eisenhower did agree to send Deputy Under Secretary of State Robert Murphy to London immediately. However, at the same time he cabled Eden to urge that the maximum number of maritime nations also be consulted about the situation.[32]

In London, the days following the nationalization were filled with frantic action. Special meetings of the Cabinet, the Defence Transition Committee, and the newly established Cabinet Egypt Committee were held. The prime minister sought the support of Commonwealth leaders. To New Zealand Prime Minister Sidney Holland, Eden wrote that if Nasser's action was allowed to pass unchallenged, "the oil supplies of the free world will be at his mercy and Commonwealth communications and trade will be greatly jeopardized."[33] This statement encapsulated the British government's avowed reasons for opposing Nasser. The canal was vital because 80 percent of Western Europe's oil passed through it.[34] Using the canal also significantly shortened the distance from Britain to India, Australia, and to British colonies.[35] In later years when Eden was asked the motivation for his stand during the Suez crisis, he said, "remember Australia."[36] This phrase embodied more than the practical matter of imperial communications. It was intolerable to a man like Eden, born in the last century and come to maturity at the apogee of empire, that an upstart like Nasser could strip Britain of one of its most glorious possessions. Ironically, a decade earlier the British government had been able to comprehend that changed circumstances made it inevitable that India, the cornerstone of the British Empire, be given independence. Two years earlier Eden himself had urged acceptance of the Suez Canal base accord because the British position in Egypt had become indefensible. Yet now Eden and his colleagues clung to the canal, the concession for which would expire in a mere twelve years, as if possession of it was an essential element in Britain's survival.[37]

Even as Eden was immersing himself in the emotions of a lost epoch of unchallenged British power, he realized the necessity for immediate American assistance in two specific areas. First, the British government needed administration help in obtaining American tankers and Western petroleum supplies in the event Nasser interfered with the passage of oil through the canal. Second, the British government needed Washington's cooperation in anti-Egyptian sanctions. British Ambassador Sir Roger Makins was dispatched to the State Department on July 28 to persuade the administration to freeze Egyptian and Canal Company assets in the United States. It was not an easy task. Hoover opposed the idea, telling the British ambassador that private action on behalf of the Canal Company would suffice. After his discussion with the under secretary, Makins perceptively observed that "the State Department do not feel themselves directly involved as principals in the dispute with Egypt and they are acutely aware of the domestic repercussions which strong action (e.g., involving the prospect of the rationing of oil) might have."[38]

Hoover conveyed the same detached attitude to the French ambassador, informing him that great care was needed in handling the Suez problem and pointing to the possible repercussions that might result from an "emotional approach." Byroade endorsed the under secretary's stance and counseled that "any participation in or even tacit condoning by United States government of British military measures against Egypt would be heavily counter productive to United States long-term or immediate interest throughout Arab countries of Near East. I can think of nothing that would set us back quicker and farther."[39]

Byroade's advice on this question coincided with Hoover's opinion but, after further discussion, the administration announced on July 31 that it was blocking the assets of the Egyptian government (which included the deposits of the National Bank of Egypt) and the Suez Canal Company.[40] While the financial ties between Egypt and the United States were not as extensive as Anglo-Egyptian connections, 75 percent of the National Bank's gold and dollar reserves were held at the Federal Reserve Bank of New York. Indeed the total amount of the Egyptian government and National Bank of Egypt assets blocked by the United States amounted to $42 million, which exceeded the amount held in London.[41]

The legal authority for this action derived from the as yet unrepealed state of national emergency declared by President Truman at the beginning of the Korean War. During a period of national emergency the president had the power to "regulate or prohibit transactions in foreign exchange, transfers of credit or payments by, through or to any banking institutions and may prevent or prohibit the use, transfer, withdrawal or exportation or any transaction involving any property in which any foreign country or a national thereof has any interest." Therefore, without any congressional advice or consent, the president could declare total economic war at will.[42]

But the administration only used part of its financial arsenal against Egypt. It cushioned the freezing order by excluding funds held by private Egyptian corporations and individuals. Furthermore, the order included only monies on deposit on July 31, not future accruals (which were covered by the French and British orders). These two major exceptions would continually be raised by the British as would the third major loophole, that American shipowners were permitted to continue to pay the user charges for the canal, known as canal dues, to Egyptian authorities, provided that such payments were made under protest.[43] Canal dues presented less of a problem for the British and French governments because their shipowners customarily paid in London and Paris, respectively. The British government urged the American government to have American ships pay the dues to the Suez Canal Company's offices in London or Paris.[44] But the administration, for the moment, refused to address this issue.

Hoover's thoroughness in keeping Dulles informed of events enabled the secretary of state to supply Murphy with extensive instructions prior to the latter's arrival in London on July 29. Dulles cabled that "it is our view that Nasser should not now be presented with an ultimatum requiring him to reverse his nationalization action under threat of force. We believe it is most unlikely he would back down and that war would accordingly become inevitable." Dulles then pointed out that American military action would require congressional authorization, an unlikely possibility except in "compelling circumstances."[45] Therefore, he instructed Murphy to seek an international conference of maritime nations to be summoned by three or more signatories of the 1888 Constantinople Convention that governed the canal's usage.[46]

At the first tripartite meeting, on July 29, Pineau proclaimed that the French government was ready to "go to the end" in dealing with Nasser because "one successful battle in Egypt would be worth ten in North Africa." At this and succeeding meetings British officials also raised the possibility of using military force within six weeks.[47] Murphy cabled Washington immediately, detailing the intransigent position of the British and French delegates. Lloyd maintained that the "whole Western position in the Middle East will be jeopardized if Nasser gets away with his action," while Pineau again alluded to the parallel with Hitler's remilitarization of the Rhineland.[48] Administration officials, understandably alarmed, agreed at a White House meeting on July 31 that Dulles should go to Britain and personally convey to the allies Eisenhower's belief (shared by his officials) that the British emphasis on military force was "out of date." Supporting the president's position was Allen Dulles, who said that if a military move were made now, the whole Arab world would be united against the West. While Foster Dulles insisted that "Nasser must be made to disgorge the Canal," he agreed that it was essential to convince the allies of the virtues of substituting a maritime conference for military force.[49]

To bolster his case Dulles took with him a letter to Eden from Eisenhower. The president emphasized the need for an international conference before using force because "public opinion here and, I am convinced, in most of the world would be outraged should there be a failure to make such efforts." While the president understood that the British government envisioned utilizing military measures, he emphasized that "I personally feel sure that the American reaction [against the use of force] would be severe and that the great areas of the world would share that reaction."[50] Eisenhower's tendency to hide his own sentiments behind the cover of "public opinion," however, weakened the effect of his words and contributed to the failure of Anglo-American understanding during the crisis.

The president's letter encapsulated the American government's position during August: force was acceptable only as a last resort, after all other options were exhausted. It was not that Eisenhower failed to understand the Anglo-French predicament; he wrote his confidant "Swede" Hazlett on August 3 that he recognized the need for a settlement that restored rather than further damaged the prestige of Britain and France. But Eisenhower thought that this time Nasser's action should be tolerated.[51]

The administration accurately read domestic opinion. Newspaper editors expressed concern about the nationalization of the canal but viewed the matter as a primarily European issue. Editorials stressed conciliation, not condemnation, and avoided all speculation involving military pressure.[52] This stance reflected the view of the American public, which was prepared neither to accept oil rationing nor the use of force for a faraway Canal about which they knew little and which had no apparent impact on their lives. Furthermore, Eisenhower's 1956 campaign emphasized the president's having ended the Korean War and the promise of continued American peace and prosperity. Eisenhower and his colleagues did not want to jeopardize either the president's reelection or a chance at a Republican-controlled Congress. Such election year considerations would play a part in all administration decisions during the Suez crisis.

THE TRIPARTITE APPROACH

The British and French were apprehensive about the arrival of Dulles; the French ambassador to London for one feared that the American government would adopt the same stance over Egypt that it had taken over Iran.[53] Indeed the two situations contained important parallels. Both cases revolved around oil. Nasser's willingness to be friendlier to the United States than to Britain and France echoed Mussadiq's reaction. In the Iranian crisis the British and American governments accepted the nationalization of AIOC while negotiating the terms on which oil would be purchased.[54] One of the most important differences between the Iranian and Egyptian cases was that in the former situation, Britain had a legal basis for its ire: the International Court of Justice had issued provisional measures of protection with which Iran refused to comply.[55]

The British government's apprehensiveness increased when Makins cabled London reporting Dulles's opinion that as long as Nasser did not interfere with navigation through the canal, he saw no occasion for the use of force. The ambassador concluded that "in prevailing conditions we can look for little help from Washington." Makins's reading would remain an accurate summary of the American position throughout the crisis.[56]

At his first meeting with British and French officials Dulles immediately set forth his ideas for the possible international conference. Several factors motivated the secretary's emphasis on this procedure. As a vehicle for settling international disputes the heyday of the conference coincided with Dulles's reign as a leading diplomat: his experience ran the gamut from the Hague Conference of 1907 and the Versailles Conference to the Dawes and Young Plan conferences and the Japanese Peace Treaty Conference of 1951. A conference would also have the advantage of smoking out Nasser's position; as Dulles had earlier told Makins, "If Nasser should refuse, or should assume a hostile attitude in attendance, he would place himself in an extremely bad light before world opinion." Both the secretary of state and the president placed great weight on public opinion; Nasser's public trial and conviction was a necessary prerequisite to any future military action.

That a conference would buy him some extra time was, to Dulles, another attraction. As he told United Nations Secretary-General Dag Hammarskjöld, one of the reasons for his trumpeting of the idea of a conference was that he "certainly thought the more delay there was the less likelihood there was it [force] would be invoked."[57] Dulles also insisted that any Western action against Nasser must be based on a violation of the Constantinople Convention of 1888; the conference route permitted such a legal structure. His intransigent attitude derived from the American concern over the implications of Nasser's action for United States control of the Panama Canal. Because the United States based its suzerainty over the Panama Canal and the Canal Zone on a treaty, it was imperative that any action against Nasser be based on the Constantinople Convention.

The specter of the Panama Canal also partly explains the American opposition to any suggestion that the allies approach the United Nations: Dulles and his colleagues did not want to create a precedent for a Panamanian demarche. Furthermore, Dulles pointed out the difficulty of basing any complaint against Nasser on his nationalization of the canal per se. The United States had previously accepted the principle of nationalization as long as there was adequate compensation, which Nasser had offered in his July 26 speech. Even British officials, albeit begrudgingly, accepted that Nasser had a legal right to nationalize an Egyptian company although they never acknowledged the obvious parallel between Britain's many postwar nationalizations and Nasser's action.[58]

Yet Dulles's trumpeting of his conference scheme contributed to the Anglo-American misunderstandings that would hamper communication during the next three months. The London Conference could only change the new status quo if the tripartite countries bolstered any resulting decision by military force. Consequently Dulles's British listeners eagerly read into his words a promise of force that never existed. His frequent use of the word *disgorge* abetted British wishful thinking. Perhaps the secretary saw it as a legal term—criminals are made to disgorge their ill-gotten profits. However, as Dulles knew or should have known, to laymen it has a very militant connotation that British statesmen eagerly accepted. Unfortunately the secretary frequently made rash statements without considering their implications.

The signatory nations to the 1888 convention governing the canal and other maritime nations such as the United States would be the main participants of such a conference.[59] The Soviet Union would necessarily be

SAVING THE NATION 85

invited as it was a signatory nation, but this did not trouble Dulles in part because his explicit model was the 1951 conference that preceded the Japanese Peace Treaty.[60] This conclave had been Dulles's finest hour, when he successfully fathered a peace treaty totally acceptable to the United States notwithstanding the presence of Soviet delegates.[61] The British and French governments went along with Dulles's scheme because it seemed the best way to mobilize American support against Nasser, although they continued full-scale military planning. Accordingly, during the first three days of August, invitations were sent to all signatory nations, major maritime nations, including the United States, and Egypt.

Israel, however, despite its protestations, did not receive an invitation.[62] Dulles believed that it was essential that the Suez Canal problem not become intertwined with the Arab-Israeli dispute. As he told Sir Robert Menzies, if the two issues became entangled, "there would be great danger that the entire Arab world would unite against the British and French." Therefore, the secretary opposed both the French suggestion to send additional French Mystère planes to Israel and the inclusion of Israel in the London Conference.[63]

Israeli officials found the fuss over the nationalization of the Suez Canal almost ludicrous. Since 1948 the Egyptian government had denied ships bound for Israel access to the canal on the grounds that a state of war existed between the two countries. Both the British government and the Canal Company had tolerated this action although it violated the Constantinople Convention. While the United Nations General Assembly in 1951 had passed a resolution condemning Egypt's action, no sanctions were levied on Egypt. But if the canal itself was relatively unimportant to Prime Minister David Ben-Gurion and his colleagues, the potential impact of the crisis on the Middle East in general and on Arab-Israeli relations in particular loomed large, particularly given the widely held Israeli assumption of an imminent "second round" of the Arab-Israeli confrontation.

On August 1 Dulles met with both Chancellor of the Exchequer Harold Macmillan and Prime Minister Anthony Eden. Macmillan, already closely aligned with the Suez Group, took a very hawkish position. He told Dulles that the Cabinet believed that "if this action was not met by the utmost firmness a chain reaction would be started which would ultimately lead to the loss of the entire British position in the Middle East. . . . They would rather die fighting than slowly bleed to a state of impotence." Rather than respond to Macmillan's points directly, Dulles reiterated his call for a maritime conference and again stressed the need to influence world opinion.

Eden now hosted Dulles at a lunch at 10 Downing Street. There the two statesmen clearly expressed their very different positions. The prime minister said that while they would prefer to have the United States participate in military action, the British did not count on it. "They did want our [the United States] moral support and economic support in terms of petroleum products diverted from our side, and would want us to neutralize any open participation by the Soviet Union."

Dulles replied that he agreed that Nasser should not "get away with it," but the issue was how he could be brought to "disgorge." The secretary then stated:

United States public opinion was not ready to back a military venture by Britain and France which, at this stage, could be plausibly portrayed as motivated by imperialist and colonialist ambitions in the general area, going beyond the Canal operation itself, which was still open. I felt that for the British and French to undertake such an operation without at least the moral support of the United States would be a great disaster because it opened the way for many future evil consequences.

Dulles then pointed out the major problems a military operation would pose, both logistically and for the future of Western relations with the Arab world. Finally, the secretary reiterated his conviction that the allies must make a genuine effort to settle the crisis in a peaceable manner.[64]

Accordingly, Dulles had clearly explained the American position: the use of force would be permissible only after all other alternatives had been explored. Moreover, the United States was not prepared to tolerate its allies taking any action that the United States deemed prejudicial to Western interests in the area.

In the meantime the administration considered the question of Western European oil supplies, first raised by the British government on July 27.[65] Anglo-American government attention to this issue was not new. Both governments had involved themselves in petroleum planning during World War II, and in the aftermath of the Iranian imbroglio, the American government had waived the antitrust laws and permitted the oil companies to decide jointly how to handle the loss of Iranian production.[66] The American and British governments also discussed the oil question in the months prior to the Suez crisis, holding a series of meetings in Washington in February and March 1956.[67] These were more important to the British government because Britain's use of petroleum was growing very rapidly, and with well over 80 percent of British and European supplies coming from the Middle East, the British government was acutely aware of its vulnerability.[68] Indeed fears about Middle Eastern oil supplies partly prompted the tough British stand against Nasser.

While the American government always cooperated explicitly with oil companies, never was this symbiosis more apparent than during the Suez crisis. The man in charge of the State Department's economic policies, Herbert Hoover, Jr., had not only worked in the oil industry but had come to prominence because of his services to both the government and the oil companies after the Iran coup. The administration shared the British government's concern because it worried that NATO's oil supplies might be jeopardized.[69] On July 30 the Suez Economic Task Force, composed of representatives of the State, Treasury, Commerce, Interior, and Defense departments, as well as Dr. Arthur Flemming, head of the Office of Defense Mobilization (ODM), and Allen Dulles, held its initial meeting. It first decided that ODM and the Interior departments should ask selected oil companies to send representatives to work with government officials on a committee soon to be known as the Middle East Emergency Committee (MEEC). The group's brief would be to initiate planning to assure a continued supply of oil to Western Europe in the event the Suez Canal were closed. To avoid alarming either Arab nations or the American public, this work would be done in total secrecy.[70]

Oil companies eagerly agreed to work with the administration. In fact, high-ranking officers of Socony-Mobil (Mobil) called on William Rountree on August 1 to discuss the situation. Executives feared the immediate impact of the Suez crisis on their operations: oil companies were the heaviest users of the canal. But equally important was their consternation concerning the possible impact of Nasser's coup on their own Middle Eastern operations. For this reason the Socony representatives urged that the administration take a tough stance. Rountree found himself advocating a cautious line, telling his visitors that while he understood their position, "the U.S. and the companies were faced with certain realities which had to be recognized and dealt with."[71]

Although Hoover initially refused to promise Makins any American help, one of the MEEC's tasks was to coordinate petroleum planning with the British government. Whitehall was relieved when the administration requested the presence of a high-ranking official at future meetings. Officials at the Ministry of Fuel and Power calculated that if the flow of Middle Eastern oil were interrupted, Europe's imports would fall to about half the normal rate. If the canal were closed but the pipelines remained open, the shortfall would be half as much. Such calculations led to the British placing a major emphasis on the position of tankers and the possibility of rerouting them as well as the need to coordinate production.[72]

By the second week of August the MEEC had drafted a plan of action. Oil company officials not only cooperated with the MEEC but met on their own in New York. The administration welcomed this assistance; Dulles went so far as to send his former partner and continuing troubleshooter Arthur Dean (who also represented Aramco) to a meeting at the Biltmore Hotel on August 7.[73] The machinery to deal with any crisis would soon be in place.[74]

But even if Anglo-American petroleum cooperation continued on track, oil would remain a major problem for the British government. If either American production or American tankers had to be substituted for British equivalents, it would greatly increase the dollar cost of oil. The effect of oil on the British balance of payments was an ongoing concern that had been eased by assiduous efforts to keep dollar costs down.[75] But now estimates of the cost of replacing Middle Eastern oil with other supplies ran at $500-$700 million each year, all of which would have to come out of the still perilously low British reserves. These alarming sums led a Foreign Office official to comment that "if Middle East oil supplies are cut off altogether, it is difficult to see how we could manage to avoid major economic disaster."[76]

The state of the British economy was never far from British minds. After their low point in February, British reserves had increased until at the end of July they stood at $2,405 million.[77] But with $2,000 million considered the bare minimum necessary for the sterling area to function, the Bank of England operated on a narrow margin. The Suez crisis caused financial problems for several reasons, not least of which were the possibility of increased oil costs and the expense of any military action. Most importantly, British officials feared that foreign holders of sterling would lose confidence in the pound and, fearing a devaluation, would sell their holdings.

Ironically, the success of the British government's earlier efforts now put the Exchequer at great risk. Reestablishing sterling convertibility had long been important to British governments because it was a prerequisite to the central goals of maintaining the pound's reserve currency status and the continued existence of the sterling area. After great sacrifice in February 1955 the Bank of England had announced that the pound had been returned to de facto convertibility.[78] Now this achievement could prove Britain's undoing since it permitted nonresident sterling holders to exchange pounds for the dollars or gold that comprised Britain's meager reserves. Any such sales would weaken the pound by dissipating the reserves backing sterling and would eventually force the British government to suspend convertibility, devalue, or do both. It was for this reason that Sir Edward Bridges, a senior Treasury official, commented on August 8 that it was obvious that British gold and dollar reserves would be under considerable strain and would face even worse difficulties if the London Conference did not reach a clear-cut solution.[79]

The importance of the strength of sterling and the continued existence of the sterling area to the British government in 1956 cannot be overemphasized. To Sir George Bolton, an executive director of the Bank of England, the need to preserve the sterling area required taking firm action against Nasser. As he wrote on August 1, "If however, we are unable to dislodge the Egyptians from full control of the Canal, there will follow a collapse of the sterling exchange and a very great weakening of the Commonwealth."[80] London deemed the sterling area important for its own sake, because it helped bind together the Commonwealth and also because it gave Britain something that appeared to offset the overwhelming power of the United States and the Soviet Union. In reality the sterling area and the consequent need to keep sterling at an overvalued exchange rate not only crippled Britain's domestic economy but left it totally dependent on the goodwill of others. Of course Britain most relied on the one country with surplus reserves that could be called upon if necessary—the United States.

While economic pressure would ultimately determine Britain's fate, as British officials had predicted in the spring, it became increasingly clear that it would not have the same effect on Egypt.[81] Countries such as Belgium, Italy, and Canada refused to take any economic action at all against Egypt and some Commonwealth countries, notably India, adjusted their arrangements for payments in order to lighten Nasser's load during the crisis.[82] This lack of cooperation obviously undermined the effect of the tripartite sanctions.[83]

Since Egypt derived much of its foreign exchange from the sale of cotton, with its own huge surpluses the United States could have ruined the price of cotton on the world market. But Eisenhower and his colleagues were not fully determined upon economic pressure against Egypt. Both World Bank President Eugene Black and John J. McCloy (who was close to Eisenhower, Dulles, and Black) expressed reservations at the freeze of Egyptian assets. While officials ultimately accepted this action because it was customary to freeze assets of a contested corporation pending a determination of ownership, no one in the administration supported extending the freeze to either current assets or to private Egyptian accounts.[84] Although Washington halted military assistance, because the administration sought to keep open a bridge to Nasser, officials refused to accede to the British desire for a total freeze on Egyptian assets.[85] Instead the State Department instructed the Cairo embassy to slow down but not stop entirely foreign aid payments made under the auspices of the ICA (the current vehicle for foreign aid).[86]

Egypt had two further advantages that Britain did not possess. First, the Communist bloc supplied an alternative source of funds. Accordingly, at the end of August the People's Republic of China bought Egyptian cotton after first having sold sterling in London for Swiss francs that were then given to Egypt.[87] Second, Egypt was not trying to maintain its pound as an international reserve currency. Consequently Egypt, unlike Britain, would prove relatively immune from economic strain.[88]

On the political front, Nasser took every care to seize the high ground. In the days immediately following the nationalization, Byroade reported that Egyptian officials painstakingly attempted to avoid offending the United States. The embassy reported that "the local atmosphere still shows no signs of a build up of animosity towards the western community." The total support the nationalization had received from all classes of the Egyptian public further strengthened Nasser's position. Byroade quoted a university professor described as "anti-regime" who nevertheless said, "We have not agreed with all these boys have been doing but the Canal decision goes to the heart of every Egyptian. We would die to maintain it even if we don't like Nasser."[89]

Egyptian authorities also ensured that the canal continued to operate normally. In particular they allowed ships whose owners had paid canal dues to frozen Canal Company accounts in London, Paris, or New York to pass through the canal. But this accommodating attitude did not extend to appearing at the London Conference. Instead Nasser suggested convening a parley that would deal with the general question of international control over canals and international waterways. Needless to say, the United States, fearful of the repercussions of the Suez crisis on its control over the Panama Canal, did not embrace this suggestion.[90]

In the meantime, Israeli government officials discussed, among themselves and also with French emissaries, possible military action.[91] As France was Israel's closest ally during the 1950s and Israel depended on France for most of its modern weaponry, such consultation was to be expected. Because France was a signatory to the Tripartite Declaration, its officials usually discouraged militant Israeli responses. But with the French government eager to inflict a decisive defeat on Nasser, Israeli-French cooperation could only make military action more likely. However, until the conclusion of the London Conference, Israeli leaders continued to watch and wait.[92]

This holding pattern was evident in Western capitals as well. Eden again wrote Eisenhower, reiterating the importance to Britain of a satisfactory outcome to this crisis. On this occasion the prime minister argued that while Nasser was not a Hitler, "the parallel with Mussolini was close." Hence "the removal of Nasser and the installation in Egypt of a regime less hostile to the West, must therefore also rank high among our objectives."[93] But while the president, in company with all his officials, expressed concern at Nasser's actions, he worried more that any British and French response would precipitate a disaster in the Middle East. Therefore, Dulles cabled Dillon that Washington considered it essential that the British and French not be blamed for blocking the canal and instructed Dillon to urge Pineau not to advise Canal Company employees to leave their positions. Similarly, on August 4 the secretary, in conversation with Australian Prime Minister Sir Robert Menzies, explained that one of the chief purposes of the conference was to bring to bear the force of moderation on Egypt and, equally importantly, on Britain and France as well. Dulles regarded such considerations as crucial because he believed that "the difficulty with the present situation is that the problem has become a matter of prestige for both sides: the British feel deeply that their prestige is at stake and that failure to act and thus allow Nasser to 'get away with it' would destroy all respect still held for Britain. Nasser on the other hand, feels that he cannot back down as he is now publicly committed." Dulles told Menzies that while he realized that the British and French governments were determined to use force, he had made it clear to them that the United States was in no way committed to military measures and had also expressed his doubts regarding the feasibility of a quick solution.

Having expressed similar sentiments to the Canadian ambassador, Dulles had now done his best to convey the American position to the most important Commonwealth countries. No doubt it was communicated to Whitehall. But at the same time as the American government sent one sign, it also transmitted contradictory signals by informing the British government that it would permit emergency purchases of military equipment as long as there was no publicity. Regrettably, this double message permitted British leaders great latitude to choose how to interpret Washington's stance.[94]

The London Conference, held from August 16 to 24, seemed a success for Dulles. With only Egypt and Greece refusing to attend, the secretary of state shepherded through his proposal, which called for the canal to be run by an authority established by treaty and associated with the United Nations. The members of the governing board would be selected by user nations; Egypt would have an increased voice but no more control than before July 26. This plan was carried 18 to 4. British officials accepted the London proposals without enthusiasm. As Sir Harold Beeley wrote, "I feel sure that the gravest consequences would follow from a failure to deprive Colonel Nasser of control over the Canal."[95] Dulles accurately reported the allies' position to the National Security Council as follows: "The British and the French had gone along with the U.S. plan very reluctantly and in the obvious hope that Nasser would not ultimately accept the plan." While it was highly unlikely that Nasser would accept internationalization of an asset he had just successfully nationalized, the British and French governments hoped that Nasser's rejection of the plan might provide a pretext to invade Egypt.[96] Furthermore, they believed that cooperation now would bring American aid later.

Consequently, a five-nation delegation led by Prime Minister Robert Menzies journeyed to Cairo to present the London plan to Nasser.[97] Macmillan had urged the secretary of state to head the delegation himself because he believed that Nasser might actually heed the secretary. But, notwithstanding Eisenhower's willingness to let Dulles go to Egypt, the arguments against his participation were too strong: he might diminish his personal prestige; for Nasser to accept a solution, Dulles would have to make a diplomatic retreat from some of his statements; and given Nasser's irrationality, no matter what he did, the secretary might fail.[98]

Instead of journeying to Egypt Dulles returned home and met with Eisenhower on August 29. When he outlined the British government's position—that it would take military action if Nasser had not accepted the eighteen-power proposal by September 10—the secretary did not express condemnation but instead observed that it might be very difficult to disengage the talks on this precise timetable. Eisenhower asked how the United States could encourage Nasser to accept the proposal; at Dulles's suggestion the president issued a message of support to Menzies and his companions.[99]

When Dulles and Eisenhower met again the next day, it was clear that both men had now rejected the use of force to dislodge Nasser. Dulles said, "I had come to the conclusion that regrettable as it might be to see Nasser's prestige enhanced even temporarily, I did not believe the situation was one which should be resolved by the use of force."[100] Eisenhower agreed with Dulles's analysis, adding that "he realized how tough it was for the British and French but that this was not the issue upon which to try to downgrade Nasser."[101]

For the American government this moment proved pivotal. While never enthusiastic about military measures, not until the end of August did the president and his secretary of state entirely rule out the use of force against Nasser. Now they had, and neither man would ever change his mind. The administration's reasoning made sense: the use of force would undermine the Western position in the Middle East and benefit the Soviet Union. But the president and Dulles only indirectly attempted to discourage the British and French governments from using force, for example, urging the American ambassadors to London and Paris to express concern at reports of British and French intransigence.[102] The reason for American reticence was the administration's belief, expressed by Dulles to a group of congressional leaders on September 6, that the American government "cannot oppose too strongly their [the British and French] taking steps which they feel to be in their own national interest; otherwise responsibility shifts to us."[103] While his was a legitimate concern, Dulles's cure proved far worse than the disease; had Dulles or Eisenhower bluntly told the British and French governments that the use of force was unacceptable, the tragedy of Suez might have been avoided. Indeed, from beginning to end, poor diplomacy significantly affected the Suez crisis: first, the mishandling of Nasser and, now, the American inability to explain squarely its position to its allies.

The British government forthrightly continued military preparations.

Eden wrote Eisenhower on August 27 explaining that the firmer the West appeared, the less likely the need for force in this situation, which the prime minister described as "the most hazardous that our country has known since 1940."[104] But neither Eden nor his colleagues ever asked the administration what it would do if Britain used force against Egypt. Such reticence was extremely hazardous given the British government's dependence on American largesse. The United States provided Britain with a large part of its military hardware, particularly aircraft, under programs whose terms mandated the equipment's use only in connection with NATO.[105] Furthermore, the British government remained well aware that Europe would depend on Western Hemisphere supplies if Middle Eastern supplies should be interrupted. Finally, the viability of sterling and the continued existence of the sterling area depended on American support.

In the past, British officials had often observed that when it came to Middle Eastern disputes the American government tended to split the difference and take a position halfway between the Arabs and the British.[106] Given this fact, it behooved the Eden government to prepare the ground carefully before launching an independent operation. While the ambivalence demonstrated by the American administration's initial reaction to Nasser's coup might have given the prime minister and his colleagues grounds for believing that their counterparts wished them to proceed without being burdened with any discussion, the American position had now solidified. As the redoubtable Makins informed Whitehall: "There is no support in the United States for the use of force in the present circumstances and in the absence of further clear provocation by Nasser." Therefore Makins advised that "a go-it alone policy of military intervention would obviously deal them [the Americans] a body blow."[107] Yet the British government continued to avoid the central question: To what extent, if any, would its American counterparts support an Anglo-French military solution to the crisis? British officials, increasingly aware of the American government's opposition to a military solution, hoped to force the United States into a position where it would have no choice but to support its closest ally. The Eden government would soon find out how wrong were its calculations.

FIVE

A FATAL MISTAKE

SEPTEMBER 5–OCTOBER 29, 1956

In this particular situation [the use of force]
. . . would be a fatal mistake.
—John Foster Dulles to Selwyn Lloyd,
October 5, 1956

The failure of the Menzies mission led to a second Dulles initiative: the Suez Canal Users' Association (SCUA). Premised on the belief that Nasser's government could not run the canal, its rationale was torpedoed when, after a walkout of European pilots on September 13, the Egyptian canal authority successfully operated the conduit. The British and French governments now appealed to the United Nations. For a time the October 1956 negotiations among the British, French, and Egyptian delegates held under United Nations auspices appeared to be making considerable progress. However, the Eden and Mollet governments refused to accept a pacific solution that would leave Nasser's prestige intact.

THE AFTERMATH OF THE MENZIES MISSION
AND THE CREATION OF SCUA

The five-nation delegation headed by Australian Prime Minister Sir Robert Menzies began meeting with Nasser on September 3. Two days later, Nasser bluntly informed the delegation that he would neither have anything to do with the eighteen-power proposal nor accept any form of international control over the canal. Yet Nasser attempted to placate Western opinion: he offered to enter into a treaty setting maximum levels for tolls and mandating against discrimination amongst canal users (presumably excepting Israel, whose shipping had not been permitted through the canal for years).[1]

Eden regarded Nasser's rejection of the eighteen-power proposal as a signal for more drastic action. At a luncheon for Senator Walter George, the prime minister reiterated how crucial was the Suez crisis. The issue was "whether Britain was prepared to be nibbled to death by Nasser or on [the contrary] disposed to fight for [its] existence." Only a dramatic step would bolster Britain's position, particularly with the Arab countries who were interpreting the current situation as a sign of British weakness. The solution, thought Eden, was to have all major nations refuse to pay any more tolls to Nasser.[2] At the same time Britain sought to bring the Suez Canal nationalization before the United Nations.[3] In this endeavor Eden's government received grudging support from the French government; American Ambassador to France C. Douglas Dillon reported that while Paris was considering economic sanctions and the United Nations option, "they look on these as merely stop gaps. . . . It is probable therefore that they would regard these measures, if adopted, merely as preliminary and as creating more favorable climate for military action in relatively near future."[4]

American policymakers now feared that the Western allies wished to use the United Nations as a stepping stone on the road to a military solution to the imbroglio. Ambassador to the United Nations Henry Cabot Lodge, Jr., labeled it "a transparent tactic designed to show as promptly as possible that the UN is ineffective and thus to lay the basis of military action by them."[5] Lodge urged Dulles to block the Anglo-French demarche to the world organization. The secretary needed no persuading—he opposed such an approach because he believed that the allies had not yet established any legal basis for bringing a case before the United Nations. Further, the secretary feared that such a move would establish a precedent that could be used to wrest control over the Panama Canal from the United States, and he also worried that Nasser might retaliate to any Security Council debate or decision by closing the canal to Western shipping. Such a blockade would make any later compromise more difficult and, if oil shortages resulted, could have important ramifications in the United States, especially in the coming election campaign.[6]

Understanding the delicacy of the situation, Eisenhower wrote Eden on

September 3, seeking to restrain his British counterpart. After expressing sympathy for the British position, the president said, "I really do not see how a successful result could be achieved by forcible means. The use of force would, it seems to me, vastly increase the area of jeopardy. . . . The people of the Near East and of North Africa and to some extent, of all of Asia and all of Africa would be consolidated against the West to a degree which, I fear, could not be overcome in a generation and, perhaps, not even in a century."[7]

Eden responded immediately, explaining again the British predicament and attempting to justify military action. To Eden the events of July 1956 were eerily similar to those of twenty years before. Just as Hitler had begun by remilitarizing the Rhineland, Nasser had expropriated the Suez Canal. If the West did not stop him, the same chain reaction that had destroyed Austria and Czechoslovakia would reoccur, this time decimating pro-Western Middle Eastern regimes such as Jordan and Iraq.[8] The prime minister then counterpoised the Berlin crisis of 1948 as an example of the positive benefits of a unified front. Eisenhower did not reject the use of historical analogies; he had raised the specter of the rise of Hitler in a 1955 letter to Churchill arguing for British support of the administration's China policy. But this time the administration believed that the comparison did not make sense.[9]

Dulles realized that he needed more than words to calm the situation. Therefore, during the first week of September he developed the idea of an association of Suez Canal user nations that would hire its own pilots to guide ships through the canal. The pilots would operate from vessels stationed at either end of the canal. While this scheme made little substantive sense, it would postpone British and French military action; the secretary welcomed any delay because he continued to believe that the passage of time was working in favor of a compromise.[10] In order to persuade the British and French governments to accept SCUA, Dulles suggested that the user nations pay their canal tolls to the new entity instead of to the Egyptian government. While he had previously opposed using this economic stick against Nasser, the secretary now offered it as a carrot to buy Anglo-French support for his scheme.[11]

Dulles spent the next few days selling his plan to the British government.[12] The nature of the scheme presented the chief difficulty; as Dulles admitted to the Canadian ambassador, it was "makeshift" and "not abounding in merit." When Eisenhower observed on September 8 that he did not think the scheme would work, Dulles said he had doubts too, but "there was no chance of getting the British and French not to use force unless they had some alternatives that seemed to have in them some strength of purpose and some initiative."[13]

The British government was under tremendous pressure. On the one hand, many in the government felt the need for immediate forceful action. In the words of the permanent head of the Foreign Office, Sir Ivone Kirkpatrick, "We were not prepared to perish gracefully in order to give satisfaction to some of our friends."[14] On the other hand, at this point British officials still sought American blessing for any initiative.

Discussions over SCUA meshed with a related problem. Nasser had been very careful not to allow any incidents that could serve as a casus belli. Eden had told the Cabinet that military action against Nasser "would be unlikely to receive general support without some further cause being provided by the Egyptian government." Now Foreign Office official Harold Beeley observed that "we shall need any luck we can get in the way of provocation by Colonel Nasser, and I would suggest that the concerted denial of Canal dues should still have a high priority among our immediate measures."[15] British officials had always overrated the importance of canal dues to Nasser; now they hoped that diverting them to SCUA would provoke Nasser into taking an action that would then provide the needed pretext for an invasion.[16]

For these reasons the British and French governments agreed to cooperate with the SCUA plan although it meant another postponement of the military invasion, now set for September 19.[17] From September 10 to 12 Dulles refined the SCUA scheme with British Ambassador Sir Roger Makins and newly arrived French Ambassador Hervé Alphand. Dulles also discussed with Makins the nature of the speech Eden was to give at the reopening of Parliament on September 12.[18] The British ambassador had told Foreign Secretary Selwyn Lloyd that it was "vitally important" that the prime minister's statement not depart from the American understanding of SCUA. However, under pressure from both left and right, ministers decided that the SCUA plan must be presented in a firm and decisive manner or Nasser's rejection of the Menzies mission's proposals would be taken as a new blow to Western influence in the Middle East. Therefore, while explaining the scheme before the House of Commons on September 12, Eden said that if the Egyptian government interfered with or refused to cooperate with SCUA, Western governments would feel free to take further steps through the United Nations or otherwise against Egypt.[19]

Dulles rejected this description of his plan, telling Arthur Flemming that Eden had "gone a little out of bounds" and "kind of knocked this plan down." A visit by Egyptian Ambassador Ahmed Hussein strengthened the secretary's impulse to correct what he saw as a major misstatement. Hussein told him that Nasser believed that Eden's scheme represented "open and flagrant aggression on Egyptian sovereignty and its implementation means war."[20] Wasting no time, at his September 13 news conference Dulles publicly challenged Eden's statement, informing reporters that "the United States did not intend to shoot its way through the Canal."[21] The secretary's words served to confirm British suspicions about Dulles's reliability as an ally and also removed the stick from SCUA (and a major incentive for Egyptian cooperation).

During the same week, events in Egypt further weakened the rationale behind the scheme. Since July 26, foreign pilots had stayed at their posts at the canal because the British government, in order to avoid the accusation that it had sabotaged canal operations, had restrained the desire of both the Suez Canal Company and the French government to encourage their departure. At the end of August, Byroade observed that the morale of the European pilots had plummeted and predicted that most of them would soon depart.[22] In the beginning of September, bowing to the inevitable, the British government permitted the company to tell the pilots that they were free to leave as of September 14.[23] Sensing that British and French leaders hoped that the pilots' resignation would lead to an inflammatory incident, Dulles objected to their departure on the grounds that if the pilots dispersed, it would be harder to recruit them to work for SCUA. This time his opinion was ignored, the Foreign Office responding that the pilots were at the end of their patience and would still remain available at short notice to work the canal.[24]

Nasser decisively won this round of the Suez confrontation. Both the British and French governments, using information supplied by the Suez Canal Company, had predicted total chaos that would further bolster their claim that Western intervention was a vital necessity and provide a perfect pretext for military action.[25] Instead, during the week following the departure of the Western pilots, Egyptian and other pilots shepherded almost the usual number of ships through the canal.[26]

Preparations for a conference to discuss SCUA continued, although

Nasser's success further undermined its meager rationale.[27] Invitations to the eighteen nations which had acceded to the majority proposal at the London Conference were sent out on September 14, and three days later Dulles left Washington to participate in a second London Conference, the purpose of which was to create an organizational structure for SCUA.[28] Dulles reported to Eisenhower that the British and French governments had isolated themselves, which forced the United States to serve as a bridge between them and the other delegations. These observations strengthened Dulles's determination to find a peaceful solution to the crisis.[29] By contrast, at the end of the conference Eden concluded that some new move would have to be taken lest the British and French governments be accused of following a policy of drift.[30] Hence the Anglo-French decision on September 22 to bring the Suez question before the Security Council. London ignored Dulles's renewed plea for a further postponement and instructed British Ambassador to the United Nations Sir Pierson Dixon to call a meeting of the Security Council for September 26 to inscribe the Suez question on the agenda and to urge that the Egyptian representatives be invited to a meeting at the United Nations on October 2.[31]

BRITAIN'S FINANCIAL PERIL AND MACMILLAN'S VISIT TO THE UNITED STATES

During the middle of September Chancellor of the Exchequer Harold Macmillan, one of the most belligerent Cabinet ministers, came to the United States for the annual IMF and World Bank meetings. In addition to seeking American goodwill by a well-publicized visit to his mother's Indiana birthplace, he held extensive meetings with Eisenhower, Dulles, and Humphrey. These were the most important Anglo-American contacts prior to the Suez invasion. One of the central areas of discussion was the precarious British financial position.

While some British officials, particularly Sir George Bolton at the Bank of England, thought that a confrontation over Suez would strengthen sterling, during August, events demonstrated the price the Suez crisis could exact on the weak British financial position. Ironically, while British officials had urged that the government take a strong stand against Nasser in order to safeguard the position of sterling, it was the British action against Nasser that now threatened the pound. During the middle of August, the Treasury considered asking Australia to sell Britain gold to bolster British reserves, an IMF borrowing and a waiver under the U.S. Agreement.[32] Officials also contemplated letting the transferable rate go below £1 = $2.77-$2.78, imposing additional controls over capital and curtailing convertibility.[33] At the end of the month the British government faced two interrelated problems. The first was the position of sterling. The raison d'être of a reserve currency is its reliability and transferability; it must be viewed as strong and open to free transfer. Both the Suez crisis and the means the British government chose to deal with it undercut both prongs. As yet the direct cost of the Suez impasse remained small, but if the government took military measures or should the canal be closed, the price would escalate.[34] Any increased expenditure would weaken the British financial position, casting doubt on the government's ability to retain the value of sterling at £1 = $2.80. In response, foreign holders who possessed the ability to exchange sterling for other currencies or gold would be encouraged to do so for economic reasons. Furthermore, the largest holders of sterling included oil companies and Arab nations with ample reasons for weakening the British government.

Many holders of sterling also feared that if Britain blocked assets once, it could do so again. For example, shortly after the Egyptian freeze, both the Sudan and Burma expressed concern about retaining balances in London.[35] Consequently, any retreat from convertibility or any resort to further exchange controls in order to strengthen sterling could paradoxically weaken it. Furthermore, measures designed to increase foreign holders' faith in sterling, such as approaching the IMF for a drawing in order to increase dollar and gold reserves, could backfire and erode their trust. Monetary strength is often a confidence game where perceptions create reality. Like a self-fulfilling prophecy, if doubts grew as to sterling's weakness, enough investors would deplete British reserves by exchanging their sterling for dollars. The fear of undermining investor confidence explains the British government's reluctance to borrow from the IMF until it was too late.

Oil presented the most immediate threat to the British economy and the strength of sterling. Should either the canal or the Iraq Petroleum Company pipelines be closed, the British would have to substitute Western Hemisphere supplies for Middle Eastern oil. The dollar cost of such an action would be, at the lowest estimate, between $500 million and $700 million per year.[36] In addition any oil rationing or disruption of supplies would affect industry, further subverting the British economic position. While this problem would damage all of Western Europe, only in Britain did it have a double-edged effect. Countries such as France and West Germany were not trying to keep up financial pretenses by living beyond their means.[37] Indeed, the French government, having postponed an inevitable devaluation for months, eagerly searched for an external excuse on which to blame its financial plight.[38] Britain was not in this fortunate position. Any industrial disruption that resulted from a shortage of oil would hurt exports, weaken the British balance of payments position, and additionally jeopardize the position of sterling. If Britain had to spend scarce dollars for dollar oil in lieu of sterling supplies, the British position would erode further. Given that, as of September 1, British gold and dollar reserves stood at $2,276 million, the problem with spending about one-quarter of them for oil payments becomes clear.

The American government kept abreast of this problem. The MEEC had met throughout August and into September.[39] Working with Arthur Flemming, head of the ODM, this group of British and American oil officials discussed increases in American production (usually strictly limited to keep up the price of oil) and the rerouting of tankers.[40] To the British government, the issue of money loomed largest. In mid-September Dulles, with Humphrey's approval, suggested a loan of $250-$500 million from the Export-Import Bank of the United States (EXIM), founded in 1934 to encourage foreign purchases of American products.[41] British officials responded without enthusiasm to this suggestion. As Sir Leslie Rowan said, at a time when the British government urgently sought a waiver of its next interest payment under the U.S. Agreement, the last thing it needed was a new loan. Macmillan agreed; he told American Ambassador to Britain Winthrop Aldrich that, because Britain had already borrowed too much, "he did not see how it could possibly assume further large dollar debts."[42] British officials also worried that a new borrowing would reduce foreign confidence in sterling.

On the other hand, as Rowan pointed out, an EXIM loan might further bind the administration to the British position. Moreover, the British government knew that without a special congressional session (something no one suggested), the administration had few available sources of aid for Britain or other European nations. Consequently, the Treasury advised Macmillan to discuss the EXIM loan during his American visit but to emphasize the need for American aid, either in lieu of the loan or thereafter.[43] Rowan urged Macmillan to stress to the administration that the more likely a protracted crisis, the greater the strain on sterling.[44] In this way the continued and deepening weakness of the pound exacerbated and hastened the need for military action.[45]

Macmillan made this point during all his Washington meetings, the first of which was with Eisenhower on September 25. According to Macmillan's unreliable memoirs, the president "was sure we must get Nasser down. The only thing was, how to do it. I made it quite clear that we could *not* play it long, without aid on a very large scale—that is, if playing it long involved buying dollar oil." Macmillan summed up this meeting by saying that he left the White House with a strong feeling that the president was really determined to stand up to Nasser and that he recognized that "by one means or another we [the British] must achieve a clear victory."[46]

But in fact, as Macmillan himself recognized at the time, Eisenhower's real views were by no means so extreme. A few hours after his meeting with the president, Macmillan cabled a report to Eden. The chancellor emphasized Eisenhower's preoccupation with the election: "I feel sure that the President understands our problems about Nasser, but he is, of course, in the same position now as we were in May 1955."[47] The reference is to the British election campaign of a year earlier. Then the administration had acceded to the British desire to announce a four-power summit in order to help the Conservative party's chances at the polls.[48] Now Eisenhower sought the same kind of cooperation from the Eden government.

Eisenhower gave Dulles his version of the encounter with Macmillan soon after the chancellor left. The president commented that "Mr. Macmillan talked very much more moderately (about the Suez) than he had anticipated. He cheerfully admitted that the issue was Nasser rather than the Canal." In part because Macmillan "was far less bitter than he had been a few weeks earlier," the two statesmen had "a nice chat." Most importantly, the president reassured Dulles that "nothing was said that might cause Dulles concern."[49] From this account it is obvious that Eisenhower and Macmillan never discussed the circumstances under which the British government would use force against Nasser or what the response of the United States would be if it did. Indeed Macmillan apparently conveyed the impression that his views on the Suez crisis had moderated. His seeming reorientation encouraged his American hosts to believe that their attempts to find a peaceful solution to the crisis had been effective and partly explains their later disappointment and anger when it became clear that the administration's efforts had been in vain.

That afternoon, Macmillan, accompanied again by Makins, met with Dulles. The first task of the British was to disarm Dulles, still angry over what he saw as lack of sufficient consultation prior to the Anglo-French initiative in the United Nations. Indeed Dulles was annoyed enough to mention the issue to numerous people and to bring it up again privately with Macmillan. The secretary's anger over not being consulted over a diplomatic step prefigured his reaction when the British, without prior notice, launched a military invasion.

Dulles turned next to canal dues. The secretary of state said that the American government remained willing to require American ships to pay them into a blocked account or to SCUA rather than to Egypt. But Dulles warned the British that not only would such a directive have a minimal effect on Nasser, but it might have a major and negative effect on Britain if Nasser, as Dulles thought quite likely, retaliated by closing the canal to Western shipping. The secretary wanted assurances that the British realized the risk: "The United States must know definitely, before it acts, whether the economic consequences of its action are understood and are acceptable to France and to the United Kingdom." Dulles then emphasized the huge potential cost rerouting oil supplies would entail. He added that while he could not gauge what Congress would be willing to offer when it reconvened next year, recent omens did not auger well. Macmillan agreed that Egypt would bear the financial warfare better than would Britain and said that "something must be done to make Nasser lose face and he did not believe rerouting would accomplish this."

During this portion of the meeting Dulles reiterated the American position: "The United States Government was prepared to do everything it could to bring Nasser down but he thought that the most effective way of doing so was to let the present situation in the Canal continue and use other means of pressure which would shortly be discussed between us."[50] This reference to "other means of pressure" may imply covert action; a similar reference was made during the private meeting between Macmillan and Dulles that immediately followed.[51] Yet even if Dulles had suggested a CIA initiative, during his two meetings with Dulles, Macmillan had received no justification for thinking that his government had carte blanche to use force. True, Dulles did say that "he quite realized that we [the British] might have to use force" and that the threat of force against Nasser was vital. But his statement was made as part of an enumeration of various policy alternatives such as sending ships around the Cape of Good Hope and importing additional oil from Venezuela. More importantly Dulles then said that while Suez as yet had not played a part in the election, "if anything happened it might have a disastrous effect. He reminded me of how he and the President had helped us in May 1955 by agreeing to the Four Power meeting at top level, which had undoubtedly been of great effect to us in our electoral troubles. Could we not do something in return and try and hold things off until after November 6th?" As Makins had earlier pointed out, Eisenhower and Dulles were very concerned about the election.[52] The last thing that they wanted was for the British and French governments to take military action that could jeopardize Eisenhower's claim to being the president who kept us out of war. The British government should not have been surprised at the angry American reaction when it disregarded this warning.[53]

When Macmillan brought up British financial difficulties and the great strain on the reserves, Dulles was very pessimistic about the prospect of congressional aid. The best that he could offer was the possibility of an amendment to the U.S. Agreement, but only after the election. Finally, Dulles cautioned Macmillan to keep secret all that was said because "the slightest hint of any relaxation to us on the Loan conditions might be fatal to their election prospects if it got out."[54] Dulles had obviously exaggerated the effect on public opinion of a proposed amendment. But Macmillan would have done well to consider that if Dulles viewed the rumor of such an amendment as fatal, the secretary would have taken an actual invasion even more seriously.

The next day Macmillan met with George Humphrey. Amending the U.S. Agreement was the principal topic discussed. Since 1951 it had been clear that the waiver provisions had been so poorly drafted as to be, by definition, inoperative.[55] Indeed during the spring of 1956 Humphrey had considered asking Congress to approve an amendment but had refrained from doing so because "any attempt at legislation this year would be dangerous."[56] The British government had chosen not to push the point, but now what the Treasury called that "hardy, annual question" had become too urgent to ignore. With British reserves bound to dip ever closer to the bare minimum working requirement of $2,000 million, the expenditure of $175.5 million was not to be viewed lightly.[57] The British government had come up with two suggestions. One would have allowed the British government to make foreign aid donations to third world nations in nonconvertible sterling in the amount of the loan payments.[58] The other, which Macmillan briefly discussed with Humphrey, was to drop the waiver in favor of "bisques"—unconditional rights to postpone payments of principal and interest a fixed number of times. But Humphrey, too, made it clear that the administration could offer no assistance until after the election.

Neither Humphrey nor Macmillan directly brought up the Suez crisis. According to Macmillan, Humphrey "said in a most emphatic way that America must see the United Kingdom through any of her troubles. He realized that we were essential and that if we got into serious difficulties the whole of the security of America would be imperilled." No doubt these sentiments were comforting to the chancellor. But he made a great mistake in taking them as carte blanche for the Suez invasion. Humphrey would indeed demonstrate that American aid to Britain could be forthcoming but not for military action taken against the administration's wishes.

The last official Macmillan met with during his trip was Robert Murphy. The veteran diplomat repeated administration reservations about the purpose and timing of the British-sponsored demarche at the United Nations, inquiring what they hoped to achieve. Macmillan reported to London that Murphy had hinted that the United States position after November 6 would be quite different and had pronounced that Nasser must be brought down.[59] But in a world where the United States placed great reliance on public opinion, economic pressure, and covert action, Murphy's statements cannot be interpreted as an American endorsement of an Anglo-French invasion of Egypt.

While the administration left its position somewhat vague, Macmillan committed a far more grievous sin by not making British financial needs and expectations absolutely clear to his hosts. Given the financial and military constraints under which the British were operating in 1956, it behooved Macmillan, who more than any other British Cabinet minister was fully aware of Britain's difficult financial position, to ensure that American help would be available in the event of a Suez invasion. Yet he never asked Eisenhower, Dulles, or Humphrey what the American reaction would be if the British government used force against Nasser. Dulles, Eisenhower, and Murphy at least warned him not to do anything before the election. Perhaps they should have been even more emphatic—but the United States did not need Britain, while Britain did need the United States.

Had it been Eden who had visited the United States, such reticence or failure to communicate would have been far more understandable. But Macmillan prided himself on his ability to get along with Americans, and his North African experience had given him the advantage of a previous relationship with Eisenhower. It is true that the British Treasury, Foreign Office, and Bank of England officials who considered the question of Britain's financial position during the fall of 1956 always presented two alternatives: active American help or covert American help. They never contemplated the possibility of actual American hostility.[60] However, officials draw their assumptions from the political leader heading their department. The financial predictions were prepared by the Treasury under the supervision of Macmillan. Treasury officials, working in Whitehall far distant from American diplomats, could not be expected to appreciate fully the problematic American attitude toward British policies during the second half of 1956. But the chancellor knew that American assistance could not be taken for granted; on September 10, in response to a Treasury paper on the British financial position, Macmillan had minuted, "Yes: that is just the trouble, U.S. are being very difficult." Given his knowledge of both Britain's financial dependency and American ambivalence, why then did he not try to ensure that at the crucial moment the United States would be cooperative?

The British Cabinet had authorized the planning of a military assault on another country. As chancellor, Macmillan bore the responsibility for ensuring that the necessary financial support for the invasion was in place. At the least, Macmillan's performance as chancellor during the Suez crisis must be assessed as incompetent. Furthermore, he misjudged not only financial questions. When Macmillan returned to London, he apparently informed his colleagues that "Ike will lie doggo until after the election."[61] The available accounts of Macmillan's various meetings in Washington provide no basis for this optimistic conclusion. Alistair Horne, Macmillan's authorized biographer, who, alone among historians, has had access to Macmillan's papers, believes that Macmillan let himself be misled by private conversations with American officials and by his "somewhat arrogant general view of Americans." Horne continues by saying that Macmillan was "evidently reassured by what he had heard in the States."[62] It is this sense of complacency that seems incomprehensible or perhaps even discreditable. For it is clear that nothing Macmillan heard in Washington should have led him to conclude that the American administration intended to aid Britain in the event of an invasion of Egypt prior to the American election.[63]

DIPLOMATIC MANEUVERS

As Macmillan returned to London, the French and Israeli governments continued their close contacts.[64] On September 25, Israeli Chief of Staff Moshe Dayan and Shimon Peres, director-general of the Ministry of Defense, returned from Paris and informed Prime Minister David Ben-Gurion that the French government was prepared to "act" against Nasser and wished to cooperate with Israel in this endeavor. Ben-Gurion decided to send a delegation to France immediately. At the same time, the last in a series of shipments of French arms arrived in Israel. This material was the positive force motivating the Israelis to cooperate with France. The negative factors included a fear of an escalation in the ongoing border clashes with Jordan (now exacerbated by King Hussein's request for Iraqi troops) and a belief that Nasser would attack Israel at the first available opportunity.[65] Interestingly, Anglo-French-Israeli collusion had been mentioned as a possibility by the CIA on September 27, but it was dismissed as an unfounded rumor.[66]

At the end of September Dulles professed to be perplexed by British and French intentions. He told Lodge that while the French were eager to get into a shooting war, he could not tell what the British government wanted, as the Cabinet was split.[67] Dulles did note to the president on October 2 that relations with the Western allies had deteriorated because both governments were blaming the United States for restraining them against military action. The two discussed various alternatives to the Suez crisis; Eisenhower explicitly rejected the possibility of a covert operation against Nasser himself. Further, Eisenhower reiterated that the canal issue could not serve to undermine the Egyptian leader. While Nasser had dangerous tendencies that needed to be curbed, the president advocated strengthening the base of alternative Arab leaders such as King Saud of Saudi Arabia.[68]

Although Dulles had emphasized French animosity toward the United States to Eisenhower, he enraged his British counterparts when he stated that there were "some fundamental differences" between the United States and its Western allies on the issue of colonialism. While this statement accurately reflected administration sentiment, Eden was bitter at Dulles's comment.[69] The secretary of state immediately apologized, but the incident exacerbated Anglo-American tensions.[70]

Although partly to blame, Dulles worried about the problem of communication between the British and the French governments on the one hand and the American government on the other. He cabled Aldrich and C. Douglas Dillon, American ambassador to France, on October 4, and complained, "I know British and French want us to 'stand with them.' But we do not know where they stand nor are we consulted."[71] However, Dulles remained disingenuous. He knew full well what the British and French governments wanted—American support for their use of force. When the secretary said that "their positions so far as we are aware are vague to the point of non-existence. We do not know and cannot find out whether they want war or peace," he was ignoring all the evidence of the last ten weeks. Furthermore, he had specifically informed Eden on August 24 that he did not want to be kept informed of Anglo-French military plans.[72] Finally, just as Eden ignored Makins, Dulles refused to pay attention to the accurate reports concerning British and French proinvasion sentiment that Aldrich and Dillon were furnishing.[73] A CIA intelligence estimate on September 19 had also predicted that "at least for the immediate future, the UK and France will almost certainly seek to keep the way open for the use of force."[74] Dulles committed a major diplomatic blunder by choosing to be reticent instead of telling the allies that the United States would oppose any military action.[75]

In his cable Dulles had observed that while American opinion, preoccupied with the election and the World Series, was paying little attention to the Suez crisis, the administration had concluded that the American people would not support giving a blank check to the allies. Newspaper reports for the period fully support this evaluation. To the limited extent that the media focused on the crisis, journalists stressed the importance of a peaceful settlement. Dulles received laudatory praise for both his London missions. Critics of the administration cited the vagueness of the SCUA proposals but never advocated military force.[76]

Anglo-American communications further deteriorated after Sir Roger Makins left Washington on October 11, bound for a position as joint permanent under secretary at the Treasury. While this move had been arranged during the previous spring and was unrelated to the Suez crisis, its effect proved enormous. Dulles admired and trusted Makins, who also got along well with Eisenhower (Makins, as well, had served in North Africa) and Humphrey. If Makins had been in Washington during the remainder of the year, at least some part of the "special relationship" would have remained intact. Instead, during the most difficult period in Anglo-American relations since the Second World War, the post of British ambassador lay vacant for almost a month.[77]

When Makins paid a farewell visit to Eisenhower on October 5, the president, in the British ambassador's words, took this opportunity to reiterate the American position:

> There was no doubt whatever that public opinion in the United States was firmly opposed to the use of force before every possibility of finding a peaceful solution had been exhausted. The effect in the country of such action at the present time could be most serious. Moreover, he himself could not see how the affair would end if force were attempted. In his opinion it could scarcely fail to lead to a chaotic situation in the Middle East which would encourage further Soviet penetration.[78]

Makins duly forwarded this message to London. Dulles also tried to calm the British and French governments. He met with Lloyd and Pineau in New York where the Europeans had arrived for the Security Council debate. There Dulles, after complaining again about the Anglo-French independent demarche to the United Nations,[79] enumerated the reasons against military action and said that "they [Eisenhower and Dulles] did not rule out the use of force as an ultimate choice although in this particular situation they thought it would be a fatal mistake."[80] Now Dulles had pulled no punches, but the British and French were too determined upon the use of force to heed his words.[81]

After talking with Lloyd and Pineau, Dulles and Eisenhower found that some cooperation with the British and French at the United Nations was possible. As Eisenhower told Hoover on October 6, international participation in the running of the canal must be part of an acceptable solution.

Hoover thought that perhaps an international consortium, such as took over the Iranian oil fields, might be the answer.[82] Eisenhower again vetoed covert action, at least during the crisis. The president believed that to use the CIA without inflaming the Arab world a quieter atmosphere was necessary.[83]

Two days later Eisenhower wrote to Hoover proposing a different kind of covert action—a clandestine encouraging of Nasser to make an offer that would allow fruitful negotiations to begin. In the same letter the president suggested issuing a statement that the United States would not support a war or warlike moves in the Suez area. Many problems could have been avoided had he made that statement.[84]

During the autumn a number of influential Americans who worked in the private sector attempted to bridge the gap with the Egyptian leader. Financier Bernard Baruch informed Dulles in late September of a private approach that had been made to him and was encouraged to pursue the initiative. John J. McCloy, former president of the World Bank and now chief executive officer of the Chase Manhattan Bank, suggested using the World Bank as an intermediary to Nasser. Eugene Black, the IBRD's current president, met with Egyptian Foreign Minister Mohammed Fawzi in early October. Egyptian diplomats made every effort to be conciliatory: both Fawzi and Ambassador Ahmed Hussein assured administration officials that they only sought a reasonable solution that would safeguard Egyptian rights. Moreover, Egyptian journalist and Nasser confidant Mohammed Heikal, together with fellow journalist Mohammed Amin, assured State Department diplomats that Nasser had no intention of allying Egypt with the Communist bloc and that the Egyptian president appreciated the American effort to build a bridge to the Arab world.[85]

From October 9 through 12, the British and French emissaries met with their Egyptian counterparts. The discussion was framed by the so-called Six Principles, adopted by the Security Council on October 14, which required free and open transit through the canal, respect for Egypt's sovereignty, nonpolitical operation of the canal, decisions on dues to be made by Egypt in consultation with user nations, the use of a fair proportion of dues for development, and arbitration in case of disputes.[86]

As negotiations continued Dulles and Lodge both reported that the British representatives seemed more reasonable although the French were not "giving" at all.[87] Lloyd in fact shared Dulles's view of Pineau, writing that the Frenchman was behaving in a "most extraordinary manner." Dulles, Lloyd initially believed, was "not uncooperative."[88] However, a snag in Anglo-American relations developed over SCUA and canal dues. Suddenly Dulles seemed to be backing away from his promise to have American ships pay tolls to SCUA, which had met again in London during the first week of October. Dulles now said that he had never intended SCUA to be used as an instrument of economic pressure against Nasser, and at least 90 percent of the dues should then go to Egypt, although they could be paid initially to SCUA. As this aspect had been one of SCUA's biggest attractions, Lloyd and his colleagues were understandably upset. On the other hand, it was the opinion of Secretary-General Dag Hammarskjöld, trusted by both Lodge and Dulles, that it would "blow things sky high" if the United States and other countries paid dues to SCUA.[89] Dulles refused to risk an explosion now, particularly as the Egyptians continued to be conciliatory.[90]

THIRD QUARTER BALANCE SHEET

By the second half of October it looked as if the Suez situation had passed the crisis stage. While Dulles told Eisenhower on October 21 that he was baffled by the Western allies, he "felt confident that the British and French would not resort to any of these [military or other] measures before the election as they did not want to make it an election issue."[91]

Britain's financial position might have acted as a brake. But for the receipt of $177 million from the sale of the Trinidad Leasehold Company to American interests, September reserve losses would have amounted to $125 million.[92] Officials exhibited little confidence that the situation would soon improve, not the least because the British economy always fared poorly in the autumn. Fearing the effects of a Suez invasion, Treasury officials again debated the possibility of borrowing from the IMF. Had the British government done so, it could have withstood far better the strains that were to affect the British economy in November. But increasing British liabilities did not seem the way to strengthen sterling, and so the government postponed any borrowing. As Governor of the Bank of England C. F. Cobbold said, financial markets would be better reassured if the bank borrowed when the reserves were on the increase, not as now when they were fast draining out of the bank's vaults.[93]

Consequently, as British, French, and Israeli officials secretly met at

Sèvres to coordinate military action, Treasury and Bank of England officials contemplated the financial problems facing the British government. Their maneuvering room was further reduced when various Commonwealth Central Bank governors informed Cobbold that a further devaluation of sterling would mean the end of the sterling area.[94] By the end of October it was clear that if the reserve losses for the month of October were $80 million, the British reserves on November 1 would stand at $2,248 million. After taking account of the $175.5 million payment due on the U.S. Agreement and companion Canadian loan in December, British reserves would be perilously close to the critical $2,000 million mark.[95] Under this threat, contingency planning for a war with Egypt continued. Again American support for Britain remained unquestioned.[96] British officials could not or would not bring themselves to consider what would happen if the United States aligned itself against Britain.

Interestingly both Egypt and France faced the coming months in a much stronger financial position. Washington had not levied full-scale financial pressure against Egypt. As Dulles had said in March, the administration must always keep a bridge open to Nasser. Consequently, during October Washington took two steps that improved Egypt's financial position. The first was to permit the ICA to continue part of its fiscal 1956 Egyptian aid program that apparently permitted Egypt to bolster its Swiss foreign currency reserves, thus partially negating the effect of the Western financial sanctions taken against Egypt.[97]

Secondly, the American Treasury now allowed Egypt to make payments from its frozen accounts "in appropriate cases involving hardship where shipments of goods have been completed or other services have already been rendered to partnerships or firms in Egypt."[98] If loosely applied, this provision would render the blocking regulations virtually meaningless. Egypt had further bolstered its financial position in September by borrowing from the IMF its gold tranche of $15 million. Under current IMF rules this was virtually an unconditional entitlement, which explains the British decision not to object to the drawing.[99]

The French government also had the foresight to go to the IMF. In early October the executive director of the IMF for France informed his American counterpart that losses to the French reserves for 1956 were likely to amount to $800-$900 million out of a total of reserves of $1.9 billion.[100] The situation seemed sufficiently serious to merit the IMF granting France on October 17 a standby credit not only of its gold tranche but also its first credit tranche,[101] for a total of $262.5 million.[102] Thus fortified, the French government could face the oncoming crisis with more aplomb than could the British.

Negotiations at the United Nations also continued, but the diplomats could not agree on the implementation and monitoring of the Six Principles. The continued positive Egyptian attitude left Dulles increasingly worried about the threat to peace from the Western allies. But he concluded that the British and French governments would heed administration warnings not to take any action until after the election. Aldrich supported the secretary's opinion when he reported on October 19 that while the British government had no intention of backing down over Suez, it was far more likely than before to accept a negotiated settlement.[103] Still, Dulles now decided to disabuse the allies of the idea that after the November 6 presidential election the administration would be more disposed to the use of force. He cabled Dillon and Aldrich to convey the president's strong objection to the use of force and added that "the views of the President and myself on this point are basic and fundamental and I do not see any likelihood of their being changed after [the] election."[104] In order to forestall postelection action, Eisenhower and Dulles agreed that they would be prepared to invite Eden and Mollet to Washington at the end of November, it being clearly understood that the invitation would be rescinded if military force were used in the interim. But what would the administration have done had the Suez invasion been launched on November 7? Most of the administration's warnings had been couched in terms of waiting until after the election. While Eisenhower and his colleagues were undoubtedly playing for time, they had given the allies good reason to count on their acquiescence if not approval for any military action taken after the first week of November. Fortunately for administration officials, their allies did not present them with this dilemma.

In the meantime the administration placed its faith in negotiations at the United Nations that appeared to be making some headway. Even Lloyd, a determined hawk, told the Cabinet that he could not have hoped for a more favorable outcome of the United Nations deliberations.[105] During the last week of October other crises took precedence over the Suez dilemma. The first was the rise in Israeli-Jordanian incidents, which began on October 10. This confrontation apparently began as a smoke screen for the Suez plan but soon took on its own reality. While the United States stepped up its surveillance, Britain, which had a defense treaty with Jordan, was forced to contemplate the possibility of military action against both Egypt and Israel simultaneously.[106]

THE HUNGARIAN COMPLICATION

The more important crisis was the Hungarian revolt that began on October 23. Nineteen fifty-six had been a tumultuous year for the Soviet bloc. First, Nikita Khrushchev, in a secret speech before the Twentieth Party Congress, denounced Stalin's murderous excesses. Hard upon this development came Polish unrest that resulted in the selection as Polish party secretary of Władysław Gomułka, who had been previously ostracized as an enemy of the state. While the Soviet Union accepted Gomułka when he pledged that Poland would remain in the Warsaw Pact, Khrushchev was not as benevolently disposed to the Hungarian rebellion, which started with massive student demonstrations on October 23 demanding free elections, the evacuation of all Soviet troops, and the installation of Imre Nagy as head of a new government.

Eisenhower had campaigned on a platform pledging the rollback of Communist borders and the liberation of Eastern Europe. But once in office, the administration had acquiesced in the reality of containment. Now at this moment of confrontation between the Soviet Union and one of its satellites, officials found themselves torn. Emotionally they supported the Hungarian cause, but intellectually no one advocated going to war for Budapest. During the last week of October the administration focused on events in Europe. Dulles and Eisenhower, among other things, considered bringing the Soviet actions in Hungary before the Security Council. Dulles explained to Lodge that "from a political standpoint [he was] worried that it will be said that here are the great moments and when they came and these fellows were ready to stand up and die, we were caught napping and doing nothing."[107] As Lodge worked on a resolution, on October 29 news came that Israeli troops had attacked Egypt. The next phase of the Suez crisis had begun.

SIX

USING FORCE

OCTOBER 29–DECEMBER 4, 1956

The British had no sooner invaded than
they recognized immediately that they couldn't
carry on a war of this scale without financial
help; and in view of the U.S. position, taken
promptly at the United Nations, we were not
prepared to finance their war effort.
—W. Randolph Burgess, Under Secretary,
United States Treasury

T he Israeli invasion of the Sinai on October 29 dealt a devastating blow to the administration's Middle Eastern policy. Eisenhower and his colleagues decided almost immediately that with or without the support of the British and French governments, the United States would bring the matter before the United Nations Security Council. On October 31, as it became clear that London and Paris backed the Israeli action, a furious Eisenhower administration, blocked at the Security Council by British and French vetoes, took the issue to the General Assembly. With American encouragement, the world body passed a resolution condemning the invasion by a vote of 64 to 5, Britain and France abstaining. Notwithstanding mounting American disapproval, the first part of a British and French expeditionary force landed at Port Said on November 5. However, on the next day, the British and French governments agreed to accept the United Nations cease-fire; the Israeli government acquiesced as well.

The British government had thought that its acceptance of the United Nations edict would produce the American financial aid it needed. But it became increasingly clear that the Eisenhower administration demanded a genuine Anglo-French withdrawal from Egypt as the price of assistance. With pressure on sterling and on oil supplies increasing daily, the British government found it impossible to maintain the position it had staked out and began to withdraw its forces. Finally, on December 3 the president and his colleagues decided that the British government had gone far enough to meet American demands. From then, financial aid flowed with unaccustomed generosity.

OPERATION MUSKETEER

Although the American government had been braced for trouble in the Middle East since the middle of October, the administration had not realized the extent of Israeli-French cooperation. On October 14 French General Maurice Challe and Acting Foreign Minister Albert Gazier first presented Prime Minister Anthony Eden and Minister of State Anthony Nutting with what became known as the Challe Plan. It called for Israeli forces to attack the Egyptian army across the Sinai border. After a short interval the British and French governments would demand that both sides withdraw, permitting Anglo-French forces to occupy the canal zone. On October 16, Eden and Foreign Minister Selwyn Lloyd flew to Paris for further discussions; within two days Eden had been converted to the idea.[1]

It was predictable that the French government would take the lead in formulating a militant response to Nasser. In early August, French ministers, because they did not have the capability to launch a military invasion alone, had bowed to British pressure and agreed to postpone an invasion until after the London Conference. When the Eden Cabinet again postponed Operation Musketeer (the Anglo-French invasion of Egypt), this time in favor of SCUA, French Premier Guy Mollet and Foreign Minister Christian Pineau decided that they must take the lead in formulating the plan of attack against Nasser.

The French public fully endorsed the Mollet government's hard line. Dillon sent to Washington a steady stream of reports detailing the militant attitude of the French public. Wounded by the debacle in Indo-China and dismayed by the conflict in Algeria, French sentiment clearly favored landing a poleax blow on Nasser; all levels of French society subscribed to the notion that such a response would bolster French prestige in the Middle East and could be the coup de grace against the Algerian independence movement.[2]

The Israeli government felt obliged to listen seriously to the French suggestion, because of the threat from Nasser and also because it appreciated the important shipments of French arms delivered to Israel during the autumn. As in France, a forceful Cabinet response would have the backing of the Israeli public; opinion increasingly supported launching a preemptive strike against Egypt before newly arrived Soviet arms could alter the military balance in Nasser's favor.

Ben-Gurion and General Moshe Dayan agreed to fly to France, arriving for a meeting at Sèvres on October 22.[3] Lloyd did not make a good impression on Dayan; the meeting proved awkward for all parties. Indeed Ben-Gurion initially doubted the wisdom of joining forces with the British, but on October 23, at Dayan's urging, the Israeli prime minister began to change his mind. When Pineau returned to Paris from London on October 24, Ben-Gurion had been persuaded, and only the details remained to be worked out. Pineau reported that the British Cabinet had now agreed to present a joint Anglo-French ultimatum that Egypt would be forced to reject. After British representatives Donald Logan and Patrick Dean arrived, the three delegations signed a protocol embodying their understandings. It provided that Israeli forces would launch their attack on October 29. The next day the British and French governments would present their ultimatum to Egypt for an absolute cease-fire and the withdrawal of forces from a ten-mile region surrounding the canal, this zone to be occupied by British and French forces. Egypt would be given twelve hours to acquiesce; if Nasser refused, Anglo-French forces would attack early on October 31. In addition, under the terms of the Anglo-Egyptian Suez Base Accord of 1954, Britain retained the right to reoccupy the Suez Canal base in the event Israel initiated hostilities against Egypt. Israel agreed not to attack Jordan, but if Jordan attacked Israel, British forces would not intervene. Israel would seize the western shore of the Gulf of Aqaba, ensuring its control of the Straits of Tiran.

What happened next foreshadowed the November debacle. Eden, dismayed that a written record existed, sent Logan and Dean back to Paris to retrieve the signed copies. After consulting Israel, the French government denied the British request. Eden alone destroyed his copy. The French and Israeli counterparts are still extant.[4] The incident illustrates the guilt and ambivalence with which the British leaders viewed the military plan they had just blessed. When Eden described a sanitized version of the plan at the Cabinet meeting of October 25, it was accepted but not unanimously. Objections raised included the following: the invasion would cause offense to the American government, Britain and France would appear to be favoring Israel, and Britain might be accused of violating the Tripartite Declaration.[5] All these points would also be brought up by the Eisenhower administration within the week.

British officials were increasingly dismayed by their participation in this joint operation, which came to be referred to as "collusion." Not only did Lloyd lie to Parliament, but both he and Eden continued the cover-up in their memoirs.[6] During the 1959 debate on the resumption of financial relations with Egypt, the Macmillan government prepared a statement about the Suez crisis that falsified the record of British-Israeli cooperation with Israel.[7] Yet governments often participate in schemes that are less than open and aboveboard, particularly in the military sphere. For example, British officials did not appear to be unduly troubled by their cooperation with the CIA's 1953 Iran operation. However, almost all British officials viewed their cooperation with Israel as dishonorable and different in kind from other British diplomatic demarches. Partly this reaction stems from the long-held Foreign Office truism that Britain must on no account openly side with Israel, which officials had not yet fully accepted as an independent and sovereign state. Furthermore, many in Whitehall were revolted by the cease-fire ruse that Eden and Lloyd had tried to perpetrate.[8]

As scheduled, Israeli forces invaded Egypt on October 29. Paratroopers were simultaneously dropped at the Mitla Pass, thirty miles east of Suez and behind the chief border posts on the southern side of the Israeli-Egyptian border. French planes dropped relief supplies to Israeli soldiers. Britain had agreed to begin bombing Egyptian airfields thirty-six hours after the Israeli incursion but, for unexplained reasons, delayed until sundown October 31. By then, Israeli airborne forces had been joined by an armored column that had sped across the desert.

The British air force accompanied their bombing of Cairo, Port Said, and various military targets with a psychological attack; almost a million leaflets were dropped on Cairo urging residents to revolt against Nasser's regime. As the bombing continued and Israeli soldiers advanced toward the canal, the Anglo-French flotilla, sailing from Malta, remained over five hundred miles from Egypt; the joint paratrooper force marked time in Cyprus.

The administration had observed the first signs of a partial Israeli mobilization on October 26. However, William Rountree, the head of the State Department's Near Eastern Affairs Desk, speculated at a White House meeting that the target of these troops was Jordan. Although Eisenhower wrote Ben-Gurion urging him to take a "peaceful and moderate approach," when Secretary of State Dulles called Eisenhower on Monday morning, the president said that things looked better on both the Hungarian and Middle Eastern fronts.[9] Within hours the sense of calm had dissipated. By afternoon, when it was clear that the Israelis had invaded Egypt, Dulles told Senator William Knowland that he guessed that the invasion had been worked out at least with the French and possibly also with the British government.[10] At a White House meeting called that evening to discuss the Israeli action, Eisenhower clearly enunciated his position: the Tripartite Declaration and various American statements made thereafter required the United States to support the victims of aggression in the Middle East. Dulles pointed out that if the Israeli invasion resulted in the disruption of the canal's operation, the British and French troops clearly would intervene. The secretary then elucidated the central issue facing the administration: "The French and British may think that—whatever we may think of what they have done—we have to go along with them." The president responded by asking "what they would think if we were to go in to aid Egypt to fulfill our pledge" and then declared that "in these circumstances perhaps we cannot be bound by our traditional alliances."

Indisputably, timing played an important part in the American response to the Israeli incursion. The administration correctly believed that the Anglo-French-Egyptian negotiations were moving toward a resolution of the crisis, thereby eliminating any justification for the use of force.[11] Furthermore, that the Suez invasion had been launched in the middle of the Hungarian crisis also influenced the American government's reaction. Soviet tanks had entered Budapest on October 24. Fighting in Hungary continued as the rebels tried to establish their independence. While the president and his colleagues had no intention of beginning a war with the Soviet Union, they hoped that the Soviet use of force would expose Communist perfidy in the court of public opinion, which Eisenhower and Dulles took very seriously. Now the attention of the world might be distracted.

Timing played another role—the administration did not want a major world crisis eight days before the presidential election. Eisenhower worried less about defeating Adlai Stevenson, who was clearly on the ropes, than about obtaining a sizable majority in order to be able to "reform and revamp" the Republican party.[12] Eisenhower had warned Makins about the election, and Macmillan had received the same message from Dulles, Humphrey, and Murphy. The president and his colleagues now deeply resented having their strongly expressed preference so blatantly ignored.[13]

American officials also deeply resented being deceived. Certainly the administration itself would not have hesitated to mislead the British government in cases where vital American interests were at stake, in the same way as the Eden Cabinet had now done. In addition, the British government had dropped enough hints of its general intention to use force. Nonetheless a general sense of betrayal, which boded ill for the British government, pervaded the administration.[14] The administration's perception of British treachery strengthened because it fed upon a long-simmering resentment in Washington against allied leaders who appeared to feel free to use and abuse the United States. Eisenhower had written to General Al Gruenther that "at times I get weary of the European habit of taking our money, resenting any slight hint as to what *they* should do, and then assuming, in addition, full right to criticize us as bitterly as they may desire."[15]

The president and his advisors agreed that the United States must go to the United Nations; Dulles said that the United States must introduce a Security Council resolution before the Soviet Union did.[16] Rather than call Congress back into session, the administration decided to ask its British and French counterparts to join the American government in approaching the Security Council. He would tell the British government, said Eisenhower, that "we recognize that much is on their side in the dispute with the Egyptians but that nothing justifies double crossing us." Concerning the election, which would take place on November 6, Eisenhower maintained that he did not care whether he won reelection, but that he did not think that under the circumstances the country would throw him out. The president reiterated that "we are moved to help Egypt at once in order to honor our commitments." The allies never understood the importance of the administration's peculiarly American mix of morality, self-righteousness, and hypocrisy. Furthermore, that the administration had jettisoned the concept of rollback in Eastern Europe and accepted containment exacerbated American anger at the British and French governments. Administration officials were undoubtedly guilt ridden and dismayed by their inability to respond meaningfully to the Soviet invasion of Hungary. Eisenhower, Dulles, and their colleagues displaced some of this anger and guilt, which they might otherwise have turned against themselves, toward the British and French cabinets. Secondly, having tacitly conceded Eastern Europe to the Soviet Union, the administration became that much more committed to a contest with the Communists for the allegiance of the underdeveloped world. Consequently it would have nothing to do with what looked like an old-fashioned imperialist plot concocted by the two archcolonialist powers.

Eisenhower and Dulles summoned to the White House the unfortunate John Coulson, who, like many of his colleagues, continued to believe in the integrity of his government.[17] The president immediately informed Coulson of his deep concern over the Israeli invasion and stated that the United States was obliged to honor its clear commitment embodied in the Tripartite Declaration. Therefore, the United States would call for a Security Council session on the next day and wanted to know if the British government would cooperate. As Coulson had been kept in the dark by the Foreign Office, he told Eisenhower and Dulles that he thought that the British government would support a Security Council resolution condemning Israel.[18] Eisenhower concluded by telling Coulson that he deeply desired a united front with the British government, but that whatever happened, he would keep his word regarding the Tripartite Declaration. The president apparently thought that the British might be misled by the French government, Coulson reported, and closed his cable to the Foreign Office by saying, "I am sure it will be of great value if you can tell them as early as possible tomorrow that you will join them in the approach to the Security Council."[19]

The events of Tuesday, October 30, clarified both the British and American positions. As Lodge prepared for the introduction of a Security Council resolution, the president and secretary of state spent much of the day exchanging messages with Eden, so much so that Dulles at one point said that "this was getting to be a sort of trans-Atlantic essay contest."[20] The Eisenhower administration assumed that the French government had conspired with the Israeli government because, among other things, a large number of French Mystère aircraft had been sent to Israel during the preceding weeks. Furthermore, on October 19 Dillon had cabled Dulles to report on his luncheon meeting with Minister without Portfolio Jacques Chaban-Delmas. The Frenchman warned the ambassador that while his government could understand the American desire for peace during early November (i.e., before the presidential election), once the election was over, France, together with Britain, would take military action.[21]

Not yet fully cognizant of the British position, Eisenhower during the morning sent two cables to Eden. The president explained his belief that if the United States did not intervene on Egypt's side, the Soviet Union would, and asked for an explanation of the British government's general intentions.[22] Eden immediately responded to the president. He began by emphasizing that, notwithstanding the Cabinet's belief that Nasser's action jeopardized Britain's national security, his government had fully cooperated with each of Dulles's schemes. Then Eden told Eisenhower that while his government had tried to restrain Israel (and had succeeded in obtaining an assurance that Israel would not attack Jordan), Egypt had largely brought the attack upon itself by insisting that a state of war between Israel and Egypt existed and by encouraging other Arab states to attack Israel. Eden ended his message with a confused statement that Britain would work with the United States at the Security Council although he believed that any resolution would be futile.[23]

Several hours later a second, even more misleading telegram from Eden arrived. The prime minister advocated that Britain and the United States should neither support nor condemn Israel's action but instead should immediately "take effective and decisive steps to halt the fighting." Therefore, the British government was presenting both Egypt and Israel with what Eden called a declaration (actually an ultimatum) ordering them to cease all fighting, withdraw from a zone around the Suez Canal, and allow Anglo-French troops to occupy Port Said, Ismalia, and Suez. If either side refused, the British and French would "use the necessary measures to enforce the declaration." The prime minister explained that his knowledge of the constitutional and other difficulties of the American system prevented him from asking Eisenhower's advice before taking this action but hoped that the administration would support the British government's action, at least in general terms.[24]

Throughout the autumn the British government had always assumed that if needed, American support or acquiescence would be forthcoming. Now the extent of the Eden Cabinet's miscalculation became apparent. Eisenhower, Dulles, and Hoover, at a White House meeting, agreed that the British and French governments did not have an adequate cause for war. Hoover observed that the British and French might have felt that they had forced the United States to a choice between them or the Arabs. Dulles, concurring, said that "their thinking might be that they will confront us with a de facto situation, in which they might acknowledge that they have been rash but would say that the U.S. could not sit by and let them go under economically." To this statement Eisenhower replied that "he did not see much value in an unworthy and unreliable ally and that the necessity to support them might not be as great as they believed."[25]

Eisenhower met immediately with Arthur Flemming, who was in charge of petroleum questions. Now the ramifications of the administration's position became clear. The president said that "he was inclined to think that those who began this operation should be left to work out their own oil problems—to boil in their own oil, so to speak." He justified his firm stance by explaining that he was "extremely angry with both the British and the French for taking this action unilaterally and in violation of agreed undertakings such as the Tri-Partite [sic] Declaration of 1950."[26] The MEEC plan of action for handling Middle Eastern oil movements in the event of a cutoff of the canal or various pipelines, which was now ready to be implemented, remained on the shelf.[27] Simultaneously the administration suspended the insignificant amount of economic aid it currently furnished to Israel.[28]

The British deception continued to be the most troublesome point for American officials. A distraught Coulson cabled Foreign Secretary Selwyn Lloyd to say that he had told Dulles that he found it impossible to believe that the British government had played any role in encouraging the Israeli action. Coulson emphasized to Lloyd his distress at the administration's suggestion that the British had deliberately concealed information from the United States and ended his cable by advising the foreign secretary that "I fear that unless something can be done to allay American suspicions on this point, there will be the most serious effect on our mutual relations."[29]

The special relationship received a further blow when the British and French ambassadors vetoed the resolution condemning Israel that the United States had introduced in the Security Council.[30] During the next day Dulles and Lodge attempted to circumvent the Anglo-French vetoes. They decided to convene the General Assembly, using the "Uniting for Peace" resolution, adopted at the start of the Korean War. In 1950 the Soviet Union had vetoed the American resolution; this time it was the British and

French governments. But Dulles was as determined to succeed now as Secretary of State Dean Acheson had been when facing Soviet obstruction six years earlier.

The secretary of state believed that the coinciding of the Hungarian revolt with the Suez invasion made this moment pivotal in history. In fact Dulles told Vice-President Richard Nixon that from the standpoint of posterity two things were important: "It is the beginning of the collapse of the Soviet Empire—the second is the idea is out that we can be dragged along at the heels of Britain and France in policies that are obsolete. This is a declaration of independence for the first time that they cannot count upon us."[31] There is no question that Dulles sincerely believed himself to be an ardent antiimperialist. He did not see it as contradictory that this belief coexisted with a willingness to overthrow other countries' governments if they appeared to be Communist led or influenced. The Anglo-French scheme inclined almost all Americans to wave their anticolonialist banners; Dulles proved no exception.[32]

The secretary of state was not alone in his view. Eisenhower also pictured himself as an ardent antiimperialist. He had written Churchill two years earlier, "Colonialism is on the way out as a relationship between peoples. The sole question is one of time and method. . . . If we are intelligent enough to make constructive use of this [anticolonialist] force, then the result, far from being disastrous, could redound greatly to our advantage, particularly in our struggle against the Kremlin's power."[33] The president now feared that at this climactic moment the British government had steered the colonial world's emerging nationalist sentiment in precisely the wrong way.

American Ambassador to the United Nations Henry Cabot Lodge, Jr., a passionate antiimperialist, reinforced the president's stand. To his credit, he had more interest in the underdeveloped world than did the rest of the administration; for example, he tried, without success, to obtain administration support for SUNFED, the United Nations scheme for aid to the underdeveloped world. Unfortunately, he had alienated Western diplomats such as British Ambassador to the United Nations Sir Pierson Dixon, who viewed Lodge as "a complicating factor" because of his uneasy relationship with Dulles and his failure to comprehend Britain's relationship with the Middle East.[34]

Lodge saw the Suez crisis as his and his country's finest hour. He had anticipated a showdown in September, telling Dulles that if the British and French governments resorted to force without overt provocation, they would be subject to condemnation as aggressors. While this eventuality would threaten the "special relationship," Lodge deemed it preferable to acquiescing in the British initiative because "if a condemnation were not voted, the United Nations would cease to be a respectable organization." Preparing to go before the General Assembly, Lodge telephoned the president to say that never was there such widespread approval of an American action and that the Afro-Asian group had endorsed the moral courage of the United States.[35]

As the Israeli invasion continued and as British and French aircraft attacked Egyptian targets, the special emergency session of the General Assembly convened on November 1 at 5:00 P.M. and ran twelve continuous hours until 4:20 A.M. when it passed a resolution calling for a cease-fire and troop withdrawal. In a dramatic gesture Dulles personally introduced the American-sponsored resolution condemning the Israeli, British, and French actions and then entered the hospital for a major operation; Canadian Minister for External Affairs Lester Pearson added an amendment providing for a United Nations Emergency Force (UNEF) to enter the canal zone.[36]

Pearson played a major role in the events of the next four months.[37] Although a leader of a Commonwealth country, "Mike" Pearson became disenchanted both with Eden and British diplomacy during the Suez crisis.[38] He stepped in and acted as the "honest broker," presenting the American position with a Canadian imprimatur. Unlike Hammarskjöld, whose *bona fides* were suspected by British, French, and Israeli leaders, Pearson earned and retained the respect of all parties throughout the crisis.

The British and French delegates were now subjected to almost universal criticism, which, among other things, permitted Soviet Ambassador Arkady Sobolev to bask in the light of moral righteousness; with his government having announced the withdrawal of Soviet troops from Budapest, he could concentrate on the immoral behavior of Britain and France. The seeming Soviet moral ascendancy particularly distressed the administration. Dulles and Eisenhower believed that the brutal crushing of the Hungarian revolt would conclusively reveal the true nature of communism to the nonaligned world. To the administration's utter dismay, world public opinion now concentrated on the Suez invasion. Furthermore, the Middle Eastern debacle had handed the Soviet Union another opportunity to align itself on the side of underdeveloped nations against the imperialist powers. Not surprisingly Dulles told Lodge on November 2 that the British and French governments perhaps were worse than the Soviet Union.[39] The administration would treat its errant allies accordingly.[40]

For all his high-minded rhetoric, Dulles labored under no illusions that the United Nations resolution would be the deciding force in changing British and French minds. When Secretary of Commerce Sinclair Weeks asked if military aid should be suspended to Britain and France, Dulles answered no because the American government would pressure them in other ways which he did not want announced. As Dulles told his brother Allen, "There would be a strain on Britain and France and it would be economic and quickly [sic]"; the secretary was undoubtedly referring to the same two issues that had been present throughout the summer and autumn months—oil and sterling.[41]

On October 31, the Foreign Office told Coulson that the Israeli invasion had made the oil situation acute and ordered him to contact administration officials to start discussions on Anglo-American oil planning as soon as possible. To Whitehall's surprise Coulson replied that he did not dare approach the State Department in its current mood and, furthermore, that the meeting of the MEEC set for November 1 had been summarily canceled.[42]

The same obtuseness marked the British government's financial calculations. On October 30, a senior Bank of England official had stated that the Israeli invasion might strengthen the position of sterling.[43] The next day Chancellor of the Exchequer Harold Macmillan told Governor of the Bank of England C. F. Cobbold that he thought it unlikely that there would be immediate attempts to transfer sterling funds in bulk, and thus it was decided that the Bank of England would "dig our toes in on the whole exchange front." Consequently, the bank would not attempt to prevent foreign holders of sterling from exchanging their holdings for dollars and withdrawing the funds from Britain.

For his part Nasser forcefully reacted to the Suez invasion. He rallied his army commanders, who had panicked in response to the success of their Israeli opponents.[44] Nasser called in Raymond Hare, the new American ambassador to Egypt, seeking American assistance in support of the Egyptian government. Hare responded that the American government had made an exceptional effort to help Egypt and urged Nasser not to ask the

Soviet Union for assistance. The American ambassador did not know that Khrushchev had already informed Nasser that he would not risk a world war for Egypt's cause. As Nasser's fellow Arab leaders also responded only with words, he had no choice but to rely on the United States to force the foreigners from his soil. As part of the Egyptian defense, canal authorities blasted and sank all types of floating equipment in order to block the canal. What the British had always feared had now become reality—the Suez Canal was closed.[45]

AMERICA TAKES CHARGE

Macmillan thought that as things developed over the next few weeks the questions of a waiver under the U.S. Agreement and an IMF loan would need to be reviewed.[46] Officials did not yet appreciate the possibility of an increased threat to sterling, nor did they realize the significance of American opposition. The two items the chancellor mentioned, a waiver and an IMF drawing, could not be obtained without American acquiescence. Although at the United Nations the American government had made its position perfectly clear, British officials still did not comprehend that Washington's assistance might not be forthcoming.

British use of American-financed military equipment revealed the same blindness. Winthrop Brown, economic minister of the U.S. embassy in London, noted that the invasion force included bombers of the type financed by American aid and pointed out to British Ministry of Defence official Richard Powell on November 1 that under the terms of American Special Aircraft Purchase Aid to the RAF, all such equipment must be used solely for NATO defense. In fact British officials knew perfectly well that they had violated signed agreements; former minister of defense Sir Walter Monckton and the prime minister had agreed that nothing should be said to the administration "in the hope that if we came to the point of operations, they would be giving us at least their moral support."[47] Now the British government had to consider how to finesse this problem as well.[48]

During the first weekend of November the American government became increasingly puzzled that the British and French governments neither accepted the cease-fire nor landed their forces at Suez. The French government bore no responsibility for this odd behavior. On November 3 Pineau, together with General Challe, flew to London in a vain attempt to urge the

British government to accelerate the timetable for Musketeer. While Pineau's idea of using Israeli troops for the needed logistical support made sense, the British Cabinet, anxious to continue its pretense of impartiality, eschewed any contact with Israel. However, one modification was made: British paratroopers were told to land on November 5, one day ahead of the naval landings.[49]

Although this adjustment had not much improved Musketeer's logic, it provided the impetus for the plan for UNEF. Adopted on November 4 by a vote of 55 to 0 with 19 abstentions, the Canadian resolution ordered Secretary General Dag Hammarskjöld to develop a plan to introduce a police force in the area within the next forty-eight hours; an Indian resolution calling on Hammarskjöld to report to the General Assembly within twelve hours on compliance with the cease-fire was also approved.[50] During the weekend Hammarskjöld worked to get a token force assembled quickly enough to forestall an Anglo-French landing and personally appealed to the British and French governments not to land their forces. Defiance of this message would be another count in the indictment against the two countries.[51]

Eisenhower confessed that he was also puzzled by Eden's willingness to proceed with the invasion when the British people did not wholeheartedly back their government; the president concluded that "Eden and his associates have become convinced that this is the last straw and Britain simply *had* to react in the manner of the Victorian period."[52] Indeed Eisenhower correctly emphasized the growing fissures in British society, the widest since Munich.[53] Anthony Nutting, minister of state at the Foreign Office and a former protege of Eden, resigned. After first waffling on Operation Musketeer, First Sea Lord Earl Mountbatten of Burma wrote to Eden on November 2 expressing grave reservations.[54] Foreign Office officials seethed with anger. Although Permanent Under Secretary Sir Ivone Kirkpatrick had made it clear that he expected obedience, senior official Sir Paul Gore Booth took the daring step of sending him a memorandum on November 2 expressing the "dismay caused throughout our ranks by Her Majesty's Government's action."[55] The Foreign Office law officers were equally upset; for example, G. G. Fitzmaurice wrote Kirkpatrick on November 5 to say that "I must have some latitude about dissociating myself from any responsibility for the legal advice given to H.M. Government about our intervention in Egypt."[56]

The Labour party registered objections to the government's policy from October 30. Aldrich labeled these objections "deep" and suggested that the trade unions might resort to industrial action.[57] Political demonstrations increased in volume, culminating in the monster rally held on the evening of November 4 in Trafalgar Square, almost within earshot of Cabinet ministers meeting at 10 Downing Street. The members of the Cabinet Egypt Committee discussed whether the Anglo-French expeditionary force should still land in Egypt since both Israel and Egypt had indicated that they would accept the cease-fire. Indeed Israel, having obtained control of the Sinai, Gaza, and the Straits of Tiran, showed itself very anxious to accept the cease-fire in order to forestall the possibility of more casualties. After some discussion Cabinet ministers decided that, notwithstanding the risk of increased criticism, the landing should take place as scheduled. They erroneously concluded, among other things, that Britain and France would be in a stronger position if they had troops in Egypt when the cease-fire was accepted.[58]

On Monday, November 5, Anglo-French airborne forces landed in Port Said. Eden sent Eisenhower two letters defending his decision. While he regretted the split between the two nations, Eden said, "I know that Foster thought we could have played this longer. But I am convinced that, if we had allowed things to drift, everything would have gone from bad to worse. Nasser would have become a kind of Moslem Mussolini." Consciously or not, Eden had drawn a parallel to the Aswan affair. Then the British had wanted to play things long, but the government had acquiesced in Dulles's decision to withdraw precipitately the offer to finance the Aswan Dam. Now the prime minister requested the same courtesy from the American government.[59]

He would not get it; instead Eisenhower told a Monday morning White House gathering that he would try to bring Eden to "an acceptable position." Hoover announced that oil supplies from the Middle East were now virtually cut off. Sunken ships completely blocked the canal, while Syrians had sabotaged three pumping stations for the Iraq Petroleum Company pipelines, rendering them useless. Only the tap line that ran from Saudi Arabian oil fields remained open. The president suggested preparing heavy tankers and oilers for immediate use, but regarding the British and French oil problem, he "felt that the purposes of peace and stability would be served by not being too quick in attempting to render extraordinary assistance."[60]

The reality of an oil embargo spotlighted the abysmal British planning. Although Whitehall had appreciated Britain's dependence on American supplies and financial sustenance in the event of a Middle Eastern oil blockade, as a Foreign Office official had pointed out on October 31, "There is still no plan which could be put into action if Middle East oil supplies to the West were interrupted." The British Ministry of Fuel and Power had prepared rationing plans that called for an immediate 10 percent cut in oil deliveries to retail outlets. Now the prime minister agreed that they should be put into effect as of November 7.

Yet other problems overshadowed the fuel blockade. Clearly, the British and French governments were almost completely isolated. Several Commonwealth governments openly condemned the British actions and, worse still, only Australia proclaimed its support. Even there opposition politicians had criticized the British government.[61] More seriously, a Soviet threat had now appeared. On the evening of November 5, Soviet Prime Minister Nicolai Bulganin sent Eden and Mollet a letter condemning their actions and suggesting the possibility of rockets raining down on London and Paris.[62] While the immediate effect of this threat was to harden the Conservative stance, the Soviet attempt at intervention strengthened the administration's determination to force British and French cooperation with the United Nations lest they give the Soviet Union an opportunity to intervene in the Middle East.

The position of sterling also continued to present a problem. During the first two days of the month the Bank of England had lost $50 million, and losses continued to mount in the days that followed.[63] Both Macmillan in his memoirs, and his official biographer, Alistair Horne, maintain that it was this loss of reserves that changed Macmillan from the most hawkish of Cabinet ministers to the leader of the doves at the crucial Cabinet meeting of November 6. In Horne's words, "He told the Cabinet that there had been a serious run on the pound, viciously orchestrated in Washington. Britain's gold reserves, he announced, had fallen by £100 million [$280 million] over the past week or by *one eighth* of their remaining total."[64]

In his memoirs Macmillan provides a more detailed account, alleging heavy sales of sterling in New York and stating that after making inquiries in New York and Washington during the Cabinet meeting itself, he was told that the American government would not countenance an IMF drawing unless the British government agreed to the cease-fire.[65] Accounts by or about Eden, Lloyd, and Butler all corroborate Macmillan's account and maintain that the chancellor's statement provided the reason that they agreed to the United Nations cease-fire.[66]

Macmillan's colleagues did not know that on November 6 Macmillan cited a clearly erroneous figure. The British Treasury could not have lost £100 million ($280 million) for the week ending November 6 because on the next day the chancellor was told that the loss for the week was $85 million (£30.4 million).[67] Indeed on November 16 the Treasury reported that losses for the month to date amounted to $200 million (£71 million), and on November 20 Macmillan announced to the Cabinet that the losses for the month "might go as high as $300 millions [£107 million]" or virtually the identical amount he apparently adduced on November 6.[68] Moreover, no Treasury or Bank of England official mentioned the reserve loss as primarily New York in origin until November 20, and the location of foreign exchange sales proves nothing about the identity, nationality, or motivation of the sellers. Indeed Treasury and Bank of England officials only began displaying concern about the trend of financial events on the day following the Cabinet meeting, and their comments remained muted until the following week.[69] Finally, there is no independent evidence for the allegation that someone in the American government discussed the possibility of a British IMF drawing on November 5 or 6.[70]

Did Macmillan knowingly make false statements to the Cabinet and if so, why? It seems obvious that Macmillan knew that he was misleading the Cabinet when he told his colleagues that £100 million ($280 million) in reserves had been lost in one week. The one alternative explanation, that Macmillan confused dollars with pounds, does not hold water. The chancellor was a shrewd man, conversant with financial information. Surely on a vital question of national security he would have made certain of his figures before making such a critical pronouncement.

What then motivated Macmillan's actions? Macmillan knew that an approach based on financial information would be effective. Ministers were aware that the pound had been under intermittent pressure since 1945 and subscribed to the gospel that sterling was crucial to Britain's global position. Furthermore, Macmillan undoubtedly discerned that his misstatements would not be discovered. As chancellor, he had primary responsibility for Britain's finances. Of his colleagues only one could have challenged his statements. Butler, who spent four years as chancellor, had both the background and the American contacts to question Macmillan. However, preoccupied with the increasingly negative consequences of the Suez invasion, which he had never favored, he had no motivation to do anything other than accept Macmillan's figures at face value. As prime minister, Eden might have rallied the Cabinet to his side, but weakened by illness and devastated by the impending catastrophe, he could not do so.

Macmillan's words bore additional weight since the chancellor had been one of the strongest advocates of taking a hard line against Nasser. The chancellor's October optimism had helped entice Eden and his colleagues into agreeing to the Sinai invasion; now his pessimism led them to reverse their positions. As Macmillan had been partly responsible for this disastrous policy and for the splintering of the special relationship, perhaps on November 6 Macmillan had simply tried to cut his and his country's losses. In that case, the chancellor, thoroughly alarmed at the situation he had helped to create, used the most effective device at hand to convince any reluctant colleagues of the danger facing Britain.

Certainly Macmillan's figures influenced fellow ministers. Not only alarmed by the growing financial peril, they feared the consequences of the ever-growing rift between Washington and London. A majority of the Cabinet, led by R. A. Butler and Lord Salisbury, now demanded that the cease-fire be accepted. The pressure on Eden was intense. Tired and overwhelmed by the opposition from the country, Parliament, and his colleagues (only Lloyd, Anthony Head, and James Stuart wanted to continue), Eden bowed to the sentiment in favor of the cease-fire.[71]

Eden first called Mollet to inform him of the decision. The French were reluctant to cave in to American pressure. For a moment rare in the history of the Fourth Republic, the French people had united behind the government's actions. Furthermore, the French treasury stood better prepared for adversity than did Britain, having arranged an IMF standby credit of $262.5 million on October 17. But given the structure of the military operation the French could not continue without British support; therefore an angry Mollet Cabinet resentfully acquiesced in the British decision.[72]

BRITAIN'S INCREASING FINANCIAL PERIL

Eisenhower had gone to Gettysburg early in the morning of November 6 in order to vote. On his return to the White House he convened a meeting of top officials at 12:30 and there received Eden's call that the British and

French governments had accepted a cease-fire to take effect at midnight. Eisenhower's reaction was one of relief. The Soviet threat worried American officials; the president told Allen Dulles and Hoover that a Russian direct attack on the British and French meant "we would be in a war, and we would be justified in taking military action even if Congress were not in session."[73] Now this threat had receded. Because the American administration refused to countenance a Soviet presence in the Middle East, when Eisenhower spoke to Eden by telephone, he urged him to accept the cease-fire unconditionally and to withdraw British troops as quickly as possible. Furthermore, in order to prevent not only the Anglo-French force but Soviet troops as well from joining UNEF, Eisenhower told Eden that no soldiers from the "big five" should be included. The British government had intended precisely that, to remain in Egypt under a United Nations cloak, but Eisenhower had no intention of tolerating a continued Anglo-French military presence in Egypt.[74]

In a message delivered to Eden later that afternoon, the president reiterated the need for unconditional acceptance of the cease-fire and emphasized that what he called the "use of technical troops to clear [the] Canal" could be handled later.[75] Eden replied that although the British government had not made it a condition of the cease-fire that British troops be permitted to clear the canal, "this is something which has got to be done most urgently in the interests of the world. We are on the spot and the only people who can do it quickly. We therefore think it right that we should be allowed to carry it through unhindered."[76] This point became a major bone of contention between Washington and London. If British and French forces could not participate in UNEF, the Eden government insisted that they should at least stay to clear the canal. However, the administration found the notion of an extended and American-sanctioned British military presence in Egypt completely unacceptable.

Word from Cairo stiffened the American resolve. Hare told the State Department that suddenly the United States appeared to the Arabs as "a real champion of right." He believed that if the United States played its cards carefully, it could improve its position in the Middle East in a manner inconceivable a few weeks earlier.[77] The administration now became determined not to squander this golden opportunity to convince Arab nations of its anticolonialism and good intentions.[78]

Eden had called Eisenhower early on the morning of November 7 to

congratulate him on his sweeping election victory and to suggest an immediate Washington meeting among Eden, Mollet, and Eisenhower.[79] Since
Eisenhower and Dulles had previously contemplated inviting the two
European premiers to the White House after the election if they continued
to follow the American lead, the president agreed to the meeting. He then
informed his close aides Colonel Andrew Goodpaster and Sherman Adams
of this meeting, and to allay their fears that an Eden visit would jeopardize
American policies, the president called Eden back to ensure that the British
government had fully accepted the cease-fire and was not planning to
renege once Eden arrived in the United States. While Eden's answers
appeared to have satisfied the president, once the phone call was over,
doubts resurfaced. Hoover exacerbated them when he said that the American government must be very careful to avoid the appearance of teaming up
with the British and French governments. Furthermore, Dulles, consulted
by telephone, strongly opposed the meeting. Consequently the president,
speaking to Eden for the third time that morning, told the prime minister
that although he wanted to see him, "I don't see how we can handle this
now with so much on our plate—we just can't handle this at the same
time."[80] When Eden protested, Eisenhower said, "I am not talking about
not meeting and talking with our friends. But I have had opposition about
the timing."[81]

Eden's biographer records that the prime minister found Eisenhower's
veto of their meeting the most traumatic event of the crisis.[82] The administration refused to associate itself publicly with the British and French
governments until they had complied with the United Nations resolutions.
The American government's interpretation of the resolutions mandated the
immediate departure from Egypt of British and French forces. Only then
would the administration give sustenance to its erstwhile allies. Nonetheless, neither Eden nor any of his colleagues perceived the American government's position; they still believed that once they accepted the cease-fire
resolution, they would have considerable room for maneuver.

The Cabinet and Egypt Committee meetings of November 7, the day on
which the Israeli government formally accepted the United Nations cease-
fire, showed that the British government still thought it had bargaining
room. While a divided Cabinet acceded to the American proposal that
UNEF exclude big power troops, this ignominious defeat exacerbated the
British government's need to salvage some token of victory.[83] On Novem-

ber 8, Eden ordered British Commander General Sir Charles Keightley to initiate troop withdrawal discussions with UNEF Commander Designate Canadian General E. L. M. Burns. However, the British government continued to insist that British forces must clear at least some parts of the canal, something the American government declined to allow.

This dispute was crucial because on November 7 the financial pressure on Britain began to take its toll. That was the day the 10 percent cut in oil deliveries began.[84] More importantly, on that day British officials began to comprehend the fierce struggle that would have to be waged if the pound were to stay at its present parity of $2.80 to the pound and if sterling were to maintain its position as the world's major trading currency.[85]

Sir George Bolton, an executive director of the Bank of England, prepared a gloomy assessment of the foreign exchange market. Britain was facing urgent technical questions that grew out of the pressure on the pound. The Bank of England was using its reserves to hold official sterling at $2.78 both in London and throughout the continent. More reserves were being expended to support transferable sterling (although at the increased discount rate of 2 percent of parity); its level was not only an indication of the strength of the currency but affected commodity transactions and the pattern of trade. Unfortunately, as Bolton stated, these operations caused a British dollar shortage that would be exacerbated if the Suez confrontation continued, because during the 1950s any international crisis increased the demand for dollars.

Bolton also pointed out that after Britain made its annual payments on the U.S. Agreement and companion Canadian loan of $175.5 million in December, British reserves would dip below the critical $2,000 million mark as of January 1, 1957. However, he remained opposed to taking the two logical protective moves: the implementation of exchange controls and a devaluation of sterling. The former would end the use of sterling as an international trading currency; the latter might be the end of the sterling area. Instead, to ensure that no doubts surfaced as to Britain's commitment to the current parity, Bolton recommended that both the official and transferable rates be held at the current levels, regardless of how much the reserves fell. Then, as soon as it became feasible, the government should consider selling its portfolio of U.S. dollar securities and approaching Washington to discuss both an IMF drawing and a renegotiation of the waiver clauses.[86] This strategy, which the British government accepted, assumed that American cooperation would be obtained before a financial crisis came; even at this point no one questioned the availability of such support.

Interestingly, no British official suggested including in British reserves the British portfolio of long-term U.S. government securities and American corporate securities. In November the market value of these instruments amounted to almost $1,000 million.[87] While the Bank of England liquidated its portfolio of short-term dollar securities during November (some $55 million in value), British officials virtually ignored the long-term holdings. As British banker Raymond Bonham Carter has written, "This was always regarded as money in the stocking kept under the bed, never for use as a last resort (whatever that was) and never to be put in the shop window." Had this amount been included in the reserves, even at a discount from market value, or at least publicized, the British position would have appeared far less precarious.[88]

Also on November 7, Macmillan and his officials met to discuss the financial situation. Beginning with the proposition that during the previous week the British reserves had dropped by $85 million, officials discussed the usual possibilities such as an IMF drawing and an EXIM loan. The tone of the financial discussion had not been very urgent; the conversation about the oil shortage was rather more so. If consumption continued at the current rate, the maintenance of supplies would cost 800 million precious dollars on an annual basis. Macmillan and his officials decided that at the parliamentary debate on the economic situation scheduled for November 12 the chancellor would only make very general remarks.[89]

As it became clear that American aid would not come soon, the British government began to consider the possibility of financial disaster. In response to a Foreign Office inquiry about the chances for an IMF drawing and an EXIM loan, newly arrived Ambassador to Washington Sir Harold Caccia reported on November 8 that the outlook for either at the present time was poor.[90] Since October 31, the administration had evaded British attempts to pin down American plans concerning European oil problems. Now the Saudi Arabian government cut off crude oil supplies to the refinery located in Britain's Bahrein protectorate and prohibited British and French tankers from loading oil at Saudi ports.

The next day Caccia went to the White House for a new ambassador's traditional first visit to the president. Eisenhower received him cordially but was adamant that no prime ministerial summit could be scheduled until UNEF arrived in Egypt and Anglo-French withdrawals began.[91] Eisenhower intended to ensure that no one could suspect a conspiracy between his government and the allies and particularly wished to forestall the Soviet Union from using the United Nations to win favor in world public opinion. He again stressed the importance of significant and visible Anglo-French troop withdrawals. When Caccia said that Nasser's power and prestige would increase if it appeared that he had scored a success over Suez, Eisenhower, repeating a comment he had made in September and October, replied that "the Canal issue was not the best for bringing him down."[92]

The cordiality if not the content of Eisenhower's meeting with Caccia encouraged the British government to believe that relations were improving; accordingly, Eden cabled Eisenhower on November 11, seconding the message Mollet had sent the day before, asking for a three-party meeting as soon as possible. The president replied that while he hoped that they could meet in the near future, the prompt arrival of UNEF and the withdrawal of Anglo-French forces had to come first.[93] The British and the French governments did not yet understand that troop withdrawals were the prerequisite to the resumption of close relations.

THE AMERICAN USE OF ECONOMIC DIPLOMACY

On November 12, as Macmillan presented a serious but not alarming financial picture to the House of Commons, officials at the Treasury and the Bank of England finally began to consider seriously the possibility of an imminent sterling crisis; as the notes of a Treasury and Bank of England meeting held that day recorded, "We cannot continue to lose reserves at the present rate, and continue at the same time to hold sterling at its present value."[94] When the participants discussed what action they should recommend, the British government's perilous situation became clear. First of all, as this and earlier memoranda indicate, although the pound had been under pressure since July 27, no serious thought had been given to taking protective measures against a major financial crisis.[95] Now officials sketched out two scenarios—one which would be feasible with American help and one which would be possible without active American assistance. That the actions envisioned in both cases depended on American aid illuminated the

British dilemma. Indeed experts listed the following steps to be taken in the absence of active administration help: an IMF drawing of 25 percent of Britain's quota, an EXIM loan, the sale of U.S. securities, and amendment of the waiver clauses. All of these items required American assistance or acquiescence. Even when British officials were endeavoring to save the pound without American help, all their proposals involved American aid.[96] To his credit Sir Roger Makins, who had now taken up his new position as joint permanent under secretary of the Treasury, clearly understood the nature of the problem Britain was facing; his cover letter to Macmillan enclosing a summary of this November 12 meeting stated that "it shows convincingly the need for American cooperation."[97]

Unfortunately neither Eden nor his foreign secretary comprehended the prerequisite for support. Lloyd now journeyed to New York to attend the regular session of the General Assembly that had just opened.[98] Remaining a hardliner, he told Lodge on November 13 that "if the United States had not led the hunt against us in the United Nations I believed we would have had a brilliant success and that Nasser by now would have gone."[99] As Lodge had been partly responsible for the American stance and also prided himself on his performance over the preceding two weeks, it is not surprising that the foreign secretary reported that Lodge had not relished his argument. That Lloyd felt he could make these comments to a man whose goodwill he needed shows how little he understood what was now required of his government. Eden's November 15 cable to Lloyd provided another example of faulty British perceptions.[100] The prime minister, still not accepting his lack of bargaining power, rejected the possibility of a total withdrawal based solely on a United Nations assurance that clearing the canal and negotiations on a canal agreement would begin thereafter.[101] The prime minister still had not grasped that he had no bargaining power.

Lloyd further displayed his incomprehension of the world around him when he arrived in Washington later that week. Together with Caccia he visited Dulles at Walter Reed Hospital.[102] Lloyd reported that Dulles had deplored Britain's failure to bring down Nasser. In reply the foreign secretary stated that although the United States by its actions at the United Nations had made Nasser's removal more difficult, the Anglo-French invasion had made the Egyptian leader highly vulnerable.[103]

The foreign secretary's interpretation of the events of November as a British victory became evident again in his conversation with former under secretary of state Walter Bedell Smith. When Smith raised the British government's failure, Lloyd "discussed with him whether in fact we had failed and pointed out the military disaster which had befallen Nasser, the economic trouble that he had brought upon himself."[104] Eden endorsed Lloyd's position, cabling the foreign secretary that "I am sure it is right to take a strong line as you have done."[105]

Makins thoroughly disagreed with the prime minister's assessment. On Friday, November 16, he wrote Macmillan that sterling had "a rough week on the exchanges and the deficit [on the month] to date is about $200 million."[106] Makins pointed out that if current trends continued, the monthly loss, which in keeping with current practice had to be announced on the third or fourth of the next month, might well be over $300 million. Makins doubted whether even with American support it would be possible to arrange any large support plan for sterling, such as an IMF drawing or the waiver, but suggested authorizing Harcourt to speak with Humphrey about the British predicament.[107]

Treasury official Sir Leslie Rowan's letter to Harcourt crossed with one written by Harcourt that, in accurate and interesting detail, described the obstacles he was facing: "We meet a brick wall at every turn with the administration. They remain extremely friendly on a personal basis but are not prepared to discuss any serious business. I think the attitude of the Administration can best be summed up by 'you have got yourselves into this mess, now get yourselves out of it.'" Humphrey was adamantly opposed to dollar aid to Britain or France on the grounds that American public opinion opposed it. However, Harcourt said, "My own view is that the feeling within the Administration is considerably more hostile than it is amongst the general public. They are hurt and piqued at our action which they look on as a blunder and they seem determined to treat us as naughty boys who have got to be taught that they cannot go off and act on their own without asking Nanny's permission first."[108]

Anticipating an instruction from Whitehall to discuss Britain's financial problems with Humphrey, Harcourt said that the secretary of the Treasury understood Britain's precarious condition and then correctly predicted that "in the end I think we shall get their help but we shall only get it when things are really desperate and only at about one minute to twelve—they look on the present as being about 11 o'clock." Finally, Harcourt urged the Treasury not to press for an IMF drawing yet. While the American government technically could not block the drawing of the gold tranche, it could block the IMF board from considering the issue.[109]

The European oil predicament was now worsening daily. Robert Anderson, former deputy defense secretary and Eisenhower's special envoy to the Middle East, told a National Security Council meeting on November 8 that the closing of the Iraq Petroleum Company pipeline and the Suez Canal necessitated the delivery of an additional 350,000 barrels of oil each day (b/d) from the American Gulf Coast to the East Coast while an additional 450,000 b/d needed to be transported from the Gulf Coast and Venezuela. Free world shipping, when fully utilized, would allow 800,000 b/d of Middle Eastern oil to travel around Cape Horn to Europe. Should these targets be met, Europe would still face a deficit of between 10 percent and 15 percent of its requirements. Should the Aramco tapline or other Middle Eastern sources be cut off, Europe would face much greater shortages.[110] This fear partly motivated the administration's refusal to allow the MEEC to meet. Government officials told major oil company executives that the administration did not intend to take any official action prior to a genuine cease-fire and troop withdrawals because they intended to convince the Arab world that the United States, not the Soviet Union was their true friend.[111]

As the days went by, the administration's position hardened. The British government, realizing the futility of any approach to the United States, decided to filter its advance to Washington through a European body. This gambit seemed to work; Sir Hugh Ellis Rees, the British ambassador to the Organization of European Economic Cooperation (OEEC), reported on November 12 that the MEEC might be reconvened if it were approached by an OEEC committee with a Swiss chairman. While this plan ruled out the OEEC's Oil Committee and seemed demeaning, the British government acquiesced. Its allies eagerly cooperated because the cutoff of oil supplies affected every country in Western Europe.[112] Unfortunately, British optimism was misplaced. On November 15 Dr. Arthur Flemming informed the National Security Council that "it had been agreed that the time had not yet come to put into operation the plans for supplying oil to Europe drawn up by the Middle East Emergency Committee." Ellis Rees confirmed this bad news to Whitehall on November 19 when he reported that his American counterpart had said that the MEEC was not meeting because the administration was "afraid that premature action . . . might move some of the Arabs to indulge in further sabotage of oil installations."[113]

Faced with continued American intransigence, Britain continued its attempt to use the OEEC to find a European solution to the oil shortage. One idea, emanating from the Bank of England, called for European creditor nations, chiefly West Germany, to create a dollar pool that all members of the OEEC could draw upon for oil purchases. Britain would benefit from the increased availability of dollars, which could then be used to make British-owned tankers and oil processing supplies available to other European nations lacking such facilities. However, the German government refused to commit itself to this scheme.[114]

EDEN'S ECLIPSE

During the autumn Eden's health had declined drastically. His gall bladder condition had left him subject to recurrent high fevers requiring potent amphetamines. While on medication the prime minister experienced periods of increased energy; thereafter he would be completely enervated. In October he had struggled with another bout, and once the first exultation of action had passed, he suffered visibly.[115] Persuaded to see his doctors on November 19, Eden found that the verdict varied as to whether he was seriously ill or merely exhausted. In any case he did not seem fit to carry on and bowed to advice to recuperate at Ian Fleming's Jamaica home, departing on November 23.[116] Eden's exit, although it was a personal political disaster, helped prop up the disintegrating special relationship.[117] The prime minister had remained determined to take the strongest possible stand against Nasser and still wanted a conditional withdrawal from Egypt. With his departure the British government regained a certain amount of flexibility. Moreover, the prime minister's relations with administration officials had never been good. In the wake of the Suez imbroglio they had deteriorated further because the administration resented having been deceived. American officials realized that Eden was not solely responsible, but as prime minister he received the lion's share of the blame.[118]

In order to improve the beleaguered special relationship, behind Eden's back both Butler and Macmillan established daily contacts with Aldrich.[119] While neither Dulles nor British officials particularly liked Aldrich, during November he served as an effective intermediary.[120] Macmillan on several occasions told the American ambassador that he would like to come to the United States immediately, but Hoover, deputizing for the recuperating

Foster Dulles told Aldrich that "we remain firm in our conviction that withdrawal of troops is of prime urgency and must be moving toward accomplishment before other important questions can be answered."[121]

On November 19 Aldrich called Eisenhower and reported, prematurely, that the British Cabinet was going to be reshuffled and that Eden would be replaced. The next day the president, together with Humphrey and Hoover, reviewed Aldrich's various messages. The president favored Macmillan to replace Eden, while Humphrey endorsed Butler, with whom he had worked closely when the latter was chancellor of the Exchequer. Humphrey's role in the repair of Anglo-American relations loomed increasingly large both because of the centrality of financial issues and because Hoover, the acting secretary of state, reposed great trust in the treasury secretary. While Harcourt believed that Humphrey was the most stubborn member of the administration, in fact all the men close to Eisenhower believed in the necessity of an immediate, unconditional British withdrawal from Egypt.[122] Economic aid would be used as the stick and the carrot: the lack of it would pressure Britain out of Egypt and the promise of assistance would encourage the British to follow American wishes.[123] Dulles had previously tried this technique on Nasser; now it proved more successful.

AMERICAN PRESSURE ON BRITAIN AT ITS HEIGHT

The administration's victorious campaign against Britain illustrated the executive branch's virtually untrammeled power to mobilize negative economic power in the field of foreign relations. While congressional leaders were kept informed of the administration's actions, the president had no need to obtain legislative approval to withhold financial assistance.[124] He and his colleagues had almost complete freedom to conduct their crusade against America's allies as they saw fit.

The president laid out the sequence of events to be followed: "First, we are ready to talk about help as soon as the pre-condition (French and British withdrawal) is established; second, on knowing that the British and French forces will comply with a withdrawal undertaking at once we would talk to the Arabs to obtain the removal of any objections they may have regarding the provision of oil to Western Europe; third, we will then talk the details of money assistance with the British." The State Department instructed Aldrich to convey this message to both Butler and Macmillan

Eisenhower meets with his senior advisors. At extreme left is Treasury Secretary George Humphrey, while Dulles is seated on the president's other side. (Courtesy Dwight D. Eisenhower Library/National Park Service)

because the American government should not appear to be playing favorites.[125]

Now the administration could play its preferred intermediary role—between the British and French on the one hand and the Arabs on the other. As Eisenhower said: "We must face the question, what *must* we do in Europe and then the question, how do we square this with the Arabs?" Therefore, the president deemed it important to obtain the agreement of Saudi Arabia, Iran, and Iraq that once the British and French had begun to withdraw, the American government should give them petroleum aid in order to "prevent the dissolution of Europe."[126] Indeed European oil supplies seemed to be approaching the critical stage; for example, on November 20 the British minister of fuel and power announced further rationing measures to cope with the expected 25 percent shortfall of oil supplies. Ellis Rees wrote Macmillan on November 23, while the OEEC's organization was in good shape, "We cannot do much more as regards oil until the Americans authorize their industry to get in touch with ours and form an expert advisory group to our Oil Committee."[127]

The British government still failed to comprehend the American stance.[128] Therefore, Lodge reiterated that the British and French governments must comply with the United Nations resolutions and immediately withdraw from Egyptian territory. Furthermore, when Hammarskjöld reported to the General Assembly on November 21, he repeated Nasser's intransigent message that clearance of the canal would not begin while British and French forces remained in Egypt.[129] Yet the Foreign Office confirmed Lloyd's stance that only one battalion would be withdrawn. The bulk of British and French forces would stay in Port Said for the foreseeable future to maintain order and to aid UNEF forces when they arrived.[130] Whitehall defended its timetable on the grounds that it would bolster the government's domestic standing. British officials further pointed out that their schedule made technical sense. But the Foreign Office had lost touch with international reality: no plan could work that (as even Whitehall admitted) violated the United Nations resolutions.[131] The General Assembly responded to the British government's attempted evasion on November 24 by censuring the British and French for their conduct and again demanded an unconditional, immediate withdrawal. After "much searching of heart," as Robert Murphy told Caccia, the United States voted for this resolution and abstained on a Belgian resolution that would have omitted the censure and lengthened the timetable for withdrawal.[132]

However painful it may have been to vote to condemn the British and French actions, the American position at the United Nations fully reflected the administration's stance.[133] When Hoover told Eisenhower at a Thanksgiving Day conference that the European oil situation was now becoming critical, Eisenhower told him to tell Caccia that while the administration viewed the oil problem as a top priority, "in order to do that, we must stay four square with the U.N., so Britain must take some preliminary actions."[134]

British attention now focused on the increasingly desperate position of sterling. November 20 and 21 were terrible days, with losses of $48 million. For the first time a British official attributed a high percentage of the drain to New York; Makins reported on November 22 that Cobbold told him that "New York seems to be in a state nearly of panic about sterling and do not trust the situation from hour to hour."[135] The next day was even worse;

with the New York market still open the reserves were down $20 million. According to Cobbold, on both days oil companies had accounted for much of the selling.[136] This result was predictable. As the seven sisters bought and sold oil for both dollars and sterling, they obviously had large sterling accounts. Given the increased likelihood of a sterling devaluation, it made good economic sense for these companies to sell their pounds as soon as possible.

As Makins said, "The real trouble is that there is absolutely nothing coming in on the plus side."[137] Much of the problem derived from the so-called leads and lags. This phrase refers to the time differential between payments by buyers and sellers in international trade. The world of foreign exchange trading is a betting game where once a currency is in trouble, investors rush in ever-increasing numbers to rid themselves of their holdings.[138] While the flow of funds is never evenly distributed, during any time of financial doubt, foreign buyers of British goods delayed paying for them in the hopes that their currencies would soon increase in value against the pound, which would make exports cheaper. By contrast, foreign sellers of goods refused to take sterling and instead insisted on dollars in payment for goods sold to British purchasers.

Britain's political problems now exacerbated its financial dilemmas. The continued Anglo-American rupture and the prolonged debates at the United Nations meant that neither American aid nor a speedy clearance of the canal would quickly materialize. If the impasse continued, sterling would certainly be devalued or left to float.[139] In either case it made perfect sense for holders of sterling to exchange their pounds for dollars before the exchange rate worsened.[140]

The selling of sterling by governments did not become a major factor during the fall of 1956. Government holdings of sterling were not extensive enough to become an important component of the massive drain of sterling during this period. For example, notwithstanding allegations to the contrary, the sterling holdings of the United States government declined only from £30 million to £26 million during the quarter September 30 to December 31, 1956. Of the countries with extensive sterling holdings, only India reduced its reserves significantly while Australian reserves actually increased.[141]

On November 23 matters had so deteriorated that Sir George Bolton told the Federal Reserve Bank of New York that the Bank of England needed to sell at least $100 million worth of gold for dollars to meet the current demand.[142] Concurrently the Treasury and the Bank of England began considering "crash action" to be taken if they could not obtain American assistance. The reestablishing of the special relationship occupied first place on this list that also included selling dollar securities in Switzerland, reducing British forces in Germany, and increasing taxes. These policies were designed to maintain the official rate of £1=$2.80 unless all "the reinforcements" were gone.[143] That officials believed that the currency was not overvalued and that its problems were political, not financial, in nature provided one of the reasons behind the government's determination to hold the rate for sterling. This view was widely shared; for example, Per Jacobssen, managing director of the IMF, told Cobbold on November 22 that he believed that "our [Britain's] present exchange rate is fundamentally sound on an international basis."[144]

One day earlier the Foreign Office had sent Caccia the text of a personal message from Macmillan to Humphrey appealing for American financial assistance. Simultaneously the Commonwealth Relations Office had authorized the British high commissioner to Canada to explain Britain's financial position to the Canadian government and to inform the government that Britain might request a waiver under the U.S. Agreement and companion Canadian credit.[145] Thereafter the Canadian government was kept fully informed of the Anglo-American financial discussions.[146] Caccia delivered the message to Humphrey on November 26, adding that in his opinion the secretary of the Treasury was the most intransigent and vindictive member of the administration.[147]

Had Caccia known of Humphrey's November 26 telephone call to Butler, he would have found confirmation of his opinion. The secretary told Butler that he wanted to get the American message across to the British government. The administration was "today opposed to the United Kingdom whom they regarded as being disobedient to the United Nations commands, and in defiance of them." World opinion, said the secretary, felt that the British still insisted on a conditional withdrawal. However, if the British government were to obey the United Nations resolutions, then the United States would be "anxious to discuss the terms of a general settlement."[148] Caccia was right about Humphrey taking a tough stand on what the British should do but wrong in implying that the secretary of the Treasury was not representative of administration opinion as a whole.

Hoover took up these same points in a cable to Aldrich, who continued to urge that the White House agree to a high-level meeting with British officials. The acting secretary of state said the basic requirement was "concrete evidence of more substantial withdrawal of British and French forces." Nonetheless, Hoover betrayed a definite softening of the American position by adding that it was not necessary that the last Western soldier leave Egypt before tripartite consultation was resumed.[149]

Humphrey took the same stance when he met with Caccia and Harcourt at a lengthy meeting on November 27. The secretary would not budge from his position that "the United States government was powerless to act until Her Majesty's Government had shown in a way which the world could accept, that we were conforming to rather than defying the United Nations."[150] Yet once the British government had met the administration's requirements, because the administration concurred in the British assessment of the reasons for sterling's plight, Humphrey pledged that the United States would help Britain as far as it could.[151]

Indeed, the treasury secretary now outlined for the first time the nature of future American assistance. The administration would support a drawing from the IMF of Britain's gold tranche and first credit tranche, for a total of $561 million, which was more than the British government had expected. An EXIM loan would quite possibly be available in an amount sufficient to pay all oil costs. On the question of the waiver, Humphrey assured the British that "the United States would examine favourably any approach we cared to make."[152]

This meeting encouraged the Treasury and Bank of England to believe that extensive American help was on the horizon. British officials were working on a constricted schedule; the reserves figure would be announced on December 3 or 4. It was likely to be below $2,000 million, which would be calamitous unless the chancellor could simultaneously announce immediate American assistance. Therefore it was decided that the statement would be made on December 4; as Makins said, "We are working with the Americans against a very tight time table, and another 24 hours might make all the difference to the tone you are able to give to your statement."[153]

An Anglo-French withdrawal from Egypt was the prerequisite to American aid however, and the British government remained unready to admit complete defeat. Macmillan told Aldrich on November 27 that he sincerely hoped that Lloyd's ongoing negotiations with Hammarskjöld and Lodge would produce an agreement on withdrawal that the Cabinet could approve.[154] However, Egyptian diplomats insisted that events had to follow in sequence: first, withdrawal; then canal clearance; and finally, negotiations for a canal settlement. Furthermore, Lloyd cabled Butler, "the hard core of [American] policy makers, some of which have been strongly pro-British in the past, are now against us. This will continue certainly until we have made what they would regard as the *amende honorable* by rapid withdrawal."[155]

Lloyd's reading was correct, at least about some administration officials. Dulles demurred at Eisenhower's suggestion that, given the indications that "the boys" in Britain were ready to go along with the United Nations, the United States could now make it clear that American oil assistance would be undertaken as soon as the British government went along with the United Nations resolutions. The secretary said, "It is awfully hard to see how we can begin to use that oil to meet their needs before they have indicated that they would comply with the UN resolution." Eisenhower then backed down and said that "his only thought was to say that we *understand* they are going to comply."[156]

Yet by November 28 the administration had begun to retreat slightly from its original stance. Hoover suggested that Aldrich ask Butler if it would help his position if the White House announced the reconvening of the MEEC on November 29. Aldrich reported that Butler, Macmillan, and Lloyd all welcomed it; the announcement was made on November 30. Dillon, the American ambassador in Paris, felt equally pleased. The French government had introduced rationing on November 29. Even before that, the strain on fuel supplies had been apparent.[157]

As Butler and Macmillan strove to persuade their colleagues of the need for surrender, another complication arose. Since Egypt did not permit Israel to use or benefit from the canal on the grounds that Israel and Egypt remained at war, the British worried that the same argument would be used to deny them the use of the canal. However, assurances from Lodge and Hoover managed to defuse British concerns on this issue.[158]

Everyone now focused on the forthcoming two British statements, the first on the troop withdrawal, the second on Britain's financial position. Butler and Macmillan struggled to obtain Cabinet approval for a withdrawal announcement. As Butler had acknowledged to the Cabinet on November 22, a strong body of Conservative backbenchers opposed any

major troop withdrawal. Their opposition made any such public pledge a
political football for Cabinet ministers.[159] Because he was deputy prime
minister, Butler bore the brunt of their reaction.[160] Simultaneously the
Treasury and Bank of England continued to hone the draft of the chancellor's speech to be given on Tuesday, December 4. A revised copy was sent
to Caccia to be shown to Humphrey; because they wanted to include in the
statement a promise of the maximum possible American assistance, Makins
and his colleagues felt it was important to clear the statement with the
administration.[161]

A Bank of England memorandum sent by Makins to Macmillan on
November 30 indicated the pressure facing the Treasury and the Bank of
England. The final November reserves loss to be announced publicly was
$279 million. However, the real loss was $401 million, the British Treasury
having made up the difference by selling U.S. Treasury securities and
including in the figures forward amounts that had not yet been received.[162]

Even using the $279 million figure, British gold and dollar reserves as of
December 1 would fall below the magic $2,000 million mark to stand at
$1,965 million. If the British had to make the $175.5 million payment due in
December on the U.S. Agreement and companion Canadian loan, without
replenishing the reserves at the end of the year could be no higher than
$1,789.5 million and would undoubtedly be lower.[163] Further, Cobbold
told Makins that sales of sterling had been very heavy during the last two
days of the month. Oil company sales accounted for a good part of the drain
as did the lack of any resumption of Anglo-American cooperation to inspire
confidence.[164]

Fortunately news from Washington slowly improved. Harcourt reported
on November 30 that Burgess had been quite encouraging about the
waiver, suggesting that the American government would approve of Britain's claiming it in December, subject to later negotiations. Nevertheless,
on December 2, Humphrey, having returned from a weekend at his
Thomasville, Georgia, plantation, telephoned Harcourt and "again emphasized that any financial support was subject to agreement on the political
side."[165] On the brink of success, the administration worried about two
potential difficulties. While the American government still insisted on a
firm Anglo-French agreement to withdraw from Egypt, it did not want its
pressure to split the Conservative party—the prospect of a Labour government alarmed American officials.[166] Also, Washington feared a French

refusal to acquiesce in the troop withdrawal. Concerned about both possibilities, Humphrey called Butler on December 2 to say that the United States was eager to furnish aid to Britain, that Eisenhower would make a statement to that effect, but that the British withdrawal announcement must be as definite as possible. Feeling that he had not been sufficiently specific, Humphrey had Aldrich call Butler on the night of December 2 to say that the main point of the secretary's telephone call was "that the American administration wished the U. K. to announce a definite date by which the withdrawal operation would be completed." Butler replied that Humphrey had not made this point, that it was impossible to set a date, but that "he could be assured that the U.K. bona fides were above reproach, and that he could say no more that night."[167]

Butler and Macmillan pressed fellow ministers to agree to the withdrawal. Significant opposition remained; as late as November 30 the Cabinet consensus was to attempt a withdrawal conditioned on some sort of guaranty about the clearance of the canal.[168] The next day, ministers reviewed the first draft of the statement on withdrawal to be made by the foreign secretary two days hence; it contained an unconditional promise to withdraw but no firm date. At the meeting of December 3 held prior to the House of Commons session, Lloyd announced that the secretary-general had reviewed the announcement and had accepted the lack of a specific date for withdrawal.[169]

As Lloyd rose in the House of Commons to announce the Anglo-French troop withdrawal, London instructed Caccia to inform the administration that the British government could not set a precise date without jeopardizing an orderly embarkation but that "we have decided to go without delay and we intend to go without delay." Caccia reminded American officials that as Hammarskjöld had accepted the uncertainty, the United States should as well. When Murphy repeated to Caccia the need for a firm date, the ambassador told Murphy that "an Englishman's word was his bond" and so this point should be "reconsidered at the highest level." Eisenhower and Dulles were reexamining this requisite; both agreed, in the president's words, that the British and French "had gone adequately to meet the requirements."[170]

Therefore, Macmillan's long-awaited December 4 statement painted a far more optimistic picture than would have seemed possible two weeks earlier.[171] After revealing that the reserves had fallen to $1,965 million,

Macmillan announced that substantial support measures, backed by the United States, would be undertaken.[172] With American approval, the British government would apply for a drawing against its IMF quota of $1,300 million. Furthermore, Macmillan added, the United States Treasury Department had said it would present the matter of a waiver under the U.S. Agreement to Congress with the "definite recommendation" that the language of the agreement be modified to permit a waiver.[173] The position at the Suez Canal had been abandoned, but sterling had been saved, at least for the moment.

SEVEN

THE AMERICAN WAY

DECEMBER 4, 1956–MARCH 23, 1957

*I said that it had occurred to me that the situation
now existing in the Middle East bore a
certain resemblance to the Greek-Turkey
situation which had arisen in 1947.*
—John Foster Dulles to Harold Caccia,
December 24, 1956

With the agreement on Anglo-French troop withdrawal, the American government began to mend its relations with its errant allies. Simultaneously, President Eisenhower and his colleagues drafted the Middle Eastern initiative soon to be known as the Eisenhower Doctrine. The administration intended to take advantage of the opportunity presented by recent events in the Middle East to restructure Arab-American relations. To keep up the momentum, the administration forced the Israeli government to withdraw its troops behind the 1949 armistice lines. During March, the Israeli army completed its evacuation as an Anglo-American summit meeting concluded in an atmosphere of mutual praise. With the canal set to reopen, the Suez crisis was over.

AMERICAN AID TO BRITAIN

Secretary of the Treasury George Humphrey told British Ambassador to the United States Sir Harold Caccia on December 2 that once the president gave his blessing, the British could look forward to "massive support."[1] Humphrey kept his word. When the British government on December 3 committed itself to an early and complete withdrawal, he wrote influential

Senator Styles Bridges that the administration supported a British government request to amend the U.S. Agreement.[2] In order to mend fences, both Humphrey and Secretary of State John Foster Dulles decided to go to the NATO meetings scheduled for December 10–12 in Paris.

On December 5, Lord Harcourt, the British economic minister in Washington, began talks with the IMF on the British drawing that Chancellor of the Exchequer Harold Macmillan had previously announced would be sought.[3] The administration's clear support motivated the British government to seek a very large amount: a drawing of Britain's gold and first credit tranche ($561.47 million) and a standby of Britain's remaining two credit tranches ($738.53 million).[4] Given the IMF's weighted voting system, American backing ensured that the British government would get its money.

However, Harcourt worried that Egyptian Director Ahmed Zaki Saad might object to the borrowings on the legitimate grounds that the British government had violated IMF rules by failing to notify the fund of its orders blocking Egyptian accounts.[5] Another subject under Anglo-American discussion was the timing of the borrowings. As the United States supplied all IMF funds, a drawing of $561.47 million on one day could negatively affect the American government's cash flow. Therefore the U.S. Treasury requested that the British borrow the drawing in two installments about ten days apart.[6]

As the IMF negotiations continued, Harcourt met Humphrey to begin discussions on an EXIM credit for the British government to be used for oil and oil-related expenses. The treasury secretary was cordial, but when Harcourt suggested the possibility of an omnibus American loan to European countries, he reacted angrily, telling the British minister that "he was perfectly prepared to lend to individual borrowers, particularly to the United Kingdom, but he was 'damned if he was going to be the sole lender to a gang of spenders.'" He said that "he disliked the OEEC and everything to do with it and always had done so."[7]

Humphrey's unaccustomed generosity to the British government partly stemmed from his belief, expounded at a meeting of the Pennsylvania Society on December 8, that "we took a stand against [the British and French governments] when their action violated the basic principles in which we believe. Just so, we must now support them in their wholehearted effort to arrive at a just and fair settlement through negotiation."[8]

Humphrey's remarks reflect two elements of American foreign policy in the Eisenhower-Dulles era: first, the successful application of the carrot and stick approach to the Western allies, and second, the air of moral righteousness and hypocrisy that permeated all administration statements on the Suez crisis. Because they convinced themselves that American foreign policy decisions were made for reasons of principle, not realpolitik, administration officials had no trouble reconciling their opposition to the British-French-Israeli action in Egypt with their support of such actions as the CIA sponsored coups in Iran or Guatemala, which prima facie were strikingly similar to the Suez imbroglio. Such moral confidence, verging on self-righteousness, bolstered the American government's ability to oppose its closest allies and stiffened the administration's resistance to compromise.

With the position of sterling improving but not yet stabilized, the British government, in keeping with long-standing central bank theory, sought to obtain the largest support credits possible from the United States.[9] Caccia and Harcourt urged the Treasury and Bank of England to "strike while the iron is hot" and obtain loan commitments sooner rather than later. They argued that "we shall almost certainly get more from the United States in the present mood than if we allow this question to simmer too long, especially with Congress in sight." Therefore they pushed for an EXIM loan of $700 million, which, together with the IMF commitment of $1,300 million, would give the British government a financial reservoir of $2,000 million, a sum exceeding the total of British reserves at the time.[10]

The IMF Executive Board took up the British requests for a drawing of $561.47 million and standby credit of $738.53 million on December 10. In what Caccia described as "an almost embarrassingly friendly atmosphere," the British representatives listened to various directors laud their efforts to retain sterling's current parity and basked in their strong American support. Altogether it was a welcome change from the British government's recent experiences with international organizations. The final vote: sixteen in favor, none opposed, with the Egyptian delegate abstaining. The Bank of England borrowed the first part of the drawing, $250 million, on December 12 and the remainder, $311.47 million, on December 21.[11] Sir Roger Makins, joint permanent under secretary of the Treasury, cabled Harcourt to say, "Congratulations on a most successful operation."[12]

The improvement in Anglo-American monetary cooperation mirrored a broader movement to repair Anglo-American ties. On December 6, Vice-

President Richard Nixon broadcast the administration's new approach in a New York speech. He fulsomely lauded the administration's Suez stance, saying, "The United States had met the test of history. The United Nations had been saved. The rule of law had been upheld." At the same time, the vice-president also spoke highly of the British and French governments. Both the American press and the British embassy perceived his encomium as a fence-mending gesture.[13]

Dulles and Humphrey arrived in Paris on December 10, and Dulles began discussions with both British Foreign Secretary Selwyn Lloyd and French Foreign Minister Christian Pineau.[14] The next day Humphrey and his aides met with Macmillan and British Treasury official Sir Leslie Rowan. Humphrey again displayed his reformed attitude toward Britain's finances. The events of November had convinced him that continued international financial stability, in which the United States had a large stake, required a strong pound. Humphrey told his British counterparts, "At present the U.S. were engaged in trying to restore confidence in the £; to be niggardly in any way in this might endanger the whole operation for some quite small amount."[15] In this atmosphere British and American officials cordially discussed the IMF drawing, the EXIM loan, and the question of a waiver under the U.S. Agreement. Both sides agreed that the waiver clauses of the U.S. Agreement should be scrapped in favor of a "bisque" scheme that would permit the British government to postpone payments of principal and interest a fixed number of times at its sole discretion. Only the number of such bisques needed to be decided.[16]

Following the next day's NATO meeting, Macmillan called on Dulles seeking both to repair Anglo-American relations and to distance himself from Prime Minister Anthony Eden. The chancellor told Dulles that "he, personally was very unhappy with the way the [Suez] matter had been handled and the timing, but that Eden had taken this entirely to himself and he, Macmillan, had no choice except to back Eden." The chancellor also indicated that his hope was that a change of government would make either him or R. A. Butler prime minister, if not immediately on Eden's return, then within six months.[17]

On December 13, Macmillan met separately with Dulles and Humphrey. Macmillan told the secretary of state that "the British action [at Suez] was the last gasp of a declining power . . . perhaps in two hundred years the United States would know how we felt." Using all his charm, the chancellor emphasized to Dulles that the secretary of state could change the course of history by carving a new Middle Eastern settlement; to both men Macmillan suggested the idea of a joint Anglo-American study group on Middle Eastern problems such as oil.[18] These discussions were cordial, for both Americans wanted a reestablished special relationship as long as it was clear that the American government would take the lead in all important decisions. Macmillan's words showed that he understood the situation very well.

Unbeknownst to Macmillan the American government had already begun to formulate the Eisenhower Doctrine, its own wide-ranging Middle East blueprint. During the spring of 1956 Eisenhower and his colleagues concluded that the United States was losing influence over Middle Eastern nations.[19] One week after Nasser's nationalization of the canal, the Joint Chiefs of Staff registered their concern about the implications of the Egyptian president's action. They feared that if left unchallenged, Nasser would emerge as the dominant symbol of Arab nationalism. If so, negative consequences could develop for American oil supplies, for American bases in other parts of the world, and on the less tangible issue of Western prestige in the area, which in turn could jeopardize American efforts to counter the Communist threat.[20]

In the wake of the Anglo-French invasion, administration officials believed that the United States should immediately occupy the void left by the precipitate decline of European influence in the Middle East.[21] Moreover, the administration wanted to use the unique opportunity presented by the climax of the Suez crisis to improve Arab-American relations. As Lodge never tired of pointing out, the reputation of the United States among the Arab nations had never been so high.[22] American intervention during the Suez invasion had apparently broken the damning nexus in Arab minds between the United States and Israel. Even Nasser had been making conciliatory gestures to American Ambassador to Egypt Raymond Hare.[23] Accordingly, officials became convinced that they should capitalize on the improved American reputation in the Middle East and build bridges to Arab countries that would strengthen their anticommunism and insure Western oil supplies into the decades ahead.[24] The president also envisioned that any plan must allow for a military force that the American government could rapidly muster against a Soviet threat to the Middle East.[25]

The fear of an imminent Soviet challenge also influenced another significant change in administration policy: the decision to drop the quest for a
solution to the Arab-Israeli conflict, formerly the centerpiece of American
Middle East policy. Two years of barren efforts had convinced Dulles of the
futility of such a search. The secretary of state told his close aide Robert
Bowie, "He believed that the root of the problem could not be eradicated.
He said he had been reading the Old Testament and they had the same
problems as we have today. He said it did not make sense that he could
solve problems which Moses and Joshua with Divine guidance could not
solve."[26] Furthermore, the administration hoped that its improved standing in the Middle East might be sufficient to bring about a major improvement in Arab-American relations even though a solution to the Arab-Israeli
impasse had not been found.

During December officials debated how best to take advantage of their
new opportunities. Dulles perceived three possible approaches: the United
States could join the Baghdad Pact, it could form a new regional grouping,
or it could deal with the Middle East on a country-by-country basis. The
president and his secretary of state agreed that, given congressional realities, the third approach probably made the most sense. Eisenhower said
that what he wanted was a "package deal" combining various elements that
would allow the United States to improve its relations with the Arab
world.[27] At a White House meeting on December 20, Dulles, on the State
Department's recommendation, advised against joining the Baghdad Pact
not only because of domestic American opposition but because the pact
was inextricably linked to Britain and was anathema to both Nasser and
King Saud of Saudi Arabia.[28] Consequently, the secretary favored asking
Congress for a resolution authorizing economic and military aid and ap-
propriating a sum such as $400 million for a two-year period.[29]

The similarities to the situation that had spawned the Truman Doctrine a
decade earlier weighed in Dulles's mind. In fact when Caccia came to see
the secretary on December 24, Dulles treated him to a reading of a portion
of Truman's address to Congress of March 12, 1947.[30] Once again, an
American administration sought to create a situation in which the countries
of the world could choose their governments free from coercion. Both
crises involved a Middle Eastern problem that had galvanized an American
administration into action. Furthermore, for all the administration's talk
about joint projects, the United States was again rejecting the use of
collective action, through the United Nations or otherwise.

On December 27 Dulles gave Eisenhower a redraft of his proposed congressional message and told Vice-President Richard Nixon that the Middle East, not Hungary, would be the president's first order of business in the new year. Two days later the secretary unveiled the plan to Caccia and French Ambassador Hervé Alphand. But Dulles cautioned the ambassadors to avoid using language in their reports to London and Paris that might imply that the administration had consulted with the Western allies. While he ascribed his admonition to congressional sensitivities, Dulles was distancing the United States from Britain and France on Middle Eastern issues. He clearly relished the new situation with the United States taking full charge in the Middle East instead of having to deal with and through the British.[31] The secretary said to David Lawrence, "We must fill the vacuum of power which the British filled for a century—not merely the ability to act in an emergency but day in and day out presence there."[32]

The president began his campaign for the Eisenhower Doctrine on December 31 at a meeting with the congressional Republican leadership. At this gathering the president only offered general remarks, principally a summary of Middle Eastern events during the past few months. Then Humphrey rose to explain the financial consequences of the Suez crisis, concentrating on the problems of oil for Western Europe and the need to help Britain retain the sterling parity.[33]

The next day, at a meeting of the Bipartisan Congressional Leadership, the president unveiled his plan and called for a large congressional appropriation for major Middle Eastern expenditures and for advance authorization to use American military force under certain conditions without further legislative permission. Eisenhower said that British and French weakness had left a vacuum in the Middle East that either the United States or the Soviet Union would fill. He justified the need for a new initiative by raising the future significance of Middle Eastern oil to the United States and the present importance of Britain and France continuing as strong powers. When Dulles spoke, he emphasized that independent American action would work better than any treaty arrangement, which could encourage local animosities. Furthermore, a congressional resolution would be reassuring to various Middle Eastern governments. However, neither the president nor his secretary of state clearly cataloged the specific goals of the Eisenhower Doctrine. Instead Eisenhower and his colleagues emphasized the need for formulating a new American policy to take advantage of a fortuitous turn in world events without specifying to what end.

The stiff questioning by congressional leaders prefigured the lack of enthusiasm that would greet the Eisenhower Doctrine.[34] In 1947 members of Congress shared the president's perception of a threat to American national interests and supported his recommendations for dealing with it. Ten years later both Democratic and Republican congressional leaders had significant doubts about both the problem and the prescription. It is a testament to the modern president's growing ability to control foreign policy that, notwithstanding these significant difficulties, Eisenhower continued on the course that he, together with his advisors, had charted.

On January 5 the president delivered in person his special message that asked for $200 million for economic aid for Middle Eastern countries and sought prior authorization for military action "to secure and protect the territorial integrity and political independence of such nations, requesting such aid, against overt armed aggression from any nation controlled by International Communism."[35] Whatever the weaknesses of the Eisenhower Doctrine, its introduction represented a major milestone in the history of Western relations with the Middle East: from now on the United States, not Britain, intended to take primary responsibility for the region.[36] A direct result of the Suez crisis, the Eisenhower Doctrine also marked another stepping stone down the road of the imperial presidency. By asking Congress to delegate war powers in advance of any specific occurrence, Eisenhower was further usurping Congress's constitutional role.[37]

MACMILLAN REPLACES EDEN

Concurrently another major development occasioned by the Suez Crisis unfolded: the retirement of Anthony Eden as prime minister and his replacement by Harold Macmillan. While recuperating in Jamaica, Eden had been informed but not consulted about the British decision to agree to a complete and early withdrawal. Eden's standing with the Conservative party and in the country was now so reduced that Butler and Macmillan felt free to bypass Eden and repair Anglo-American relations as best they could.[38]

Eden returned to London on December 14 and made his first appearance in the House of Commons three days later. His speech was coolly received not only by Labour party members but by his own backbenchers. To Conservative party members Eden had done the unpardonable: he had lost.[39] At the December 18 meeting of the backbenchers' 1922 Committee, MPs again gave Eden a hostile reception.[40] The government suffered another setback on December 20 when the Conservatives' majority at a by-election caused by the resignation of Anthony Nutting was reduced from 11,000 at the previous general election to 2,300.[41] On the same day, as British and French troops completed their withdrawal from Egypt (the last troops left on December 21), Eden, who remained an unreconstructed hardliner, made his final appearance in the House of Commons. He alienated Conservatives of all complexions by maintaining that "I would be compelled . . . if I had the same very disagreeable decisions to take again, to repeat them."[42]

The final blow to Eden was physical. The debilitation and fevers that had sent the prime minister to Jamaica lingered, and on the advice of his doctors, Eden informed the queen on January 8 that he felt he had no choice but to resign.[43] While this was a tragic blow for Eden, who had waited for so long to reach the top position only to lose it after eighteen months, it proved a blessing for the Conservative party.

It was not immediately apparent who would succeed Eden. Before the Suez crisis Butler, as a senior member of the Cabinet and acting prime minister, would most likely have been chosen as Eden's successor.[44] The events of October and November had changed this. Although events vindicated Butler's hesitant approach to the Suez invasion, his attitude had diminished his popularity with his party. Macmillan, by contrast, had appeared firm and strong although in reality he had done a volte-face. Their joint appearance at a 1922 Committee meeting on November 22 had boosted Macmillan's star while dimming Butler's. Butler faltered and stumbled as he attempted to explicate the events that had overtaken the Cabinet's Suez plans. In contrast Macmillan, while proclaiming that his advanced age obviated any possibility of personal ambition, made a resounding plea for party unity.

As soon as Eden's resignation was announced, Macmillan's campaign to succeed him, which had already begun, went into high gear.[45] With Churchill's endorsement, the final step was the polling of Conservative ministers who virtually unanimously supported Macmillan.[46] On January 10, he went to Buckingham Palace to accept officially the royal summons to form a government.[47]

The administration greeted the news of Eden's resignation with relief;

Eisenhower told Ann Whitman that "he had always liked him—but that he had not proved himself a good first man." While Dulles would have preferred Butler, the change in tone in Anglo-American relations was immediately clear from the fact that the president sent Macmillan both an official letter of congratulations and a personal note.[48]

Macmillan moved quickly to create closer ties with the administration. He had been keeping in touch with American Ambassador to Britain Winthrop Aldrich prior to becoming prime minister; now through more direct channels he sought an early meeting with Eisenhower. By the end of January the two men agreed to a March meeting in Bermuda after Eisenhower first met with French Premier Guy Mollet in Washington.[49]

Anglo-American financial cooperation matched the political collaboration. During December British embassy representatives had discussed with administration officials an EXIM loan for the British government to pay for oil and oil-related expenses. On December 21 the administration announced that EXIM had authorized a line of credit of $500 million in favor of the British government collateralized by U.S. securities owned by the British government.[50] Thereafter negotiations continued on both the terms of an EXIM agreement and on an amendment of the U.S. Agreement.[51]

Britain, however, was not yet out of the financial woods. The December reserve figures indicated an increase of $168 million to a total of $2,133 million. Adding in the $175.5 million in respect of the Anglo-American and Canadian loan agreements, which had been placed in escrow accounts pending a settlement of the waiver question, brought a total of $2,308.5 million. But this figure reflected the IMF infusion of $561 million, without which the amount of British reserves would have stood no higher than $1,747.5 million and probably considerably lower.[52] This financial reality, which Macmillan fully appreciated, provided one more reason for the British government to keep its policies in line with those of the United States.

GETTING ISRAEL TO WITHDRAW

With the special relationship on the mend, and the Eisenhower Doctrine launched, the administration turned all its attention toward obtaining a full Israeli withdrawal from the territory it had occupied during the Suez campaign. In the wake of the Israeli invasion of Egypt on October 29, the administration immediately began considering sanctions against Israel. Initially Dulles took a very hard position. He told the president early on the morning of November 1 that Israel's aggression could not go unpunished. However, Eisenhower pointed out that not only had the United Nations not yet condemned any country as an aggressor, but if sanctions were applied against Israel, they would have to be applied against Britain and France as well. The implications of such an eventuality for NATO deeply disturbed the president.

Administration officials discussed this question in depth at the National Security Council meeting of November 1. Although Dulles continued to favor sanctions, Eisenhower's more moderate view prevailed. While the administration suspended its insignificant economic assistance to Israel ($24 million in fiscal 1957), Washington neither froze Israeli bank balances nor levied sanctions against Israel.[53] Furthermore, the administration permitted both aid in transit and ongoing projects to continue.[54]

Prime Minister David Ben-Gurion on November 8 agreed to comply with the United Nations resolutions and withdraw Israeli troops "as soon as satisfactory arrangements were concluded" with UNEF. During November American officials, viewing Israel as (in Dulles's words) a "cat's paw," exerted its pressure primarily on Britain and France.[55] Therefore, Israeli troops, knowing they had the support of the British and French governments, remained in their new positions.[56]

Israeli leaders particularly valued the French endorsement. During the 1950s the Fourth Republic, motivated by its bitter battle to retain *Algérie Française*, had become Israel's closest ally. Moreover, pursuant to secret agreements entered into during and after December 1955, France began sending Israel vital shipments of arms, well in excess of what the United States would have permitted. The crucial French-Israeli meeting took place on June 22, 1956. Negotiators agreed that the Israelis would receive seventy-two Mystère fighter planes, forty Super Sherman tanks, and other miscellaneous equipment. On August 18 the first of these Mystères arrived in Israel.[57]

During the Suez invasion French military aid proved vital. According to the American air attache in Tel-Aviv, U.S. F-84 fighter planes belonging to the French air force flew to Israel where they were immediately repainted with Israeli markings and dispatched on interceptor missions with Israeli and French crews. The American embassy also reported the arrival of additional Mystère F-4 planes.[58]

British and French troops completed their evacuation of Egypt on December 21, but the Israeli government, having begun to withdraw its forces from the Sinai desert, delayed its evacuation from the Gaza Strip and from a small part of the Sinai overlooking the Straits of Tiran and the Israeli port of Elath in the hope of receiving some tangible benefits in exchange for territory. Gaza, populated by 200,000 Palestinian refugees, officially belonged to no country but had been ruled by Egypt since 1949. Because it maintained that the region had been the base for deadly fedayeen raids into Israel, the Israeli government wanted some sort of international control over the area.

The waters of the Gulf of Aqaba posed a different problem. In violation of the 1949 armistice accord, the Egyptian government had occupied the islands in the channel and used this strategic position to fire upon ships approaching the port of Elath. Israel sought both United Nations recognition of the gulf's status as an international waterway and a commitment to keep the waterway open. Finally, the Israeli government intended to ensure access to the Suez Canal, which the Egyptian government had blocked since 1948, on the grounds that a state of war existed between the two nations.

When Ben-Gurion discussed these problems with British Ambassador to Israel Sir John Nicholls on January 7, the latter said that "the United States' attitude would be of decisive importance."[59] The administration's stance was already clear—Israel would not be rewarded for its resort to arms. Officials stated their reasons in moralistic terms: "The guiding principle has been that of the United Nations Charter . . . that the parties will settle any international disputes in which they may be involved by peaceful means and will refrain in their international relations from the threat or use of force in any manner inconsistent with the United Nations."[60] Therefore, the administration insisted that Israel first had to withdraw completely from all captured territories before questions such as passage through the Gulf of Aqaba and security from raids could be addressed.[61]

The Israeli government recognized that to withdraw without any international guarantees would be to acquiesce in the Egyptian government's positions. With the Afro-Asian bloc in the United Nations growing each year, the international organization would provide little support for its cause once Israel had given away its bargaining chips. France, embroiled in

Algeria and afflicted by mounting economic troubles and perennial political crises, was a weak reed. Britain had always maintained a pro-Arab and anti-Israel stance. Its unaccustomed support of Israel during the Suez crisis was clearly a temporary state of affairs. Although the Soviet Union had voted for the partition resolution that had led to the creation of Israel, Moscow had long since changed its pro-Zionist orientation. That left Israel heavily dependent on the United States, which, given the nature and opinions of administration officials, did not bode well for Israeli goals.

The administration's coolness toward Israel had several sources. First, Eisenhower and Dulles felt uncomfortable dealing with Jews. Although not blatantly anti-Semitic, the president was unable to reach out to Jews in the way that he did with other groups.[62] As his papers reveal, the secretary of state felt distinctly uncomfortable with Jews and took a blunt and often harsh approach toward the Jewish state.[63] Senior State Department officials such as Loy Henderson, who had been the chief State Department opponent of partition, held pronounced anti-Zionist views. Other important diplomats who were more or less hostile to Israel included American Ambassador to the United Nations Henry Cabot Lodge, Jr., and United Nations Secretary-General Dag Hammarskjöld. Their bias would play an important role in the events that followed.[64]

A desire for improved Arab-American relations also influenced officials against Israel. Dulles told Senator Lyndon Johnson on November 13 that "the United States faced an almost insoluble problem in the [Middle East] area because of our identification with the State of Israel which above all the Arabs hated."[65] Having launched the Eisenhower Doctrine, administration officials wanted nothing to jeopardize what they saw as an excellent opportunity to improve Arab-American relations and therefore attempted to ensure that international opinion could not perceive American policy as pro-Israel.[66]

In Eisenhower's America, Jewish or other support for Israel was far less pervasive than it would later become. Administration officials prided themselves on their willingness to put this issue above politics and not pander to the Jewish vote and indeed resented advice from men such as Thomas Dewey and Jacob Javits that they do more to cultivate Jewish voters.[67] Congressional support for Israel set the outer limits of what the administration could do, and Eisenhower and his colleagues were left with sufficient latitude to accomplish their goals.

In the meantime Nasser, exploiting his power, was delaying the clearing of the canal until Israeli forces withdrew totally. Clearance operations had begun at the end of December, but it became evident during January that Nasser was using the canal as a lever to force the Western powers to make Israel leave all captured territory.[68] While Nasser's tactics stiffened the British government's resolve to try to wrest a certain degree of control over the canal from Egypt, the American government still naively believed that a continued uncompromising stance against Israel would reap the best dividends from Nasser and the rest of the Arab world.[69]

Israel informed the secretary-general on January 14 that it would not withdraw its troops from Gaza and from Sharm el Sheik, which overlooked the Gulf of Aqaba. The Afro-Asian bloc responded by introducing a resolution noting with regret Israel's failure to comply with previous resolutions and requesting that Hammarskjöld continue his efforts to secure compliance. Administration officials faced a quandary. While not wanting to side with Israel openly, both Dulles and Eisenhower conceded that Israel's position on the Gulf of Aqaba had sufficient merit to deserve more than an outright dismissal.[70]

Yet even when they recognized the justice of some of Israel's complaints, American officials remained determined that Israeli soldiers should follow the precedent set by their British and French allies and withdraw from Egypt expeditiously. The administration now used several tactics simultaneously, beginning with private diplomacy. For this delicate mission Dulles selected his former law partner Arthur Dean, who had participated in the MEEC discussions.[71] During December 1956, and continuing into January and February 1957, Dean met secretly with Israeli Ambassador to the United States Abba Eban and Israeli Foreign Minister Golda Meir.[72] Concurrently Dulles put formal diplomatic pressure on Israel directly and also through Hammarskjöld.

Finally, the administration used economic weapons. In 1956, the Israeli economy remained weak. After October 29, Israel received no further American grants in aid for a loss to the Israeli budget of $24 million. As a result, by the end of January 1957 Israel's dollar income had already dropped approximately $80 million out of an annual dollar income of about $470 million. Furthermore, until 1955 Israel had depended heavily on the Soviet Union for one-third of its oil imports. The termination of Soviet supplies had already hurt the Israeli economy; the Suez invasion caused further sharp increases in the cost of oil imports. The United States remained the most likely source of Israel's future oil supplies.[73] As Dulles said to Eisenhower, the United States had the sticks and the carrots.[74]

The General Assembly vote of January 19 reiterating its demand for prompt and complete Israeli withdrawal confirmed the stalemate. For its part, the Israeli government, for both strategic and domestic political reasons, now suggested an Israeli administration in Gaza. Ben-Gurion was facing significant pressure from his party's right wing to obtain some gains from the loss of life that had purchased the Sinai victory. Furthermore, Israeli public opinion took an increasingly bellicose view of the situation. According to the American embassy in mid-January, the Israeli public now regarded retention of Gaza and Sharm el Sheikh as vital national interests. Finally, the prime minister, in the first euphoria after the Israeli army's spectacular victory, had proclaimed the armistice agreement dead.[75]

While Israel's Gaza proposals were problematic, the nation's reluctance to return to the status quo ante regarding the Gulf of Aqaba was understandable to most outside observers; as Britain's ambassador to Israel said, "They [the Israeli government] could not be expected to accept a return to the armistice agreement as an adequate assurance of free access to Elath, since they did not enjoy this before."[76] Unfortunately neither the secretary-general nor American officials who were in charge of the negotiations yet accepted the logic of the Israeli position.

During the week of January 21 Hammarskjöld worked on his draft report to the General Assembly recounting Israeli compliance with the resolutions of November 1956. Although he made the usual complaints about Israeli intransigence, the report was more favorable to Israel than had been expected.[77] General debate began on January 28. Lodge said that while the United States believed that Israel must withdraw unconditionally, his country endorsed the deployment of UNEF forces on the demarcation line.[78] Through the efforts of Canada's Minister for External Affairs Lester Pearson and various European delegates, on February 2 the General Assembly passed two resolutions that focused on both Egypt and Israel. The first deplored Israeli noncompliance with the earlier General Assembly resolution that had mandated a complete Israeli withdrawal from all occupied territory and called upon Israel to complete its pullback without delay. The second resolution called upon both countries to observe the armistice agreement and, after Israeli troops withdrew, mandated the stationing of UNEF troops on the Israeli-Egyptian border.[79]

While on the question of Gaza this resolution offered some comfort to

Israel, it did not deal with the Gulf of Aqaba. Eisenhower attempted to obtain Israeli acquiescence by writing Ben-Gurion on February 3 to emphasize the importance with which he viewed Israeli compliance with the United Nations resolutions. But the Israeli government was not persuaded and held out for adequate guarantees of access to the gulf as well as protection from the return of Egyptian forces to Gaza. As Lodge accurately perceived on February 4, some further pressure would have to be applied before Israel would agree to withdraw.[80] The dilemma facing the United States and Britain was not whether to apply their own pressure but what to do if the General Assembly voted to require economic and other sanctions on Israel as the Afro-Asian bloc now threatened. British Foreign Office official I. T. M. Pink explained his country's problem as follows: "To vote in favor of sanctions would not be understood in this country; to vote against or even to abstain would cause more trouble in the Arab world."[81]

The exigencies of the president's new Middle Eastern policy now shaped the administration's response to this impasse. On January 29 Saudi Arabian King Saud began a week-long official visit to the United States.[82] Although he was treated extremely deferentially and received the promise of an enormous aid package, he angrily criticized the February 2 resolution as too mild.[83] As the administration had chosen Saud as a rival Middle Eastern leader to Nasser, the king's attitude signaled trouble for a more interventionist American policy.[84]

Congressional opinion on the Eisenhower Doctrine and on the administration's treatment of Israel constituted an equally important problem. Joint Senate committee hearings held in January on the Eisenhower Doctrine and on the events of the previous six months indicated that the president would have to coax congressional approval of his initiative.[85] Congressional leaders such as Republican Senate Minority Leader William Knowland and Democratic Senate Majority Leader Lyndon Johnson were anxious that the United States treat Israel fairly; Senator Knowland thought that the United States should only support sanctions against Israel if they were also levied against the Soviet Union for its treatment of Hungary.[86] Dulles dealt with congressional doubts strenuously but disingenuously. For example, he told Senator H. Alexander Smith, a key administration supporter, on February 10 that "we have no reason to doubt that the Canal will be open to Israel traffic." Actually Dulles had every reason to question such a denouement.[87]

Legislative support for Israel's position provided one reason for Ben-

Gurion's continued hard line. The prime minister expressed his dismay at the resolutions and contrasted the treatment of Israel with that meted out to India, whose invasion of Kashmir had also violated armistice accords, and to the Soviet Union and Egypt.[88] The Israeli leader may have calculated that if he stood firm until the canal was cleared, Egyptian interference with British, French, and Israeli shipping would improve Israel's bargaining position.[89]

At his press conference of February 5 Dulles made it clear that Israeli calculations were wrong—the United States would not permit Israel to play it long. The secretary of state said that while the United States would not impose economic or other sanctions on Israel unilaterally, if, on the other hand, the United Nations did so, the administration would give the matter serious consideration. His assertion led Dixon to fear that the Arab countries, encouraged by this signal, would introduce a resolution calling for sanctions in the near future.[90] British diplomats were extremely troubled by the possibility of such a resolution in part because they appreciated the justice of the Israeli position on the Gulf of Aqaba. Furthermore, the French government would almost certainly vote against such sanctions, and the United States would probably endorse them. This dilemma led Foreign Secretary Selwyn Lloyd to ask Caccia if he thought a message from the prime minister to the president urging American restraint on the sanctions' issue would be in order. Caccia advised against it for two reasons. First, "the United States have let us know as clearly as they can that they do not wish yet to be associated with us too closely in Middle Eastern affairs." Second, Eisenhower was currently vacationing at Humphrey's Georgia plantation.[91]

In Eisenhower's absence Dulles and State Department colleagues began to realize that a resolution calling for sanctions would set a bad precedent. Also, American officials increasingly took cognizance of the merits of the Israeli position on the Gulf of Aqaba, perhaps in part because of the widespread newspaper support Israel was receiving.[92] But Dulles believed that if the United States voted against a resolution calling for sanctions, it would be "the end of any hope for us in the M[iddle] E[ast]."[93] Therefore, the secretary concluded that the United States must somehow induce Israel to withdraw before such a resolution came up for a vote.

Consequently, making a major concession, Dulles (with the president's knowledge and acquiescence) gave Eban an aide-mémoire stating that the

American government considered the Gulf of Aqaba an international waterway and, provided that Israel fully withdrew from the captured territories, the United States would insist upon the right of free and innocent passage and join with others to secure this right. On the subject of the Gaza Strip, the aide-mémoire stated that the UNEF force should move into the area and serve as a buffer between Israel and Egypt, while recognizing that the armistice agreement had given it to Egypt.[94]

This about-face testifies to Dulles's ability to work behind the scenes for a pragmatic compromise while simultaneously publicly maintaining a hard line. Although ideology occupied an important place in the secretary's approach to diplomacy, the secretary of state could, if the situation demanded and as long as his authority was not under public attack, violate the same principles he had recently labeled sacred. This flexibility allowed Dulles to make compromises such as he now proposed to Eban.[95]

Eban, realizing that the aide-mémoire represented a significant improvement in the administration's position, urged his government to accept the terms that the United States had proposed and to use them as the basis for further bargaining. Notwithstanding Eban's explanation and attempts by Cabinet ministers such as Golda Meir to persuade him to the contrary, Ben-Gurion, pushed by his right-wing supporters and believing that he had room to maneuver, refused to accept the memorandum as a basis for withdrawal. Instead, on February 15 Eban presented Dulles with his government's reply, which expressed qualified approval of the proposals on the Gulf of Aqaba but rejected as unsatisfactory the American position on Gaza. To solve the resulting impasse, the Israeli government suggested that the United States and Israel jointly determine the future of the Gaza Strip.[96]

The Israeli rejection of what he believed had been a substantial concession on the part of the American government infuriated Dulles. He now headed down to Thomasville, Georgia, to meet with Eisenhower, Humphrey, and Lodge. The secretary's conviction that if the Israeli forces did not withdraw from the captured territory the whole of the Middle East would be lost to the Soviet Union, helped convince the president to commit all his prestige to an Israeli withdrawal. Lodge told the president that time was of the essence because the Arab nations were pushing for a resolution calling for immediate sanctions against Israel. The president said that he would support such a resolution if Israel did not withdraw from the captured territories and would also advocate prospective sanctions against Egypt if it blocked the Gulf of Aqaba. To increase the pressure on Israel to accept the American compromise, Eisenhower agreed that private American assistance and the sale of Israel bonds in the United States should be forbidden.[97] No new legislation would be needed; the same Korean War powers that had allowed the administration to freeze Egyptian assets would suffice. Finally Eisenhower told Humphrey to get in touch with "one or two leading Jewish personalities who might be sympathetic to our position and help to organize some Jewish sentiment."[98]

On his departure from Thomasville Dulles told the press that a main topic of his discussions with the president was Israel's failure to respond to the United Nations' repeated calls for withdrawal. Dulles took the same hard line in conversations with Knowland and with Eban; the secretary told the latter that if he did not see any merit in the American proposals, the Israeli government could "try [its] luck elsewhere."[99]

The White House's public relations campaign against Israel began on February 17 when the State Department released the text of the February 11 aide-mémoire simultaneously with a detailed statement from the president that outlined the American position and asserted, among other things, that Egypt had cooperated more with the United Nations than had Israel.[100] This barrage roused American public opinion to the president's side; for example, the New York *Journal American*, consistently friendly to Israel, wrote on February 19, "President Eisenhower has placed his tremendous prestige behind his assurances to Israel. Further than that he does not feel he should go. Further than that we do not think he should go." The *New York Times*, albeit reluctantly, joined in the chorus calling for withdrawal; after defending the Israeli position, it concluded, "Nevertheless in view of all the circumstances surrounding the tangled affair, we believe that it would be part of a greater wisdom and higher statesmanship if Israel did withdraw from the last strong points it holds beyond the armistice lines. It would thereby put itself on the side of the angels."[101]

Dulles also sought to increase public approval for the administration's position. He called Dr. Roswell Barnes, associate general secretary of the National Council of Churches, to ask him to drum up non-Jewish support to counteract "the Jewish influence here [which] is completely dominating the scene."[102] Dulles wanted Barnes to arrange for sermons in Protestant churches on Sunday, February 24, lauding the administration's stance because "we got no support from the Protestant elements of the country. All we get is a battering from the Jews." The secretary followed up this phone call with another to Dr. Edward Elson of the National Presbyterian Church. Dulles told him that the president was a little discouraged and that "if the Jews have the veto on US foreign policy, the consequences will be disastrous. The future of the UN is at stake." Elson said that "he was preaching on an Old Testament subject and he thought he could do something about it."[103]

Dulles also attempted to ensure the success of any economic pressure levied against Israel. Restitution payments made by the West German government stemming from the holocaust constituted Israel's second largest source of foreign income. As West Germany did not belong to the United Nations, it would not be bound by a resolution calling for sanctions. Attempting to ensure the effectiveness of his economic diplomacy, Dulles contacted a member of the West German embassy to ask if the German government would suspend these payments that amounted to $30-$40 million each year. When the German envoy expressed his government's reluctance to take such a step, the secretary urged him to ask Bonn to do something to "make [Israel] get nervous."[104]

These gambits were sideshows; administration officials concentrated their attention on convincing congressional leaders to accept their Middle Eastern policy. Knowland had already indicated that legislative acquiescence would not come easily; on February 16 he had told Dulles that he would resign from the United States delegation to the United Nations rather than vote in favor of sanctions against Israel. As Senate Majority Leader Lyndon Johnson strongly opposed sanctions as well, Eisenhower returned to Washington and summoned congressional leaders to the White House on Wednesday, February 20.[105]

During the meeting the president and his secretary of state raised familiar themes: Dulles said that "if Israel should not withdraw there would be increased guerrilla warfare, stoppage of oil supplies, and growth of Russian influence." Furthermore, Dulles said that "the firmness of the US position thus constituted the crucial issue particularly since much of the world, including the Israeli government, believed Israel could in crucial moments control US policy. Should Arab nations see any confirmation of this belief, they would feel compelled . . . to turn to Russia."

After framing matters in such an apocalyptical fashion, administration officials rejected various compromises proposed by the legislators. The meeting ended with congressional leaders obviously unpersuaded of the justice of the administration's course. True, Senator Smith said that he agreed that the administration had made a concerted effort to deal with Israeli doubts and added that Israel should comply with the United Nations resolutions. But Smith also added that "sanctions against Israel would be inconsistent unless we applied sanctions to other violators of UN resolutions."[106] The administration knew that it was only a matter of time before Congress blocked anti-Israeli sanctions; Dulles had told Lodge on February 12 that "we were going to be in very serious trouble and indeed may lose our authority to impose sanctions."[107] Equally problematic was the fact that public opinion still opposed sanctions. As Clare Boothe Luce observed, the administration appeared to be "punishing the small country with a good case and overlooking the biggest offenders, Nehru, Nasser and Moscow."[108]

The president went to the nation in a television address on February 20. He asked, "Should a nation which attacks and occupies foreign territory in the face of United Nations disapproval be allowed to impose conditions on its own withdrawal?" However, Eisenhower disingenuously minimized previous Egyptian violations of the armistice agreement and implied misleadingly that if Egypt now violated this or previous United Nations resolutions, sanctions would be applied against it. Eisenhower knew that a two-thirds vote of the General Assembly would never approve of a resolution mandating sanctions against Egypt.[109] Indeed the United Nations had taken punitive action against Egypt neither for its invasion of Israel in violation of the 1947 partition resolution nor for its refusal to allow Israeli shipping through the Suez Canal.

Ben-Gurion's reply came the next day. In what was meant to be a conciliatory speech, he stated that Israel had only three requirements: Israel's right to the Gulf of Aqaba be guaranteed, the Egyptians' return to Gaza not be permitted, and the Gaza border be secured. However, these criteria still put Israel at odds with the United States on the question of Gaza's future.[110]

The text of the resolution calling for sanctions circulated at the United Nations on February 22 and 23. It condemned Israel and "call[ed] upon all States to deny all military, economic or financial assistance and facilities to Israel in view of its continued defiance of the aforementioned Resolutions."

No mention was made of Egypt.[111] The British and Canadian governments continued to try to head off what many European and old Commonwealth countries believed would be a disastrous outcome. Macmillan wrote to Eisenhower pleading with him either to agree to a less onerous resolution or to bolster American guarantees to Israel. The president sent a noncommittal reply.[112] Pearson drafted an alternative resolution that included both sanctions and affirmative promises to Israel if it cooperated.[113] Dixon worried that Pearson would be outsmarted by Lodge who would introduce another resolution, even tougher on Israel, which would be immensely popular with the Afro-Asian bloc. Once again Britain would be forced to choose between offending the United States and Arab countries on the one hand or France and Israel on the other.[114]

The American and Israeli governments faced off against each other. As Caccia pointed out to Lloyd, congressional opposition to sanctions put the administration under pressure to find a quick solution.[115] On February 24, before Congress had an opportunity to show how it would handle this problem, Eban returned from Israel and offered Dulles significant concessions: Israel would consent to the separation of the Gaza and Gulf of Aqaba issues; it would not condition its withdrawal from Gaza on a satisfactory settlement of the Gulf of Aqaba problem, nor would Israel make a long-term solution to the Gaza question a prerequisite to a troop withdrawal.[116] These admissions marked the beginning of the end of the crisis; the Israeli government had significantly retreated.

The United States now obtained a postponement of the United Nations debate on the question of Israeli withdrawal. As Dulles and his staff drafted a new resolution that included a precise description of the status of the Gulf of Aqaba, Eban discussed the Gaza problem with Hammarskjöld.[117] The administration regarded the continued focus on Israel as undesirable in two respects. It did not want to see congressional and public support for the Eisenhower Doctrine divided over the question of the administration's treatment of Israel. While Eisenhower's Middle East policy enjoyed overwhelming American support, the prospect of economic sanctions applied against Israel provided every indication of being divisive. For example, on February 25 a mass rally held at Madison Square Garden called upon the administration not to impose such sanctions. The administration could ignore the largely Jewish audience, but it could not disregard the various senators who either personally spoke or sent messages of support.[118] From

Eisenhower and Dulles confer with French Prime Minister Guy Mollet (seated) and French Foreign Minister Christian Pineau, February 26, 1957. (Courtesy Dwight D. Eisenhower Library/National Park Service)

the standpoint of foreign policy, the administration knew that any compromise with Israel risked alienating moderate Arabs whose support it needed for the Eisenhower Doctrine to succeed.[119]

Dulles met again with Eban to reiterate the dangers of an aggressive Israeli policy. Among other things, the secretary contended that if Israel insisted on proclaiming the 1949 armistice agreements null and void, it would be bound by the 1947 partition agreement. Obviously the Israeli government would reject such an interpretation because its victories during the war of independence had significantly increased the size of the Jewish state.[120] Leaving Eban to ponder his advice, the secretary of state went to the White House where Eisenhower was meeting with French Prime Minister Guy Mollet and Foreign Minister Christian Pineau. Their visit was part of the administration's effort to patch up the rifts in the Atlantic Alliance. Middle Eastern topics occupied a substantial part of these cordial meetings, which stretched over two days. When Pineau proposed that France would recognize Israel's right to protect itself against fedayeen raids from Gaza bases in the same way as the American government had recognized Israeli rights in the Gulf of Aqaba, the administration grasped at this offer that provided a way out of a confrontation no one desired.[121]

For their part, once they learned of the French proposal, Israeli leaders realized that they must accept the compromise. France had provided too much public support and military help for its efforts to be publicly spurned. On March 1, before the General Assembly, Israeli Foreign Minister Golda Meir delivered a speech written at the State Department, announcing a rapid and full Israeli withdrawal but reserving Israel's right to exercise "its inherent right to self-defense under Article 51 of the Charter" should its shipping be interfered with.[122] The French delegate reaffirmed Israel's right to take action should its security be threatened.[123] Only Lodge's speech deviated from what had been decided; instead of leaving the question of Gaza open, he referred to the armistice agreement that gave the territory to Egypt.[124]

Lodge's disregard of what Dulles and Eban had agreed upon almost triggered an Israeli about-face; Ben-Gurion had only reluctantly accepted the inevitability of an Israeli withdrawal. Lodge's speech appeared to signal an administration attempt to alter the terms of the understanding between the United States and Israel. Only after a considerable struggle did Eban and his colleagues convince a furious Ben-Gurion that Israeli withdrawal must continue without delay. Faced with the reality of American intransigence and comforted by the knowledge that with American recognition of the international status of the Gulf of Aqaba and a French undertaking concerning the Gaza Strip, Israel had gained something tangible to show for the Sinai campaign, Ben-Gurion allowed the withdrawal to go forward.[125] Eisenhower, for his part, professed himself "deeply gratified" at the Israeli government's acquiescence.[126] Withdrawal negotiations between Israeli General Moshe Dayan and United Nations commander General E. L. M. Burns began on March 4 and were completed within three weeks.[127]

However, economic sanctions did not determine the issue. In 1957 Israel had not yet developed the addiction to American capital that would later characterize its economic and foreign policies. Dulles fully grasped the situation. As he told Lodge, Israeli officials "do not want to antagonize the

Eisenhower Administration for four years. That is more important than any sanctions."[128] Israel, surrounded on all sides by hostile nations, needed the support of one of the global powers in order to survive. The Soviet Union had made it clear that its patronage was being directed elsewhere; that left the United States. Eban, confirming Dulles's conclusion, had this to say about the Suez crisis in his memoirs: "Henceforward U.S.-Soviet hegemony was virtually ensured. Israeli policy makers were harshly reminded that no other country except the United States could help us redress the adverse balance arising from the geopolitical predominance of the Arabs and their alliance with Soviet power. This is still the central truth of Israel's foreign policy."[129]

Furthermore, while maintaining its hard-line public stance, the American government had made a significant concession. The administration had recognized the international character of the Gulf of Aqaba, had assumed the responsibility of defending the reaffirmed status quo, and had acquiesced in French support for the Israeli position on the Gaza Strip.[130] In this case public steadfastness combined with private compromise proved effective.

CANAL DIPLOMACY

Surveying their handiwork in mid-March, the president and his colleagues felt proud of all that they had accomplished. By joint resolution Congress had affirmed the Eisenhower Doctrine on March 9. The General Assembly adjourned the next day, and according to Lodge, the standing of the United States among underdeveloped nations was higher than ever before.[131] Yet the Middle East remained in flux; Israeli forces had not even completed their withdrawal when on March 11, Egyptian administrators returned to Gaza. To Eban, Dulles professed surprise and dismay, although he had told Lodge a week earlier that the American government had always made clear to Israel the inevitability of an Egyptian return to Gaza. When the Israeli government on March 13 delivered to Dulles a letter of protest containing a veiled threat of military action, the secretary of state immediately cabled Hare in Cairo.[132] He instructed the ambassador to urge the Egyptian government to use restraint in exercising its rights in Gaza and to suggest that if Nasser complied with UNEF requests the United States might consider a resumption of economic relations.[133]

A consultation between Dulles and Hammarskjöld provided another example of the tensions present in American-Egyptian relations. To the secretary-general, who was about to visit Egypt, Dulles said that "the situation is deteriorating in the sense [that] the expectations which H[ammarskjöld] and we had, and the Israelis had, at the time of their withdrawal are being diluted by the Egyptians." Worse still, the secretary worried that Nasser's provocations might lead the Israeli government "to the use of force under conditions where it would be difficult to get a UN condemnation of them."[134] The secretary of state had assumed that Nasser would be content with Israeli withdrawal from Gaza and would not be so precipitate as to order the return of Egyptian officials into the area before all Israeli troops had evacuated it. Dulles could not envision that the Egyptian leader would immediately press his advantage to the limits rather than pragmatically bide his time.

Certainly Dulles did not believe that the situation was irremediable. He told Knowland on March 19 that "we have a few assets to bring to bear against Egypt" and he was "fully resolved in his own mind to be as tough and strong as we need to be to get Egypt to live up to its part." But Dulles then sent a conciliatory message to Nasser urging the Egyptian leader "to act as to evidence a willingness on your part to contribute to security and tranquility."[135]

The British government was also reassessing its Egyptian policy. Following final British troop withdrawal from Egypt on December 21, Whitehall became increasingly preoccupied with this subject. In the wake of the Suez invasion the Egyptian government had sequestered British, French, and Egyptian Jewish property.[136] As difficult as this problem appeared, it paled in significance to the ongoing negotiations over reopening the Suez Canal.

Before the canal could be reopened it had to be cleared. For reasons of practicality and prestige, beginning in December both the British and French demanded that their salvage ships, already in the Middle East, be part of the salvage operation.[137] While Nasser eventually permitted UNEF to use British resources in the clearance operations, Hammarskjöld failed to give the necessary orders to allow British participation. British diplomats were furious. Not only did they dislike the result, but, reflected Peter Ramsbottom, this "sad story . . . reveal[s] only too clearly that Hammarskjöld is far from being a satisfactory choice for conducting important negotiations on our behalf in the Middle East."[138]

During January, against a backdrop of continuing clearance operations, officials of all concerned countries pondered the future of the canal. Both the British and French governments took the position that their diplomats should resume tripartite negotiations with Nasser on the basis of the Six Principles. But while in October Nasser had been willing to compromise in order to forestall an Anglo-French military expedition, he was no longer as amenable to diplomacy once European troops had ignominiously retreated.[139]

Seeking again to internationalize the problem, the American government began to consider the World Bank as a possible intermediary. In early January Eugene Black, the World Bank's president, took a first step in this direction by agreeing that his institution would act as fiscal agent for the canal's clearance, holding and disbursing the estimated $40 million necessary to complete the job.[140] At the same time former World Bank head and current administration advisor John J. McCloy began working on a plan for the IBRD to take over the task of international supervision of the canal after it was reopened.[141]

The stalemate concerning the canal's future increasingly troubled British officials. The Foreign Office concluded that "the economic harm caused by keeping canal closed even for a few days longer than necessary is immense." Estimates of the monthly cost of the canal's closure to the British balance of payments ranged from £30-£40 million, or $84-$112 million (of which half was attributable to oil). Western diplomats feared that if no agreement concerning control over the canal was reached, when the canal reopened (now scheduled for early March), Egypt would obtain control by default.[142]

Once again Egypt proved more immune to economic pressure than did Britain. While Egypt clearly found the Anglo-American economic sanctions troublesome and suffered from a shortage of oil, the nature of its economy combined with the availability of aid from Communist and developing world nations ensured that Egypt could easily withstand continuing sanctions.[143] As a State Department official concluded, "The blocking of Egyptian funds by the United States has had little effect on the Egyptian economy."[144]

Because the British and French trusted McCloy, they took seriously his doubts about the possible role of the World Bank. On January 24 the foreign secretary admitted to Caccia that Egypt would certainly control the canal in the future. Lloyd held out the hope that the canal dues could serve as a sufficient carrot to compel Egyptians to agree to a "satisfactory settlement." As he had done in September, Dulles again encouraged these hopes. He told Caccia and visiting Minister of Defense Duncan Sandys on January 28 that he was considering sending Hammarskjöld a letter urging that dues be paid not to Egypt but to an international body such as the World Bank or SCUA.[145] Although Lloyd continued to advocate using economic pressure against Egypt, at the end of January he confessed to the Cabinet that he was "rather pessimistic about the possibility of users avoiding paying dues direct to the Egyptian authority."[146]

During February, diplomatic efforts had focused on Israel rather than the status of the canal. However, on February 7, Admiral Arthur Radford, chairman of the Joint Chiefs of Staff, informed the National Security Council that the Joint Chiefs hoped that "the Israelis would prove themselves smart" and legally force the issue of Israeli use of the canal. Once Egypt refused Israeli ships passage, Egypt would be clearly in the wrong, and "we and the UN would be in a position to impose sanctions on Nasser."

Dulles responded by pointing out that "after all, the United States was not anxious to get in to a war in the Middle East in place of the British and the French." As the United States had used economic sanctions against Egypt, it could only rely on Hammarskjöld's diplomacy. But the secretary of state recognized the need to spur the secretary-general along. Consequently on February 7 Dulles instructed Lodge to explain to Hammarskjöld American ideas concerning an interim settlement for the canal: all dues should be paid in the first instance to a neutral agency that would immediately hand over half the amount to Egypt, with the remaining sums impounded pending a final settlement in accordance with the Six Principles.[147]

Once this approach collapsed, the State Department dressed up the same ideas as the Four Power Proposal. Cosponsored by France, Britain, and Norway, as well as the United States, it was presented to Nasser at the beginning of March.[148] Still awaiting a reply, British and French leaders met in Paris on March 9. Pineau emphasized to his British counterparts that "from the point of view of French opinion it would be impossible to pay the Canal dues to Nasser." British leaders had no desire to enrich their Egyptian foe either. Unfortunately the Western allies knew that other user countries would not boycott the canal. And, as Cabinet Secretary Sir Norman Brook informed the prime minister, the cost of a British boycott of the canal without the support of other countries would be extremely high.

When the Egyptian government issued a reply to the Four Power Proposal on March 18, the time for a decision on British policy had arrived. While affirming its willingness to respect the Constantinople Convention, Egypt totally rejected the idea of international control over the canal or canal dues.[149] Macmillan expected to discuss the future of the canal, as well as other Middle Eastern issues, at his Bermuda summit with Eisenhower set for March 21.[150]

Macmillan had much to be pleased about as he prepared for a meeting that he hoped would restore the special relationship. The EXIM loan agreement for a line of credit for $500 million had been executed on February 25.[151] An amendment to the U.S. Agreement had been signed on March 6. It substituted for the incomprehensible waiver clause a British unconditional right to postpone payments of principal and interest seven times (each a bisque).[152]

PETROLEUM AND THE SUEZ CRISIS

The prime minister also drew comfort from the denouement of Western Europe's oil crisis. Showing the same solidarity they had exhibited during the Iranian crisis, during November American oil companies had cooperated with their British counterparts on their own to ease the situation.[153] After the reconvening of the MEEC on November 30, American cooperation on oil-related issues had steadily increased. The administration blessed a program for diversionary tanker movements on December 7, and the following day Sir Hugh Ellis Rees, the British ambassador to the OEEC, reported that the joint American-European discussions were proceeding satisfactorily. The United States government lifted load line limitations of coastal tankers, increasing capacity by 30 percent. Additionally, eighteen tankers were reactivated from the "mothball" fleet.[154]

As the allies attempted to present their petroleum requirements to the United States, Secretary of the Interior Fred Seaton explained the principles that would govern the administration's handling of the problem: (1) the petroleum industry should manage the crisis with the least possible government interference, (2) the increased flow of Western Hemisphere oil to Europe must not result in any shortages for American customers, and (3) efforts should be made to insure that the adverse effects of the crisis on the petroleum industry would be kept to a minimum.[155]

The various American and European committees decided to assume a 25 percent shortfall in supplies and proceeded to plan how to alleviate the crisis.[156] The laggard pace and squabbling evident in Paris and Washington alarmed Whitehall. Having imposed a second round of cuts on oil consumption in December, officials now had before them an alarming report that predicted that the outlook for fuel oil consumption would become increasingly "gloomy."[157] The German government continued reluctant to fund a European dollar pool for oil.[158] The decision by the Texas Railroad Commission in early January not to expand significantly Texas production seemed to be an important setback.[159] Therefore, British officials planned further cuts in oil consumption.[160]

At the same time administration officials found themselves under fire from a joint Senate committee investigating the "oil lift." These hearings, held in February and March 1957, laid bare the administration's policy of collusion with the oil industry and provided the precedent for later investigations of the petroleum industry.[161] Among other things, industry executives and administration officials revealed that their chief concern remained stable American prices and profits irrespective of the effect on Europe.[162]

Yet during February it became increasingly clear that the oil shortage had not brought the anticipated consequences for Europe in general and Britain in particular. Three factors accounted for this result. Petroleum supplies proved more abundant than had been estimated; according to Arthur Flemming, who was in charge of the administration's petroleum supply program, Western Europe had received 90 percent of its oil requirements. Furthermore, the mild winter of 1956–57 permitted consumers to conserve oil supplies.[163] Finally, in 1956 Western Europe did not depend on oil for the majority of its energy demands. Oil satisfied only 17.2 percent of Western Europe's energy needs; coal provided 70 percent and hydroelectric power the balance. In Britain, industry depended on oil for only 7 percent of its energy requirements; in total, oil fulfilled 13 percent of all British needs for energy supplies.[164] Not surprisingly then, British officials concluded that the fuel oil restrictions had not caused any serious drop in production.

Unfortunately the satisfactory ending to the oil crisis of 1956–57 allowed both the United States and Britain to avoid any hard questions about their relations with oil companies or their national petroleum policies. While civil servants in both London and Washington considered broad questions affecting the production and sale of Western petroleum supplies, they always came to the conclusion that all was well in the best of all possible worlds. For example, Foreign Office official Stephen Falle, asked to look at the workings of the "Gulf posted price" method, concluded that "before the present crisis, we had no reason to be dissatisfied with our sales of oil in dollar markets, and as the United States demand increases we can expect our sales there also to increase." A State Department official cavalierly dismissed the concerns of independent oil consultant Walter Levy who, in a study of the Suez oil crisis, stressed the weakness of the Western bargaining position vis-à-vis the oil-producing states.[165]

RECONCILIATION AT BERMUDA

The happy resolution of the oil crisis had not prevented the question of oil supplies from dwelling on the prime minister's mind as he left for Bermuda, but the omens preceding the summit had been propitious.[166] The administration had also worked to reestablish Anglo-American relations. For example, when British Defense Secretary Duncan Sandys visited Washington at the end of January, Caccia wrote, "Certainly this week he [Dulles] and [Secretary of Defense Charles] Wilson have gone out of their way to be friendly." Eisenhower confided in his diary that he was going to Bermuda "to focus our attention, in a personal meeting, upon Anglo-American relations."[167]

Eisenhower, Macmillan, and their entourages met at Bermuda's Mid-Ocean Club beginning with an informal session on March 20. From the beginning an atmosphere of friendship and trust prevailed. Eisenhower commented in his diary that "the meeting was by far the most successful international meeting that I have attended since the close of World War II." The president ascribed the cordial atmosphere to three causes: the pressing importance of the problems raised, the atmosphere of frankness and confidence (which Eisenhower partly attributed to his and Macmillan's wartime friendship), and the fact that each side had made excellent preparations. To these a fourth might be added—Macmillan not only had committed him-

Eisenhower greets Macmillan, now prime minister, at the start of the Bermuda Conference (March 20–24, 1957), which marked the Anglo-American rapprochement. (Courtesy Dwight D. Eisenhower Library/U.S. Navy)

self to the special relationship but, like Churchill, understood that in this relationship the United States' position must always remain dominant.

The future of Western relations with Nasser proved to be one of the most important topics discussed. Lloyd, not surprisingly, said that "Nasser was not only an evil, unpredictable and untrustworthy man, but was ambitious to become a second Mussolini." Dulles and Eisenhower had again grown frustrated with Nasser; the heady days of December and January when the administration had believed that a new day was dawning for American-Egyptian relations were long gone. However, well aware of the strength of Nasser's position in Egypt, the Americans believed that, given Europe's dependence on the Suez Canal, the West had no choice but to deal with him. Indeed Dulles had said to the president on March 20, "To have the best chance of obtaining a satisfactory settlement, we must 'do business with Nasser,' and try to lead him into cooperating with us, giving him concessions etc. which would have the incidental effect of building him up."[168] Accordingly, Eisenhower and Dulles recommended and the British accepted a return to the carrot and stick approach; if Nasser was cooperative, he would be rewarded with such boons as the resumption of normal relations, the unblocking of funds, access to PL 480 wheat, and technical assistance.[169] If Nasser chose instead to threaten other Arab governments, the administration would protect them using the powers granted by the Eisenhower Doctrine. One year after the British and American governments had shifted to a hard line against the Egyptian leader, events had come full circle.

EIGHT

CONCLUSION

THE IMPORTANCE OF HAVING MONEY

*The British action [at Suez] was the last gasp of
declining power . . . perhaps in two hundred years
the United States would know how we felt.*
—Harold Macmillan to John Foster Dulles,
December 12, 1956

The Suez crisis did not so much end as fade away. On April 8, 1957, the Suez Canal, totally under Egyptian control, reopened to shipping. One month later the British government announced that it would permit British ships to pay dues to the Egyptian canal authority and use the canal. Thereafter, Western governments continued their attempt to impose some form of international control over the waterway. Nasser rejected all such efforts until, at year's end, British, French, and American diplomats conceded the futility of their endeavors and accepted Nasser's complete control over the canal.

Concurrently British and Egyptian negotiators began discussions in Rome concerning the blocked Egyptian accounts and compensation for British property that had been sequestered by Egyptian authorities. In July 1958, the Suez Canal Company reached a settlement with the Egyptian government. In exchange for full legal possession of all Canal Company assets outside Egypt and compensation for the Egyptian nationalization, the company would assume the liabilities of the canal as of July 1956 and surrender immediately any and all rights to the canal and to the company's franchise.[1] Six months later, after the intervention of World Bank President Eugene Black, the British and Egyptian governments resolved outstanding financial issues and resumed diplomatic relations that Nasser had severed after the Anglo-French invasion.[2] On May 1, 1958, the American government announced that it had released the Egyptian assets it had frozen almost two years earlier.[3]

By that time the Suez crisis seemed long distant. Close Anglo-American ties had been reestablished. A British presence in the Middle East remained visible; notwithstanding the Eisenhower Doctrine the United States had not fully usurped Britain's traditional role. France became increasingly obsessed with the Algerian revolt while Egypt still refused Israeli ships passage through the Suez Canal. In short it almost appeared as if the Suez crisis, while full of sound and fury, had signified nothing. Actually the Suez crisis had important consequences for each of the five countries involved.

AFTERMATH OF THE CRISIS

Egyptian President Gamal Abdel Nasser emerged as the chief victor of the Suez crisis. Seizing the Suez Canal allowed Nasser to strike a blow against the Western leaders who had humiliated him by the withdrawal of the Anglo-American offer to finance the Aswan High Dam. He masterfully conducted Egyptian foreign policy during the three months between the nationalization of the shares of the Suez Canal Company on July 26, 1956, and the Israeli attack on October 29. By resisting all temptations to be provocative and taking a moderate stance at the United Nations, Nasser so positioned his country that when the Anglo-French-Israeli invasion came, Egypt appeared to be an innocent victim.

In the aftermath of the onslaught Nasser successfully insisted on full control of the canal even though Western nations had underwritten and actually performed the work of clearing the canal.[4] The Egyptian leader's position in the Arab world greatly benefited from his symbolic victory over the British and French governments; this triumph together with Nasser's successful nationalization of the canal completely overshadowed the humiliation of the Egyptian army by smaller Israeli forces.

The crisis irrevocably changed the basis of Egyptian power in the society that Nasser ruled until his death in 1970. The Free Officers government had initially left the strong European business community in Egypt virtually unfettered. The events of November 1956 altered this state of affairs: Nasser ordered the sequestration of all British, French, and Jewish property and made it clear that non-Muslims were no longer welcome in Egypt. When these foreign nationals, together with most Egyptian Jews, departed, they took with them some of the cosmopolitan elements that had previously distinguished Cairo and Alexandria from other Arab cities.[5]

Israel also profited from the Suez crisis. The trouncing Israeli armies gave to their Egyptian opponents enhanced Israel's standing in Western eyes; the 1948 victory no longer seemed to be a fluke. By cooperating with France and Britain, Israel cemented its relations with the former and improved them with the latter. While the actions of the Israeli government in January and February 1957 offended the Eisenhower administration, thereafter American-Israeli relations gradually improved. Having taken responsibility for forcing Israel to withdraw to the 1949 armistice lines, the American government increasingly felt an obligation toward Israel that it had not previously acknowledged. The resolution of the Gaza and Gulf of Aqaba issues, while not ideal, represented an improvement over the previous status quo. Israeli shipping now freely used the port of Elath, and the presence of UNEF troops in Gaza ended fedayeen raids. Indeed the withdrawal of UNEF forces in May 1967 triggered the Six Day War.

The two confrontations shared other connections. The leaders of Israel and Egypt in June 1967—Nasser, Meir, and Eban—had participated in the Suez crisis. Both sides assumed that the United States, cast again in a pivotal role, would behave as it had before. Nasser felt safe in expelling UNEF forces; he believed that the American government would prevent Israel from retaliating. Because Israel also feared that the United States might attempt to constrain its actions, it rapidly launched a preventive war. But the lessons learned in 1956 did not apply. Johnson was not Eisenhower, times had changed, and the outcome in June 1967 proved very different from what it had been a decade earlier.

France continued to sink deeper into an Algerian morass. This conflict both destroyed the Fourth Republic and brought Charles De Gaulle back to power as head of the more stable Fifth Republic. British and American actions during the Suez crisis reinforced two central tenets of Gaullist foreign policy. First, the United States was not to be trusted.[6] Hence De Gaulle's insistence on an independent nuclear force, the so-called *force de frappe*, and the eventual withdrawal of French forces from NATO. Second, Gaullists believed that if forced to choose, Britain would always prefer the United States to continental Europe. From these principles stemmed the 1963 French veto of British membership in the Common Market.[7]

De Gaulle was right about Britain, at least as led by Harold Macmillan. Macmillan took office seeking above all to restore the special relationship. Both with Eisenhower and, later, John F. Kennedy, Macmillan reestablished the close Anglo-American relationship he sought. The prime minister's success was due in part to his personality and partly to his realization that Britain's role must always be subservient to that of the United States.[8]

This perception subsumed another, even more basic one. For the decade after World War II, Britain claimed to be one of the "Big Three." That this status had become a sham was not acknowledged, either in Britain or abroad. After the Suez crisis no one harbored any doubts. A nation that was forced to recant an action, which it had labeled in its vital national interest, at the command of another country because it had run out of money was, at least temporarily, a client state, not a superpower. Britain would never claim a leading role again.

Such a change might have led British leaders to a reassessment of their world position and to a reorientation away from past goals and toward the European continent. Britain might have joined the Common Market as a founding member and played a leading role ab initio in the European Economic Community. Certain members of the British establishment did hope that the Suez crisis would cause such a reexamination. For example, during November 1956, British Ambassador to Washington Harold Caccia urged the Foreign Office henceforward to regard the Anglo-American relationship unsentimentally as a business relationship. Indeed Caccia told a Whitehall colleague that "I personally am quite glad that the post-war period of 'old-boyism' is at an end. It was getting phoney and maybe the end had to be sharp." His perceptions of a new turn in the special relationship led the ambassador in January to undertake an exhaustive survey of British and American positions on a host of issues.[9]

Others in the British government believed that the post-Suez calm provided an opportunity for Britain to join the new European order. Minister of Education Sir David Eccles wrote Macmillan on December 3 that "the best prospect for England now is the formation of a balance of power inside the free world, i.e., the leadership of Western Europe."[10] Interestingly the Eisenhower administration shared Eccles's perception. At a meeting of the National Security Council held on October 4 Dulles noted with approbation the "very encouraging revival of interest in European unity manifested in the course of the last few weeks." Even at the height of the Anglo-

Eisenhower and Dulles greet Macmillan and Lloyd upon the British visitors' arrival for an informal White House dinner on October 23, 1957, Macmillan's second visit with Eisenhower in six months. (Courtesy Dwight D. Eisenhower Library/U.S. Navy)

American impasse, the administration continued to take appreciative note of this development; Colonel Andrew Goodpaster's minutes of a White House meeting held on November 20 recorded that "the President and the others saw the possibility of some blessings in disguise coming to Britain out of this affair, in the form of impelling them to accept the common market."[11] But Macmillan was not the man for such a realignment.[12] Furthermore, his emphasis on Britain's special relationships, both with the United States on the one hand and the Commonwealth on the other, echoed the still predominant view in Britain where most people were not yet ready to view their nation as just another European country.

During his term as prime minister, which lasted until 1963, Macmillan presided over a significant reduction in the scope of Britain's foreign policy. As the epigraph to this chapter makes clear, Macmillan understood the ramifications of the precipitate decline in British power that had occurred over the past decade.[13] While chancellor of the Exchequer, Macmillan had kept a close eye on Britain's precarious financial condition and had called for a significant reduction in defense expenditures. He made these cuts when he became prime minister.[14] Furthermore, Macmillan realized that the days of Britain's empire were numbered. Ghana, formerly the Gold Coast, became independent in 1957; the prime minister's famous 1960 "winds of change" speech signaled the rapid British retreat of the 1960s from its African and Middle Eastern possessions and prefigured Prime Minister Harold Wilson's 1967 decision that Britain would no longer retain a presence east of Suez.

But neither Macmillan nor his government made the hard choices necessary to give Britain real financial independence. The position of sterling had been Britain's Achilles' heel during the Suez crisis, and only devaluation or a floating pound could restore to Britain control over its own currency. Because the strength of sterling and the existence of the sterling area both acted as a link between Britain and other countries, particularly those in the Commonwealth and empire, and served as an illusory symbol of British strength, the British government sacrificed the well-being of the British economy in order to retain the parity of $2.80 to the pound. Another major sterling crisis occurred in September 1957, this time triggered largely by a French refusal to devalue sufficiently and a German refusal to revalue upward. A regular succession of such crises and the "stop-go," "zig-zag" British economic roller coaster ride defined British economic life in the 1960s and into the following decade as well.[15] By that time the state of the British economy had so deteriorated that the overdue 1967 devaluation to £1=$2.40 had little positive effect.

One of the prime reasons for the British government's acquiescence in the Franco-Israeli Suez scheme was its concern over Britain's position in the Middle East. Ironically, the Suez invasion, particularly the Cabinet's cooperation with Israel, then brought Britain's standing in the region to its lowest point ever. While Britain's reputation recovered from this nadir, clearly the era of British Middle Eastern suzerainty had almost ended.

The Suez crisis underscored what everyone knew: as elsewhere, the United States was the predominant power in the Middle East. Unfortunately, the Eisenhower administration did not know which way to direct its Middle Eastern policy.[16] The first appearance of American troops in the region, during the July 1958 landing in Lebanon, revealed the hollowness of administration thinking. The American government had been confident that it could succeed where the British and French governments had failed and that it could win the region for the West. Instead Arab nations grew increasingly alienated from the United States, which became closely aligned with Israel.

THE IMPORTANCE OF ECONOMIC DIPLOMACY

The history of the Suez crisis provides a comprehensive case study of the utility and limitations of economic diplomacy, that is to say, the use of economic means to influence relations among states. While the evolution of American Middle Eastern policy was important, the Suez crisis did not have the far-reaching effect on the United States that it had on the other four countries involved. The Suez Canal had never been of vital interest to the United States. American officials only intervened when the Anglo-French-Israeli invasion threatened to obstruct the fight against world communism and Western access to Arab oil, which were identified as vital national interests. The administration interceded through economic pressure; as has been seen, officials utilized American financial muscle against Britain, France, Israel, and Egypt with varying degrees of success.[17]

Anglo-American sanctions against Egypt had little effect on Nasser and his nation. First, American pressure remained halfhearted. Because Eisenhower and Dulles always wanted to keep a bridge open to Nasser, they did not block private Egyptian accounts and, more significantly, never attempted to drive down the price of cotton, which was Egypt's largest export. Given the massive American cotton surpluses of the period, the administration could have engineered a price war that would have significantly harmed if not destroyed the Egyptian economy. Second, Egypt had alternative sources of funds. China made sterling available, India aided Egypt, and the Soviet Union offered to build the Aswan Dam. Finally, as a developing nation Egypt did not need large amounts of foreign exchange in order to exist, nor was it trying to live beyond its means.

This last factor also contributed to France's immunity to American pressure. The French government knew that its economy in general and the franc in particular faced serious financial problems. But ministers believed that the risk to the economy was a small price to pay for the opportunity to destroy Nasser, whom French officials excoriated for his aid to the Algerian rebels. Furthermore, with no appearances to keep up, France had no hesitation in borrowing from the IMF in October 1956, thereby provisioning itself to face the November crisis with equanimity.

The American government used the threat of American economic sanctions to force Israel to withdraw from the territory it had captured in November 1956. However, as Dulles himself recognized, the importance of economic sanctions was symbolic. Israel could afford to do without American aid; it could not afford to be without American approval. Surrounded by hostile states, aware of the weaknesses in its relations with Britain and France, Israel needed the United States as an ally. The threat of the Eisenhower administration's lasting enmity forced Prime Minister David Ben-Gurion to agree to the withdrawal of Israeli forces behind the 1949 armistice lines on March 1, 1957.

While Britain could forgo American approval and friendship, it could not forfeit American money. Indeed the Eisenhower administration's use of economic sanctions against Britain presents one of the most successful examples of this type of pressure. Several factors account for the American government's success. Britain did not have an alternative source of funds; the United States not only controlled access to its own markets but to the IMF and the World Bank as well. Furious with Britain, the administration showed itself willing to use all the economic means at its disposal to force the British government back in line. Furthermore, both the timing of the Suez crisis and the use of negative economic pressure ensured that Eisenhower and his colleagues suffered little in the way of congressional constraints.

Most importantly, the British government had left itself completely vulnerable to an attack of this kind. For the previous decade it had been conducting a foreign policy beyond its means, relying on the United States government to pay the bills. Britain simply could not afford to "go it alone."[18] The defenselessness of British and European oil supplies to Arab and American pressure further contributed to the British decision to withdraw.

Britain's economic policy reinforced its decision to accept the American government's dictates. The persisting allegiance of postwar British governments to the strength of the pound and to the continuance of the sterling area caused a succession of financial crises. The United States government in 1956 had reserves of $22,000 million; Britain was attempting to run its economy and that of the sterling area with reserves of $2,000–$2,400 million.[19]

Moreover, during the Suez crisis Britain faced problems beyond its inadequate reserves. The insistence of British governments on making the continued strength of the pound and the maintenance of the sterling area chief national priorities presented the American government with the perfect weapon to use against Prime Minister Anthony Eden and his colleagues. When it came to the test in November 1956, too much importance had been placed on the pound and the sterling area for the British to sacrifice them; therefore, the Eden government had no choice but to withdraw British troops ignominiously from Egypt. Even after the November 1956 sterling crisis, Macmillan could not envision a world without the sterling area. He wrote Eden on December 31:

> There is no way of avoiding the dangers to sterling which come from our being bankers to the sterling area. We have inherited an old family business which used to be very profitable and sound. The trouble is that the liabilities are four times the assets. In the old days a business of this kind, like Coutt's or Cox's Bank, would have been sold to one of the big five. The trouble is I do not know who is to buy the sterling area banking system. I tried it out on Humphrey but he was not taking it. So we must either carry on the business with all its risks, or wind it up and pay 5s in the £.[20]

However, this embarrassing finale to one of the most puzzling episodes in twentieth-century history only occurred because the British government acted in an almost incomprehensibly foolish manner. British officials had long predicted that in a conflict between an Arab nation and Britain the United States would try to carve out a middle position, and they had also recognized that Britain was far more vulnerable to economic pressure than was Egypt. From 1940 it had been apparent that Britain needed the United States to pay for its military ventures. Yet once Nasser nationalized the Suez Canal, in what can only be described as a "midsummer of madness," Eden and his fellow ministers plunged into an ill-conceived adventure that demanded a transformation of the world of 1956 into that of 1882. This willful ignorance led them to discount completely the certain American opposition they knew they would face. And this blindness gave the American government the opportunity to use its economic power to humiliate and defeat Britain in a fashion that Germany in two world wars had not been able to do.

APPENDIX A:

THE ANGLO-AMERICAN FINANCIAL AGREEMENT

Section 5 of the Anglo-American Financial Agreement provided that Britain would be eligible for a waiver of interest if

(A) The government of the United Kingdom finds a waiver is necessary in view of the present and prospective conditions of international exchange and level of its gold and foreign exchange reserves and,

(B) The International Monetary Fund certifies that the income of the United Kingdom from home-produced exports plus its net income from invisible current transactions in its balance of payments was on the average over the preceding five calendar years less than the average annual amount of United Kingdom imports during 1936–8, fixed at £866 million, as such figure may be adjusted for changes in the price level of these imports.

For the years 1951–55 average income was to be computed for the calendar year in which the request was made.

However, the United States was also concerned that Britain did not prefer other obligations over the debt owed to the American government. Thus Section 6(iii) provided that no waiver of interest may be requested unless the aggregate of the releases or payments in that year of sterling balances accumulated to the credit of overseas governments, monetary authorities and banks (except in the case of colonial dependencies) before the effective date of the Agreement is reduced proportionately.

The problem was that although the intent of the waiver clauses was apparent, that is, to allow Britain to obtain a waiver of interest payments in a year in which it had balance of payments difficulties, the mechanics were faulty. For one thing, it was not clear what "year" was referred to. Practically speaking the year referred to would have to be the next succeeding year so that after a waiver was received the British government would reduce sterling payments proportionately. Instead, the agreement appeared to call for simultaneous proportionate reductions of payments in respect of the sterling balances and of interest payments. This was not feasible because sterling payments were made throughout the year as opposed to interest payments, which were made at the end of the year.

Further, by 1955 most of the sterling balances were no longer blocked, making it very difficult to reduce withdrawals. In fact Egypt was the only country with significant blocked accounts. In the fall of 1955 and thereafter the British government was loath to approach the Egyptian government and ask for a renegotiation of the problematic Anglo-Egyptian accord on Egyptian sterling balances.

APPENDIX B:

THE TRIPARTITE DECLARATION,

MAY 25, 1950

The governments of the United Kingdom, France and the United States, having had occasion during the recent Foreign Ministers meeting in London to review certain questions affecting the peace and stability of the Arab states and of Israel, and particularly the supply of arms and war material to these states, have resolved to make the following statements:

1. The three Governments recognize that the Arab states and Israel all need to maintain a certain level of armed forces for the purpose of assuring their internal security and their legitimate self-defense and to permit them to play their part in the defense of the area as a whole. All applications for arms or war material for these countries will be considered in the light of these principles. In this connection the three Governments wish to recall and reaffirm the terms of the statements made by their representatives on the Security Council on August 4, 1949, in which they declared their opposition to the developments of an arms race between the Arab states and Israel.

2. The three Governments declare that assurances have been received from all the states in question, to which they permit arms to be supplied from their countries, that the purchasing state does not intend to undertake any act of aggression against any other state.

Similar assurances will be requested from any other state in the area to which they permit arms to be supplied in the future.

3. The three Governments take this opportunity of declaring their deep interest in and their desire to promote the establishment and maintenance of peace and stability in the area and their unalterable opposition to the use of force or threat of force between any other states in that area. The three Governments, should they find that any of these states was preparing to violate frontier or armistice lines, would, consistently with their obligations as members of the United Nations, immediately take action, both within and outside the United Nations, to prevent such violation.

APPENDIX C:

INFORMATION CONCERNING THE SUPPLY
OF MIDDLE EASTERN OIL IN 1956[1]

PRODUCTION

Prior to the Suez invasion, Middle Eastern oil production was tabulated at the following rates (million tons per annum):

Kuwait	60
Saudi Arabia	50
Iraq	33
Iran	26
Qatar	5.7
Neutral Zone	1.8
Egypt	1.8
Bahrein[2]	1.5
Total	179.8

World production in 1955 was approximately 770 million tons.

APPROXIMATE REVENUES OF MAIN PRODUCERS
(in millions of dollars, 1955)

Kuwait	280
Saudi Arabia	in excess of 280

Iraq	240
Iran	86.8
Qatar	36.4

OPERATING COMPANIES

Kuwait—Kuwait Oil Company
Shareholders: British Petroleum, 50 percent; Gulf Oil Corporation, 50 percent.

Saudi Arabia—Arabian American Oil Company (Aramco)
Shareholders: Standard Oil of California, Texaco, Standard Oil of New Jersey—all 30 percent; Socony Mobil, 10 percent.

Iraq—Iraq Petroleum Company Limited
Shareholders: British Petroleum, 23¾ percent; Shell, 23¾ percent; Compagnie Française des Petroles, 23¾; Near East Development Corporation (shares held equally by Standard Oil of New Jersey and Socony Mobil), 23¾ percent; Participation and Explorations Corporation (Gulbenkian[3]), 5 percent.

Iran—Iranian Oil Consortium
Shareholders: British Petroleum, 40 percent; Shell, 14 percent; Compagnie Française des Petroles, 6 percent; Standard Oil of New Jersey, Standard Oil of California, Texaco, Gulf Oil Corporation, Socony Mobil—all 7 percent; Iricon Agency Limited,[4] 5 percent.

Qatar—Qatar Petroleum Company
Same ownership as Iraq Petroleum Company.

Bahrein—Bahrein Petroleum Company
Shareholders: Standard Oil of California, 50 percent; Texaco, 50 percent.

Neutral Zone—American Independent Oil Company
Shareholders: Aminoil, Getty Oil Company, Kuwaiti and Saudi interests.

Egypt—Anglo-Egyptian Oil Company
Shareholders: Shell and British Petroleum, 30.895 percent each; Egyptian government, Socony Mobil, private interests.[5]

EUROPE'S OIL SUPPLIES (in millions of tons)

	Gross Imports	Imports from Canal	Middle East IPC	Exports (mainly to Europe)
United Kingdom	39.8	23.3	3.5	7.2
France	26.0	13.8	10	4.8
Italy	18.2	8.6	7	5.8
Germany	10.4	1.5	2	1.0

Source: *The Economist*, November 10, 1956.

MIDDLE EAST OUTPUT AND SHIPMENTS WEST OF SUEZ

(in millions of tons)

	Crude Oil	Shipments to West Via Canal	Via Pipeline
Kuwait	59	44	
Saudi Arabia	51	8	16
Iraq	34	4	25
Iran	25	10	
Qatar	6	5	
Bahrein	1.5	3	

Source: *The Economist*, November 10, 1956.

APPENDIX D:

PRINCIPAL ASPECTS OF THE ANGLO-AMERICAN
OFFERS TO FUND THE ASWAN HIGH DAM[1]
DECEMBER 1955

1. The United States and Great Britain would together contribute a grant of $70 million to cover the foreign exchange cost of the first phase of the construction, estimated to take about four years. The Egyptians would put up $65 million for local expenditures toward which the United States would contribute about $20 million in PL 480 wheat.

2. The World Bank would supervise the initial phase of construction as agent for the expenditure of the Anglo-American funds. During the first two years of Phase I, the World Bank would proceed with the preparation of plans for Phase II, the main dam and electrical works.

3. The World Bank would now give the Egyptian government a letter of intent indicating its readiness to lend $200-$250 million for the foreign exchange costs of Phase II, subject to the following points being worked out: (a) agreement with the Sudan on the division of Nile waters, (b) agreement with Egypt on internal financing of the local costs and stabilization of the local economy,[2] and (c) agreement for additional outside financing of foreign exchange costs (as of December 1955, estimated at $80 million–$130 million, the United States and Britain remaining the obvious source).

4. The United States and Britain would advise Egypt that they would "consider sympathetically lending its further support through participation

in the financing of the remaining foreign exchange costs of the project, in the light of conditions then existing and of the programs and performance during the first stage of construction, and subject to necessary legislative action. Among the conditions referred to will be the satisfactory resolution of the Nile water rights matter."

5. The United States aide-mémoire stated that the American proposal was made on the conditions that (a) the United Kingdom would provide as a grant £5.5 million; (b) the World Bank would supervise the expenditure of Anglo-American monies under an arrangement satisfactory to the United States and Britain; (c) the World Bank would make a loan of $200 million; (d) the Egyptian government would proceed "expeditiously and economically in cooperation with the Bank and will allocate its resources in a manner designed to assure high priority to the development, carrying on and completion of the Project, and will ensure that the necessary local currency costs of the project are met"; and (e) international competition under procedures developed by the bank would be the method used for the selection of contractors and for the procurement of all supplies and equipment for which foreign exchange is required.

6. In addition, the United States offer letter stated: "These proposals are, of course, subject to review by the United States Government in the event that extraordinary circumstances intervene."

7. The United States finds that "a direct negotiated contract with the consortium is not feasible and competitive bidding is required."

8. In order to make funds immediately available for the first phase, the United States contribution would have to come out of current fiscal 1956 Mutual Security Aid appropriations. This would require application of at least $20 million of the total of $30 million of funds programmed for Egypt in the current year. The balance would come from contingency reserves, etc. It might even be necessary to draw on some of the funds scheduled for Egypt in fiscal 1957.

9. Construction was expected to commence in July 1957 although preparatory work would begin earlier.

APPENDIX E:

STERLING ASSETS

PART I (in millions of £)

	September 30, 1956	December 31, 1956	Change
Sterling Area			
Australia	206	259	+53
New Zealand	102	88	−14
South Africa	18	24	+6
India	475	412	−63
Pakistan	80	77	−3
Ceylon	62	60	−2
Hong Kong	144	143	−1
Malaya	378	369	−9
British West Africa	496[a]	481	−15
British East Africa	192	192	
British West Indies	138	132	−6
Other British Africa	127	124	−3
Other colonies	131	136	+5
Irish Republic	163	171	+8
Other countries[b]	375[c]	384	+9
Total	3,087[d]	3,052	−35

	September 30, 1956	December 31, 1956	Change
Non-Sterling Area			
Belgian monetary area	7	5	−2
French franc zone	69	59	−10
Greece	15	11	−4
Italian monetary area	11	10	−1
Netherlands monetary area	26	18	−8
Norway	24	17	−7
Portugal	13	14	+1
Other Europe	120c	113	−7
United Statesf and dependencies	30	26	−4
Canada	16	13	−3
Argentina	27	26	−1
Brazil	2	3	+1
Israel	3	2	−1
Egypt	131g	128	−3
Sudan	31	34	+3
Iran	10	18	+8
Thailand	20	20	
China and Formosa	16	9	−7
Other countriesh	48	44	−4
Total	619	570	−49
Total Both Areas	3,706i	3,622	−84

Source: United Kingdom Treasury and Supply Delegation to the State Department. See NA, SD, 841.10/2-1857, Jordan-Moss to Lister, February 18, 1957.
aRevised.
bSee Sterling Assets, Part 2.
cRevised.
dRevised.
eRevised.
fIncludes the American government's segment of Counterpart Funds.
gRevised.
hSee Sterling Assets, Part 2.
iRevised.

STERLING ASSETS, PART 2 (in millions of £)

	September 30, 1956	December 31, 1956	Change
Sterling Area			
Persian Gulf territories	164	169	+5
Iraq	130	127	−3
Jordan	25[a]	27	+2
Burma	42	46	+4
Iceland	0[b]	0	
Libya	14	15	+1
Total	375[c]	384	+9
Non-Sterling Area			
Sweden	21	23	+2
Switzerland	18	12	−6
West Germany	35	34	−1
Other	46[d]	44	−2
Total	120[e]	113	−7
Other American account countries	−3	−3	
South America[f]	4	4	
Japan	38	35	−3
Other	9	8	−1
Total	48	44	−4

Source: United Kingdom Treasury and Supply Delegation to the State Department. See NA, SD, 841.10/2-1857, Jordan-Moss to Lister, February 18, 1957.
[a]Revised.
[b]Revised.
[c]Revised.
[d]Revised.
[e]Revised.
[f]Excluding Argentina and Brazil.

NOTES
~

ABBREVIATIONS

AW   Dwight D. Eisenhower Papers, Ann Whitman File
B/E   Bank of England
CAB   Cabinet Office
DD   Declassified Documents
EC   Exchange Control
EL   Dwight D. Eisenhower Presidential Library
FO   Foreign Office
FRBNY   Federal Reserve Bank of New York
FRUS   *Foreign Relations of the United States, 1955–1957* (citations include volume
          number followed by document number and page numbers, e.g., *FRUS*,
          vol. 17, 199:367–79)
G   Governor's Files
NA   National Archives
NSC   National Security Council
OV   Overseas Finance
PREM   Prime Minister's Private Office
PRO   Public Record Office
SD   General Records of the Department of State
T   Treasury
TD   General Records of the Department of the Treasury
WHC   Dwight D. Eisenhower Papers, White House Central Files
WHM   White House Memoranda

INTRODUCTION

1. See, e.g., Finer, *Dulles over Suez*, Love, *Suez*, and Neff, *Warriors at Suez*. One of the earliest books written on the Suez crisis, Thomas, *Suez*, remains the most accurate account of economic diplomacy during the crisis, although it too contains gaps and inaccuracies. Works covering the Suez crisis during the last decade predominantly took the form of biographies of major British leaders, such as James, *Anthony Eden*; Howard, *RAB*; and Horne, *Macmillan, 1894–1956* and *Macmillan, 1957–1986*. While each of these books adds extensively to our knowledge of the Suez crisis, they present flawed accounts of the American use of its financial clout during 1956–57.

2. This book is based on documents from the 1950s. Consequently the study employs the terminology of the time, most notably the use of the phrase *underdeveloped nation*.

3. PRO, FO 371/119133, Memorandum by Sir Ivone Kirkpatrick, September 7, 1956.

4. Samuel Johnson, *The Adventurer* (London, 1753).

CHAPTER ONE

1. Kennan, *American Diplomacy* (Chicago, 1950, 1984), p. 50.

2. Between 1941 and 1945 Britain received a total of £3.8 billion ($15.3 billion) in lend-lease aid (net of its contribution in "reverse lend-lease"—those services and goods Britain rendered to the United States). Concurrently with the execution of the U.S. Agreement, Britain agreed to pay $650 million (£161.29 million) in final settlement of its lend-lease obligation.

3. Pollard, *Development of the British Economy*, p. 219. In 1945 £1 equaled $4.03; therefore, British sterling debts equaled $13.52 billion.

4. The sterling area was formed after Britain departed from the gold standard in 1931. Originally it consisted of a loose association of countries that agreed to link their currency with sterling rather than gold. Once World War II began, the system became regularized with the acceptance of British exchange control by those countries wishing to remain in the sterling area. In the postwar period the sterling area (by then formally known as the "scheduled territories") consisted of Britain, its empire, and most of the Commonwealth (Canada never was a member; its currency was always linked to the dollar). The sterling area steadily shrank—by 1979, when exchange control was ended, it consisted only of Britain, Northern Ireland, the Channel Islands, and Gibraltar.

5. B/E, OV 31/119, J. M. Keynes, "The Problem of Our External Finance in the Transition," June 12, 1944.

6. Morgan, *Labour in Power*, p. 144.

7. See, e.g., John Morton Blum, *V Was for Victory* (New York, 1976), pp. 309–13.

8. E. M. Bernstein, interview for "An Ocean Apart," Public Broadcasting Network, May 1988.

9. See, e.g., Acheson, *Present at the Creation*, p. 122.

10. The "Ottawa system" referred to the network of trade protection and tariffs fashioned in 1932 by Britain and members of the empire and Commonwealth in Ottawa, Canada. Among other things, it accorded "imperial preference" (i.e., lower tariffs) to products produced in British empire and Commonwealth countries.

11. A currency that is not convertible may not be freely exchanged for another currency. During the Second World War, the British government enacted regulations that prevented holders of pounds from exchanging them for dollars without government permission. Authorization was granted only for products necessary for the war effort that could not be purchased within the sterling area. This procedure severely limited the amount of goods American companies could sell in Britain or in the rest of the sterling area because Commonwealth and empire governments had enacted comparable regulations that allowed London to control their dollar reserves through the so-called dollar pool.

12. Simultaneously the British government was granted a loan of Canadian $1.25 billion (U.S. $1.159 billion) on virtually the same terms and conditions. See Cairncross, *Years of Recovery*, pp. 115–16.

13. The text of the relevant provisions of the U.S. Agreement is in Appendix A.

14. FRBNY, C261, England 1940–46, Keynes to Sproul, December 21, 1945.

15. Morgan, *Labour in Power*, p. 149.

16. Edmonds, *Setting the Mould*, p. 102.

17. During the interwar period, the American refusal to cancel World War I loans to European nations earned the government the sobriquet "Uncle Shylock."

18. The importance of American anticolonialist sentiment that influenced people from Franklin Roosevelt down should not be underestimated. As *Life* magazine editorialized in an "Open Letter to the People of England," "One thing we are sure we are *not* fighting for is to hold the British Empire together." The best study of American wartime attitudes toward the British Empire is found in Louis, *Imperialism at Bay*. The above quotation is found on p. 198.

19. For example, nearly one-half of the total United States prewar trade was with countries of the sterling area where Britain obviously played a dominant role.

20. See, e.g., Gardner, *Sterling-Dollar Diplomacy*, pp. T 236–54.

21. The Tehran Conference Declaration of 1943 provided that the United States, the Soviet Union, and Britain would withdraw all troops from Iran (previously jointly occupied by American, Soviet, and British troops) within six months of the end of the war. American troops left in January, the British forces on March 2, 1946. Soviet soldiers remained until a combination of an American show of force and Iranian appeals to the United Nations led to their removal at the end of March.

22. Cairncross, *Years of Recovery*, pp. 131–32.

23. Ibid., pp. 139–40.

24. Concerning the 1949 devaluation, see Ibid., pp. 165–211, and Morgan, *Labour in Power*, pp. 379–88.

25. See, e.g., PRO, T 236/3913, "Note of a Meeting on the Waiver Clause," February 21, 1950; T 236/3916, M. Stevenson, "The Waiver—1952," October 16, 1952; and T 236/3917, O. Franks to Butler, November 15, 1952.

26. The best source on this subject is Kaufman, *Trade and Aid*.

27. See, e.g., Ambrose: *Eisenhower: Soldier*, p. 542, where the author states, "The right wing never came out of its room to meet him halfway. But he never stopped trying to educate the Old Guard."

28. See, e.g., the president's diary entry of April 1, 1953: "The happenings of the past few weeks emphasize again how difficult it is for a party that has been in the minority for twenty years to take up the burdens of responsibility for the operation

of the government. . . . This is especially true because of the fact that for so long a time the Republican Party has been opposed to, and often a deadly enemy of, the individual in the White House" (EL, AW, Eisenhower Diaries, box 9).

29. The Bricker amendment, sponsored by Senator John Bricker of Ohio, grew out of the senator's anger at the Yalta agreements and American membership in the United Nations. This proposed constitutional amendment, designed to limit the president's treaty-making power, stated that "a treaty shall become effective as internal law in the United States only through legislation which would be valid in the absence of a treaty." Among other problems, no one knew what the ramifications of such an amendment would be. Eisenhower spent huge amounts of his time fighting the Bricker amendment through 1956, when it was finally buried.

30. Eisenhower also coddled conservatives over internal security issues such as the instituting of loyalty oaths and the tolerance of Senator Joseph McCarthy's behavior.

31. See Ambrose, *Eisenhower: The President*, pp. 78–79, 155–56 and 252; and Kaufman, *Trade and Aid*, pp. 25–26, 223–24, 115–20, 122–29.

32. In order to pave the way toward the goal of convertibility, the Eisenhower administration sponsored two major financial studies. In July 1953, Lewis Douglas, formerly Roosevelt's director of the budget and ambassador to Britain, delivered the first one, on the subject of British economic problems. Douglas's main conclusion was that the economic health of Britain and the rest of the sterling area significantly affected American prosperity. The United States had a vested interest in Britain's return to convertibility, which could happen only if the United States contributed by expanding trade. Clarence Randall, former chief executive officer of Inland Steel Corporation, chaired the Randall Commission, whose report, delivered in January 1954, was meant to convince Congress that American aid to Europe was on the right track. Thus while the report echoed Douglas by stating that the United States must lower its tariffs, it also insisted that such action should not be unilateral. See FRBNY, Sproul/Cobbold Correspondence, Eisenhower to Randall transmitting report of Lewis Douglas, August 24, 1953; B/E, OV 31/49, "The Report of the Randall Commission," January 29, 1954.

33. "Butskellism" was derived from the combination of the names of R. A. Butler, Conservative chancellor of the Exchequer from 1951 to 1955, and his Labour counterpart and later Labour leader, Hugh Gaitskell. It represented a commitment by both parties to the welfare state and to the continued nationalization of basic British industries and services such as the health system, and the railroad, telephone, and coal industries.

34. The percentage of British imperial trade grew dramatically in the postwar period. Immediately prior to the war the empire had accounted for 39.5 percent of Britain's imports and 49 percent of its exports. After the war the proportion was much greater: in the 1946–49 period the respective percentages were 48 percent and 57.5 percent, and for the 1950–54 period, 49 percent and 54 percent. Porter, *The Lion's Share*, p. 320.

35. The best account of ROBOT is found in Cairncross, *Years of Recovery*, pp. 234–71.

36. These terms refer to the following repetitive cycle that characterized the British economy in the fifties and sixties: When British business was booming,

inflation would increase. This jump would frighten foreign investors who would dump sterling in anticipation of a devaluation. In order to attract them back, the Bank of England would raise the bank (base) rate. While foreign deposits would return, the increased cost of money would squelch internal investment and often lead to a recession.

37. For example, a significant portion of the cost of "Plan K"—the Royal Air Force modernization scheme—was paid for from Mutual Security Act funds. See NA, SD, 841.10/5-255, Raynor to Merchant, May 2, 1955.

38. A very interesting comparison of the British and German financial positions is found in the *Financial Times* editorial of January 1, 1956.

39. In 1955 British defense expenditures amounted to £1,569 million ($4,393 million), which represented 9.4 percent of its gross national product as compared with 4.1 percent for Belgium, 7.7 percent for France, and 5.3 percent for West Germany. American military expenditures in 1955 amounted to 14 percent of GNP. In 1955 United States military aid to Britain amounted to £23 million or $64.4 million. See B/E, OV 46/21, Leckley to Parsons, October 18, 1956; PRO, FO 371/120798, Foreign Office to Washington, No. 3033, June 28, 1956; EL, AW, Administrative Series, box 21, "British and U.S. Defense Costs and Related Data," January 15, 1957.

40. Ernest Bevin (1881–1951) rose to prominence as a trade union leader. By 1931 he was a leader of the Trades Union Congress, serving as chairman in 1936. He first entered the Cabinet under Churchill, serving as wartime minister of labour and national service. With no experience in foreign affairs, he was a surprising choice for foreign secretary when Labour returned to power in 1945. Yet many would argue that it was at the Foreign Office that Bevin made his greatest contribution—not only with his Middle East policy but by his strong advocacy of the Atlantic Alliance and his early appreciation of the threat posed by the Soviet Union.

41. Prior to World War II the area between the Persian Gulf and the Mediterranean Sea was known as the Near East. Because the Middle East Command was located in Cairo, the terminology began to change during the war. During the 1950s both terms were used (for example, the relevant State Department area office was the Bureau of Near Eastern Affairs), but *Middle East* was clearly winning.

42. Louis, *British Empire*, p. 3.

43. Bullock, *Ernest Bevin*, p. 44; Gilbert, *Never Despair*, pp. 30–31.

44. The final evacuation of French troops from Syria and Lebanon took place in 1946.

45. In that year the British government issued a white paper that provided for freezing the Jewish population in Palestine at one-third the number of the Arab majority. Further immigration would be permitted after five years but only with Arab consent, which, under the circumstances, was extremely unlikely.

46. Louis, *British Empire*, provides the best account of British postwar policy toward Palestine. See pp. 381–571.

47. David Ben-Gurion (1886–1973) emigrated to Israel from Russia where he helped found the Histadrut labor organization and headed the Mapai Labor party from 1930 to 1965. Willing to accept the United Nations sponsored partition plan, he served as prime minister from 1949 to 1953 and again from 1955 to 1963. In the 1950s he was viewed as a hawk, but his positions were to the left of those later taken by the Likud party.

48. In 1949 the nations belonging to the Arab League were Egypt, Iraq, Lebanon, Saudi Arabia, Syria, Jordan, and the Yemen. Libya joined the league in 1951 as did Sudan five years later.

49. See Appendix B for the text of the Tripartite Declaration.

50. DD, 78-282B, State Department, "Crisis in Britain's Near East Policy," OIR Report No. 4690, June 11, 1948, p. iv.

51. During the 1950s, however, most of the American need for petroleum products was satisfied by domestic production. EL, White House Office, NSC, Office of National Security Advisor, Policy Papers, box 3, "A Report to the National Security Council on National Security Problems Concerning Free Petroleum Demands and Potential Supplies," January 6, 1953.

52. These companies are Exxon (also known as Esso or Standard Oil of New Jersey), Shell, BP (or British Petroleum, the successor company to the Anglo-Iranian Oil Company), Gulf, Texaco, Mobil (formerly Socony Mobil), and SoCal (also known as Chevron or Standard Oil of California).

53. The Iraq Petroleum Company, the prototype of the Middle Eastern joint-venture company, was owned by BP, a consortium of French oil companies and seven American oil companies. CalTex was a joint venture between SoCal and Texaco, and Aramco was owned by SoCal, Texaco, Exxon, and Mobil. Appendix C contains a breakdown of ownership of joint-venture oil companies in 1956.

54. The pricing mechanism provided in this and other agreements helped ensure that oil companies generated large profits. Host governments had reason to resent these agreements. They received their profits in the form of a "royalty" on each barrel of oil produced in their country. Because the As Is Agreement restricted production, a given government would find its oil-derived revenues arbitrarily restricted.

55. John M. Blair, *Control of Oil*, p. 196. See also Anderson, *Aramco*.

56. Painter, *Oil and the American Century*, p. 171.

57. Iran was called Persia until 1935.

58. Louis, *British Empire*, p. 9.

59. Throughout 1952 Iran continued to produce oil although the oil-company-sponsored boycott kept most of Iranian production off world markets.

60. Painter, *Oil and the American Century*, p. 174.

61. Muhammed Reza Pahlevi (1919–80) was proclaimed "Shah-in-Shah" of Iran when British and Russian troops forced his father (who was suspected of pro-German sympathies) to resign in 1941. Initially he governed with an uncertain hand, but after the 1953 coup the Shah, aware of his strong American backing, ruled Iran in an autocratic and increasingly repressive manner. While he sought the modernization of his country, much poverty remained in a land increasingly enriched by oil. Open protests began in 1977; the Shah was forced to flee Iran on January 16, 1979.

62. Mohammed Mussadiq (1881–1967) was born to a wealthy landowning family in Iran. He served as foreign minister from 1922–24 and in other government positions but then withdrew from politics until 1942 when he was elected to the Majlis. He began to attract an increasingly large following because of his militant speeches against AIOC. Becoming prime minister in 1951, he proved to be less than adept at handling the government, quarreling in turn with every important interest group in Iranian society. After the coup, he served three years in solitary confinement on the charge of unconstitutional behavior.

63. Bill, *The Eagle and the Lion*, p. 75.

64. As Acheson explained to Eisenhower and Lodge, "The Iranians are fanatics and the British take the position that the whole future of British investments is imperiled" (Lodge Papers, box 71, "Meeting with Truman, Acheson and Eisenhower," November 18, 1952).

65. Painter, *Oil and the American Century*, p. 175.

66. Carlton, *Britain & the Suez Crisis*, p. 9.

67. On the Anglo-Iranian confrontation, see Bill, *The Eagle and the Lion*, pp. 50–86; Louis, *British Empire*, pp. 632–89; and Painter, *Oil and the American Century*, pp. 174–79.

68. Hopwood, *Egypt*, p. 24.

69. Louis, *British Empire*, p. 9; Sattin, *Lifting the Veil*, p. 274.

70. See, e.g., Hahn, "Containment and Egyptian Nationalism"; Rubin, *Arab States*, pp. 217–19.

71. Hopwood, *Egypt*, pp. 32–33; Louis, *British Empire*, pp. 691–735; Rubin, *Arab States*, pp. 216–21; Sadat, *A Woman of Egypt*, pp. 124–32 (Jehan Sadat is the widow of Anwar Sadat); Sattin, *Lifting the Veil*, pp. 274–76.

72. Concerning American-Egyptian relations, see Aronson, *From Sideshow to Center Stage*, and Hahn, *The United States, Great Britain, and Egypt, 1945–1956*.

73. PRO, FO 954/20, Churchill to Cranborne, April 3, 1945.

74. DD, 78-415A, State Department Intelligence Report No. 5980, "The British Position in the Middle East," October 2, 1952.

75. EL, AW, Eisenhower Diaries, box 9, January 6, 1953.

76. Yet Eisenhower did hold Churchill in special esteem, writing, "For my part, I think I would say that he [Churchill] comes nearest to fulfilling the requirements of greatness in any individual that I have met in my lifetime" (EL, AW, Eisenhower Diaries, box 8, Eisenhower to Hazlett, December 8, 1954). The president's high regard for Churchill gave the latter leverage that his successor would not enjoy.

77. While in Washington Eisenhower had watched MacArthur unmercifully eject the Bonus Army during the summer of 1932 in disregard of President Hoover's orders.

78. The best secondary source on Eisenhower's career remains Ambrose's two-volume biography cited above. Eisenhower's own memoirs of his years as president, *The White House Years* (2 vols.), are exceedingly useful for historians. For background on his wartime experiences, see David Eisenhower, *Eisenhower at War*. An excellent study of Eisenhower's years as president is Greenstein, *The Hidden Hand Presidency*.

79. For further background on Dulles, see "John Foster Dulles: Speak Loudly and Carry a Soft Stick" in Brands, *Cold Warriors*; Hoopes, *The Devil and John Foster Dulles*; Immerman, *John Foster Dulles*; and Prussen, *John Foster Dulles*.

80. At the Paris Peace Conference, Dulles earned himself a footnote in history books for drafting a provision, in an attempt to solve the reparations tangle, that actually limited Germany's liability but became know as the "war guilt" clause and contributed to the rise of the Nazis.

81. Author's interview with Lucius Battle.

82. John Foster Dulles Papers, Personal Papers, box 50, Dulles to Churchill, January 17, 1952; Acheson, *Present at the Creation*, pp. 603–5.

83. Ambrose, *Eisenhower: The President*, p. 21; James, *Anthony Eden*, p. 359.

84. EL, AW, Eisenhower Diaries, box 9, February 19, 1953.

85. Ibid., May 14, 1953.

86. George Humphrey (1890–1970) practiced law in Cleveland before joining the Hanna Company as its general counsel. Not only did his companies run large profits, but Humphrey was one of the first industrialists to diversify, entering the plastics and banking fields, among others. No biography exists of George Humphrey. As the Humphrey Papers, located at the Western Reserve Historical Association, Cleveland, Ohio, are very skimpy, the best source for information on his activities are various collections at the Eisenhower Library.

87. EL, AW, Eisenhower Diaries, box 9, May 9, 1953.

88. On the subject of foreign loans, see, e.g., Humphrey Papers, reel 9, Humphrey to Dulles, December 12, 1953, where Humphrey detailed his opposition to an American loan to the European Coal and Steel Community.

89. According to one Dulles biographer, Townsend Hoopes, the secretary of state "was determined to concentrate his energies on what he regarded as the transcendent issues facing a world in turmoil." Apparently, economic questions did not fit within this definition (Hoopes, *The Devil and John Foster Dulles*, p. 141).

90. Herbert Hoover, Jr., (1903–69) followed in his father's footsteps, not only in his Anglophobe prejudices but in his choice of career, finding success both as an engineer and as a businessman. With his specialty being the oil industry, he served as a consultant to various countries, including Venezuela and Iran. This experience led Dulles to appoint him as his special advisor on international petroleum problems in 1953. Hoover's successful participation in the negotiations on Iranian oil questions led to his appointment as under secretary of state in succession to Walter Bedell Smith. With no papers extant, information about Hoover comes from other sources. These reveal a narrow-minded, not particularly diplomatic man who was unsympathetic to the problems of European nations. The fact that he was hard of hearing exacerbated the difficulties emissaries had in dealing with him.

91. See, e.g., interview with Clarence Randall, Dulles Oral History Collection, Princeton University, Princeton, N.J.; author's interview with C. Douglas Dillon. It is a mark of the intimacy between Hoover and Humphrey that they gave a joint interview for the Dulles Oral History Collection.

92. Author's interview with Lord Sherfield (formerly Sir Roger Makins), London, November 17, 1987.

93. B/E, OV 31/55, Washington to Foreign Office, No. 2441, December 7, 1956.

94. In January 1956 the perceptive British ambassador to the United Nations, Sir Pierson Dixon, offered this description of Lodge: "Cabot Lodge is a complicating factor from my point of view. With a seat of his own in the Cabinet, he has a great many irons in the fire. One gets the impression that his relations with Foster Dulles are not very easy, and although I am sure that he is genuinely friendly to us and convinced of the need for cooperation between the two Delegations, I am not sure that he has at all a clear picture of the Middle East problems as a whole" (PRO, FO 371/121270, Dixon to Schuckburgh, January 6, 1956; Lodge Papers, box 71, Transition Diary, November 21, 1952, and General Correspondence, box 7, Lippmann to Lodge, July 1, 1943). For an account of Lodge's tenure at the United Nations, see "The Discovery of the Third World: Henry Cabot Lodge at the United Nations" in Brands, *Cold Warriors*.

95. DD 1986-1411, State Department, "Relative US-UK Roles in the Middle East," November 27, 1953, pp. 3–4.

96. Eban, *Autobiography*, p. 175.

97. Yungher, "United States-Israel Relations," p. 57.

98. Spiegel, *The Other Arab-Israeli Conflict*, p. 54; Hoopes, *The Devil and John Foster Dulles*, p. 184.

99. Eban, *Autobiography*, p. 172.

100. For an excellent statement of the American attitude, see Hoover's conversation with British ambassador to the United States Sir Roger Makins in Chapter 2.

101. Painter, *Oil and the American Century*, pp. 191–92; Taheri, *The Cauldron*, pp. 138–40.

102. The ownership of the Iranian oil consortium was Anglo-Iranian, 40 percent; Shell, 14 percent; Exxon, Mobil, SoCal, Texaco, and Gulf, 7 percent each; Compagnie Française Petrole, 6 percent; and 5 percent for various American independents working together under the name "Iricon."

103. Author's interview with Adam Watson; author's interview with Sir Denis Wright.

104. EL, AW, Eisenhower Diaries, box 8, Eisenhower to Edgar Eisenhower, November 8, 1954.

105. Gilbert, *Never Despair*, p. 1234.

106. See, e.g., EL, AW, Eisenhower Diaries, box 3, Eisenhower to Churchill, March 19, 1953 (draft); International Series, box 16, Churchill to Eisenhower, March 19, April 5, 1953, and Eisenhower to Churchill, April 7, 1953.

107. See, e.g., DD, 1987-3222, State Department Cable No. 4805, Washington to London, January 19, 1953; EL, AW, International Series, box 16, Eisenhower to Churchill, May 16, 1953.

108. The best account of the base negotiations is found in Louis, "The Tragedy of the Anglo-Egyptian Settlement of 1954," in Louis and Owen, *Suez 1956*.

109. *New York Times*, April 3, 1955, p. 22.

110. The two major books on Eden (1897–1977) take sharply divergent approaches. James, *Anthony Eden*, is quite favorable while Carlton, *Anthony Eden*, is sharply critical.

111. Author's interview with Lord Sherfield, May 25, 1989.

112. Louis, "Anglo-Egyptian Settlement"; EL, AW, International Series, box 17, Churchill to Eisenhower, June 21, 1954.

113. John Foster Dulles Papers, Personal Papers, box 87, State Department Press Statement No. 594, October 19, 1954.

CHAPTER TWO

1. In 1942 Sir Miles Lampson, the British ambassador to Egypt, gave King Farouk the alternative of appointing Nahas Pasha prime minister or abdicating. Knowing that Lampson had the military power to enforce his ultimatum, Farouk acceded and appointed Nahas. See Vatikiotis, *Modern History of Egypt*.

2. The best books in English on Nasser's life are Lacoutre, *Nasser*, and Nutting, *Nasser*. Nasser himself set down the principles of the Egyptian revolution in *Egypt's Liberation*, which Eden, during the Suez crisis, often referred to Nasser's *Mein Kampf*.

3. Nutting, *Nasser*, pp. 45–46.

4. Raymond O. Hare, EL, Eisenhower Oral History Collection; Sadat, *A Woman of Egypt*, pp. 152–53.

5. In retrospect senior British diplomats who espoused a policy of nonintervention believe that one of their chief mistakes was too much faith in the "Iraq card," the belief that the moderate Nuri Said would continue to be an important force in the Middle East.

6. An excellent account of the origins of the Baghdad Pact and the American perception of its purpose and meaning is found in Hermann Frederick Eilts, "Reflections in the Suez Crisis: Security in the Middle East," in Louis and Owen, *Suez 1956*.

7. In a related move, in October 1953, at the request of the United Nations Truce Revision Organization the administration suspended aid to Israel, already lowered from Truman administration levels, when Israel refused to stop work on a hydroelectric project on the Upper Jordan. Israel caved in to American pressure and ceased work on the project, and aid was resumed.

8. On Project Alpha, see Shimon Shamir, "The Collapse of Project Alpha," in Louis and Owen, *Suez 1956*; and Schuckburgh, *Descent to Suez*, pp. 242–356.

9. NA, SD, RG 59, 611.74/3-2055, Cairo to State Department, No. 1373, March 20, 1955.

10. A first dam at Aswan had been built by the British between 1898 and 1902. Enlarged twice thereafter, it was 53 meters high and 1,952 meters long and stored water at 121 meters above sea level.

11. The dam was planned to store water at 182 meters above sea level. The structure would be 111 meters high and 5,000 meters long. The reservoir would have a capacity of 130 billion cubic meters and would be three times the size of Lake Mead (behind the Hoover Dam), which in 1956 was the largest man-made reservoir in the world. PRO, FO 371/119048, Memorandum, "High Aswan Dam," January 19, 1956; T 236/4673, A. K. Potter, "High Aswan Dam," October 18, 1955; NA, SD, 874.2614, 4-2356, Rountree to Hollister, April 23, 1956.

12. The Egyptian pound was worth slightly more than one British pound.

13. The Egyptian sterling balances largely originated from the British and American use of Egypt as their Middle Eastern headquarters and as an outgrowth of the desert war. In effect the British government borrowed the cost of the Middle Eastern campaign from the Egyptian government but after the war found it could not repay its debts.

14. The British government would have been more willing to return inconvertible sterling to Egypt, that is to say, sterling that could not be exchanged for other currencies, because that would not have hurt British reserves. But the Egyptian government sought sterling it could exchange for dollars, marks, or other currencies.

15. B/E, OV 43/59, R. Earland, "Egypt's No. 2 Account," January 1, 1955.

16. It should be recalled that London held the reserves for the whole of the sterling area.

17. B/E, OV 43/9, Foreign Office to Cairo, No. 2027, September 22, 1955; See also Burns, *Economic Aid*, pp. 39–43.

18. B/E, OV 43/62, J. S. J. Margetson, "Egypt: An Assessment of Creditworthiness," November 14, 1955; see also OV 43/59, M. J. Balfour, "Egypt—High Assuan Dam," March 17, 1955, and OV 43/9, C. E. Loombe, "Egypt," June 1, 1955.

19. Of course Egypt did have sufficient foreign exchange to pay for the dam if it were allowed to reclaim its sterling balances. However, as the British government had no intention of returning the balances immediately, it never included them in its calculations of Egyptian creditworthiness.

20. Eugene Black (1898–) was a former senior vice-president of the Chase National Bank. In 1947, at the request of the World Bank's new president, John J. McCloy, he joined the World Bank as United States executive director, where they implemented "sound, non-political lending policies." In 1949 Black succeeded McCloy as president. He continued to emphasize conservative financial practices that would please the New York banking community, such as the early retirement of World Bank bonds and the limiting of new loans to between $200 million and $250 million annually.

21. The World Bank had been formed as part of the Bretton Woods accords that also created the IMF and set the pattern of international financial relations for twenty-five years. The World Bank's role was to lend money for development projects, while the IMF would deal with currency stabilization programs. Up to this point, however, both institutions had been characterized more by inactivity than by what they had accomplished.

22. B/E, OV 43/60, "Note of a Meeting held on Wednesday, April 6, 1955, to discuss arrangements for financing the construction of the High Aswan Dam"; NA, SD, 874.2614/4-2255, Hart to Allen, April 22, 1955.

23. B/E, OV 43/60, A.H.D. Letter 13, May 18, 1955.

24. B/E, OV 43/62, Washington to Foreign Office, No. 2860, April 23, 1955.

25. PRO, T 236/4672, M. T. Flett to William Armstrong, June 20, 1955; B/E, OV 43/60, "Egypt—High Aswan Dam," June 30, 1955. While Black wanted the British to release more sterling to Egypt, he did not want the British government to tie the release to specific contractual payments.

26. PRO, FO 371/118961, "Exchange of Notes between the Government of the United Kingdom of Great Britain and Northern Ireland and the Government of Egypt Concerning Financial Matters."

27. B/E, OV 43/61, A.H.D. Letter 38, September 24, 1955.

28. Eban, *Autobiography*, pp. 179–80; Lacoutre, *Nasser*, p. 156; Sadat, *A Woman of Egypt*, pp. 154–55.

29. From 1948 through April 1956, American sales of arms to Egypt from military and commercial sources amounted to $1,820,925. In addition, sales of aircraft and spare parts (mostly commercial) totaled $8,490,836. NA, SD, Lot File 57 D 616, "Ambassador Richards' Mission," February 11, 1957.

30. On the 1955 Czech arms deal, see Burns, *Economic Aid*, pp. 30–35; Lacoutre, *Nasser*, pp. 160–62; Nutting, *Nasser*, pp. 101–30.

31. John Foster Dulles Papers, Telephone Conversations, box 5, telephone call to Allen, September 28, 1955; telephone call from Hoover, September 22, 1955.

32. Ibid., JFD/DDE, Chronological Series, box 12, Dulles to Hoover et al., September 22, 1955; Schuckburgh, *Descent to Suez*, p. 281.

33. B/E, OV 43/62, C. E. Loombe, "Egypt: High Aswan Dam," October 24, 1955.

34. John Foster Dulles Papers, JFD/DDE, Chronological Series, box 12, Dulles to Nasser, September 27, 1955.

35. Ibid., JFD/DDE, WHM, box 3, "Memorandum of a Conversation with the President," October 11, 1955.

36. Ibid., JFD/DDE, Chronological Series, box 12, "Memorandum of Conversation with Mr. Macmillan," October 3, 1955.

37. The debate in administration circles concerning the wisdom of informing the British government about Eisenhower's letter to Bulganin illustrated that the American government saw Anglo-American cooperation as less than total. The British appear to have had no such hesitancy about telling Washington about Eden's letters to the Soviet leadership. See ibid., JFD/DDE, Chronological Series, box 12, Dulles to Murphy et al., October 11, 1955.

38. Eden had been operated on for a gall bladder condition in April 1953. The surgeon's knife slipped, severing the bile duct. Finally, after two more operations, the second of which was performed in Boston, Eden recovered, but thereafter he suffered debilitating attacks accompanied by high fevers. James, *Anthony Eden*, pp. 362–66.

39. The Suez Group was a body of right-wing Conservatives that had been formed to oppose British withdrawal from the Suez Canal base and thereafter proclaimed itself vociferously opposed to a policy of "imperial scuttle." Led by Julian Amery, son of Leo Amery (a leading exponent of imperial greatness) and son-in-law of Harold Macmillan, the group was small but commanded the support of many influential fellow travelers, such as Churchill and much of the Conservative press.

40. This is clear from the Schuckburgh diaries. See also author's interview with Watson, and Colville, *Fringes of Power*, pp. 631–709.

41. PRO, FO 371/108742, Foreign Office to UKDEL, New York, June 24, 1954; Colville, *Fringes of Power*, p. 694.

42. See, e.g., Ambrose, *Eisenhower: The President*, pp. 178–83; James, *Anthony Eden*, pp. 375–79.

43. John Foster Dulles Papers, JFD/DDE, Telephone Conversations, box 5, telephone call with Brownell, October 17, 1955.

44. PRO, T 236/4673, Washington to Foreign Office, No. 2513, October 18, 1955, and Cairo to Foreign Office, No. 1442, October 14, 1955; B/E, OV 43/62, Washington to Foreign Office, No. 218 E., October 17, 1955, A. K. Potter, "High Aswan Dam," October 19, 1955.

45. Harold Macmillan (1894–1986) wrote four volumes of memoirs and published his Second World War diaries. These are informative and interesting although not very reliable especially as regards controversial questions such as the Suez crisis. Alistair Horne has written a two-volume official biography, *Macmillan 1894–1956* and *Macmillan 1957–1986*.

46. Sir Roger Makins (1904–) was perhaps the most successful British emissary ever to serve in Washington. With an American wife (whose father was responsible for beginning the Davis Cup tennis tournaments) and long experience in the United States (he had served in the embassy in the 1930s under Sir Ronald Lindsay), Makins got along splendidly with Dulles and Humphrey. He always understood the administration's motives and correctly interpreted and predicted American actions. As time went on, 10 Downing Street and Whitehall increasingly disregarded his voice.

47. B/E, OV 43/62, Foreign Office to Washington, Nos. 4813 and 4815, October 20, 1955.

48. See, e.g., B/E, OV 43/62, A.H.D. Letter 42, October 20, 1955.

49. PRO, T 236/4673, Foreign Office to Washington, No. 4814, October 20, 1955.

50. Made in connection with Indo-China, Eisenhower's comment was: "Even at this moment France wants nothing except commitments from us—so far as I know they have made no real concessions to our frequently repeated convictions, messages and recommendations that at times almost approached the characteristics of entreaties. Thailand, the Philippines—and in a more clandestine way—Australia, have all shown far more statesmanship and have all recognized the basic requirements of a cooperative effort more than our principal European allies, France and Britain" (EL, AW, Eisenhower Diaries, box 7, Eisenhower to Gruenther, June 8, 1954).

51. William Harcourt, 2d Viscount Harcourt (1908–79), was a descendant of Junius Spencer Morgan and a partner in the London investment bank of Morgan Grenfell & Co., which had been the London branch of the House of Morgan. He served with much success as the Treasury's chief representative in Washington from 1951 to 1957. Harcourt fit right into Washington society, having rented his house from John Davis Lodge, brother of Henry, and becoming quite close with Humphrey. Not the least of Harcourt's talents was his mastery of both the Washington and the New York banking worlds.

52. British officials worried that if the Consortium went ahead with the project without World Bank or American funding, the Bank of England would face insurmountable pressure to use the Egyptian sterling balances to pay the Consortium's costs should the Egyptian government default on its payments.

53. B/E, OV 43/62, Washington to Foreign Office, No. 2584, and Foreign Office to Washington, No. 4906, October 25, 1956.

54. John Foster Dulles Papers, JFD/DDE, Telephone Conversations, box 5, telephone call with Humphrey, December 5, 1956.

55. Sir Ivone Kirkpatrick (1897–1964) was the highest-ranking permanent official (i.e., nonpolitical appointment) in the Foreign Office from 1953 through 1956. As much as anyone, he exemplified the end of an era. Deeply affected by his years in the Berlin embassy during the late 1930s where he served as the resident Cassandra, Kirkpatrick advocated a firm policy throughout the Suez crisis, invariably comparing Nasser to Hitler. His reputation suffered, for many blamed him for the debacle. Kirkpatrick, who had gone straight from school to active service during World War I (where he was severely wounded), was the only senior member of the Foreign Service who had never attended university.

56. PRO, T 236/4673, Washington to Foreign Office, No. 2598, October 26, 1955; B/E, OV 43/62, Washington to Foreign Office, No. 2621, October 28, 1955.

57. Ecological considerations did not appear to play any part in either the initial determination to fund the dam or the later American and British decisions to withdraw their offers.

58. NA, SD, 874.2614/10-2255, Allen to Hoover, October 22, 1955; 874.2614/10-2755, Hoover to Dulles, October 27, 1955; 874.2614/11-755, Hoover to Cairo, No. 929, November 7, 1955; 874.2614/11-1455, Memorandum of Conversation between Hoover, Makins et al., November 14, 1955.

59. PRO, T 236/4674, Washington to Foreign Office, No. 2649, November 1, 1955, and D. N. V. Rickett to Petch, November 2, 1955; B/E, OV 43/62, "Egypt—High Aswan Dam," October 31, 1955, and "Egypt—High Aswan Dam: Meeting at Trea-

sury, Friday, 4 November," November 7, 1955; NA, SD, 874.2614/10-2255, Allen to Hoover, October 22, 1955.

60. Lippmann and Black quotes both from B/E, OV 43/62, Washington to Foreign Office, No. 2667, November 3, 1955.

61. The British government was especially concerned with local currency costs, believing that if they were too high, they would jeopardize Egypt's financial position, which could first deplete Egyptian reserves and ultimately result in Britain being forced to release sterling balances at a faster than expected rate. See PRO, T 236/4673, Potter to Rickett, October 28, 1955.

62. The final project cost as estimated in December 1955 amounted to $1.1 billion. However, the State Department also calculated that Egypt would require an additional $.7 billion for development projects over the next decade. NA, SD, 874.2614/1-3055, State Department to Cairo, No. 1139, December 2, 1955.

63. B/E, OV 43/62, Washington to Foreign Office, No. 2648, November 1, 1955.

64. Ibid., OV 43/62, Foreign Office to Washington, No. 5337, November 12, 1955.

65. R. A. Butler (1902–82) was one of the men responsible for the more moderate form of conservatism that defined Tory ideology during the first three decades after World War II. He had given his name to the important Butler Act of 1944, which determined the direction of postwar British education, and after the war he played a major part in running the Conservative Central Office. Twice he had the opportunity to become prime minister and twice he was outsmarted by Harold Macmillan. The best book on his life is Howard, *RAB*.

66. During the period of nonconvertibility sterling was divided into several types. One form of sterling was available only for use within the sterling area. American account sterling by contrast, which was always convertible into dollars, was used for transactions with North and South America. Transferable account sterling, the sterling used by countries neither in the sterling area nor in the Americas, remained in a middle category. This form of sterling achieved de facto convertible status after February 1955. See, e.g., PRO, T 236/3941, Rowan, "External Policy and Action Following the Decisions Announced on February 24, 1955," March 9, 1955.

67. *Financial Times*, January 5, 1956, p. 1.

68. PRO, T 236/3943, "Meeting Held in Ballroom, British Consulate General, Istanbul, September 13, 1955."

69. The text of the relevant provisions of the U.S. Agreement is set forth in Appendix A.

70. PRO, T 236/4296, Washington to London, No. 2701, November 5, 1955.

71. Ibid., T 236/4674, Thorneycroft to Eden, November 2, 1955.

72. B/E, OV 43/62, Washington to Foreign Office, No. 2676, November 3, 1955, and No. 2699, November 5, 1955; Foreign Office to Washington, No. 5159, November 4, 1955, and No. 5240, November 8, 1955; PRO, T 236/4674, Foreign Office to Washington, No. 5158, November 4, 1955, and Washington to Foreign Office, No. 2700, November 5, 1955.

73. Dr. Abdul Kaisouni, in his mid-forties in 1955, had been Egyptian finance minister for over a year. Known as a capable man with Western ties (he had attended the London School of Economics and had a British wife), Kaisouni obviously preferred an Anglo-American agreement over a Soviet-built dam. His position became increasingly more difficult.

74. B/E, OV 43/62, Foreign Office to Washington, No. 5269, November 9, 1955, and No. 5337, November 12, 1955; PRO, T 236/4674, A. K. Potter, "High Aswan Dam," November 2, 1955.

75. B/E, OV 43/62, Washington to Foreign Office, No. 2763, November 14, 1955; No. 2783, November 16, 1955; No. 2797, November 17, 1955; No. 2810, November 18, 1955; Foreign Office to Washington, No. 5335, November 12, 1955; No. 5470, November 18, 1955, No. 5477; November 19, 1955.

76. Ibid., OV 43/62, Cairo to Foreign Office, No. 1774, November 23, 1955.

77. Ibid., OV 43/62, Washington to Foreign Office, No. 2831, November 20, 1955; No. 2834, November 21, 1955; No. 2859, November 23, 1955; No. 2871, November 25, 1955; Foreign Office to Washington, Nos. 5564 and 5565, November 24, 1955.

78. PRO, PREM 11/1117, Foreign Office to Washington, No. 5631, November 26, 1955.

79. See, e.g., PRO, CAB 128/30, CM 37(55), CM 39(55), CM 40(55).

80. During Eisenhower's first term, Humphrey, Hoover, and Hollister, known in Washington as the "three Hs," spoke out often against American foreign aid. Author's interview with C. Douglas Dillon.

81. PRO, T 236/4276, Washington to Foreign Office, No. 2960, December 5, 1955.

82. Ibid., T 236/4676, Washington to Foreign Office, No. 3002, December 8, 1955.

83. EL, WHC, Confidential Files, Subject Series, box 70, Hoover to Humphrey, December 14, 1955; NA, TD, RG 198, George Humphrey Files, Humphrey to Hoover, December 19, 1955.

84. The British and American negotiators agreed that the United States would provide $54.6 million of the hard currency costs of Phase I of the project and Britain the remaining $15.4 million. PRO, T 236/4676, Washington to Foreign Office, No. 3069, and Foreign Office to Washington, No. 5940, December 13, 1955.

85. Thomas Leslie Rowan (1908–72) served in many important posts including principal private secretary to Winston Churchill and head of the office of economic affairs of the Treasury. From 1949 to 1951 he was economic minister in the Washington embassy. Thereafter he became head of the overseas finance division of the Treasury, where he had major responsibility for the position of the pound and the state of the reserves.

86. FRBNY, C261, British Government, John Exter memorandum dated December 13, 1955, concerning conversation with Sir Leslie Rowan on December 12, 1955.

87. PRO, T 236/4676, Rickett to Sir Bernard Gilbert et al., and Washington to Foreign Office, No. 3041, December 12, 1955.

88. B/E, OV 43/63, Foreign Office to Washington, No. 6012, December 15, 1955; EL, WHC, Confidential Files, Subject Series, box 70, Hoover to Sherman Adams, December 16, 1955; DD 1985-163, Hoover to Dulles, December 16, 1955; DD 1988-818, Dulles to Hoover, December 16, 1955.

89. The most important aspects of the offers are detailed in Appendix D.

90. B/E, OV 43/63, Washington to Foreign Office, No. 3097, December 15, 1955; Nos. 3116 and 3121, December 16, 1955; Foreign Office to Washington, No. 6007, December 15, 1955.

91. PRO, FO 371/119052, Washington to Foreign Office, No. 3130, December 17, 1955; T 236/4677, Washington to Foreign Office, No. 3131, December 17, 1955.

CHAPTER THREE

1. They mandated that the bank "feel reasonably satisfied that the additional foreign exchange and the local currency be available as required" and made Egypt agree that its own contribution be made in such a way as not to cause inflation or impair its creditworthiness. Egypt and the World Bank together would review Egypt's investment program, and the Egyptian government was to promise not to incur any new foreign debts beyond those that the bank agreed "to be prudent in the light of Egypt's circumstances."

2. PRO, FO 371/119052, Washington to Foreign Office, No. 3130, December 17, 1955; B/E, OV 43/63, Foreign Office to Washington, No. 6140, December 21, 1955.

3. PRO, T 236/4677, Washington to Foreign Office, No. 3187, December 29, 1955.

4. In this regard Hermann Frederick Eilts, a former American ambassador to Egypt, has written, "One wonders whether Nasser's realization that the administration, at least in its early days, seemed willing to tolerate his political excesses may have encouraged his increasingly strident challenge to western interests and his self assured impression of political invincibility" (Eilts in Louis and Owen, *Suez 1956*, p. 356).

5. B/E, OV 43/63, Cairo to Foreign Office, No. 1997, December 27, 1955; PRO, T 236/4677, Washington to Foreign Office, No. 3187, December 19, 1955.

6. B/E, OV 43/63, Cairo to Foreign Office, No. 2021, December 30, 1955.

7. See, e.g., ibid., OV 43/63, Cairo to Foreign Office, No. 2, January 1, 1956; PRO, FO 371/119047, Cairo to Foreign Office, No. 93, January 16, 1956.

8. PRO, FO 371/119047, Washington to Foreign Office, No. 93, January 14, 1956; No. 122, January 18, 1956; Foreign Office to Washington, No. 250, January 16, 1956; FO 371/119048, Washington to Foreign Office, No. 148, January 20, 1956; B/E, OV 43/64, Washington to Foreign Office, No. 169, January 23, 1956.

9. Ibid., FO 371/119048, "Memorandum of Understanding Between the Government of Egypt and the International Bank for Reconstruction and Development," draft, January 19, 1956; FO 371/119049, Cairo to Foreign Office, Nos. 179 and 180, January 29, 1956; FO 371/119050, Cairo to Foreign Office, No. 219, February 4, 1956; T 236/4680, M. E. Johnston, "High Aswan Dam," February 8, 1956; F. Milner to Johnston, February 9, 1956; NA, SD, 874.2614/1-2956, Cairo to State Department, No. 1424, January 29, 1956; 874.2614/1-3056, Cairo to State Department, No. 1439, January 30, 1956.

10. NA, SD, 874.2614/2-1056, Hoover to Cairo, No. 1897, February 10, 1956.

11. Ibid., 874.2614/2-2456, Cairo to State Department, No. 1683, February 24, 1956.

12. Ibid., 874.2614/3-1756, "Joint Statement of the Government of Egypt and the International Bank for Reconstruction and Development, Cairo," February 9, 1956; PRO, FO 371/119051, Cairo to Foreign Office, No. 265, February 19, 1956.

13. The compromise provided that Britain would contribute up to $16 million to Phase II's foreign exchange costs, which were estimated at $130 million. The administration initially demanded an exchange guaranty that would have protected the United States had Britain devalued the pound. After much discussion the British government finally dissuaded American officials from insisting on such protection. When it was a question of potential American expenditure, the administration could be fully cognizant of the British financial position.

14. (John) Selwyn Lloyd (1904–78) was foreign secretary under both Eden and Macmillan. Thereafter he served as chancellor of the Exchequer until Macmillan fired him during the so-called night of the long knives. When Alec Douglas Home replaced Macmillan as prime minister, Lloyd became Conservative leader of the House. He is remembered as the "confidant whose discretion could always be trusted; the lieutenant whose loyalty was unshakable." More unkindly, Peter Thorneycroft, who served in the Eden and Macmillan Cabinets, labeled Lloyd a "stooge" (author's interview with Lord Thorneycroft).

15. EL, AW, Eisenhower Diaries, box 9, February 8, 1956.

16. R. A. Butler, who had been chancellor of the Exchequer, became lord privy seal and leader of the House.

17. The biggest area of contention at these meetings concerned the disputed oasis of Buraimi claimed by Saudi Arabia but also by the British protectorates now known as Oman and the United Arab Emirates. During the 1950s British troops invaded the area several times, where they fought against soldiers allegedly supplied by Aramco to the Saudi government. Administration officials believed that British policy jeopardized Western standing in the area and also offended Saudi Arabia.

18. DD, 1981-581B, State Department, "Eden Talks," January 30, 1956, 2:15 P.M., DD, 1981-582A, State Department, "Eden Talks," January 30, 1956, 4:00 P.M., DD, 1981-585B, State Department, "Eden Talks," February 1, 1956, 4:00 P.M.; EL, AW, International Series, box 20, press release concerning Eden talks, February 1, 1956.

19. Burns, *Economic Aid*, pp. 63–64.

20. Schuckburgh, *Descent to Suez*, p. 340.

21. PRO, FO 371/121271, Foreign Office to Washington, No. 1246, March 5, 1956.

22. Carlton, *Anthony Eden*, pp. 388–90; Clark, *From Three Worlds*, pp. 154–55; James, *Anthony Eden*, pp. 425–26.

23. The British financial position deteriorated further during January. While Eden was in the United States Macmillan had threatened to resign unless Eden agreed to major budget cuts. It was a no-lose proposition for the chancellor. He would get the credit for any improvement in the financial situation, and Eden would invariably be blamed for these unpopular actions.

24. James, *Anthony Eden*, pp. 429–33.

25. Tory politician Anthony Nutting, in 1956 minister of state in the Foreign Office, later recalled that after Glubb's dismissal Eden became almost irrational on the subject of Nasser, at one point actually stating, "Can't you understand that I want Nasser murdered" (Lapping, *End of Empire*, p. 262).

26. NA, SD, 641.74/3-156, London to State Department, No. 2037, March 1, 1956; 641.74/2-756, London to State Department, No. 3791, March 7, 1956; Lloyd, *Suez: 1956*, pp. 46–47.

27. On March 21 Makins handed to Dulles a confidential paper approved by Eden on British Middle East policy. Strongly evincing the British disillusionment with Nasser and Eden's own appeasing policy toward the Egyptian leader, the paper mooted the isolation of Egypt from other Middle Eastern countries, the strengthening of the Baghdad Pact, and the withdrawal of economic aid, including the Aswan offers. See *FRUS*, vol. 15, 208:383–87, Makins to Dulles, March 21, 1956. See also PRO, FO 371/118842, Karachi to Foreign Office, No. D 33, March 7, 1956.

28. The Anderson Mission represented an American attempt to find its own

(rather than an Anglo-American) solution to the Arab-Israeli impasse. Indeed, as Francis Russell, the American coauthor of the Anglo-American Project Alpha, wrote: "In view of the British desire to direct the course of events in the Middle East and the lengths to which this has recently driven them. . . . I would be inclined not to go further with them at this time." Therefore, Makins was not to be told of Anderson's journey until the last moment. See *FRUS*, vol. 14, 470:888–89, Russell to Dulles, December 28, 1955; *FRUS*, vol. 15, 5:9, Memorandum of Conversation at the State Department, January 5, 1956.

Robert B. Anderson (1910–89) was born and educated in Texas. After receiving a law degree in 1932, he entered the state legislature as a Democrat and during the next two decades filled a variety of state offices. He switched parties in 1952 and served in the Eisenhower administration as secretary of the navy in 1953–54 and deputy secretary of defense for the following two years. In these positions he earned the president's respect and trust and, when George Humphrey retired in 1957, became secretary of the Treasury. In 1960 Eisenhower unsuccessfully urged Anderson to run for president. During the 1960s Anderson carried out diplomatic missions for his fellow Texan and friend Lyndon Johnson. However, in 1987 he received a prison sentence for income tax evasion and operating an illegal offshore bank. In January 1989 the Appellate Division of the New York State Supreme Court disbarred him for "unconscionable activities."

29. EL, AW, Eisenhower Diaries, box 8, Eisenhower to Hazlett, December 8, 1954.

30. Ibid., box 13, March 8, 1956; Memorandum dated March 13, 1956, concerning conversation with Anderson, March 12, 1956.

31. By this time the State Department had already begun a major reassessment of American policy toward Egypt. Most of the suggestions embodied in this memorandum emerged intact in Dulles's memorandum to Eisenhower of March 28 (see n. 33, below). One very important idea that was not readily apparent in the Dulles document was the recommendation that the British government delay its rapid reduction of forces from the Suez base (the final 25 percent of the contingent were due to depart before June 18). It is possible, however, that this suggestion was listed in the part of the document that the State Department censored. See *FRUS*, vol. 15, 192:352–57, "United States policy in the Near East," March 14, 1956.

The secretary's new attitude toward Egypt did not translate into a change of heart about Israel. On March 27, in a letter to his former colleague and confidante Arthur Dean, Dulles dismissed the idea of sending arms shipments to Israel to compensate it for the Soviet shipments to Egypt. He also took the opportunity to complain that "one of the troubles we have is that the Israelis will not sit down and talk with us with any intimacy. . . . They insist on working with us at arm's length and, indeed, are carrying on a very highly organized and high-powered campaign directed to force our hand irrespective of our judgment. I do not think that these tactics will succeed. But their pursuit does not help matters" (John Foster Dulles Papers, JFD/DDE, Subject Series, box 10, Dulles to Dean, March 27, 1956). See also *FRUS*, vol. 15, 199:367–70, Memorandum of Conversation at the State Department, March 15, 1956; 200:370–71, Hoover to Dulles, March 16, 1956; 221:405–9, Memorandum of Conversation at the State Department, March 28, 1956.

32. John Foster Dulles Papers, JFD/DDE, Subject Series, box 10, March 24, 1956.

33. This new American approach to Egypt received the code word *Omega*. Douglas

MacArthur II (son of the general and counselor of the State Department) became coordinator of the program while Francis Russell, who had worked on the now defunct Project Alpha, took on the responsibility of planning new measures. See *FRUS*, vol. 15, Editorial Note, pp. 461–62; John Foster Dulles Papers, JFD/DDE, Subject Series, box 5, Memorandum for the President, March 28, 1956. See also *FRUS*, vol. 15, 225:423–24, Memorandum of Conversation at the White House, March 28, 1956.

34. EL, AW, Eisenhower Diaries, box 13, March 28, 1956; Memorandum dated March 29, 1956, of conference with the president, March 28, 1956.

35. PRO, FO 371/119052, Cairo to Foreign Office, No. 405, March 1, 1956; FO 371/119053, Bishop to Granham, March 3, 1956; B/E, OV 43/9, Foreign Office to Cairo, No. 651, March 3, 1956; NA, SD, 874.2614/3-956, Rountree to Hoover, March 9, 1956; 874.2614/4-356, Rountree to Hoover, April 3, 1956.

36. NA, SD, 874.2614/2-2056, Hoover to Cairo, No. 1633, February 20, 1956; 874.2614/3-3056, Dulles to Cairo, No. 1935, March 30, 1956; PRO, FO 371/119054, Washington to Foreign Office, No. 843, April 3, 1956.

37. John Foster Dulles Papers, JFD/DDE, Chronological Series, box 13, Suggested Message for the President, April 4, 1956; Personal Papers, box 100, Department of State Release No. 172, April 3, 1956.

38. On April 1, Dulles, Hoover, and MacArthur met with Makins and British Embassy Counselor R. W. Bailey for a detailed discussion of future Anglo-American policy toward the Middle East. (See *FRUS*, vol. 15, 232:435–45, Memorandum of Conversation at Dulles's Residence, April 1, 1956.) During the visit of Air Marshall and Chairman of the British Joint Chiefs Sir William Dickson, American and British diplomats met for a second such far-ranging discussion. Among other things, Dulles suggested that Britain should undertake a comprehensive study of the effects of a cutoff of Middle Eastern oil supplies. Dickson, for his part, observed that "if the Egyptians initiated action which would lead to the closing of the Canal, it might be necessary to undertake military operations to open up the Canal under UN auspices" (*FRUS*, vol. 15, 240:457–61, Memorandum of Conversation at Dulles's Home, April 4, 1956). See also PRO, FO 371/118861, Trevelyan to Schuckburgh, April 5, 1956.

39. The outbreak during April of renewed clashes on the Israeli-Egyptian border complicated Washington's attempt to reorient American Middle Eastern policy. Eisenhower had obliquely signaled this shift on April 9 when he announced that the United States would observe its commitments to oppose aggression and would support and assist any nation subjected to aggression. Operation Stockpile, which called for the storage of major military hardware in a Mediterranean location within easy access of Israel, became a major part of the new administration thinking. While Washington still refused to sell weapons to Israel, Stockpile would allow military equipment to be sent quickly to Israel in the case of Arab-initiated hostilities. See *FRUS*, vol. 15, 259:496–98, Memorandum of Conversation at the State Department, April 9, 1956; 282:532–57, MacArthur to Dulles, April 14, 1956; 305:575–77, "Proposal For Statement by The United States That It Will Make Weapons Available to Victim of Aggression in the Middle East," April 25, 1956; 315:589, Eisenhower to Ben-Gurion, April 30, 1956; Lodge Papers, General Correspondence, box 4, Meeting with Congressional Leaders, April 10, 1956.

40. PRO, FO 371/118862, Watson Memorandum, April 11, 1956.

41. See PRO, T 236/4778, "Egypt: The Economic Implications of a Possible New Policy," March 29, 1956; "Ways of Bringing Pressure on Egypt," April 1956; Rickett to Rowan, April 10, 1956, enclosing "Use of Exchange Control Powers Against Egypt"; Rickett to Rowan, April 16, 1956, enclosing a draft of "Ways of Bringing Pressure on Egypt" revised to reflect comments of various ministries; T 236/4841, Rampton to Johnston, April 20, 1956, concerning the effect of a closure of the Suez Canal.

42. PRO, FO 371/118862, Schuckburgh to British Ambassadors, May 28, 1956. See also FO 371/121273, "Discussions with Mr. Dulles," May 3, 1956.

43. See John Foster Dulles Papers, Personal Papers, box 100, Press Release No. 272, May 22, 1956; EL, AW, Eisenhower Diaries, box 8, Pre-Press Conference briefings, May 23, 1956.

44. Military planners at this time also cooperated in drawing up an Anglo-American plan for military action against Israel should it, as was widely feared, launch a preventive war against Egypt. The Tripartite Declaration provided the justification for these precautions. See, e.g., PRO, FO 371/121273, Chiefs of Staff Committee, "Joint United States-United Kingdom Action in the Event of Arab-Israel War," April 18, 1956.

45. NA, SD, 874.2614/3-2756, Cairo to State Department, No. 1910, March 27, 1956; 874.2614/5-1856, "Position Paper: Aswan Dam," May 18, 1956; 874.2614/5-2356, State Department to Khartoum, etc., May 23, 1956; 874.2614/5-2456, Dulles to Cairo, etc., May 24, 1956; 874.2614/5-2656, Cairo to State Department, Nos. 2346 and 2347, May 26, 1956; 874.2614/5-1956, Hoover to Addis Ababa, No. 549, May 29, 1956; 874.2614/6-656, Rountree to Dulles, June 6, 1956; PRO, FO 371/119055, Treasury Memorandum to Phillips, June 6, 1956. See also Watson Memorandum, June 6, 1956; Milord to Hancock, June 6, 1956; FO 371/119054, Kirkpatrick Memorandum, June 7, 1956.

46. PRO, FO 371/118862, Trevelyan to Watson, April 9, 1956.

47. An American observer commenting on the base ceremonies observed that "the motif of the Egyptian celebration is Nasser's success in ridding Egypt of imperialism and strengthening himself by the Soviet arms purchase." NA, SD, 974.7301/6-1856, Rountree to Hoover, June 18, 1956.

48. The British and American governments knew that this eventuality might occur because they had been receiving reports indicating Nasser's renewed interest in definitive financing agreements since early May. See, e.g., B/E, OV 43/10, Washington to Foreign Office, No. 377S, May 11, 1956; PRO, FO 371/119054, Trevelyan to Watson, May 26, 1956.

49. FRBNY, 797.5, Foreign Economic Assistance, Egan to Exter, January 20, 1956.

50. John Foster Dulles Papers, JFD/DDE, Telephone Conversations, box 5, telephone conversation with Congressman Richards, May 22, 1956.

51. For example, the State Department reported in January 1956 that since the announcement of the Aswan offer, "significant opposition" to the administration's position had developed in the cotton and rice producing regions (NA, SD, 874.2614/3-1756, State Department to Cairo, A-170, January 5, 1956).

52. Black told Lloyd on June 6, "This position [of Congress] could be overcome if the Administration really wanted to" (PRO, FO 371/119072, "Conversation between Secretary of State and Mr. Eugene Black on June 6, 1956"). See also FRUS, vol. 15, 360:658-67, Rountree to Dulles, May 23, 1956.

53. Ibid., FO 371/119055, Makins's Record of Conversation with Black, June 29, 1956.

54. Such an offer would not have been entirely unwelcome because a prevalent American theory held that the Russians were financially overextending themselves and would not be able to fulfill the financial offers they had made. See, e.g., C. L. Sulzberger's column in the *New York Times*, December 26, 1955, p. 18; NA, SD, 874.2614/7-356, Allen to Hoover, July 3, 1956.

55. PRO, FO 371/119056, "Aswan High Dam," July 3, 1956, Foreign Office to Washington, No. 3153, July 10, 1956; FO 371/119057, Record of Conversation in Washington, July 13, 1956.

56. Ibid., FO 371/119056, Washington to Foreign Office, No. 1488, July 11, 1956. The Aswan affair was meant to be Byroade's last major issue as American ambassador to Egypt. Dulles had grown more and more concerned that Byroade's increasing partiality toward Nasser had limited his effectiveness; during January the two had discussed a change of post, and on June 28 the secretary cabled Byroade suggesting that he take the position of U.S. ambassador to South Africa. See *FRUS*, vol. 15, 414:759–60, State Department to Cairo, No. 3099, June 28, 1956.

57. Ambrose, *Eisenhower: The President*, p. 329.

58. NA, SD, 874.2614/7-1356, Cairo to Secretary of State, No. 70, July 13, 1956.

59. The visit to Egypt by Soviet Foreign Minister Dmitri Shepilov during the June celebrations for the final British evacuation of the Suez Canal base fueled speculation concerning a Soviet offer to fund the Aswan Dam. See NA, SD, 874.2614/7-356, Allen to Hoover, July 3, 1956.

60. The report stated that "the Committee directs that none of the funds provided in this act shall be used for assistance in connection with the construction of the Aswan Dam, nor shall any of the funds heretofore provided under the Mutual Security Act as amended be used on this dam without prior approval of the Committee on Appropriations" (NA, SD, 874.2614/3-1756, Mutual Security Appropriations Bill 1956, Senate Report to Accompany HR 1230).

61. John Foster Dulles Papers, JFD/DDE, Chronological Series, box 13, Memorandum for the President, July 16, 1956; Dulles to Hayden, July 17, 1956; Telephone Conversations, box 5, telephone call from Knowland, July 17, 1956.

62. PRO, FO 371/119056, Washington to Foreign Office, No. 1545, July 19, 1956; NA, SD, 874.2614/7-1956, Memorandum of Meeting with Sir Roger Makins, July 19, 1956.

63. Given their mutual dislike, it is ironic that it took the combined mistakes of Eden and Dulles to bring the Aswan effort to its tragic end. World Bank President Eugene Black, for one, urged Dulles to explain to Nasser his problems with Congress. See *FRUS*, vol. 15, 410:748–51, Memorandum of Conversation at the State Department, June 25, 1956.

64. PRO, FO 371/119056, Ross Memorandum, July 16, 1956; FO 371/118864, Memorandum by the Secretary of State for Foreign Affairs, July 19, 1956.

65. NA, SD, 874.2614/7-1956, Memorandum of Conversation, July 19, 1956.

66. During the morning of July 19 Dulles had discussed with Eisenhower his proposed statement to the Egyptian ambassador concerning the administration's withdrawal of its funding offer and had also shown the president his draft statement. (See *FRUS*, vol. 15, 473:861–62, Memorandum of Conversation at the White House, July 19, 1956.) Dulles defended his actions with respect to the dam in a letter

to Eisenhower written on September 15, 1956. He stated that the decision was not abrupt and that Egypt, by "flirting with the Soviet Union," had consciously jeopardized the offer. Dulles cited the mounting congressional opposition, saying, "If I had not announced our withdrawal when I did, the Congress would certainly have imposed it on us, almost unanimously. As it was, we retained some flexibility." Actually Dulles had completely squandered all the flexibility he possessed (John Foster Dulles Papers, JFD/DDE, WHM, box 3, Dulles to Eisenhower, September 15, 1956). See also Robert Bowie, "Eisenhower, Dulles, and the Suez Crisis," in Louis and Owen, *Suez 1956*. Bowie's account is particularly instructive because as the head of the State Department's Policy Planning Staff he was involved in the department's discussions leading up to the decision not to fund the dam.

67. John Foster Dulles Papers, Personal Papers, box 100, State Department Press Release No. 401, July 19, 1956; JFD/DDE, Telephone Conversations, box 5, telephone call with Allen Dulles, July 19, 1956.

68. In its discussion with the Egyptian ambassador to Britain, the Foreign Office took the same tack as the Eisenhower administration. Officials emphasized three points: the decision was made on economic grounds, it would not have any effect on future Anglo-Egyptian relations, and Britain remained interested in the development of the Nile valley. NA, SD, 874.2614/7-2056, Memorandum of Conversation, July 20, 1956; PRO, FO 371/119057, Commonwealth Relations Office to Commonwealth High Commissioners, W. No. 286, July 20, 1956.

CHAPTER FOUR

1. PRO, T 236/4111, Cairo to Foreign Office, No. 36 S, February 26, 1955.

2. See, e.g., B/E, OV 43/62, Memoranda, November 3 and 15, 1955. Interestingly, the State Department's Near East desk considered the merits of the transfer of company reserves during December. The evaluating officer concluded that given Egypt's desperate need for foreign exchange, the demand that the Suez Canal Company comply with Egyptian law was understandable. He did question whether the company ought to be entitled to retain some of its reserves in order to pay non-Egyptian expenses such as dividends and pensions. NA, SD, 974.7301/12-2255, Shaw to Geren, December 22, 1955.

3. PRO, FO 371/119069, Wylie to Watson, February 29, 1956.

4. Ibid., FO 371/119073, Suez Canal Company General Letter, January 26, 1956.

5. Ibid., FO 371/119045, "Suez Canal: Future Policy," draft, March 9, 1956.

6. Shortly after taking up his post in Egypt, Byroade observed, "It is characteristic of the Management [of the Canal Company] never to be happy with the state of affairs in the Canal Zone. The Management has something of a genius for seeing and foreseeing difficulties" (NA, SD, 974.7301/3-1555, Byroade to State Department, March 15, 1955).

7. Concerning the future of the canal, various economic considerations needed to be taken into account. The first was that the demand on the canal from oil tankers had grown in direct proportion to the increased worldwide demand for oil (up over 18 percent each year during the first half of the 1950s). However, the larger tankers now coming on stream could not fit through the canal. These facts seemingly dictated an expansion of the canal's capacity. Certainly, the economics of any new

construction would have to be weighed against the availability of alternatives to the canal, both the shipping routes around the Cape of Good Hope and the possibilities of building larger and more extensive pipelines. See, e.g., McCloy Papers, SC1/38, Habachy to McCloy, February 2, 1957; PRO, FO 371/119069, Cairo to Foreign Office, No. 610, March 31, 1956.

8. Canal Company sources, not surprisingly, painted a different financial picture. In a Canal Company report furnished to John J. McCloy, the following figures were given (in thousands of U.S. dollars):

	1953	1954	1955
Canal Company gross income from dues	83,904	88,077	93,516
Egyptian entitlements			
Allocation taxes	4,354	7,456	12,106
Egyptian taxes on shareholders	4,953	4,939	5,048
Share of net profits allocated by statute to the Egyptian government	4,485	4,485	4,609
Total	13,792	16,880	21,763
Net profits			
To reserves	2,870	2,870	2,870
Paid to shareholders	19,570	19,567	20,141
Total	22,440	22,437	23,011

Source: McCloy Papers, SC1/19, Spofford to Rosen, December 28, 1956.

See also B/E, OV 43/9, "Egypt: Suez Canal Company," April 10, 1956; PRO, FO 371/119070, Paris to Foreign Office, No. 91, April 20, 1956, and Watson, "Suez Canal Company," April 24, 1956.

9. PRO, FO 371/119070, Watson minute, April 28, 1956.

10. In 1955 the company earned £32 million in canal dues. After all expenses, including about £1 million given to the Egyptian government, approximately £10.5 million was available to be paid out as dividends. While these sums seem paltry, the company felt aggrieved because the current dividends represented an increase from earlier years; from 1937 to 1948 the company only paid about E £4 million, and for the period 1949–56 total Egyptian receipts from canal royalties were only E £2.45 million. See NA, SD, 974.7301/9-556, Liebesny to Maktos, September 5, 1956; *Economist*, August 4, 1956, p. 422.

11. Author's interview with Watson. British officials did consider what would happen if the canal was closed to British shipping but even then did not contemplate Nasser's nationalization of the Canal Company. See, e.g., PRO, T 236/4841, Rampton to Johnston, April 20, 1956.

12. PRO, FO 371/119071, Brenchley to Watson, May 12, 1956.

13. See, e.g., ibid., FO 371/119071, Issacson to Watson, May 16, 1956.

14. The agreement, which was initialed on May 30, required the company to turn over the sterling equivalent of E £15 million by January 1, 1959, and a further amount equal to 7 percent of net profits each year until 1963, approximately E £22 million in total. An Egyptian law was promulgated on June 14. See, PRO, FO 371/119072, Cairo to Foreign Office, No. 939, June 1, 1956; B/E, OV 43/10, Wylie to Watson, June 14, 1956; OV 43/11, Margetson, "Suez Canal Company," July 18, 1956.

15. Heikal, *Cutting the Lion's Tail*, p. 117; Lacoutre, *Nasser*, pp. 166–81; Nutting, *Nasser*, pp. 142–44.

16. A State Department paper prepared on July 17 had also predicted that Nasser, in response to the Anglo-American withdrawal of funding for the dam, might launch a propaganda war against the United States. While the author thought that "the Suez Canal problem and Middle East oil will also be considered as fertile fields for Egyptian action against us," the possibility of a takeover of the canal was not mooted. See *FRUS*, vol. 15, 467:849–53, Allen to Dulles, July 17, 1956, enclosing a memorandum concerning Egyptian reactions to the withdrawal of offer on Aswan High Dam; NA, SD, 774.5-MSP/7-2556, Rountree to Hoover, July 25, 1956; 874.2614/7-2556, Memorandum of Conversation concerning Aswan, July 25, 1956.

17. Simultaneously with Nasser's announcement Egyptians took physical charge of the canal. See *FRUS*, vol. 15, 511:906–8, Cairo to State Department, No. 146, July 26, 1956; Heikal, *Cutting the Lion's Tail*, pp. 119–29; Fawzi, *Suez 1956*, pp. 33–46.

18. James, *Anthony Eden*, pp. 453–54.

19. DD, 1987-1475, London to Secretary of State, No. 481, July 27, 1956; PRO, CAB 128/30, CM 54 (56), July 27, 1956.

20. NA, SD, 974.7501/7-2756, London to State Department, No. 481, July 27, 1956.

21. PRO, FO 800/726, Foreign Office to Washington, No. 3358, July 27, 1956.

22. DD 1987-1476, Paris to State Department, No. 469, July 27, 1956.

23. Guy Mollet (1900–1975) was a Socialist whose government, which lasted from January 1956 until May 1957, endured longer than any other coalition during the Fourth Republic. He considered it his mission to bring peace to Algeria; like all others, he failed.

24. Horne, *A Savage War of Peace*, pp. 161–65; Maurice Vaisse, "Post-Suez France," in Louis and Owen, *Suez 1956*.

25. It should be recalled that since February 1955 the Bank of England had supported transferable sterling within 1 percent of parity, around $2.77. Trading in transferable sterling was the main determinant of the position of sterling at this time.

26. PRO, T 231/715, Memorandum to Sir Leslie Rowan, July 27, 1956.

27. The Bank of England could so quickly enact these complicated regulations because, at the request of the Treasury, it had prepared a draft of such measures in March 1956 that now needed only to be implemented. See, e.g., B/E, EC 3/356, Rickett to Hawker, April 11, 1956; "Use of Exchange Control Powers Against Egypt," April 11, 1956; "Blocking Powers," April 12, 1956; "Egypt," April 19, 1956; EC 5/356, 1956 No. 1164, Supplies and Service Finance, The Control of Gold and Securities (Suez Canal Company) Direction, 1956.

28. No further releases under the sterling releases agreement were due until January 1957. PRO, CAB 128/30, CM 54 (56), July 27, 1956.

29. Colonel (later General) Andrew Goodpaster from 1954 to 1960 handled "White House communications." Among other things he joined many of the president's meetings, serving as secretary.

30. PRO, FO 371/119078, Washington to Foreign Office, No. 1597, July 27, 1956.

31. In January 1952, French officials had proposed an international conference on the future of the Suez Canal. The British government eagerly supported this idea, and on taking office, European diplomats presented the Eisenhower administration with a detailed blueprint that called for the United States and other maritime

nations to guarantee the canal's international status. From January until June 1953 the American government waffled. Finally in July, after participating in five preliminary sessions, the administration, fearing the effect this maneuver would have on Egyptian and Arab opinion, informed the British and French governments that it would not take part in the wider, secret conference the allies had suggested. See, e.g., PRO, T 236/4179, Allen to Beeley, March 3, 1953; Ledward to Duke, April 11, 1953; Paris to Foreign Office, No. 200, May 29, 1953; Allen to Serpell, June 15, 1953; Washington to Foreign Office, No. 1385, June 29, 1953; "Draft Note for Discussion at an Interdepartmental Meeting at the Foreign Office at 11:30 on August 6, 1953."

32. The State Department also immediately instructed American Ambassador to Israel Edward Lawson to contact Israeli Prime Minister Ben-Gurion to stress that the American government hoped for Israeli "restraint." See *FRUS*, vol. 16, 12:22–23, Tel Aviv to State Department, No. 97, July 27, 1956. See also EL, AW, Eisenhower Diaries, box 16, Memoranda of Conferences with the President, July 27, 1956; Minutes of Cabinet Meeting, July 27, 1956; Phone Calls, July 27, 1956; Notes of Conversation with the President, July 28, 1956; International Series, box 19, Washington to London, No. 545, July 27, 1956.

33. PRO, FO 371/119080, Eden to New Zealand Prime Minister, July 28, 1956.

34. During the previous decade Europe's dependence on oil supplies had grown both because of increasing automobile ownership and, more importantly, because oil increasingly replaced coal and gas in industrial production.

35. For example, the Aden-Liverpool route was 10,450 miles via the Cape of Good Hope but only 4,420 miles using the Suez Canal. The Adelaide-Liverpool route was 11,550 miles using the cape and 9,640 miles via the canal.

36. Author's interview with David Dilks.

37. What makes the British response even more puzzling is that the government realized that Egypt would never have renewed the Canal Company's franchise. See, PRO, CAB 134/1298, "The Suez Canal-Future Policy," May 1956.

38. PRO, FO 371/119078, Washington to Foreign Office, Nos. 1605, 1607, 1609, July 28, 1956; T 236/4625, Washington to Foreign Office, No. 1608, July 28, 1956.

39. NA, SD, 944.7301/7-2756, Cairo to State Department, No. 157, July 27, 1956; 974.7301/7-2756, Memorandum of Conversation, July 27, 1956.

40. Treasury official Andrew Overby told John Exter of the FRBNY on August 3 that "there was considerable opposition to it [the Egyptian blocking] in the United States government" (FRBNY, C261 Egypt, Exter Memorandum to the Files, August 6, 1956).

41. The assets of the Suez Canal Company located in the United States amounted to $40 million. The American restrictions, which also covered the earnings of blocked accounts, were enacted as Sec. 510.201 to Sec. 510.801 of the Foreign Assets Control Regulations. FRBNY, C260.2, Egyptian Assets Control Regulations, July 31, 1956; B/E, OV 31/55, Exter to Bank of England, August 1, 1956; PRO, FO 371/125465, Ford to Beeley, March 18, 1957; SD, NA, Lot File 62 D 11, box 7, Arnold Memorandum concerning blocked and free accounts, October 2, 1956.

42. The statutory support for this action was U.S.C. Title 50, Appendix Section 5(b), commonly known as the Trading with the Enemy Act. See, NA, SD, 974.7301-72856, Raymond to Dulles, July 28, 1956; PRO, T 236/4635, Pitblado to Armstrong, September 4, 1956.

43. FRBNY, C260.2, License Granted Pursuant to Authorization 8.03—Payment of Suez Canal Transit Charges, August 10, 1956. Because paying tolls without protest could constitute acquiescence in Nasser's seizure of the canal, ships' captains were required to pay under protest.

44. PRO, FO 371/119078, Foreign Office to Washington, No. 3371, July 27, 1956.

45. Yet on the previous day Dulles had advised Eisenhower that the United States should be prepared to use force if necessary to keep the canal operating. See *FRUS*, vol. 16, 23:38–39, Telephone Conversation with the President, July 29, 1956; NA, SD, 974.7301/7-2856, Hoover to Dulles, July 27, 1956; 974.7301/7-3056, No. 574, Dulles to Murphy, July 30, 1956.

46. Article 1 of the convention attempted to ensure that the Suez Canal would always be open "in time of war as in peace, to every vessel without distinction of flag." Article 9 authorized the Egyptian government to take steps necessary to guarantee the execution of the treaty. Turkey was authorized to take all proper measures to ensure the defense of Egypt, but article 11 stated that such measures could not interfere with the free passage of ships through the canal. For an excellent analysis of the convention, see Bowie, *Suez 1956*.

47. PRO, FO 371/119106, "Summary Record of the Tripartite Conference Held in London from July 29, 1956 to August 2, 1956."

48. Simultaneously Barbour confirmed the bellicose British position, cabling Washington that Chancellor of the Exchequer Macmillan "stressed that if they [the British] had to go down now the Government and he believed British people would rather do so on this issue and become perhaps another Netherlands" (*FRUS*, vol. 16, 33:60–62, London to State Department, No. 550, July 31, 1956). See also NA, SD, London to State Department, No. 521, July 29, 1956.

49. EL, AW, Eisenhower Diaries, box 16, Memorandum of Conference with the President, July 31, 1956.

50. John Foster Dulles Papers, JFD/DDE, Subject Series, box 11, Eisenhower to Eden, July 31, 1956.

51. EL, AW, Eisenhower Diaries, box 17, Eisenhower to Hazlett, August 3, 1956.

52. NA, SD, 974.7301/7-3056, State Department to London, No. 583, July 30, 1956; 974.7301/7-3156, State Department to London, No. 606, July 31, 1956.

53. PRO, FO 371/119078, Foreign Office to Paris, July 30, 1956. French doubts about Dulles were no doubt exacerbated by a conversation between the secretary and Pineau that took place earlier in the summer. According to Pineau, "Dulles had been very unhelpful as regards the Middle East. He had turned out to be a stout defender of Colonel Nasser and thought that we ought to continue to give the latter the benefit of the doubt" (PRO, FO 371/124436, Paris to Foreign Office, No. 277S, July 13, 1956).

54. See, e.g., PRO, FO 371/119080, Cairo to Foreign Office, No. 1330, July 30, 1956.

55. See NA, SD, 974.7301/8-3156, Bloomfield to Wilcox, August 31, 1956.

56. PRO, FO 371/119080, Washington to London, No. 1613, July 30, 1956.

57. John Foster Dulles Papers, JFD/DDE, G, C & M, box 1, Memorandum of Conversation with Hammarskjöld, August 10, 1956.

58. NA, SD, 974.7301/7-3056, Dulles to Murphy, No. 574, July 30, 1956; 974.7301/7-3056, Memorandum of Conversation with Makins, July 30, 1956; 974.7301/7-3156, Howard to Maktos, July 31, 1956; 974.7301/7-3156, Memorandum of Conversation with Lloyd et al., July 31, 1956.

59. Interestingly, during the spring of 1956 the State Department had considered the potential benefits and detriments of American accession to the Suez Canal Convention. See NA, SD, 974.7301/4-356, Bevans to Phleger, April 3, 1956.

60. The State Department concluded that because the Soviet Union had never repudiated the treaties signed by Czarist Russia, it would be impossible to convene a conference based on the 1888 convention without inviting the Soviet Union. See NA, SD, 974.7301/7-3156, Raymond to Phleger, July 31, 1956.

61. PRO, FO 371/119091, Johnston to Private Secretary, August 1, 1956.

62. As part of its campaign to keep Israel and therefore the Arab-Israeli dispute from becoming entangled with the Suez crisis, the administration again utilized the services of Robert Anderson. The American special envoy lunched with Israeli Ambassador to Washington Abba Eban on August 3. Eban contended that the crisis showed that Israel was America's only reliable ally in the Middle East; therefore, the administration should arm Israel in order that it become a "bastion of strength." Without directly responding to this suggestion, Anderson said that "it would be greatly to Israel's advantage to keep quiet during the coming period" (*FRUS*, vol. 16, 60:136–38, Russell to Dulles, August 4, 1956). See also PRO, PREM 11/1098, Foreign Office to Washington, No. 3483, August 1, 1956; FO 371/119083, Foreign Office to Addis Ababa et al., Nos. 378 and 379, August 2, 1956.

63. At this point the British government shared these sentiments. For example, a Foreign Office memorandum written on August 4 concluded that "it is, therefore, important that we and the French (and the Americans) should agree to use our influence to keep Israel right out of the dispute." PRO, T 236/4635, "France and the Middle East, August 4, 1956; NA, SD, 974.7301/7-2756, Paris to State Department, No. 469, July 27, 1956; 974.7301/8-456, Memorandum of Conversation, August 4, 1956.

64. NA, SD, 974.7301/8-156, Murphy's Memorandum of Conversation, August 1, 1956; Aldrich's Memorandum of Conversation, August 1, 1956; Memorandum of Conversation with Eden, August 1, 1956; Memorandum of Conversation between Eden and Dulles, August 1, 1956.

65. PRO, FO 371/120830, No. 3389, July 28, 1956; John Foster Dulles Papers, JFD/DDE, Telephone Conversations, box 5, telephone call to Mansfield, July 30, 1956.

66. Painter, *Oil and the American Century*, pp. 172–210.

67. PRO, FO 371/120828, Middle East Oil I through V, Records of Meetings held at the State Department, February 29–March 5, 1956.

68. An instructive note presented to the Cabinet by Macmillan in October 1955 stated that at the current rate, British petroleum imports during the next twenty years would have to be trebled to meet British needs and that the Middle East provided the only possible source of supply. PRO, CAB 128/78 CP (55)152, October 14, 1955.

69. As the National Security Council's staff had prepared a paper on the Middle East oil situation in the spring, the administration was well aware of what the allies faced. EL, White House Office, NSC, Office of National Security Advisor, box 14, Economic Intelligence Committee's *Ad Hoc* Working Group on Middle East Oil, May 3, 1956.

70. The MEEC was created pursuant to the Defense Production Act of 1950, as amended, which allowed the government to designate private corporations to assist

in government actions undertaken for purposes of national security. Under this authorization Flemming approved a Voluntary Agreement Relating to Foreign Petroleum Supply and invited United States oil companies to participate. The agreement enabled the American government to secure current information on foreign petroleum supply and production and appointed a Foreign Petroleum Supply Committee, composed of oil company executives. The committee was authorized to prepare appropriate plans of action in the event of an emergency; Flemming now requested such a plan and approved it on August 10. Among other things the plan called for the formation of the MEEC. On August 19 Attorney General Brownell rendered a ruling that the MEEC did not violate antitrust laws.

71. NA, SD, 974.7301/7-305/6, Memorandum of Conversation, July 30, 1956; 974.7301/8-156, Memorandum of Conversation, August 1, 1956.

72. PRO, FO 371/120830, Foreign Office to Washington, No. 3289, July 28, 1956; "Suez Canal Oil Supplies," August 2, 1956; FO 371/119081, Foreign Office to Washington, Nos. 3486 and 3487, August 2, 1956; FO 371/119084, Washington to Foreign Office, Nos. 1641 and 1652, August 3, 1956; FO 371/119085, Washington to Foreign Office, No. 1649, August 3, 1956; FO 371/119260, Washington to Foreign Office, No. 1659, August 3, 1956.

73. Arthur Dean had been a member of the Korean Armistice Commission. For further details see chap. 7, no. 71.

74. John Foster Dulles Papers, Telephone Conversations, box 5, telephone call to Humphrey, August 6, 1957.

75. PRO, FO 371/120829, Gummer to Rampton, April 30, 1956.

76. The oil-related drain of the reserves resulted from, first, the additional costs of substituting for consumption Western Hemisphere oil for cheaper Middle Eastern oil and, second, the loss of foreign exchange British companies earned by producing, selling, and transporting Middle Eastern oil. See PRO, FO 371/120799, D. Wright, "The Egypt Crisis and the British Economy," August 27, 1956.

77. In the pre-1971 world of fixed exchange rates a country's currency was backed by dollars and/or gold reserves. If a currency was convertible, holders of the currency could obtain these same dollars from the central bank on demand.

78. The Bank of England reached this goal by allowing trading in transferable sterling on world markets. When necessary the Bank intervened in trading to ensure that transferable sterling never slipped below $2.77-$2.78.

79. PRO, T 236/4188, Bridges to Macmillan, August 8, 1956.

80. B/E, G 1/124, "Sterling and the Suez Canal Situation," August 1, 1956.

81. American officials also believed that economic pressure would not be enough to destroy Nasser. For example a State Department intelligence report dated August 10, 1956, concluded that while the tripartite sanctions would hurt Egyptian development plans and necessitate a retrenchment in social spending, "the resultant pressures upon the Nasir [sic] regime would probably not be sufficient within a year's time or even longer to threaten its survival" (EL, White House Office, NSC, Office of National Security Advisor, box 9, Intelligence Report No. 7312, "Possible Effects of Economic Sanctions on the Egyptian Economy," p. ii).

82. B/E, OV 43/11, Ottawa to Foreign Office, No. 729, July 28, 1956; PRO, FO 371/118943, Brussels to Foreign Office, No. 166, August 3, 1956; Rome to Foreign Office, No. 517, August 3, 1956; Economist, September 1, 1956, p. 740.

83. See, e.g., PRO, FO 371/118945, "Measures of Economic Pressure Against Egypt," August 1956; *New York Times*, August 5, 1956, sec. 4, p. 3.

84. Black had been devastated by the administration's decision not to fund the Aswan project, calling it "the greatest disappointment of my professional life." During August Macmillan attempted to persuade Dulles to tighten American economic sanctions against Egypt with no success. However, in keeping with customary practice, interest accruing on blocked accounts was frozen (Dulles Oral History Collection, Princeton University, Princeton, N.J., interview with Eugene Black). Also see, e.g., FRBNY, C260.2, Exter Memorandum to Files, August 8, 1956; PRO, T 236/4635, Macmillan minute, August 19, 1956, on Rickett memorandum, "Economic Pressure on Egypt," August 16, 1956. NA, SD, 974.7301/8-2256, Arnold to Chief, International Finance Division, August 22, 1956.

85. NA, SD, 974.7301/8-356, London to State Department, No. 684, August 3, 1956; 974.7301/8-856, London to State Department, No. 750, August 8, 1956; Bliss to Hoover, August 8, 1956; 974.7301/8-956, Dulles to Cairo No. 340, August 9, 1956; Lot file 62 D 11, box 7, Arnold Memorandum to Files, August 13, 1956, 974.7301/8-1156, State Department to Oslo, No. 201, August 11, 1956.

86. In 1956 American aid to Egypt totaled approximately $62 million. The largest segment consisted of development assistance under the Mutual Security Aid Program. In fiscal 1955, Egypt was allocated $40 million. American aid paid for railroads, commodity imports, potable water, highways, and machine shops. PRO, T 236/4635, Washington to Foreign Office, No. 1709, August 14, 1956; DD, 1980-109A, Staff Notes No. 11, August 25, 1956; NA, SD, 774.5-MSP/8-1656, State Department to Cairo, No. 403, August 16, 1956; 774.5-MSP/9-1956, Rountree to Hoover, September 19, 1956.

87. Accordingly, this transaction had the dual effect of strengthening the Egyptian financial position while simultaneously weakening British finances. The Bank of England, however, chose not to object because one of the attributes of a reserve currency is that holders can shift out of it at will. See PRO, PREM, 11/1135, Macmillan to Eden, August 29, 1956; *Economist*, September 1, 1956, p. 740.

88. At the end of August the American embassy in Cairo estimated Egyptian liquid assets outside the United States, Britain, and France to amount to E £80 million, including £60 million in gold in Egypt and some E £8 million in clearing accounts in Egypt's favor held with the Soviet bloc. At that time the Egyptian government was receiving about one-third of the canal dues with the remainder being paid into blocked accounts. The embassy staff concluded that Egypt's financial position was serious but not desperate. More importantly, Byroade presciently predicted that if the Egyptians ultimately blamed their financial problems on the West, Nasser would withdraw his backing from pro-Western ministers such as Kaisouni. NA, SD, 974.7301/8-2856, Cairo to State Department, No. 486, August 28, 1956.

89. NA, SD, 974.7301/7-3056, Cairo to State Department, Nos. 170 and 176, July 30, 1956; 974.7301/7-3156, Cairo to State Department, No. 182, July 31, 1956; 974.7301/8-456, Cairo to State Department, No. 240, August 4, 1956; 974.7301/8-656, Cairo to State Department, Nos. 268 and 272, August 6, 1956; 974.7301/8-756, Cairo to State Department, No. 294, August 7, 1956.

90. Ibid., 974.7301/8-1556, Cairo to State Department, No. 379, August 15, 1956; 975.7301/8-2256, Memorandum of Conversation, August 22, 1956.

91. Selwyn Ilan Troen, ed., "Ben-Gurion's Diary," in Troen and Shemesh, *Suez-Sinai Crisis*, pp. 291–96. The Israeli prime minister's entries also clearly reflect his skepticism concerning Anglo-French military plans.

92. This attitude is clearly reflected in Ben-Gurion's diary entries for August 1956. See ibid.

93. PRO, PREM 11/1117, Foreign Office to Washington, No. 3568, August 5, 1956.

94. Some State Department officials now began to take a harder line toward Nasser. For example, Francis H. Russell, a special assistant to Dulles, concluded on August 4 that "the possibility of our establishing a cooperative relationship with Nasser no longer exists." His judgment was especially significant because Russell had been one of the architects of Project Alpha—the ill-fated Arab-Israeli peace plan launched the previous year. See *FRUS*, vol. 16, 62:140–43, "U.S. Policies Toward Nasser," August 4, 1956. See also NA, SD, 974.7301/8-456, Memorandum of Conversation, August 4, 1956; 974.7301/8-756, Memorandum of Conversation, August 7, 1956; 974.7301/8-856, Dulles to London et al. August 9, 1956.

95. PRO, FO 371/119128, Beeley, "Suez Canal: Implications for Middle East Policy," August 18, 1956.

96. EL, AW, NSC Series, box 8, "Discussion at the 295th Meeting of the National Security Council, August 30, 1956"; see also Clark Papers, box 7, Clark Diary, August 23, 1956.

97. The countries were Australia, the United States, Sweden, Iran, and Ethiopia.

98. EL, AW, Eisenhower Diaries, box 17, Eisenhower to Dulles, August 20, 1956; WHC, Confidential Files, Subject Series, box 72, Dulles to Hoover, August 22, 1956; DD 1982-323, Dulles Memorandum of Conversation with Macmillan, August 21, 1956; NA, SD, 974.7301/8-2156, No. 43, Hoover to McCardle, August 21, 1956; Clark Papers, box 7, Clark Diary, August 22, 1956.

99. John Foster Dulles Papers, JFD/DDE, WHM, box 4, Memorandum of Conference with the President, August 29, 1956.

100. This statement should be contrasted with Dulles's comment to a National Security Council meeting on August 9, 1956: "Should we try to stop use of force by the British and French? He did not favor this course, but it should be considered. How much help should we give the British and French? He felt the United States must make it clear that we would be in the hostilities if the Soviets came in" (EL, AW, NSC Series, box 8, memorandum dated August 10, 1956, of the discussion at the 292d meeting of the National Security Council).

101. While virtually all civilian members of the administration shared the Eisenhower/Dulles point of view, the Joint Chiefs of Staff consistently took a more prointerventionist position on the grounds that Nasser's takeover of the canal, if not immediately, would ultimately have serious ramifications for American military, political, and economic interests. See, e.g., *FRUS*, vol. 16, 68:154–55, JCS Memorandum to Secretaries of Defense Wilson, August 3, 1956; John Foster Dulles Papers, JFD/DDE, WHM, box 4, Memorandum of Conversation with the President, August 30, 1956.

102. EL, AW, International Series, box 19, Hoover to American Embassy London et al., No. 1590, September 2, 1956; box 43, Suez Summary, September 4, 1956.

103. Dulles also allowed the British Suez expeditionary force to use radio elec-

tronic equipment provided through Mutual Defense Aid because of its "relative unimportance" with the caveat that no precedent would thereby be created. See *FRUS*, vol. 16, 73:176–77, Dulles Telephone Conversation with Gray, August 9, 1956; John Foster Dulles Papers, JFD/DDE, Subject Series, box 7, Memorandum Concerning Congressional Consultation on Suez, September 6, 1956.

104. PRO, FO 800/726, Foreign Office to Washington, No. 3913, August 27, 1956.

105. The ongoing discussions during the fall of 1956 on the subject of additional American Plan K military aid to the Royal Air Force illustrates the British dependent position. See, e.g., PRO, T 234/129, Serpell to Clarke, October 2, 1956, Clarke, "Plan K Aid," October 15, 1956.

106. PRO, FO 371/120812, "Harmonisation of Anglo-United States Policy in the Middle East," July 24, 1956.

107. PRO, FO 800/740, Washington to Foreign Office, No. 1849, September 9, 1956.

CHAPTER FIVE

1. See, e.g., PRO, FO 371/118946, CRO to U.K. Commissioner Canada et al., No. 1467, August 31, 1956; FO 371/119125, Cairo to Foreign Office, No. 1874, September 3, 1956; FO 371/119126, Cairo to Foreign Office, No. 1919, September 5, 1956; FO 371/119127, Cairo to Foreign Office, No. 1936, September 6, 1956; FO 371/119128, Cairo to Foreign Office, No. 1942, September 6, 1956; EL, AW, International Series, box 43, Suez Summaries, September 4 and 5, 1956; NA, SD, 974.7301/9-556, Cairo to State Department, No. 613, September 5, 1956.

2. NA, SD, 974.7301/9-656, London to State Department, No. 1335, September 6, 1956.

3. PRO, FO 800/739, Foreign Office to Washington, No. 3931, August 28, 1956. British legal experts were dubious about the efficacy of such a scheme. See FO 800/747, Fitzmaurice to Vallat, October 9, 1956.

4. Similarly Lloyd reported to the Cabinet that the French government believed it would be a mistake to go to the United Nations without what amounted to a prior American guarantee of support for the Anglo-French position. See PRO, CAB 128/30, CM (56) 63, September 6, 1956; NA, SD, 974.7301/9-756, Paris to State Department, No. 1126, September 7, 1956.

5. NA, SD, 974.7301/9-556, Lodge to Dulles, September 5, 1956.

6. The imminence of the election had earlier led Lodge to seek to postpone the opening of the General Assembly from September to November 12 to avoid its being in session during the presidential campaign. The Suez affair made such a maneuver increasingly desirable. Lodge Papers, HCL General Correspondence, box 59, Lodge to Eisenhower, May 5, 1956; PRO, FO 800/739, Washington to Foreign Office, No. 1761, August 29, 1956; Foreign Office to Washington, Nos. 3948 and 3949, August 30, 1956.

7. PRO, FO 800/726, Foreign Office to Washington, No. 4060, September 6, 1956.

8. In his memoirs Eden had this to say about Nasser's resemblance to the dictators of the 1930s: "Nowadays it is considered immoral to recognize an enemy. Some say that Nasser is no Hitler or Mussolini. Allowing for a difference in scale I am not so

sure. He has followed Hitler's pattern, even to concentration camps and the propagation of *Mein Kampf* to his officers. He has understood and used the Goebbels pattern of propaganda in all its lying ruthlessness. Egypt's strategic position increases the threat to others from any aggressive militant dictatorship there" (Eden, *Full Circle*, p. 481).

9. EL, AW, Eisenhower Diaries, box 10, Eisenhower to Churchill, March 19, 1955; PRO, FO 800/740, Foreign Office to Washington, No. 4061, September 6, 1956. The parallel with the Anglo-American position on the Far East did not escape the British, but, as Kirkpatrick wrote Makins, the difference was that "we, rightly or wrongly, believe that if we are denied the resources of Africa and the Middle East, we can be wrecked within a year or two" (PRO, FO 800/740, Kirkpatrick to Makins, September 10, 1956).

10. John Foster Dulles Papers, JFD/DDE, WHM, box 4, Memorandum of Conversation with the President, September 6, 1956. See also *FRUS*, vol. 16., 161:351–52, Dulles Memorandum, September 2, 1956; 170:369–72, State Department to Cairo, No. 640, September 4, 1956.

11. For example, Lloyd informed the Cabinet on August 21 that Dulles had been very dubious about denying the canal dues to Egypt. See PRO, CAB 128/30 CM (56) 60, August 21, 1956.

12. Initially Dulles, pleading the need for secrecy, sought to keep the French in the dark on the SCUA proposals. See *FRUS*, vol. 16, 198:451–55, "Outline of Proposal for a Voluntary Association of Suez Canal Users," September 9, 1956; NA, SD, 974.7301/9-956, Memorandum of Conversation, September 9, 1956.

13. In a report dated September 5, the Watch Committee (composed of senior representatives from the Departments of State, Army, Navy, and Air Force; the Joint Intelligence Committee; the CIA; the Atomic Energy Commission; and the FBI) concluded that while the British and French governments would not take military action as long as the Menzies mission remained in Cairo, they would begin hostilities "if they decide that their objectives are not obtainable within a reasonable time by negotiations or by other non-military means" (*FRUS*, vol. 16, 174:378–81, SC 05194/56, "Conclusions on British-French Intentions to Employ Force Against Egypt," September 5, 1956). See also *FRUS*, vol. 16, 175:382–91, "Probable Repercussions of British-French Military Action in the Suez Canal," SNIE 30-4-56, September 5, 1956; John Foster Dulles Papers, JFD/DDE, WHM, box 4, Memorandum of Conversation with the President, September 8, 1956; NA, SD, 974.7301/9-756, Memorandum of Conversation, September 7, 1956; 974.7301/9-856, Memorandum of Conversation, September 8, 1956; 974.7301/9-956, Memorandum of Conversation, September 9, 1956; 974.7301/9-1256, Memorandum of Conversation, September 12, 1956. Dulles also took time to brief a bipartisan congressional delegation on his scheme. See *FRUS*, vol. 16, 179:396–98, Memorandum of Conversation at the State Department, September 6, 1956.

14. PRO, FO 371/119133, Kirkpatrick Memorandum, September 7, 1956.

15. Ibid., FO 371/119129, Foreign Office to Washington, No. 4126, September 9, 1956; Washington to Foreign Office, Nos. 1844 and 1845, September 9, 1956; FO 371/119130, No. 1851, September 9, 1956; CAB 128/30, CM (56) 59, August 14, 1956; CAB 134/1216, Egypt Committee Minutes, September 9, 1956; FO 371/119128, Beeley, "Suez Canal," August 31, 1956.

16. In April 1956, the State Department legal advisor had told Hoover that because it had long been an international waterway, if the Suez Canal were closed to traffic, under international law the British and Americans would have the right to move in. But Nasser was very careful not to take such a belligerent step. See PRO, FO 371/119060, Washington to Foreign Office, No. 823, April 1, 1956.

17. John Foster Dulles Papers, JFD/DDE, Subject Series, box 11, Eisenhower to Eden, September 8, 1956.

18. NA, SD, 974.7301/9-1056, Memoranda of Conversations, September 10, 1956; Makins to Dulles, September 10, 1956; 974.7301/9-1156, Memoranda of Conversations, September 11, 1956.

19. Aldrich reported to the State Department on September 17 and described the back-bench pressure on Eden. He also said that the embassy had heard that while Butler and Monckton had urged Eden to bring the Suez question to the United Nations, Macmillan had sided with the right wing, hard-line faction of the Tory party. NA, SD, 974.7301/9-1756, London to State Department, No. 1520, September 17, 1956; PRO, FO 371/119129, Foreign Office to Washington, No. 4136, September 10, 1956; James, *Anthony Eden*, p. 514.

20. NA, SD, 974.7301/9-1356, Memorandum of Conversation, September 13, 1956.

21. PRO, FO 800/740, Washington to Foreign Office, Nos. 1892 and 1896, September 11, 1956; John Foster Dulles Papers, JFD/DDE, Telephone Conversations, box 5, telephone call from Dr. Flemming, September 12, 1956; Personal Papers, box 110, State Department Press Release No. 486, September 13, 1956.

22. NA, SD, 974.7301/8-2556, Cairo to State Department, No. 462, August 25, 1956.

23. The British government attempted to ensure that this statement not appear to be an Anglo-French governmental order to the pilots to leave. See PRO, FO 371/119136, Record of a Meeting at the Foreign Office, September 8, 1956.

24. Ibid., FO 371/119130, Washington to Foreign Office, No. 1848, September 8, 1956; FO 800/740, Foreign Office to Washington, No. 4143, September 10, 1956; FO 371/119137, "Record of Conversation between the American Ambassador and the Secretary of State on September 12, 1956"; NA, SD, 974.73-1/9-1156, State Department to Paris, No. 936, September 12, 1956.

25. See, e.g., Monckton Papers, box 7, Wilkinson to Monckton, September 5, 1956.

26. The legal advisor to the State Department had confirmed that a departure of pilots and a consequent blockage of traffic through the canal might suffice as a justification for Western action against Nasser under the Constantinople Convention. Hence the importance placed on this eventuality by the British and French governments (NA, SD, 974.7301/9-1556, "Memorandum on Certain Legal Questions Relating to the Suez Canal," September 15, 1956).

27. The administration believed that congressional authorization was not required for the United States to join SCUA because it was a valid executive action taken under the president's constitutional authority as a means of effectuating rights of the United States under a treaty (the Constantinople Convention) made for its benefit, among others. See NA, SD, Lot file 62 D 11, box 8, Hill to McCardle, October 4, 1956.

28. PRO, FO 371/119193, Foreign Office to Washington, No. 4247, September 14, 1956; Washington to Foreign Office, No. 1948, September 17, 1956.

29. NA, SD, 974.7301/9-1956, London to State Department, No. Dulte 2, September 19, 1956.

30. PRO, FO 371/119177, Eden to Lloyd, September 21, 1956.

31. PRO, PREM 11/1102, Foreign Office to Washington, Nos. 4389 and 4403, September 22, 1956; Washington to Foreign Office, No. 1979, September 22, 1956; FO 371/119178, Foreign Office to UKDEL, New York, No. 876, September 22, 1956; Washington to Foreign Office, Nos. 1974 and 1975, September 22, 1956.

32. Under its Articles of Agreement the IMF is permitted to make two kinds of credit arrangements. A "drawing" is an actual loan as opposed to a "stand-by" arrangement, which represents an unconditional promise of the fund to make dollars (or a similarly strong currency) available to a country against payment in its own currency at a future time should the country so request it. A country is permitted four tranches, the amount of which is linked to the amount of its subscription to the IMF. During the 1950s the first or so-called gold tranche was virtually automatic under fund rules while further drawdowns were not. Until the Suez crisis little use of the fund's borrowing facilities had been made.

33. PRO, T 236/4188, Brook to Bridges, August 11, 1956; B/E, G 1/124, Governor's Note, August 15, 1956.

34. The budgetary cost of precautionary measures for August and September 1956 was estimated at £11.9 million. See PRO, PREM 11/1135, "The Egypt Crisis and the British Economy," August 27, 1956.

35. PRO, T 231/716, Foreign Office to Rangoon, No. 308, August 24, 1956; FO 371/120796, "The Egypt Crisis and the British Economy," August 27, 1956.

36. The American estimates ranged up to $1,000 million.

37. For example, West Germany was flush with reserves and would have had no problem paying for dollar denominated supplies of oil.

38. See B/E, G 1/99, Jebb to Lloyd, June 26, 1956; Rowan to Cobbold, June 28, 1956; Cobbold to Rowan, June 29, 1956.

39. The MEEC was composed of fifteen representatives from oil companies, including the five American "majors," four of their subsidiaries, and three other companies. All participants were given antitrust immunity.

40. See, e.g., EL, WHC, Confidential Files, Subject Series, box 82, Vaughan to Toner, September 10, 1956; PRO, T 236/4841, Washington to Ministry of Fuel and Power No. 39 ELFU, August 11, 1956; Washington to Ministry of Fuel and Power, No. 41F, August 13, 1956; Ministry of Fuel and Power to Washington, Nos. 36 and 37 Fuel, August 14, 1956; FO 371/119260, Washington to Foreign Office, No. 1693, August 10, 1956; Washington to Foreign Office, No. 1713, August 15, 1956; Washington to Foreign Office, No. 1842, September 10, 1956; Washington to Foreign Office, No. 1894, September 11, 1956; Foreign Office to Washington, No. 4224, September 13, 1956.

41. See, e.g., PRO, FO 371/120796, Washington to Foreign Office, No. 1934, September 14, 1956; T 230/302, "U.S. Aid and Suez," September 14, 1956; NA, SD, 841.10/9-1456, Burgess to Dulles, September 14, 1956.

42. NA, SD, 974.7301/9-1456, London to State Department, No. 1477, September 14, 1956.

43. B/E, OV 31/55, Rowan to Macmillan, September 12, 1956; PRO, T 230/302, "Note of a Meeting held on 12 noon on Monday, 17 September 1956"; T 234/78, "The Oil Operation: U.S. Aid," September 19, 1956.

44. PRO, T 236/4188, Rowan to Macmillan, September 20, 1956.

45. Eden had told Dulles on September 20 that while a military action might be costly, it would be better for Britain in the long run than a protracted crisis. Eden undoubtedly based his conclusion on Macmillan's Cabinet statement of September 12: "This [bringing the issue to a head] was of great importance from the point of view of the national economy. If we could achieve a quick and satisfactory settlement of this issue, confidence in sterling would be restored; but, if a settlement was long delayed, the cost and the uncertainty would undermine our financial position." However, Eden also reassured Dulles that for the time being, Britain could hold its military operation in abeyance without undue expense. See PRO, CAB 128/30, CM 64 (56), September 12, 1956; John Foster Dulles Papers, JFD/DDE, Subject Series, box 11, Dulles Memorandum of Conversation with Sir Anthony Eden, September 21, 1956.

46. Macmillan, *Riding the Storm*, pp. 133–35. See also Horne, *Macmillan, 1894–1956*, pp. 418–25.

47. In a letter written to Eden on September 26, Macmillan could be no more definite than to say that his "feeling" was that Eisenhower was determined "to bring Nasser down" (PRO, FO 800/740, Washington to Foreign Office, No. 2004, September 25, 1957; PREM 11/1102, Macmillan to Eden, September 26, 1956).

48. Dulles told Makins in May 1955 that on the subject of a four-power summit, "we were deeply torn between two points of view. The first was our very great desire to help Sir Anthony under the existing circumstances. Second, the proposal itself was against our better judgment" (NA, SD 611.41/5-655, Memorandum of Conversation, May 6, 1955).

49. Eisenhower also commented that "Macmillan was far more reasonable on the Suez business than he had expected" (EL, AW, Eisenhower Diaries, box 8, September 25, 1956, telephone calls, September 25, 1956).

50. PRO, PREM 11/1102, Washington to Foreign Office, Nos. 2001 and 2002, September 25, 1956; FO 800/740, Washington to Foreign Office, No. 2003, September 25, 1956; NA, SD, 974.7301/9-2556, Memorandum of Conversation, September 25, 1956.

51. According to Macmillan's memoirs, "Dulles went on to talk about different methods of getting rid of Nasser. He thought that the new SCUA plan might prove successful. But of course it would take six months." The American account of the meeting is quite different in tone: Dulles "questioned whether we should embark on such a problematic course [as rerouting ships] and thought that other means of deflating Nasser should be explored. Nasser is now facing a difficult economic situation due to the loss of trade and tourists and further action might be taken to accentuate this situation." No one reading this account would take Dulles's words as suggesting covert action. See Macmillan, *Riding the Storm*, p. 136; NA, SD, 974.7301/9-2556, Memorandum of Conversation, September 25, 1956.

52. See PRO, FO 800/740, Washington to Foreign Office, No. 1942, September 17, 1956, where Makins writes that "it remains true that the great Republican trump card, which the Democrats do not yet know how to overtrump, is peace. So, although the President and Dulles have been careful not to exclude the possibility that force may have to be used, there is in my judgement no prospect as the international outlook appears today, that the United States will themselves participate in military action before November 6."

53. A comparison of the totally different way Macmillan presented this meeting in the fourth volume of his memoirs, *Riding the Storm*, pp. 135–37, is instructive. The message from Dulles that Macmillan conveyed contemporaneously is absent from Macmillan's retrospective account. See also *FRUS*, vol. 16, 265:580–81, Memorandum of Conversation at the State Department, September 25, 1956.

54. PRO, PREM 11/1102, Macmillan, "Note of a Private Talk with Mr. Dulles," September 25, 1956. The American version of the private discussion held by Dulles and Macmillan emphasizes to an even greater degree the cautious and cautioning American attitude. According to a memorandum written by the secretary of state when Macmillan said that he hoped that the president would certainly be reelected, Dulles replied, "I said that I hoped that nothing drastic would happen through British action which might diminish our chances. Macmillan said he recalled that we had been helpful in their election situation and he would bear that in mind. I said I felt that there was a basis for some reciprocity and he said he quite agreed." As to how to deal with Nasser, Dulles recorded, "We discussed the plans for diminishing Nasser's prestige and I expressed the view that this could be done by economic and political means more effectively than by military means." Finally, Macmillan, reiterating Eden's comment of September 20, heartened the secretary by stating that "the present military situation was such that they could without expense hold action in abeyance" (*FRUS*, vol. 16, 265:581, "Memorandum of a Conversation Between Secretary of State Dulles and Chancellor of the Exchequer Macmillan, Department of State, Washington, September 25, 1956").

55. The waiver provisions are contained in Appendix A.

56. PRO, FO 371/120796, Laskey, "Anglo-American Loan Agreement: The Waiver," April 19, 1956.

57. The amounts due and payable as principal and interest under the U.S. Agreement and companion Canadian credit not only changed from year to year but differed in various official and unofficial reports. This study uses what appear to be the most reliable numbers, culled from the figures supplied by the State Department and the FRBNY. See NA, SD 841.10/12-556, Ottawa to State Department, No. 445, December 5, 1956; FRBNY, C261 Bank of England, Roche Memorandum to Files, January 3, 1957; C261 British Government, Clarke to Exter, January 4, 1957.

58. See, e.g., PRO, FO 371/120796, "Alternative Approach to the Question of the Waiver in the U.S. and Canadian Loan Agreements," September 5, 1956.

59. Ibid., FO 371/120342, Makins to Kirkpatrick, September 30, 1956.

60. See, e.g., PRO, T 236/4188, Bridges to Macmillan, September 7, 1956: "As regards the hypotheses, the first would be that we were acting in accordance with United Nations wishes, and most importantly with overt U.S. and Commonwealth support, and support from a good number of other countries. At the other extreme would be the possibility that we would be acting with the French and perhaps with one or two others, but that the U.S. was not overtly supporting us." Bridges did state that without American support the strains, at the worst, might be such that the Treasury and the Bank of England could not maintain the value of the pound. But then he hedged again, stating that "the factors are so imprecise that it is impossible to make precise plans in advance." This assessment remains the most apocalyptic Treasury paper.

There is one memorandum in the PRO entitled "Planning for War with Egypt" that professes to examine the possibility of American aid on two assumptions: "(a) American participation in war, and therefore her co-operation, and (b) American non-participation, and therefore her non co-operation." However, the paper only dealt with American commodity aid to Britain, not the financial aspects, which were far more important. See T 234/129, Symons to France, October 4, 1956.

61. Thomas, *Suez*, p. 88.

62. Horne, *Macmillan, 1984–1956*, pp. 424–25.

63. It is difficult to be certain of Macmillan's motives without access to his papers. But his long-standing rivalry with Eden suggests that he may have had good reasons for not keeping the prime minister fully informed of American reservations. Eden had been under attack since the spring of 1956. If the Suez crisis ended badly for Britain, his chances of remaining prime minister were virtually nil. (For example, Eden's press secretary William Clark had noted in his diary that "if Nasser does get away with it—in fact if Nasser is still dictator of Egypt next year—the Eden government is doomed.") As Macmillan was one of two possible successors, he had a strong motive to ignore and underestimate American opposition to a Suez invasion. If this was his strategy, it worked quite well though at great cost to his country. See Clark Papers, Clark Diary, box 7, August 7, 1956.

64. During the spring of 1956 Israeli diplomats had discussed with Canadian counterparts obtaining F-86 jets manufactured in Canada under American license. The Canadian government initially expressed reluctance to approve this transaction, but in July the State Department decided to intervene and offered to supply other military equipment to Canada if the Canadian government allowed the Israeli government to purchase twelve F-86s. During the autumn the order was increased to twenty-four airplanes. See *FRUS*, vol. 15, 227:426, Memorandum of Conversation at Dulles's Residence, March 28, 1956; 487:881–82, Ottawa to State Department, July 23, 1956; 488:881–82, Ottawa to State Department, July 23, 1956; 492:886–87, Allen to Dulles, July 24, 1956; *FRUS*, vol. 16, 204:465–69, Memorandum of Conversation at the State Department, September 10, 1956. See also Mordechai Bar-On, "David Ben Gurion and the Sevres Collusion," in Louis and Owen, *Suez 1956*.

65. Selwyn Ilan Troen, ed., "Ben-Gurion's Diary," in Troen and Shemesh, *Suez-Sinai Crisis*, pp. 299–300.

66. DD, 1978-339C, CIA Briefing, September 27, 1956.

67. Dulles told senators on September 27 that the influential Macmillan and Lord Salisbury were in favor of force, that the majority of the Cabinet opposed military action, and that Eden occupied the middle ground. He told Senate Majority Leader Lyndon Johnson on October 4 that "we don't know what the British and French are up to—they are not very forthgiving in keeping us informed" (John Foster Dulles Papers, JFD/DDE, Subject Series, box 7, "The Secretary's Briefing on the Suez Situation with Members of Senate Foreign Relations Committee," September 27, 1956; Telephone Conversations, box 5, telephone call to Johnson, October 4, 1956).

68. Ibid., JFD/DDE, Telephone Conversations, box 5, telephone call from Lodge, October 2, 1956; WHM, box 4, Memorandum of Conversation with the President, October 2, 1956.

69. Clark Papers, box 7, Clark Diary, October 2, 1956; PRO, PREM 11/1174, Washington to Foreign Office, October 3, 1956. Eden devoted three pages of his memoirs to this incident. See Eden, *Full Circle*, pp. 557–59.

70. In spite of the British reaction, Dulles's comment garnered newspaper support for the administration and also ignited a favorable response in the underdeveloped world. See, e.g., H. Alexander Smith Papers, box 126, "Colonialism and Mr. Dulles" by Marguerite Higgins in the *New York Herald Tribune*, October 8, 1956.

71. DD, 1982-000958, Dulles to Dillon and Aldrich, Nos. 1261 and 2465, October 5, 1956.

72. PRO, PREM 11/1176, Foreign Office to Washington, No. 3984, September 1, 1956.

73. See, e.g., DD, 1987-1480, London to Secretary of State, No. 1249, September 1, 1956; DD, 1982-959, London to Secretary of State, No. 1932, October 9, 1956; DD, 1987-2764, Paris to Secretary of State, No. 1408, September 24, 1956; DD, 1987-1483, Paris to Secretary of State, No. 1649, October 6, 1956.

74. DD, 1978-9D, Special National Intelligence Estimate Number 30-5-56, September 19, 1956.

75. British and French leaders entirely reciprocated Dulles's sentiments, stating repeatedly that they did not understand what Dulles wanted. For example, Mollet told General Al Gruenther toward the end of October that "even now I do not know what Secretary Dulles really wants" (John Foster Dulles Papers, G, C & M, box 2, Gruenther to Dulles, October 29, 1956).

76. PRO, FO 371/120313, Washington to Foreign Office, No. 575 Saving, August 11, 1956; NA, SD, 974.7301/8-1756, State Department to London, No. 19, August 17, 1956; 974.7301/8-2856, State Department to London, No. 36, August 20, 1956; 974.7301/8-2156, State Department to London, No. 43, August 21, 1956; 974.7301/8-2256, State Department to London, No. 44, August 22, 1956; 974.7301/8-2356, State Department to London, No. 48, August 23, 1956; 974.7301/9-1956, State Department to London, No. 17, September 19, 1956; 974.7301/9-2056, State Department to London, No. 24, September 20, 1956.

77. Part of the gap resulted from the fact that Makins's replacement, Sir Harold Caccia, by his own request traveled to Washington by sea.

78. PRO, FO 371/120329, Makins to Eden, October 5, 1956.

79. Dulles's persistent harping on this point brought Eden to cable a rejoinder to Makins stressing that "he [Dulles] has clearly got his facts mixed" (PRO, PREM, 11/1102, Foreign Office to Washington, No. 4539, October 1, 1956).

80. Ibid., PREM 11/1102, UKDEL to Foreign Office, No. 785, October 5, 1956.

81. As Eden cabled Lloyd on October 8: "When I read the record of your conversation with Dulles and Pineau on October 5 it made me fear more than ever that our position is being eroded. . . . We have been misled so often by Dulles' ideas that we cannot afford to risk another misunderstanding" (PRO, FO 800/741, Foreign Office to New York, No. 1078).

82. In fact McCloy had mentioned to a British official several days earlier the possibility of using the World Bank to internationalize the canal. See PRO, FO 371/119155, Rundall to Chancery, September 27, 1956. Black followed up these contacts, meeting with Egyptian Foreign Minister Mohammed Fawzi in October. See EL, AW, International Series, box 43, Suez Summary, October 26, 1956; PRO, FO 371/119155, Washington to Foreign Office, No. 2123, October 15, 1956; FO 371/110158, Washington to Foreign Office, No. 2170, October 23, 1956.

83. EL, AW, Eisenhower Diaries, box 19, Memorandum dated October 8, 1956, of Conference with the President, October 6, 1956.

84. John Foster Dulles Papers, JFD/DDE, WHM, box 3, Eisenhower to Hoover, October 8, 1956.

85. NA, SD, 974.7301/9-2456, Memorandum of Conversation, September 24, 1956; 974.7301/10-256, Memorandum of Conversation, October 2, 1956; 974.7301/10-556, Memorandum of Conversation, October 5, 1956; 974.7301/10-1156, Memorandum of Conversation, October 11, 1956; 974.7301/10-1256, Memorandum of Conversation, October 12, 1956; John Foster Dulles Papers, JFD/DDE, Telephone Conversations, box 5, telephone call from Baruch, September 24, 1956; EL, AW, International Series, box 43, Suez Summaries, October 4, 9, and 25, 1956.

John J. McCloy (1895–1989) was one of the most influential members of the American establishment. Having graduated Amherst College and Harvard Law School, he began his legal practice at the prestigious Wall Street firm of Cravath Henderson & de Gerstorff (now Cravath Swaine & Moore). While working on the "Black Tom" case, he met former secretary of state Henry Stimson. When Stimson became secretary of war in 1940, McCloy moved to Washington as well, becoming assistant secretary of war. In 1947 he became president of the World Bank and then, two years later, the first civilian high commissioner of West Germany. During the 1950s McCloy headed the Chase National Bank and then became senior partner of the Wall Street firm of Milbank Tweed Hadley & McCloy, a position McCloy retained well into his eighties. During the 1960s and 1970s McCloy's most important action was to form, coordinate, and keep on the right side of the antitrust laws the "McCloy group," a forum for regular meetings of the major multinational oil companies. Given the serious nature of the canal blockage, McCloy seemed the natural choice to take charge of the sensitive task of coordinating its clearance. McCloy insisted on serving without compensation.

86. The Soviet Union vetoed the second half of the resolution, which stated that these principles were embodied in SCUA and in the proceedings of the London Conference.

87. According to Dillon the French public wholeheartedly supported its government's hard-line approach. See NA, SD, 974.7301/10-656, Paris to State Department, No. 1649, October 6, 1956.

88. John Foster Dulles papers, JFD/DDE, Telephone Conversations, box 5, telephone call from Ambassador Lodge, October 11, 1956; EL, AW, International Series, box 43, Suez Summaries, October 12, 1956; AW, NSC Series, box 8, "Discussion at the 300th Meeting of the National Security Council, October 12, 1956"; PRO, FO 800/728, Lloyd, Memorandum re Pineau and Dulles in New York, October 15, 1956.

89. John Foster Dulles Papers, JFD/DDE, Telephone Conversations, box 5, telephone call with Lodge, October 17, 1956.

90. See, e.g., EL, AW, International Series, box 43, Suez Summaries, October 15 and 19, 1956; PRO, PREM 11/1121, UKDEL to Foreign Office, No. 847, October 13, 1956; T 236/4626, UKDEL to Foreign Office, No. 882, October 18, 1956; FO 371/119203, UKDEL to Foreign Office, No. 846, October 13, 1956; FO 371/119205, Dulles to Lloyd, October 15, 1956; FO 371/119206, Lloyd to Dulles, October 20, 1956; NA, SD, 974.7301/10-1656, Memorandum of Conversation, October 16, 1956;

974.7301/10-1756, State Department to London, No. 2170, October 17, 1956; 974.7301/10-1956, London to State Department, No. 2170, October 19, 1956.

91. John Foster Dulles Papers, WHM, box 4, Memorandum of Conversation with the President, October 21, 1956.

92. As it were they rose $52 million to $2,328 million. *Financial Times*, October 3, 1956, p. 1. Permission to sell Trinidad Leasehold, a private company, had been granted by the British government in the beginning of 1956 and was not undertaken in response to the crisis. Because British residents were not permitted to hold dollars, the sale of this company to American interests meant that the Treasury received the dollars while Trinidad's owners were given nontransferable sterling.

93. PRO, T 236/4188, Hall to Bridges, October 2, 1956; Rickett to Rowan, October 4, 1956; B/E, OV 38/50, Note of Conversation with Rowan and Rickett, October 24, 1956.

94. PRO, T 236/4188, Cobbold to Macmillan, October 17, 1956.

95. Ibid., T 236/4188, Rowan to Makins, October 26, 1956.

96. For example, senior Treasury official R. W. B. Clark sent Rickett a memorandum on October 15 entitled "Planning for War with Egypt," which began, "I think that what all this means is that if we get into a situation in which we need aid (with the Americans prepared in principle to give it) there will have to be fresh [American] legislation" (PRO, T 234/129).

97. EL, AW, Eisenhower Diaries, Staff Notes, No. 25, October 2, 1956; FRBNY, C260.2, Davis to Files, October 17, 1956.

98. B/E, OV 31/55, Arnold to Atkins, Chairman, Foreign Exchange Committee, October 29, 1956.

99. See PRO, FO 371/120822, "International Monetary Fund—Egypt," September 14, 1956; B/E, "Suez: IMF Drawing," September 14, 1956; NA, TD, NAC, box 3, Minutes of National Advisory Council Meeting No. 250, September 13, 1956.

100. French problems stemmed from growing inflationary pressure on the economy, primarily as a result of high domestic demand to which growing military outlays on Algeria, high fixed investment, and rising labor costs all contributed. France also suffered from the effects of the rapid decline in American aid that followed the Indochina Settlement of 1954. See B/E, OV 46/21, "Review of French Economic Position, 1956"; OV 45/45, "The French Economy: Periodical Report No. 1, July 1957"; NA, TD, NAC, National Advisory Council Document No. 1999, October 10, 1956.

101. *Tranche* is a financial term referring to a portion of a loan.

102. The standby credit ran for one year, from October 17, 1956, until October 16, 1957. See, e.g., NA, TD, National Advisory Council Document No. 1999, October 10, 1956; National Advisory Council Document No. 88, October 17, 1956; PRO, T 236/4188, Allen to France, October 19, 1956.

103. NA, SD, 974.7301/10-1956, London to State Department, No. 2170, October 19, 1956.

104. Ibid., State Department to Paris and London, No. 1448, October 22, 1956.

105. PRO, CAB 128/30, CM (56)71, October 18, 1956; FO 371/119158, CRO to Canada et al., No. 330, October 22, 1956; John Foster Dulles Papers, JFD/DDE, Telephone Conversations, box 5, telephone calls with Lodge, October 23 and 24, 1956; WHM, box 4, Memorandum of Conversation with the President, October 24, 1956.

106. On October 15 Eisenhower told Dulles to make it very clear to the Israelis that they must halt all border raids against Jordan. Among other things, the president declared: "Our position in this matter could not and should not be influenced by domestic political considerations. . . . He would not under any circumstances permit the fact of the forthcoming elections to influence his judgment" (*FRUS*, vol. 16, 344:722–74, "Memorandum of Conversation in Washington," October 15, 1956). See also EL, White House Office, Office of Staff Secretary, Security Series, Alpha 7, CIA impression of Israel-Jordan affair, October 11, 1956; Eisenhower Diaries, box 9, Memorandum for the Record, October 15, 1956; Thomas, *Suez*, pp. 103–4.

107. John Foster Dulles Papers, JFD/DDE, Telephone Conversations, box 5, telephone call to Lodge, October 24, 1956.

CHAPTER SIX

1. James, *Anthony Eden*, pp. 527–32.

2. NA, SD, 974.7301/9-2456, Paris to State Department, No. 1387, September 24, 1956; 974.7301/9-2256; Paris to State Department, No. 1413, September 25, 1956; 974.7301/9-2956, Paris to State Department, No. 1516, September 29, 1956; 974.7301/10-356, Paris to State Department, No. 1586, October 3, 1956.

3. The meeting was held at the villa of the Bonnier de la Chappelle family, the scion of which had assassinated Admiral Darlan in 1942.

4. See Mordechai Bar-On, "David Ben Gurion and the Sevres Collusion," in Louis and Owen, *Suez 1956*; Dayan, *Story of My Life*, pp. 183–234; James, *Anthony Eden*, pp. 528–32; Logan Papers, Logan reminiscences; Teveth, *Moshe Dayan*, pp. 253–57.

5. PRO, CAB 128/30, CM (56) 74, October 25, 1956; James, *Anthony Eden*, pp. 534–36. It should be noted that the minutes of British Cabinet meetings are entitled "Conclusions." Their specificity varies greatly. Sometimes speakers are identified; other times they are not, and the passive voice is used. On this particular occasion the phrase used to introduce the objections to the Suez invasion was *doubts were expressed on the following grounds*.

6. Eden, *Full Circle*, pp. 575–600; Selwyn Lloyd, in his book *Suez: 1956*, pp. 167–94, does discuss the Sevres meeting and the Anglo-French-Israeli discussions but downplays the British role.

7. PRO, PREM 11/2653, Sir Norman Brook to Macmillan, March 5, 1959.

8. Another example of the British attitude toward Israel is found in a cable from Aldrich to the State Department. There Aldrich details the Foreign Office concern that Dulles's draft for SCUA would allow Israel to become a member, something that Foreign Office official Sir Harold Beeley insisted must be avoided at all costs. NA, SD, 974.7301/10-256, London to State Department, No. 1809, October 2, 1956; Logan Papers, Logan comments, January 1988.

9. *FRUS*, vol. 16, 379:785, Tel Aviv to State Department, No. 415, October 26, 1956; EL, AW, International Series, box 29, Eisenhower to Ben-Gurion, October 27, 1956; Eisenhower Diaries, box 18, Telephone Calls, October 28 and 29, 1956; box 19, Memorandum of Conference with the President, October 27, 1956. On October 28 the Watch Committee had summarized the significant amount of evidence that

indicated the possibility of an Israeli attack on Egypt without, however, concluding that an attack was imminent. See *FRUS*, vol. 16, 392:799–800, "Memorandum from the Director of the National Indications Center to the Intelligence Advisory Committee," October 28, 1956.

10. To Dillon, Dulles cabled: "Bits of evidence are accumulating which indicate that French government, perhaps with British knowledge, is concerting closely with Israelis to provoke action which would lead to Israeli war against Egypt with probable participation by French and British." NA, SD, 684A.86/10-2956, State Department to Paris, No. 1537, October 29, 1956; John Foster Dulles Papers, JFD/DDE, Telephone Conversations, box 5, telephone call from Senator Knowland, October 29, 1956.

11. Dulles told the White House meeting of October 30 that "the British were practically in agreement with Egypt on a resolution of the Suez dispute at the recent UN meeting, but have been delaying any solution since then." (*FRUS*, vol. 16, 419:851, Memorandum of Conference at the White House, October 30, 1956).

12. EL, AW, Eisenhower Diaries, box 20, Eisenhower to Hazlett, November 2, 1956.

13. While Stevenson tried to use the Middle Eastern and Hungarian crises to give his campaign a much needed lift, it was Eisenhower who benefited from these international events. See *New York Times*, November 4, 1956, p. 3.

14. Makins later said that Eisenhower particularly hated having the Suez scheme concealed from him by Britain. Chaban-Delmas's comments to Dillon on October 19 and his clean breast of matters to Dillon on November 2 as well as lower expectations protected the French from the same accusation. While Dulles cabled Aldrich on October 26 complaining that Britain was deliberately keeping the United States in the dark concerning its Middle Eastern intentions, the administration never suspected British-Israeli collusion. See *FRUS*, vol. 16, 384:790, State Department to London, No. 3009, October 26, 1956; Horne, *Macmillan, 1894–1956*, p. 439; EL, AW, Eisenhower Diaries, box 19, Phone Calls, November 2, 1956, Dulles to Rountree.

15. EL, AW, Eisenhower Diaries, box 20, Eisenhower to Gruenther, November 23, 1953.

16. Dulles had told Lodge during the afternoon of October 29 that part of the motivation for going to the Security Council was to "smoke them [the British and French] out to see where they stand" (John Foster Dulles Papers, JFD/DDE, Telephone Conversations, box 5, October 29, 1956).

17. Ibid., WHM, box 4, Memorandum of Conference with the President, October 29, 1956.

18. From the middle of October the British Cabinet had imposed a news blackout concerning Musketeer. Consequently the invasion came as a surprise to most of the Foreign Office, British diplomats abroad, and Commonwealth countries as well as the United States government.

19. PRO, FO 800/741, Washington to Foreign Office, No. 2200, October 29, 1956; EL, AW, Eisenhower Diaries, box 19, Memorandum of Conference with the President, October 29, 1956.

20. EL, AW, Eisenhower Diaries, box 18, Telephone Calls, October 30, 1956.

21. NA, SD, 974.7301/10-1956, Paris to State Department, No. 1839, October 19, 1956.

22. EL, AW, International Series, box 19, State Department to London, Nos. 3081 and 3083, October 30, 1956.

23. PRO, FO 800/741, Foreign Office to Washington, No. 5010, October 30, 1956.

24. Ibid., No. 5025, October 30, 1956.

25. EL, AW, Eisenhower Diaries, box 19, Memorandum of Conference with the President, October 30, 1956.

26. Ibid.

27. EL, WHC, Confidential Files, Subject Series, box 82, Vaughan to Toner, October 30, 1956.

28. NA, SD, Lot File 62 D 11, box 6, Hollister to Dulles, October 31, 1956.

29. PRO, FO 800/741, Washington to Foreign Office, Nos. 2205 and 2206, October 30, 1956.

30. This occasion marked the first British use of the veto. After learning of the Anglo-French ultimatum, Dulles told French Ambassador to the United States Herve Alphand that "he felt that this was the blackest day which had occurred in many years in the relations between England and France and the United States. He asked how the former relationship of trust and confidence could possibly be restored in view of these developments." See *FRUS*, vol. 16, 431:867–68, Memorandum of Conversation at the State Department, October 30, 1956.

31. John Foster Dulles Papers, JFD/DDE, Telephone Conversations, box 5, telephone call from the vice-president in Detroit, October 31, 1956.

32. For example, at the National Security Council meeting of November 1, 1956, Dulles stated that "unless we now assert and maintain this leadership [of the third world], all of these newly independent countries will turn from us to the USSR. . . . In short, the United States would survive or go down on the basis of the fate of colonialism if the United States supports the French and the British on the colonial issue" (EL, AW, NSC Series, box 8, "Discussion at the 302nd Meeting of the National Security Council").

33. Ibid., Eisenhower Diaries, box 4, Eisenhower to Churchill, July 22, 1954.

34. PRO, FO 371/121270, Dixon to Schuckburgh, January 6, 1956.

35. NA, SD, 974.7301/9-3056, Lodge to State Department, No. 273, September 30, 1956; EL, AW, Eisenhower Diaries, box 18, Phone Calls, October 31, 1956.

36. John Foster Dulles Papers, Personal Papers, box 102, Press Release No. 566, November 2, 1956.

37. Lester Pearson (1897–1972) was born in Ontario, Canada. He served with Canadian forces in Salonika during the First World War and then attended both Toronto University and Oxford. He rose rapidly in the Canadian diplomatic service and then became deputy minister to Foreign Secretary Louis St. Laurent. The two men became very close, and when St. Laurent became prime minister and Liberal party leader in 1948, Pearson succeeded him as minister of external affairs. This position totally suited Pearson. The Suez crisis revealed his talents, and for his quiet diplomacy he received the Nobel peace prize. When the Conservatives returned to office in 1957, "Mike" Pearson became leader of the opposition for the next five years. From 1963 to 1968 he served as prime minister and had the dubious distinction of leading the first Ottawa government to deal with the Quebec separatist movement, which had just begun to gather steam.

38. On October 30 Pearson told Dulles that the Suez invasion was "stupid" and that "he did not see what they [the British] are going to make of it" (John Foster

Dulles Papers, JFD/DDE, Telephone Conversations, box 5, telephone call to Pearson, October 30, 1956).

39. Ibid., telephone call to Lodge, November 2, 1956.

40. At this point the administration concentrated its ire on the British and French in part because officials felt that Israel was being used by the British and French governments. See, e.g., telephone call to Ambassador Lodge, October 30, 1956.

41. Ibid., telephone call to Secretary Weeks, telephone call to Allen Dulles, November 1, 1956.

42. PRO, FO 371/120832, Foreign Office to Washington, Nos. 5052 and 5053, October 31, 1956; Washington to Foreign Office, No. 2218, October 31, 1956.

43. B/E, G 1/124, C. Hamilton, "Israel/Egypt, October 30, 1956."

44. *New York Times* correspondent Osgood Caruthers reported on November 4 that although clearly under siege, Cairo was remarkably calm. Caruthers partly attributed this atmosphere to "the excellent control the Nasser Government is able to exercise over the actions and even the emotions of the Egyptian masses, which less than five years ago sacked and burned Cairo in desperate anti-foreign riots" (November 4, 1956, sec. 4, p. 5).

45. NA, SD, 641.74/10-3156, Cairo to State Department, No. 1240, October 31, 1956; 641.74/11-356, Cairo to State Department, No. 1308, November 3, 1956; 974.7301/11-256, Port Said to State Department, No. 96, November 2, 1956; Nutting, *Nasser*, pp. 170–78.

46. B/E, G 1/124, Governor's Note, October 31, 1956.

47. Sir Walter Monckton had resigned as minister of defense on October 18 because of his opposition to Eden's belligerent policy. However, to avoid a public break he had agreed to stay in the Cabinet as paymaster general.

48. PRO, PREM 11/1093, Powell to Minister, November 1, 1956.

49. Even this minor modification troubled the British naval task force commander who feared that if bad weather came, the naval armada could not reach Egypt on November 6. Thomas, *Suez*, p. 137.

50. Dag Hammarskjöld (1901–61), second secretary general of the United Nations, served in that position from 1953 until his death in 1961. Hammarskjöld inspired great respect, especially in the hearts of Americans enamored of the United Nations, but many found him difficult to deal with. British Ambassador to the United Nations Sir Pierson Dixon described Hammarskjöld as "a very obstinate creature with a unique gift for combining high moral principles with an obscurity of thought and expression which makes it almost impossible to understand what he is saying. The result . . . is a constant series of misunderstandings" (PRO, FO 371/119189, Dixon to Kirkpatrick, December 22, 1956). Ben-Gurion labeled him "our number 1 enemy after Russia" (Selwyn Ilan Troen, ed., "Ben-Gurion's Diary," in Troen and Shemesh, *Suez-Sinai Crisis*, p. 321).

51. EL, AW, Eisenhower Diaries, box 19, Memorandum, dated November 5, 1956, concerning Conference with the President November 4, 1956.

52. Ibid., box 20, Eisenhower to Gruenther, November 2, 1956.

53. British newspaper opinion reflected these divisions. The *Economist* castigated the Eden government for joining a scheme which at best would "produce a local victory and ultimate defeat" (November 3, p. 429). The *Manchester Guardian* took an even dimmer view; its editorial on November 2 predicted that "our action will

leave a legacy all over the world which temporary success can never obliterate" (p. 6). By contrast, the *Daily Telegraph* justified the Suez invasion on the grounds that it served to protect both the West in general and Britain in particular (p. 6). See also Epstein, *British Politics in the Suez Crisis*, and Thomas, *Suez*, pp. 132–33.

54. PRO, PREM 11/1090, Mountbatten to Eden, November 2, 1956.

55. Paul Gore Booth Papers, Bodleian Library, Oxford University, Oxford, England, Booth to Dean and Kirkpatrick, November 2, 1956.

56. PRO, FO 371/747, Fitzmaurice to Kirkpatrick, November 5, 1956.

57. NA, SD, 641.74/1-156, London to State Department, No. 2428, November 1, 1956.

58. PRO, CAB 134/1216, Cabinet Egypt Committee, Confidential Annex E.C. (56) 40th Meeting Minutes, November 4, 1956. Anglo-French airborne troops landed on November 5; the naval flotilla arrived the next day.

59. PRO, FO 800/726, Foreign Office to Washington, No. 5181, November 5, 1956.

60. John Foster Dulles Papers, JFD/DDE, WHM, box 4, Memorandum of Conference with the President, November 5, 1956.

61. On November 2 Hoover had told Eisenhower that the State Department had received messages of support from the prime ministers of India, Ceylon, and Libya. EL, AW, Eisenhower Diaries, box 19, Phone Calls, November 2, 1956; PRO, CAB 134/815, D.T.C. (56), November 5, 1956.

62. A National Intelligence Estimate of November 6 discounted a Soviet threat to London and Paris because such an attack would almost certainly precipitate a general war but did not foreclose the possibility of small-scale attacks on Anglo-French forces in the Mediterranean. See *FRUS*, vol. 16, 521:1018–20, SNIE 11-9-56, "Sino-Soviet Intentions in the Suez Crisis," November 6, 1956; 529:1030–32, "Summary of Meeting Held in the Department of State," November 6, 1956. See also PRO, FO 800/747, Moscow to Foreign Office, No. 1563, November 6, 1956.

63. B/E, G 1/114, Rickett, "Emergency Action," November 2, 1956.

64. Horne, *Macmillan, 1894–1956*, p. 440.

65. Macmillan, *Riding the Storm*, p. 164.

66. Eden stated in his memoirs that "a run on the pound, at a speed which threatened disaster to our whole economic position had developed in the world's financial markets" and presented a worse danger to Britain than did Soviet threats (*Full Circle*, p. 622). In his biography of Butler, Anthony Howard states that the Cabinet accepted the bitter pill of a cease-fire after Macmillan announced the loss of $270 million (£95 million) (*RAB*, p. 237). See also Horne, *Macmillan, 1894–1956*, (who quotes both Macmillan and Lord Head) pp. 440–43; James, *Anthony Eden*, pp. 573–75; Lloyd, *Suez: 1956*, pp. 210–11.

While the Cabinet minutes of November 6 do not discuss this subject, the omission proves nothing because Cabinet minutes do not purport to be a full record of proceedings. There are two references to financial matters in the November 6 Cabinet minutes. The first is Lloyd's statement: "It was equally important that we should shape our policy in such a way as to enlist the maximum sympathy and support from the United States Government." The second is a point made during discussion to the effect that if the Anglo-French occupation of the canal continued, the United Nations might impose "collective measures, including oil sanctions, against the French and ourselves" (PRO, CAB 128/30, CM 80 [56], November 6, 1956).

67. PRO, T 236/4189, "Note of a Meeting at 11 Downing Street on Wednesday, 7 November 1956."

68. Ibid., Makins to Macmillan, November 16, 1956; CAB 128/30, CM 85 (56), November 20, 1956. As of November 24, the reserve loss of the month to date was $232 million (PRO, T 236/4309, "Gold and Dollar and EPU Position: Report for the week ending 24 November 1956"). On November 29 Macmillan told the Cabinet that "in November, the final net loss which would be announced was likely to be about $270 millions" (CAB 128/30, CM 91 (56) November 29, 1956).

69. This is also true about comments in the press; for example, the *Times* editorial of November 6 was very sanguine about the performance of sterling.

70. Macmillan, *Riding the Storm*, pp. 163–67; Thomas, *Suez*, pp. 145–46. For the historian, the problem with these statements is that there is no independent evidence for them. The Macmillan papers are unavailable, and there is no reference in Treasury, Bank of England, or American archives indicating any Macmillan phone call on November 6. If Macmillan did call Washington, it is likely that he called Lord Harcourt, economic minister in the British embassy. Harcourt, whose shrewd reading of the Americans will be seen later, was, among other things, a great friend of Humphrey and would certainly have known enough to say that no borrowing would be possible until and unless the British and French governments agreed to the cease-fire. Author's interview with Raymond Bonham Carter.

71. James, *Anthony Eden*, pp. 573–75.

72. Dillon gives the following account of events in Paris: "They—the French, particularly the French government, were quite disturbed because they thought this, Mr. Mollet was very emotionally involved in his dislike of Nasser. So they were quite upset by this [the American intervention at the United Nations]. But they were more upset I think by the British decision to stop, because the British were controlling the military venture, and I was in Mollet's office at night one night when he was talking to Eden, and when the decision was made. Eden told him that the British were going to stop. The French would have continued a little further in the hope of taking the whole Canal before they stopped but they had to stop" (C. Douglas Dillon interview, Columbia Oral History Collection, Columbia University, New York, New York).

73. A day earlier at a White House meeting Eisenhower had said that the Soviet Union needed to be given a clear warning that the United States would block their move into the Middle East. The president believed that "the Soviets, seeing their position and their policy failing so badly in the satellites, are ready to take any wild adventure" (EL, AW, Eisenhower Diaries, box 19, Memorandum of Conference with the President, November 6, 1956; John Foster Dulles Papers, JFD/DDE, WHM, box 4, memorandum dated November 7, 1956, of conference with the president, November 5, 1956).

74. EL, AW, Eisenhower Diaries, box 8, telephone transcript, November 6, 1956.

75. Ibid., International Series, box 19, State Department to London, No. 3285, November 6, 1956.

76. PRO, PREM 11/1117, Eden to Eisenhower, November 6, 1956.

77. EL, WHC, Confidential Files, Subject Series, box 72, Cairo to State Department, No. 1339, November 5, 1956.

78. Eisenhower and his colleagues now also considered a revival of the offer to

finance the Aswan High Dam. Indeed, the president told Humphrey on November 8, "I will go back in the Aswan Dam, but I want these people to see we will deal with them. Willing to give $75 million loan to Egypt" (EL, AW, Eisenhower Diaries, box 19, Phone Calls, November 8, 1956).

79. The victory had been sweeping, with the popular vote totals 35,581,003 for Eisenhower to 25,738,765, giving the president a plurality almost double that which he received in 1952. However, Eisenhower was disappointed that the Republicans did not regain control of Congress (Ambrose, *Eisenhower: The President*, p. 370).

80. No British copies of the transcripts of Eisenhower's two telephone calls to Eden can be found. The American records provide a complete version of Eisenhower's side of the conversations; Eden's replies have been completely censored.

81. EL, AW, Eisenhower Diaries, box 8, Telephone Calls, November 7, 1956; box 19, Memorandum for the Record, November 7, 1956.

82. James, *Anthony Eden*, pp. 576–77.

83. Ibid., pp. 579–80; Lloyd, *Suez: 1956*, pp. 209–11.

84. PRO, T 234/78, Statement by the Minister of Fuel and Power to the House of Commons, November 7, 1956.

85. See, e.g., B/E, C261.3 England, Roche to Files, November 7, 1956; C261 England, Bank of England, Roche memorandum concerning telephone call with Bridge, November 7, 1956.

86. B/E, G 1/124, Bolton, "The Foreign Exchange Market," November 7, 1956.

87. These securities, which included 900,000 shares of Shell Oil, 430,000 shares of General Motors stock and 180,000 shares of Esso, had been nationalized by the British government during the Second World War and were used to secure the wartime loan to Britain made by the Reconstruction Finance Corporation.

88. Bonham Carter to author, August 30, 1989; B/E, G 1/124, Memorandum, November 19, 1956; PRO, T 236/4190, Rowan to Makins, November 28, 1956.

89. PRO, T 236/4189, "Note of a Meeting at 11 Downing Street on Wednesday, 7 November 1956."

90. According to Frank Southard, a U.S. Treasury official who served as the American executive director of the IMF, the administration considered the possibility of canceling the French IMF standby but decided that it could not be done absent a United Nations resolution calling on member nations to apply economic sanctions (Ibid., T 236/4309, Washington to Foreign Office, No. 2327, November 21, 1956).

B/E, OV 38/50, Foreign Office to Washington, No. 5271, November 8, 1956; Washington to Foreign Office, No. 2273, November 8, 1956; OV 31/55, Foreign Office to Washington, No. 5272, November 8, 1956; Washington to Foreign Office, No. 2271, November 8, 1956. This information was based on the visit that Harcourt had with Humphrey on November 7 (Humphrey Papers, Cleveland, reel 16, November 7, 1956). Thomas, *Suez*, p. 134, alleges that unreported to the Foreign Office, Harcourt and Humphrey met every day, with Harcourt entering through a back door. However, when Harcourt wrote Sir Leslie Rowan at the British Treasury on November 19, he said, "I have seen George Humphrey two or three times" (B/E, G 1/124, Harcourt to Rowan, November 19, 1956).

91. The *New York Times* at this time placed great weight on a resumption of cordial relations among the United States, Britain, and France. For example, an editorial on

November 9 urged that "Western ranks must be closed again—and quickly" (p. 28). The next day the lead editorial proclaimed: "What we do know is that it is a critical moment in modern history. At such moments the United States, Britain and France must stand together" (p. 18).

92. PRO, PREM 11/2189, Washington to Foreign Office, No. 2277, November 9, 1956; EL, AW, Eisenhower Diaries, box 19, Memorandum of Conference with the President, November 9, 1956.

93. PRO, FO 800/742, Foreign Office to Washington, No. 5321, November 11, 1956; FO 800/726, Foreign Office to Washington, No. 5326, November 12, 1956.

94. The first press speculations of financial trouble appeared at this time, the best report being that of Susan Strange in the *Observer* of November 11. By contrast, the *Times* editorial of November 14, while less sanguine than earlier columns, remained relatively optimistic, as were the *Financial Times* editorial of November 16 and the *Economist* editorial of November 17, 1956.

95. The same lack of foresight was evident in the 1931 battle fought by the Bank of England to keep Britain on the gold standard. See, e.g., Kunz, *Battle for Britain's Gold Standard*.

96. PRO, T 236/4189, "Note of a Meeting held in Sir Leslie Rowan's room, 3:00 P.M., 12 November 1956"; B/E, G 1/124, Rowan to Makins, November 13, 1956.

97. PRO, T 236/4189, Makins to Macmillan, November 14, 1956.

98. Brian Urquhart, a British diplomat serving in the United Nations Secretariat, writes that "virtually everyone I knew was violently opposed to the Suez expedition, which we regarded as a doomed, dishonest and contemptible aberration by the British and French governments. It was therefore with some embarrassment that I greeted the British Foreign Secretary" (Urquhart, *A Life in Peace and War*, p. 134).

99. Lloyd added that "on the question of moral guilt I talked to him [Lodge] about Guatemala and said that the United States, on his arguments, had been guilty of aggression there." This comparison was one no one in the administration ever saw as apt (PRO, FO 371/118873, UKDEL to Foreign Office, No. 1216, November 14, 1956).

100. Aldrich observed at this time that "anti-American feeling is at a very high pitch and yet is accompanied by the somewhat contradictory but nonetheless complacent assumption that the U.S. is bound to come to its senses and pick up the check" (NA, SD, 741.00/11-2256, London to State Department, No. 2866, November 22, 1956).

101. PRO, FO 371/118873, UKDEL to Foreign Office, No. 1216, November 16, 1956; Foreign Office to UKDEL, No. 1896, November 15, 1956; Lodge Papers, Lodge Diary, November 13, 1956.

102. Although he was recovering from major surgery, Dulles was exceedingly active. As Caccia noted, while Dulles was in the hospital he was continually on the telephone. PRO, PREM 11/2189, Washington to Foreign Office, No. 2277, November 9, 1956.

103. In his memoirs Lloyd elaborated on Dulles's comment: "Dulles said at once with a kind of twinkle in his eye, 'Selwyn, why did you stop? Why didn't you go through with it and get Nasser down'" (Lloyd, *Suez: 1956*, p. 219). Other authors have picked up on this apparent evidence of Dulles's ambivalence and posited the possibility that events might have taken a different course had he not been stricken

ill on November 2. True, this comment was one Dulles repeated several times; for example, on November 12 he told the president: "The British having gone in should not have stopped until they had toppled Nasser. As it was they had now got the worst of both possible worlds. They had received all the onus of making the move and at the same time had not accomplished their major purpose" (John Foster Dulles Papers, JFD/DDE, WHM, box 4, Memorandum of Conversation, November 12, 1956). Yet it is clear from this quotation that Dulles was not suggesting that he would have approved the British action but instead was deploring the fact that the British government had managed to place itself in the worst possible situation. As to the general speculation, two comments need to be made. The first is that the tone of the administration's response was set on October 30 and 31, when Dulles was fully participating in decisions. The second point is that from and after November 7 Dulles was extensively consulted by Hoover and others.

104. PRO, FO 371/118873, Washington to Foreign Office, No. 2308, November 17, 1956; PREM 11/1176, "Record of Conversation between the Secretary of State and General Bedell Smith at Her Majesty's Embassy, Washington, on November 18, 1956."

105. PRO, FO 800/742, Foreign Office to Washington, No. 5422, November 18, 1956.

106. On the British reserves problem, see also FRBNY, C261 Bank of England, Roche memoranda concerning telephone calls with Bridge and Preston, November 16, 1956; B/E, G 1/124, Cobbold to Makins and Macmillan, November 16, 1956. This last memorandum is amusing because Cobbold reiterated the classic central bank governor approach—that the crisis provided an opportunity for the government to improve its financial situation fundamentally by making budget cuts.

107. PRO, T 236/4189, Makins to Macmillan, November 16, 1956. Makins's instincts throughout the crisis remained sound. For example, he suggested that Harcourt, not Caccia, speak to Humphrey and recommended that no mention be made of the sterling area because Humphrey did not understand it very well and because Makins did not believe that "appeals on the basis on the sterling area or of the Commonwealth is the right psychological approach at this moment to the United States Treasury" (Ibid., Makins to Macmillan, November 21, 1956).

108. While the *Wall Street Journal* fully subscribed to the president's hard-line stance, lauding the administration's devotion to principle (editorial, November 12, 1956), other newspapers took a more moderate posture. In the *New York Times*, columnist Arthur Krock, on November 20, 1956, urged the administration to begin giving European allies petroleum aid notwithstanding policy disagreements. The *New York Times* on the same day carried an interesting editorial urging Britain and France to use the Suez crisis as an impetus toward Western European unity.

109. B/E, G 1/124, Rowan to Harcourt, November 16, 1956; Harcourt to Rowan, November 19, 1956.

110. EL, AW, NSC Series, box 8, Minutes, dated November 9, 1956, of discussion at the 303d meeting of the National Security Council, Thursday, November 8, 1956.

111. PRO, FO 371/120833, Washington to Foreign Office, No. 2291, November 13, 1956.

112. By this time every country in Western Europe had instituted some form of rationing. Ibid., D. Wright, "Middle East Oil and OEEC," November 12, 1956;

Wright, "Oil and OEEC," November 13, 1956; CAB 134/815, D.T.C.(56), November 12, 1956; CAB 128/30, CM 84 (56), November 16, 1956.

113. EL, AW, NSC Series, box 8, Minutes, dated November 16, 1956, of discussion at the 304th meeting of the National Security Council, Thursday, November 15, 1956; PRO, FO 371/120834, Ellis Rees Memorandum, November 19, 1956.

114. PRO, T 237/79, Leslie to Bancroft, November 28, 1956; FO 371/120835, "German Participation in Middle East Oil," December 1, 1956. I am indebted to Marc R. Bloch for summarizing the material in these documents.

115. The rampant speculation on his political future had not helped his physical condition. For example, the *Economist*'s editorial of November 10, 1956, began, "Let us be frank. . . . There is only one subject in domestic politics. It is the Prime Minister—should he go or stay?"

116. James, *Anthony Eden*, pp. 582–83.

117. An interesting question is the extent of the administration's negative feelings about Eden. The senior Shell representative in Washington, Tim Wilkinson, told Beeley and Wright on November 19 that a senior White House advisor whom he named (but the memorandum does not) had said that "while the President attached the greatest importance to rebuilding the Anglo-American alliance, 'he would never forgive Eden for what he had done'" (PRO, FO 371/120342, Wright, "The Anglo-American Alliance," November 19, 1956).

The *Economist* on November 24 observed that "the political consequences of his very necessary holiday in Jamaica cannot easily, or sensibly, be assessed" (p. 670).

118. This change of government also allowed the administration to mend quickly its relations with the British government once Eden was no longer prime minister. The irony is that Macmillan, who succeeded Eden, was initially far more hawkish on Suez than was Eden.

119. Although Lloyd was in New York, the administration did not involve him in these talks. He would have been an inappropriate negotiator as he remained an unreconstructed hardliner and also had not built up personal relations with American government officials as Butler and Macmillan had done. Unaware of what Butler and Macmillan were doing, Lloyd tried to arrange high-level administration discussions without success. See EL, WHC, Confidential Files, Subject Series, box 82, State Department to London, No. 3666, November 21, 1956; PRO, FO 371/121274, Washington to Foreign Office, No. 2330, November 21, 1956.

120. Butler's comment was that Aldrich had "for once exerted himself" (Butler Papers, G 31, Butler manuscript, April 18, 1957).

121. NA, SD, 974.7301/11-1956, London to State Department, No. 2791, and State Department to London, No. 3665, November 19, 1956; 684a.86/11-2256, London to State Department, No. 2871, November 22, 1956; 974.7301/11-2256, London to State Department, No. 2869, November 22, 1956; 974.7301/11-2356, State Department to London, No. 3698, November 23, 1956; 841.10, Aldrich to State Department, No. 2716, November 15, 1956.

122. In National Security Council meetings the only real dissenters from this policy were Harold Stassen and Admiral Arthur Radford. Neither man had the influence with Eisenhower possessed by Dulles, Humphrey, and Hoover.

123. During these crucial weeks the administration largely ignored France on the theory that it would follow Britain's lead. Dillon, who sent a steady stream of

messages to the State Department, found Washington's approach extremely frustrating. See, e.g., EL, WHC, Confidential Files, Subject Series, box 72, Paris to State Department, No. 2185, November 5, 1956, and Paris to State Department, No. 2272, November 8, 1972; White House Office, Office of Staff Secretary, Subject Series, Diplomatic, box 7, Memorandum of Conversation at the French Embassy, November 16, 1956; AW, International Series, box 12, Dillon to State Department, No. 2238, November 7, 1956; Lodge Papers, General Correspondence, box 4, Lodge to Dillon, November 9, 1956; DD 1984-1841, Paris to State Department, No. 2349, November 12, 1956.

124. See, e.g., John Foster Dulles Papers, JFD/DDE, Subject Series, box 7, "Congressional Briefing on Current Developments, October 31, 1956"; G, C & M, box 1, "Memorandum of Conversation with Senator Lyndon Johnson, November 13, 1956."

125. EL, AW, Eisenhower Diaries, box 19, Phone Calls, November 19 and 29, 1956; Memorandum dated November 21, 1956, of Conference with the President, November 20, 1956; WHC, Confidential Files, Subject Series, box 72, State Department to London, No. 3631, November 20, 1956.

126. Ibid., AW, Eisenhower Diaries, box 19, Memorandum of Conference with the President, November 21, 1956.

127. Noel-Baker Papers, 4/668, "Statement by Minister of Fuel and Power on Oil Supplies, November 20, 1956"; PRO, FO 371/120835, Ellis-Rees to Macmillan, November 23, 1956.

128. Another example of certain ministers' unrealistic beliefs occurred at a meeting of the Egypt Committee held on November 21; a considerable amount of time was devoted to discussing how to obtain immediate American adherence to the Baghdad Pact (PRO, CAB 134/1216, Cabinet Egypt Committee, EC [56], 46th meeting).

129. PRO, FO 371/118875, UKDEL to Foreign Office, No. 1333, November 21, 1956.

130. The government's situation worsened during the week of November 19, when right-wing Conservative party sentiment hardened against unconditional withdrawal. It took speeches by both Butler and Macmillan (whose performance was rated one of the best of his career) at the backbenchers' 1922 Committee meeting of November 22 to quell an incipient rebellion. See Howard, *RAB*, pp. 240–42; Horne, *Macmillan, 1894–1956*, pp. 455–57; *Economist*, November 24, 1956, p. 670; see also PRO, FO 371/118875, Foreign Office to UKDEL, No. 2087, November 21, 1956.

131. PRO, FO 371/118875, Foreign Office to UKDEL, No. 2086, November 21, 1956.

132. The vote on the censure motion was 63 to 5. PRO, FO 371/118877, UKDEL to Foreign Office, No. 1401, November 24, 1956; Washington to Foreign Office, No. 2342, November 24, 1956; FO 371/118880, "Resolution adopted by the General Assembly at its 594th Plenary Meeting on November 24, 1956."

133. Not surprisingly, the American vote increased anti-American sentiment in Britain. For that reason, Butler told Aldrich that "he had expressed hope that 'there will be no more UN resolutions'" (EL, WHC, Confidential Files, Subject Series, box 82, London to State Department, No. 2948, November 27, 1956).

134. EL, AW, Eisenhower Diaries, box 19, Memorandum of Conference with the President, November 23, 1956.

135. In his memoirs Macmillan discussed the heavy selling of sterling in New York on November 5 and 6 (*Riding the Storm*, p. 164). The documents provide no substantiation for this allegation as of the date that he gives; it is after November 20 that evidence accumulates about heavy New York selling.

136. The nature of the business of multinational oil companies ensured that they would be regular buyers and sellers of sterling. Therefore the selling of sterling by oil companies at this point does not necessarily indicate a nefarious intent on their part; both the economic and political aspects of the Suez crisis provided an impetus to exchange sterling for dollars.

137. PRO, T 236/4190, Makins to Macmillan, November 22 and 23, 1956. See also FRBNY, C261, Bank of England, Roche Memorandum to Files, November 21, 1956.

138. As Robert Hall, economic advisor to the British government, wrote Makins on November 27, "We must be rapidly approaching the danger point at which people suspect that we will be forced to take some action that will impair the value of their holdings of sterling. At this point it becomes worth while to get out of sterling for speculative reasons even if you think it likely that in the long run it will be a strong currency" (PRO, T 236/4190).

139. It remains puzzling that during late November British officials did not give much consideration to floating the pound as an offensive measure. Surely a contributing factor was the extremely negative reaction of the United States and Commonwealth governments to the ROBOT scheme of 1952 (which had called for a floating pound), which frightened them away from such a solution to the problems of sterling. Just as important, to many Bank of England and Treasury stalwarts the very concept of a floating pound remained anathema for two decades after the Second World War.

140. The fixed rate system increased the financial incentive for substantial holders of sterling to sell their pounds: the risk/reward ratio was completely in the seller's favor. If a holder retained his pounds, a devaluation would hurt him considerably. But if he sold the pounds, should there not be a devaluation, because sterling would go no higher than the fixed price of £1 = $2.80, he could always repurchase them for the same price he had sold them for initially.

141. A complete breakdown of government holdings of sterling is contained in Appendix E.

142. FRBNY, C261, Bank of England, Exter Memorandum to Files, November 23, 1956, and Roche Memorandum to Files, November 23, 1956.

143. See, e.g., PRO, T 236/4190, Rowan to Makins, "Crash Action," November 22, 1956.

144. B/E, G 1/124, Cobbold to Makins, November 22, 1956. See also Foreign Office to Washington, No. 5488, November 22, 1956.

145. During the 1950s the Commonwealth Relations Office handled Britain's foreign relations with Commonwealth countries. Britain and her former colonies then and now exchange high commissioners, not ambassadors.

146. See, e.g., PRO, T 236/4190, CRO to Canada, No. 1878, November 22, 1956; CRO to Canada, No. 1912, December 1, 1956; B/E, G 1/124, CRO to Canada, No. 1891, November 27, 1956.

147. B/E, G 1/124, Foreign Office to Washington, No. 5488, November 22, 1956; Washington to Foreign Office, No. 2335, November 22, 1956; Washington to Foreign Office, No. 2347, November 26, 1956.

148. PRO, FO 371/118885, "Record of a Conversation between Mr. Humphrey and the Lord Privy Seal on Monday, November 26, 1956."

149. NA, SD, 684a.86/11-2656, State Department to London, No. 3749, November 26, 1956.

150. He also annoyed Caccia because he "more than once used the simile that the United Kingdom was an armed burglar who had climbed in through the window while Nasser was the householder in his nightshirt appealing to the world for protection."

151. Humphrey had not lost his customary financial cautiousness. When the president suggested an OEEC meeting on November 21, Humphrey responded that he was afraid that the OEEC would try to get in and decide how to distribute American funds, and "he did not want another Marshall Plan" (EL, AW, Eisenhower Diaries, box 19, telephone calls, November 21, 1956).

152. B/E, G 1/124, Washington to Foreign Office, Nos. 2352, 2353, 2354, 2355, and 2356, November 27, 1956.

153. PRO, T 236/4190, Makins to Macmillan, November 27, 1956.

154. EL, WHC, Confidential Files, Subject Series, box 82, London to State Department, No. 2950, November 27, 1956. Aldrich was now speaking daily with Macmillan; see Ibid., London to State Department, No. 2948, November 27, 1956.

155. PRO, FO 371/118877, Dixon Memorandum concerning the Middle East, November 26, 1956; FO 800/742, UKDEL to Foreign Office, No. 1431, November 27, 1956.

156. EL, AW, Eisenhower Diaries, box 19, Phone Calls, November 27, 1956.

157. PRO, FO 371/120836, Commercial Department, French Embassy to Foreign Office, November 29, 1956; author's interview with Dillon; NA, SD, 974.7301/11-2856, State Department to London, No. 3796, November 28, 1956; 974.7301/11-2956, No. 3837, November 29, 1956; 880.2553, London to State Department, No. 3036, November 30, 1956. Worried about the European oil predicament, on November 25 the president had agreed that Flemming and his associates should on the next day begin the process of reconvening the MEEC. See *FRUS*, vol. 16, 613:1195, "Memorandum of Conversation at the State Department," November 25, 1956.

158. PRO, FO 371/118879, UKDEL to Foreign Office, Nos. 1475 and 1478, November 29, 1956; T 236/4627, UKDEL to Foreign Office, No. 1477, November 29, 1956.

159. Newspapers continued to send mixed signals to the government. The *Economist* urged a speedy withdrawal, although its lead writer reflected that "the withdrawal of the British and French forces is unavoidable, but it will not wipe out the blunder of sending them in" (November 24, 1956, p. 663). The *Manchester Guardian* persisted in its praise of the United States and lauded the United Nations while the *Daily Telegraph* grew increasingly bitter. On December 4, in response to Lloyd's announcement of a full British withdrawal, it stated: "We are surrendering to an United Nations force which by no stretch of the imagination can measure up to the epithet 'effective.' We are abandoning every purpose and every duty down, it appears to the protection of our own nationals in Egypt" (p. 6).

160. PRO, CAB 128/30, CM 87 (56), November 22, 1956.

161. See, e.g., PRO, T 236/4190, Foreign Office to Washington, No. 5491, November 22, 1956, and No. 5637, November 29, 1956; B/E, G 1/124, Washington to Foreign Office, No. 2394, December 1, 1956.

162. Macmillan apparently kept knowledge of the true reserve loss of $401 million from Eden and all other Cabinet ministers.

163. Under the terms of the agreements governing the European Payments Union, Britain owed $70 million to other European nations, which would have to be paid in December; the $47 million lost during the last two days of November, by tradition, was included in the next month's figures. That translated into a December guaranteed drain of $292.5 million, leaving the British with year-end reserves of $1,672.5 million before any December losses were included. When the real November loss figure of $401 million is used, the bank and Treasury were projecting a year-end figure of $1,550.5 million, not much higher than the lowest postwar figure for British reserves, $1,340 million at the time of the 1949 devaluation, and far lower than the post–Korean War low point of $1,846 million at the end of 1952. Obviously, foreign purchases of sterling would raise British gold/dollar reserves, but under the circumstances such transactions were highly unlikely. See PRO, T 236/4190, Rowan to Makins, November 30, 1956. See also *FRUS*, vol. 16, 647:1291–93, Paris to State Department, December 11, 1956; 654:1302–4, Memorandum of Conversation at Palais de Chaillot, December 14, 1956; 655:1304–6, Memorandum of Conversation at Palais de Chaillot, December 15, 1956.

164. The last week of November had been a true disaster for the reserves. As of November 24, the reserve loss to date had stood at $232 million. Using the $401 million figure for total losses on the month nets a loss of $169 million for the period November 25–30. PRO, T 236/4309, "Gold and Dollar and EPU Position: Report for the week ending 24 November 1956," T 236/4190, Makins to Macmillan, November 30, 1956.

165. B/E, OV 31/55, Washington to Foreign Office, No. 2384, November 30, 1956; G 1/124, Washington to Foreign Office, No. 2396, December 2, 1956.

166. EL, AW, NSC Series, box 8, "Discussion at the 305th Meeting of the National Security Council, Friday, November 30, 1956." On the subject of a possible Labour government, a Dulles memorandum of a conversation with the president recorded: "We both agreed that it would be difficult to get along with the Labor [*sic*] Government, particularly as now they had made Bevan the 'Foreign Minister' in the Shadow Cabinet" (John Foster Dulles Papers, JFD/DDE, WHM, box 4, Memorandum of Conversation with the President, December 3, 1956).

167. PRO, FO 371/118883, "Note of a Conversation," December 2, 1956; "Note of a Conversation," December 3, 1956; FO 371/120816, Note for Secretary of State, December 3, 1956.

168. Concurrently, British and French statesmen met in London in order to concert their withdrawal statements in person, the French as usual bowing to British pressure. See PRO, FO 371/118872, "Record of a Meeting held at No. 10 Downing Street at 3 P.M. on Friday, November 30."

169. PRO, CAB 128/30, CM 92 (56), November 30, 1956; CM 94 (56) and 95 (56), December 1, 1956; CM 96 (56), December 3, 1956.

170. B/E, G 1/124, Foreign Office to Washington, No. 5681, December 3, 1956; Washington to Foreign Office, No. 2401, December 3, 1956; John Foster Dulles Papers, JFD/DDE, Telephone Conversations, box 5, "Memorandum of Telephone Conversation with the President," December 3, 1956.

171. B/E, G 1/124, Statement in the House of Commons, by the Rt. Hon. Harold Macmillan, Chancellor of the Exchequer, December 4, 1956.

172. As discussed above, the Treasury had only reached the $1,965 million figure by a trick of financial legerdemain.

173. Even on December 3 Humphrey remained concerned that when Macmillan described the American administration's attitude toward a request for a waiver in his statement to Parliament, the chancellor should make it clear that the British and American governments had not colluded in any fashion. See PRO, T 236/4309, Washington to Foreign Office, No. 2405, December 3, 1956.

CHAPTER SEVEN

1. B/E, G 1/124, Washington to Foreign Office, No. 2396, December 2, 1956.

2. NA, TD, RG 56, George Humphrey Files, No. 198, Humphrey to Bridges, December 3, 1956, and NAC, box 6, National Advisory Council Staff Committee Minutes Meeting No. 592, December 3, 1956; PRO, FO 371/120816, Washington to Foreign Office, No. 2412, December 4, 1956.

3. PRO, PREM 11/1826, Washington to Foreign Office, No. 2423, December 5, 1956. When Harcourt began lobbying IMF executive directors, the Brazilian representative told him not to wait until after the NATO meeting; Harcourt quoted the man as saying, "Get your money before Dulles can see any of your Ministers otherwise he will try to do a trade of policy for cash."

4. See, e.g., B/E, OV 38/51, Foreign Office to Washington, No. 5711, December 4, 1956; Foreign Office to Washington, No. 5744, December 5, 1956; Washington to Foreign Office, Nos. 143 Eager, 144 Eager, 147 Eager, December 5, 1956.

5. The British government had considered notifying the fund of its restrictions on transfers of Egyptian pounds but had acquiesced in the administration's desire not to inform the IMF of the British and American orders blocking Egyptian assets. This decision provides another example of the same action having different consequences for both countries. As the United States had no intention of borrowing from the IMF, it did not have to worry whether its monetary decisions were in violation of fund rules. The British government was not in as fortunate a position. See, e.g., B/E, OV 38/51, Washington to Foreign Office, No. 146 Eager, December 5, 1956; Foreign Office to Washington, No. 198 Eager, December 6, 1956.

6. Ibid., London to Washington, No. 36, December 6, 1956, Washington to London, No. 16, December 6, 1956.

7. B/E, OV 31/55, Washington to Foreign Office, No. 2441, December 7, 1956. Humphrey's animus against European cooperation, however, was not shared by other administration officials.

8. Dulles Papers, Personal Papers, box 104, Burgess to Dulles, December 7, 1956.

9. The first detailed discussion of British policy in the event it proved impossible to maintain the present sterling parity was held on December 5. See B/E, G 1/99, "Policy If We Do Not Succeed in Holding the Rate for Sterling," December 6, 1956; PRO, T 236/4190, Rowan to Makins, December 6, 1956. On the improvement in sterling, see FRBNY, C261, Bank of England, Roche Memoranda to the Files, December 4, 6, and 7, 1956.

10. B/E, OV 31/55, Washington to Foreign Office, No. 2447, December 8, 1956.

11. FRBNY, IMF Files 798.3, IMF to FRBNY, No. 9157, December 11, 1956.

12. The British government utilized its entire IMF quota as it received a total drawing of $561.47 and a standby credit of $738.53 million. The standby credit ran for

one year, from December 22, 1956, until December 21, 1957. NA, TD, RG 56, NAC Documents, box 22, National Advisory Council Document No. 128, Supplement No. 120, February 2, 1957; B/E, OV 38/51, Washington to Foreign Office, Nos. 160 Eager and 161 Eager, December 10, 1956; Foreign Office to Washington, No. 206 Eager, December 10, 1956; PRO, T 236/4309, Washington to Foreign Office, No. 159 Eager, December 10, 1956.

13. PRO, FO 371/120329, Washington to Foreign Office, No. 2433, December 6, 1956.

14. DD, 1987-738, Paris to State Department, No. Dulte 7, December 10, 1956.

15. B/E, G 1/124, "Record of a Discussion at the Hotel Tallyrand, Paris, at 3 P.M. on Tuesday, December 11, 1956."

16. Simultaneously with the Humphrey talks, British officials discussed adopting a comparable change in the Canadian loan agreement. See, e.g., EL, WHC, Confidential Files, Subject Series, box 82, State Department to London, No. 3777, November 27, 1956; NA, SD, 841.10/12-556, Ottawa to State Department, No. 276, December 5, 1956; PRO, FO 371/120796, Garner to Gilbert, December 10, 1956.

17. Dulles also took the opportunity to complain to Macmillan that relations between the administration and the British embassy in Washington had deteriorated due to the replacement of Caccia for Makins. John Foster Dulles Papers, JFD/DDE, G, C & M, box 1, "Memorandum for the Record," December 12, 1956.

18. PRO, FO 371/121230, Macmillan to Lloyd, December 13, 1956, "Note for the Record," December 13, 1956. See also Horne, *Macmillan, 1894–1956*, pp. 450–53.

19. For example, in a conversation with Admiral Radford on March 13, 1956, Eisenhower said, "He did not think we were worse off with regard to the USSR. Where we are badly off is with respect to the rising Arab nations in the Middle East." EL, White House Office, Office of Staff Secretary, box 4, JC 5 (2), Memorandum of Conference with the President, March 13, 1956, dated March 14, 1956.

20. DD, 1988-82, Memorandum for the National Security Council, August 7, 1956.

21. The reports of anti-British rioting in Iraq during the first week of November 1956 provide an excellent example of the damage done to British standing in the Middle East by the Suez invasion. In order to appease public opinion, Nuri Pasha, who had encouraged the British government to take a strong stance against Nasser, broke diplomatic relations with France and refused to meet with British Petroleum's British representatives. NA, SD, 641.74/11-1056, Baghdad to State Department, No. 804, November 10, 1956.

22. EL, AW, Administrative Series, box 24, Lodge to Eisenhower, December 21, 1956. Lodge went on to write that "you [Eisenhower] have given us a position of moral *authority* which in turn has created a degree of *respect* which transcends the mere counting of noses."

23. John Foster Dulles Papers, JFD/DDE, WHM, box 4, "Suggested Draft Cable, December 19, 1955"; EL, AW, Eisenhower Diaries, box 20, "Visit of Prime Minister Nehru with the President," December 19, 1956.

24. Administration officials, wedded to their view of American exceptionalism, never understood that the Arab world largely believed that the United States shared the imperialism of Britain and France.

25. Dwight D. Eisenhower, *White House Years: Waging Peace*, pp. 177–79.

26. John Foster Dulles Papers, Telephone Conversations, box 6, telephone call to Mr. Bowie, January 12, 1957.

27. EL, AW, Eisenhower Diaries, box 20, Telephone Calls, December 8, 1956.

28. Administration officials were afraid that a decision to join the Baghdad Pact would bring strong congressional pressure to offer some sort of American guarantee to Israel.

29. EL, AW, Eisenhower Diaries, box 20, Memorandum of Conference with the President, December 20, 1956.

30. DD, 1987-3263, "Memorandum of Conversation with Sir Harold Caccia," December 24, 1956; PRO, FO 371/121274, Washington to Foreign Office, No. 2545, December 24, 1956.

31. Indeed, two years earlier, in connection with the Guatemala affair, Dulles had told Lodge that "the happiest day in his life would be when we don't have to modify our policies, etc. to keep a facade of unity" (John Foster Dulles Papers, JFD/DDE, Telephone Conversations, box 2, telephone call to Lodge, June 25, 1954).

32. EL, AW, Eisenhower Diaries, box 20, memorandum dated December 28, 1956, of conference with the president, December 27, 1956; John Foster Dulles Papers, JFD/DDE, Telephone Conversations, box 5, telephone call to Nixon, December 27, 1956; telephone call to Lawrence, December 29, 1956; PRO, FO 371/121230, Washington to Foreign Office, No. 2570, December 29, 1956.

33. EL, AW, Eisenhower Diaries, box 20, Notes on Legislative Leadership Meeting, December 31, 1956.

34. Ibid., box 21, "Notes on Presidential-Bipartisan Leadership Meeting, January 1, 1957."

35. Ambrose, *Eisenhower: The President*, p. 382.

36. Dulles, for one, recognized the full implications of this change. Among other things, he told congressional leaders on January 1 that "the United States had not previously made such arrangements here because of the primary British responsibility" (EL, AW, Eisenhower Diaries, box 21, "Notes on Presidential-Bipartisan Congressional Leadership Meeting, January 1, 1957").

37. While the Formosa straits resolution also contained an advance delegation of power, its scope was far more limited than what was now proposed. This aspect did not trouble the *New York Times*, which on January 10, 1957, gave the Eisenhower Doctrine a ringing endorsement that lauded Eisenhower's decision to "come forward . . . in declaring America's concern in the Middle East upheaval."

38. For example, on December 1, he cabled 10 Downing Street to say that while the government seemed to be having a difficult time with the Americans, "I am sure that the only thing is to stand firm on the ground that we have chosen and I believe that they will come round. I quite understand that the financial position can meanwhile become difficult, but after all we have resources which I would rather not put into a telegram but which I would rather use than yield" (PRO, PREM 11/1826, Jamaica to London, No. 102, December 1, 1956).

39. NA, SD, 741.00/12-1756, London to State Department, No. 3358, December 17, 1956.

40. Ibid., 741.00/12-1956, London to State Department, No. 3389, December 19, 1956.

41. Ibid., 741.00/12-2056, London to State Department, No. 3425, December 20, 1956.

42. James, *Anthony Eden*, p. 592.

43. Eden lived another two decades. Ennobled as the Earl of Avon, he spent much time writing his memoirs. They were prepared in nonchronological order, with the volume on the Suez crisis, *Full Circle*, written first. Published in 1960, its purpose was obviously to vindicate Eden's decisions. On Eden's resignation, see James, *Anthony Eden*, pp. 594–98.

44. Lord Salisbury, in 1956 leader of the House of Lords and lord president of the council, was senior in age and Cabinet service to Butler. But he was not considered as a successor to Eden because, since the 1920s, it was accepted that the prime minister should not sit in the House of Lords. As of yet the statute permitting an aristocrat to renounce his title had not been enacted.

45. For example, as soon as Eden's resignation was announced, Macmillan put on a masterful performance, chatting with newspaper reporters and parading down Whitehall in front of 10 Downing Street and ostentatiously visiting party dignitaries such as Lord Woolton, the former chairman. See Howard, *RAB*, pp. 246–47.

46. Butler was never very popular with his colleagues, who disliked his "mandarin" air of superiority. He also had been a loyal junior minister in Neville Chamberlain's government and had enthusiastically supported the Munich agreement, a fact not yet easily overlooked. Finally, Butler clearly allowed himself to be outmaneuvered by Macmillan. (When Macmillan retired in 1963, his successor, Sir Alec Douglas Home, was not hampered by his support for Chamberlain's appeasement policies.)

47. Horne, *Macmillan, 1894–1956*, pp. 450–61; Howard, *RAB*, pp. 242–48.

48. Dulles opted for Butler because he feared that Macmillan, taking advantage of his previous relationship with Eisenhower in North Africa, would emphasize top-level diplomacy, thereby cutting out Dulles. Humphrey preferred Butler because of the successful relationship they had enjoyed when the latter was chancellor of the Exchequer. Eisenhower thought Butler would have been easier to work with because he viewed Macmillan and Eden as sharing a vision of Britain as a colonial power. See John Foster Dulles Papers, Telephone Conversations, box 6, telephone call to Humphrey, January 10, 1957; EL, AW, Ann Whitman Diary, box 8, January 10, 1957; AW, Eisenhower Diaries, box 21, Phone Calls, January 10, 1957; Eisenhower to Macmillan, January 10, 1957; PRO, FO 371/126682, Foreign Office to Washington, Nos. 184 and 185, January 14, 1956.

49. DD, 1987-3264, London to State Department, No. 3709, January 11, 1957; PRO, FO 371/126682, Caccia to Kirkpatrick, January 11, 1957; FO 371/126683, Kirkpatrick to Caccia, January 18, 1957; EL, AW, International Series, box 20, January 23, 1957.

50. B/E, OV 31/55, Washington to Foreign Office, No. 26 Remac, December 20, 1956. News that the British government intended to pledge these holdings rather than sell them calmed Wall Street, which had feared that the unloading of such large holdings would significantly depress share prices. See the *New York Times*, December 11, 1956, p. 58.

51. See, e.g., B/E, OV 31/55, Washington to Foreign Office, Remac 1 Saving, December 28, 1956; PRO, T 236/3924, No. 3 Camer, January 1, 1957.

52. FRBNY, C261 Bank of England, Roche Memorandum to Files, January 3, 1957; C261, British Government, Clarke to Exter, January 4, 1957.

53. The American aid was allocated as follows: $22.3 million in economic assistance, $1.3 million in technical assistance, $.3 million for information services, and $.1 million for educational exchanges (DD, 1980-386, NSC Report No. 5280/1, dated November 4, 1958, "United States Policy towards the Near East, Financial Appendix").

54. Therefore, while Eban repeatedly, during October, requested an EXIM loan for water development, Dulles refused to commit the administration. The administration kept American aid to Israel low for financial as well as political reasons. For example, Humphrey told Eisenhower and Dulles on October 3 that he thought the credit risk on loans to Israel was "excessive." By December 3 the administration had memorialized its position on aid to Israel; in the words of a State Department official: "We are to 'drag our feet' but this should be done as inconspicuously as possible." Fiscal 1957 programs would not be approved, while fiscal 1956 or prior year programs were to be delayed as much as possible. See FRUS, vol. 16, 632:1236–38, Memorandum from Seager to FitzGerald, December 3, 1956; John Foster Dulles Papers, WHM, box 4, Memorandum of Conversation with the President and Secretary Humphrey, October 3, 1956; Telephone Conversations, box 5, telephone calls to and from Humphrey, October 30, 1956; WHM, box 4, Memorandum of Conference with the President, October 30, 1956; EL, WHC, Confidential Files, Subject Series, box 82, "Record of Decision," October 31, 1956; AW, Eisenhower Diaries, box 19, Telephone Calls, November 1, 1956, Dulles to Eisenhower; AW, NSC Series, box 8, "Discussion at the 302nd Meeting of the National Security Council, Thursday, November 1, 1956." See also FRUS, vol. 16, 322:682–84, Memorandum of Conversation, October 10, 1956.

55. The American decision not to use heavy pressure on Israel at this time was exemplified by the administration's approval of an increase in Israel's IMF quota from $4.5 million to $7.5 million on December 21. See NA, TD, RG 56, NAC, Document No. 88, Action No. 957, December 21, 1956; John Foster Dulles Papers, JFD/DDE, Telephone Conversations, box 5, telephone call to Lodge, October 30, 1956.

56. EL, AW, International Series, box 29, Ben-Gurion to Eisenhower, November 8, 1956; Economist, December 1, 1956, p. 762.

57. In December 1955 a contract for twelve Mystères fighter planes was signed; they arrived April 11, 1956, while simultaneously a contract for twelve additional fighters was executed. See Selwyn Ilan Troen, ed., "Ben-Gurion's Diary," in Troen and Shemesh, Suez-Sinai Crisis, p. 328. The best book concerning French arms shipments to Israel is Kolodziej, Making and Marketing Arms.

58. EL, WHC, SS, DD, box 4, Kearney to Radford, November 6, 1956; NA, SD, 784A.00(W)/11-856, Tel Aviv to State Department, November 11, 1956.

59. PRO, FO 371/128126, Tel Aviv to Foreign Office, No. 17, January 7, 1957.

60. John Foster Dulles Papers, Personal Papers, box 106, "Outline of Thoughts for Background Press Conference," December 6, 1956. See also the statement of the Deputy Secretary for NEA, who told Caccia that "the Israelis could not hope to achieve any advantage as a result of their military action" (PRO, FO 371/128126, Washington to Foreign Office, No. 56, January 10, 1957).

61. PRO, FO 371/128126, Tel Aviv to Foreign Office, No. 33, January 10, 1957.

62. Even Stephen Ambrose, who has written a thoroughly favorable account of

Eisenhower's career, admits that Eisenhower could not come to terms with two groups: Jews and Blacks. See *Eisenhower: The President*, p. 387.

63. Instances of Dulles's negative attitude toward American Jews and Israel abound. For example, on June 18, 1956, he responded to Cardinal Spellman's comment that "Jewish activities are becoming excessively arrogant and demanding" by saying that this "was one of my problems, that I felt it very important to try to demonstrate that the Jews did not in an election year dictate the foreign policy of the United States." To Lodge on February 12, 1957, he "mentioned the terrific control the Jews had over the news media and the barrage which the Jews have built on Congressmen." The next day, in conversation with the very anti-Israeli Congressman John Vorys, the secretary said, "We face a critical situation as far as the Arab world is concerned because they are watching closely to decide re [*sic*] even if a Republican Administration finds it impossible to have a foreign policy the Jews don't approve of and if that is their conclusion they will line up with the Soviets" (John Foster Dulles Papers, JFD/DDE, G, C & M, box 1, Memorandum of Conversation with Cardinal Spellman, June 18, 1956; Telephone Conversations, box 6, telephone call to Lodge, February 12, 1957; telephone call from Vorys, February 13, 1957).

64. Hoover told the president that "the Arabs had been very clever in their dealings with Hammarskjöld—much more so than the British, French and Israelis—with the result that they have frequently appeared to be in full concord with his efforts and objectives." Hammarskjöld's opinion of Israel was revealed by his January 10 statement to British Ambassador to the United Nations Sir Pierson Dixon: "The Israelis were always trying to trap him and he had to go very carefully" (John Foster Dulles Papers, JFD/DDE, Memorandum of Conference with the President, December 15, 1956; PRO, FO 371/128126, UKDEL to Foreign Office, No. 112, January 11, 1957).

65. John Foster Dulles Papers, JFD/DDE, G, C & M, box 1, Memorandum of Conversation with Senator Lyndon Johnson, November 13, 1956.

66. Henry Cabot Lodge encouraged this approach by continually emphasizing the credit with the "Afro-Asian" nations that the United States had garnered for its position on Israel. The ambassador to the United States often expressed disdain for Israel. For example, he dismissed Israeli worries about security as exemplifying the idea of "everybody picking on poor little Israel." He urged that the administration take its case against Israel public because "once the Secretary and he [Lodge] and the President start talking back we can do a great deal. Knowland, Javits and Ives have had the field to themselves but their logic is fallacious." On the question of Israeli withdrawal, Lodge wrote to Dulles, "Thirty years ago, when I first became a newspaperman in Washington, I observed the extent to which minority groups could paralyze Congress and then get Congress to paralyze the Executive Branch. As a Senator for thirteen years I saw exactly how it was done—and how very *little* it took to create a wave of fear in Congress and in the Executive Branch" (EL, AW, Administrative Series, box 24, Lodge to Eisenhower, December 21, 1956; John Foster Dulles Papers, JFD/DDE, Telephone Conversations, box 6, telephone calls from Lodge, February 11, 1957, 9:04 A.M. and 4:30 P.M.; Personal Papers, box 118, March 7, 1957).

67. The administration's cavalier attitude toward Javits's attempts to woo Jewish

voters is particularly instructive. See, e.g., John Foster Dulles Papers, JFD/DDE, Special Assistant Chronological File, box 10, Hanes to Macomber, September 18, 1956; G, C & M, box 5, Hanes to Dulles, Memoranda for the Record, October 30, 1956; Telephone Conversations, box 5, telephone call from Javits to Hanes, November 1, 1956.

68. See, e.g., PRO, FO 371/118884, Paris to Foreign Office, No. 457, December 10, 1956; FO 371/125505, UKDEL to Foreign Office, No. 104, January 10, 1957; FO 371/125508, "Suez Canal Re-opening and Settlement," February 9, 1957; FO 371/125548, CRO to Canada et al., Nos. 1 and 3, January 1, 1957; UKDEL to Foreign Office, No. 2 Saving, January 4, 1957; FO 371/125552, UKDEL to Foreign Office, No. 541, February 2, 1957; B/E, OV 43/15, Washington to Foreign Office, No. 2541, December 10, 1956; John Foster Dulles Papers, JFD/DDE, Telephone Conversations, box 5, telephone call from Hoover, December 28, 1956. Clearance operations were directed by American General Raymond Wheeler, whom John J. McCloy had recommended to Secretary General Dag Hammarskjöld. Wheeler had served as the chief of engineers during World War II and in that capacity had gotten to know McCloy, who was assistant secretary of war. The two men had kept up their connection—during McCloy's tenure as head of the World Bank, Wheeler worked on various IBRD projects. See McCloy Papers, SC1/8, McCloy to Hoover, December 12, 1956.

69. Ivone Kirkpatrick, permanent undersecretary of the Foreign Office, wrote to Lloyd on January 14: "It seems clear that Nasser is determined to use the Suez Canal as a form of pressure on the countries which use it. French and British ships will not be allowed through until Gaza is evacuated by the Jews. And we must expect access to the Canal to be closed to us later because of what is happening in Aden; and closed to the French because of Algeria; and possibly to the Portuguese because of Goa, etc., etc. In a word, Nasser has not the slightest intention of abiding by the 1888 convention or adhering to his promise to divorce the Canal from politics" (PRO, FO 371/125505).

70. EL, AW, Eisenhower Diaries, box 21, Phone Calls, January 21, 1957; John Foster Dulles Papers, JFD/DDE, Telephone Conversations, box 6, telephone call to Lodge, January 16, 1957.

71. Arthur H. Dean (1898–1987) had a long and distinguished career in government service. His most famous role was as chief representative for the United Nations Command in the fruitless attempt to arrange a post–Korean War peace conference. Dean also served as the chief of the U.S. delegation to the nuclear test ban negotiations that led to the signing of the partial test ban treaty in Moscow in August 5, 1963. Dean joined the firm of Sullivan & Cromwell in 1923 and succeeded John Foster Dulles as senior partner in 1949. Dean remained head of the firm until 1972.

72. See, e.g., John Foster Dulles Papers, JFD/DDE, Telephone Conversations, box 5, telephone call from Arthur Dean, December 3, 1956; Note to Dulles, December 26, 1956; Telephone Conversations, box 6, telephone calls from Arthur Dean, February 11, 19, 20, and 26, 1957, and telephone call from Allen Dulles, March 1, 1957; Eban, *Autobiography*, pp. 236, 245.

73. *Economist*, January 5, 1957, pp. 42–43; February 23, 1957, pp. 649–50.

74. John Foster Dulles Papers, JFD/DDE, WHM, box 6, "Memorandum of

268 NOTES TO PAGES 167–68

Conversation with the President," January 17, 1957; see also Telephone Conversations, box 5, telephone call to Lodge, December 26, 1956.

75. That the Israeli forces had vanquished Egypt's army helps explain Ben-Gurion's hubris. John Foster Dulles Papers, JFD/DDE, Telephone Conversations, box 6, telephone call to Lodge, January 18, 1957; PRO, FO 371/128128, Tel Aviv to Foreign Office, Nos. 69 and 72, January 21, 1956; NA, SD, 784A.oo(W)/1-1857, Tel Aviv to State Department, January 20, 1957.

76. PRO, FO 371/128128, Tel Aviv to Foreign Office, No. 77, January 23, 1957.

77. The report was premised on the assumption that scrupulous observance of the 1949 armistice agreement and immediate Israeli withdrawal from all captured territory should be the starting point for any settlement. It failed, however, to take sufficient notice of the blockades, boycotts, and terrorist raids to which Israel had been subjected for the past seven years. A summary of Hammarskjöld's report is contained in the February 2, 1957, issue of the *Economist*, p. 367.

78. PRO, FO 371/128128, UKDEL to Foreign Office, No. 234, January 21, 1957; Nos. 265 and 266, January 24, 1956; and No. 310, January 28, 1956.

79. EL, White House Office, Office of Staff Secretary, box 15/8, "Resolution II adopted by the General Assembly at its 652nd plenary meeting on 2 February 1957"; *FRUS*, vol. 17, 51:78–79, United Nations General Assembly Resolution 1124 (XI), General Assembly Resolution 1125 (XI).

80. This entry also provides one explanation for the British dislike of Lodge; the latter told Dulles that while under the Truman administration the American government had always taken a tripartite approach at the United Nations, now the United States was going its own way without Britain and France. Lodge Papers, General Correspondence, box 5b, Lodge's Confidential Journal, February 5, 1957. See also EL, AW, International Series, box 29, Eisenhower to Ben-Gurion, February 2, 1957; NA, SD, 784A.oo(W)/2-1157. Tel Aviv to State Department, February 12, 1957; *FRUS*, vol. 17, 54:82–84, Eisenhower to Ben-Gurion, February 3, 1957.

81. PRO, FO 371/128131, Pink, "Israeli Withdrawal," February 8, 1956.

82. His visit marked the first state visit of any Arab leader to the United States; no Israeli leader was invited to officially visit the United States during the Eisenhower years.

83. In connection with the renewal of the American lease of base facilities, the administration promised to help King Saud develop the Saudi military establishment, sell over $100 million in arms, and help train Saudis to use the new equipment. Caccia expressed his concern over the magnitude of the aid, which was far in excess of what the British government could offer its client states. See John Foster Dulles Papers, JFD/DDE, G, C & M, box 5, Memorandum of Conversation with the British Ambassador, February 7, 1957.

84. EL, AW, Eisenhower Diaries, box 21, Phone Calls, February 1, 1957; John Foster Dulles Papers, JFD/DDE, G, C & M, box 1, "Memorandum of Conversation with the British Ambassador," February 7, 1957.

85. On January 29 the Senate Committees on Foreign Relations and Armed Services unanimously adopted a resolution requesting the State Department to "provide a chronological statement, together with classified and unclassified supporting documents, telegrams, and the like of all the events that have contributed significantly to the present situation in the Middle East, with particular reference to

the period beginning January 1946." During these hearings Dulles again insulted the British; he observed that "if I were an American soldier who had to fight in the Middle East I would rather not have a British and French soldier, one on my right and one on my left. I think I would be a lot safer without them." The secretary profusely apologized but had further damaged his reputation in Britain. See PRO, PREM 11/1178, Washington to Foreign Office, No. 144, January 26, 1957, and No. 155, January 28, 1957. The record of the published hearings is found in U.S. Senate Foreign Relations Committee, *Executive Sessions*.

86. EL, AW, Eisenhower Diaries, box 21, Phone Calls, February 6, 1957; Eban, *Autobiography*, p. 237.

87. John Foster Dulles Papers, JFD/DDE, Telephone Conversations, box 6, telephone call to Senator Smith, February 10, 1957.

88. EL, AW, International Series, box 29, Tel Aviv to State Department, No. 912, February 3, 1957; PRO, FO 371/128130, Tel Aviv to Foreign Office, No. 105, February 3, 1957. See also *FRUS*, vol. 17, 68:109–12, Ben-Gurion to Eisenhower, February 8, 1957; 69:112–15, Memorandum of Conversation at the State Department, February 8, 1957.

89. Nicholls provided this explanation for Ben-Gurion's behavior. See PRO, FO 371/128131, Tel Aviv to Foreign Office, No. 111, February 7, 1957.

90. Ibid., FO 371/128130, Washington to Foreign Office, No. 254, February 6, 1957; FO 371/128131, UKDEL to Foreign Office, No. 431, February 8, 1957; *New York Times*, February 6, 1957, p. 1.

91. PRO, FO 371/128139, Jebb to Lloyd, February 9, 1957; FO 371/128131, UKDEL to Foreign Office, No. 431, February 8, 1937; Foreign Office to Washington, No. 582, February 9, 1957; Washington to Foreign Office, No. 295, February 9, 1957.

92. Eban, *Autobiography*, p. 236. For example, an editorial from the *New York Times* of February 11, 1957, castigating the president for refusing to give Israel guarantees on both the Gulf waters and Gaza issues stated, "It is surely illogical to the point of nonsense to contend that the Egyptians should be rewarded for losing a war, and the Israelis punished for winning a war in which neither side was blameless." Dulles warned Lodge on February 10 that "we would have a terrible time on sanctions." See *FRUS*, vol. 17, 74:120, Dulles Telephone Conversation with Lodge, February 10, 1957.

93. PRO, FO 371/128131, Washington to Foreign Office, No. 296, February 9, 1957; John Foster Dulles Papers, Telephone Conversations, box 6, telephone call from Mr. Luce, February 11, 1957.

94. *FRUS*, vol. 17, 77:125–32, Memorandum of Conversation at the State Department, February 11, 1957; 78:132–34, "Aide-Mémoire from the Department of State to the Israeli Embassy," February 11, 1957.

95. That Dulles possessed this skill is not surprising, for it is the hallmark of a successful corporate lawyer (and during the 1930s Dulles was one of Wall Street's most successful practitioners) to stake out an extreme position initially but then agree to a compromise. Both John Lewis Gaddis and Richard Immerman have also emphasized Dulles's pragmatism. Contributing to Dulles's reassessment was Ambassador Lawson's report that the issue of the Straits of Tiran had become so charged with emotion in Israel that Lawson doubted whether Ben-Gurion's government would survive if he did not emerge from the impasse having secured Israeli

rights of passage. See *FRUS*, vol. 17, 5:8–9, Tel Aviv to State Department, No. 801, January 4, 1957; Gaddis, *The Long Peace*, and Immerman, *John Foster Dulles*.

96. PRO, FO 371/128133, Tel Aviv to Foreign Office, No. 127, February 14, 1957; FO 371/128134, "Gulf of Aqaba," February 14, 1957; *FRUS*, vol. 17, 103:181–87, Memorandum of Conversation at Dulles's Residence, February 16, 1957; Eban, *Autobiography*, pp. 241–42.

97. According to Humphrey, the Internal Revenue Service's estimate of the amount of assistance Israel was receiving annually was $40 million in private (tax deductible) contributions and $60 million worth of Israel bonds. The *New York Times's* estimate was higher; on February 24, 1957 (sec. 4, p. 3), it reported that private American contributions to the United Jewish Appeal totaled $60 million and also quoted the $60 million figure as the amount of Israel bonds sold each year. Such a prohibition was briefly considered at the NSC meeting of November 1 but rejected on the grounds that Israel had not yet been labeled an aggressor by the United Nations. See EL, AW, NSC Series, box 8, "Discussion at the 302nd Meeting of the National Security Council, Thursday, November 1, 1956"; Ambrose, *Eisenhower: The President*, p. 386.

98. During the 1950s American Jewish support for Israel had not yet solidified. Because influential organizations such as the American Council for Judaism took strident anti-Zionist positions, an approach such as officials discussed was far more practical than it would become in future decades. See Ambrose, *Eisenhower: The President*, pp. 386–87; Dwight D. Eisenhower, *White House Years: Waging Peace*, pp. 185–86.

99. EL, White House Office, Office of Staff Secretary, SS, SD, box 1, Statement by Secretary Dulles, February 16, 1957; John Foster Dulles Papers, Telephone Conversations, box 6, telephone call from Senator Knowland, February 16, 1957; Eban, *Autobiography*, p. 242.

100. Both Eisenhower and Dulles deemed it essential to obtain public support for their policy: "Dulles said he was working on a formal Resolution. . . . He does not propose to go as far as a lot of people like to have him go—he feels in his opinion it is no use going further than public opinion. The President agreed that in general he and the Secretary had to keep public opinion and the thinking of the American people behind them 'or we will lose'" (EL, AW, Eisenhower Diaries, box 21, Telephone Calls, February 21, 1957).

101. EL, White House Office, Office of Staff Secretary, IS, box 8, Press Statement, February 17, 1957; PRO, FO 371/128133, Washington to Foreign Office, No. 379, February 17, 1957; newspaper quotation from Eban, *Autobiography*, p. 243; *New York Times*, February 22, 1957.

102. John Foster Dulles Papers, Telephone Conversations, box 6, telephone call to Barnes, February 19, 1957.

103. Ibid., JFD/DDE, Telephone Conversations, box 6, telephone call to Barnes, February 22, 1957; telephone call to Elson, February 22, 1957.

104. Ibid., Telephone Conversations, box 6, telephone call to Lodge, February 18, 1957; *Economist*, January 5, 1957, p. 42.

105. Johnson had written Dulles on February 11 to express his opposition to United Nations sanctions levied solely against Israel. See *New York Times*, February 19, 1957, p. 1.; John Foster Dulles Papers, JFD/DDE, Chronological Series, box 14, Dulles to Johnson, February 21, 1957.

106. EL, AW, Eisenhower Diaries, box 21, Bipartisan Legislative Meeting, February 20, 1957; H. Alexander Smith Papers, box 125, Memorandum, February 20, 1957.

107. John Foster Dulles Papers, JFD/DDE, Telephone Conversations, box 6, telephone call to Lodge, February 12, 1957.

108. Ibid., G, C & M, box 5, Rabb to Adams, February 11, 1957.

109. Ibid., Subject Series, box 7, Text of Address by the President, February 20, 1957.

110. PRO, FO 371/128135, Tel Aviv to Foreign Office, No. 144, February 21, 1957; No. 152, February 22, 1957.

111. Ibid., FO 371/128136, UKDEL to Foreign Office, No. 660, February 23, 1957.

112. Ibid., FO 371/128135, Foreign Office to Washington, No. 843, February 21, 1957; FO 371/128136, Washington to Foreign Office, No. 441, February 23, 1957.

113. See, e.g., Ibid., FO 371/128135, UKDEL to Foreign Office, No. 655, February 22, 1957; No. 674, February 23, 1957; EL, AW, Eisenhower Diaries, box 21, Phone Calls, February 23, 1957.

114. PRO, FO 371/128135, UKDEL to Foreign Office, No. 655, February 22, 1957.

115. Ibid., FO 371/128135, Washington to Foreign Office, No. 427, February 21, 1957. See also *New York Times*, February 19, 1957, p. 1, and February 20, 1957, p. 1; *Economist*, February 23, 1957, p. 649.

116. *FRUS*, vol. 17, 143:254-67, Memorandum of Conversation at Dulles's Residence, February 24, 1957; Eban, *Autobiography*, pp. 246-47.

117. See, e.g., EL, AW, Eisenhower Diaries, box 21, Phone Calls, February 26, 1957; John Foster Dulles Papers, JFD/DDE, February 27, 1957, telephone call to Weaver, February 27, 1957; PRO, FO 371/128137, UKDEL to Foreign Office, No. 703, February 26, 1957; Washington to Foreign Office, No. 466, February 26, 1957.

118. *New York Times*, February 26, 1957, p. 8.

119. Newspaper opinion provided another reason for the administration's willingness to compromise with Israel. For example, the *New York Times* on February 26, 1957, stated, "Contrary to widespread assumption in the United Nations and in Washington, the issue is not originally the result of Israel's armed invasion of Egypt. The issue was raised by Egypt's long-standing insistence on maintaining a 'state of war' with Israel and implementing it by both guerilla raids and a double blockade in the Suez Canal and the Strait of Tiran. It was this Egyptian maintenance of a 'state of war' and the exercise of belligerent rights which Egypt derives therefrom that resulted in Israel's military counter-action, Egypt has made no public move or promise to end the 'state of war' or to renounce the belligerent rights."

120. The French foreign minister had earlier made it clear to Dulles that his country's "tilt" toward Israel had been strengthened by the Suez invasion. See *FRUS*, vol. 17, 15:21-25, Memorandum of Conversation at the State Department, January 11, 1957; EL, AW, International Series, box 12, Memorandum of Conversation between the President, the Secretary of State Premier Guy Mollet et al., February 26, 1957. See also *FRUS*, vol. 17, 162:299-303, Memorandum of Conversation at the State Department, February 27, 1957; 165:306-9, Memorandum of Conversation at the State Department, February 27, 1957; 167:311-17, Memorandum of Conversation at the State Department, February 28, 1957. The worsening French economy provided strong motivation for the French government to seek a firm rapprochement with Washington. While France, unlike Britain, had made the required payments on its American and Canadian loans at the end of December

($39.2 million and $11.2 million, respectively), by February Paris was forced to draw down $40 million of its IMF standby. See B/E, OV 45/44, "France: Economic Report No. 12: Period Ending December 1956"; OV 45/45, "The French Economy: Periodical Report No. 1, July 1957." The French government was also in the process of arranging for a series of credits from American bankers to finance the import of crude oil and other petroleum products. See McCloy Papers, SC1/22, Barth Memorandum, February 14, 1957.

121. EL, WHC, Confidential Files, Subject Series, box 73, Elbrick to Dulles, February 19, 1957; AW, International Series, box 12, Memoranda of Conversations between Eisenhower and Mollet and others, February 26 and 27, 1957; Eban, *Autobiography*, pp. 247–50.

122. According to Eban not only was Meir's statement prepared in the State Department, but Dulles himself took a hand with the drafting process. See Eban, *Autobiography*, p. 250.

123. PRO, FO 371/128137, Washington to Foreign Office, No. 498, February 28, 1957; FO 371/128138, Nos. 724 and 727, February 28, 1957.

124. The British representatives at the United Nations had suspected that Lodge would cause problems. For one thing he had lied to them by saying that he had no prepared text of his speech to show them in advance. Furthermore, according to the minister of state for foreign affairs, Lodge "looks upon it as his mission to achieve 'two-thirds' and said to Dixon and myself the other day that 'God had apparently willed it so.'" PRO, FO 371/128137, No. 707, February 27, 1957; EL, White House Office, Office of Staff Secretary, Official Files, Subject Series International, box 8, "United States Delegation to the General Assembly, Statement by Ambassador Henry Cabot Lodge," March 1, 1957; Meir, *My Life*, p. 255; Spiegel, *The Other Arab-Israel Conflict*, p. 80.

125. PRO, FO 371/128138, Tel Aviv to Foreign Office, No. 188, March 6, 1988; *FRUS*, vol. 17, 178:337, Memorandum of Conversation at the State Department, March 1, 1957; 181:340–47, Memorandum of Conversation at Dulles's Home, March 2, 1957; 185:351–55, Memorandum of Conversation at Dulles's Residence, March 3, 1957.

126. EL, AW, International Series, box 29, Eisenhower to Ben-Gurion, March 2, 1957.

127. PRO, FO 371/128138, Tel Aviv to Foreign Office, No. 179, March 4, 1957; FO 371/128138, UKDEL to Foreign Office, No. 752, March 4, 1957; Tel Aviv to Foreign Office, No. 211, March 14, 1957.

128. Examining the probable effects of an American-supported United Nations resolution applying sanctions to Israel, the CIA had concluded that while economic sanctions would eventually force Israel to acquiesce, the chances were "better than even" that Israel would not yield but would rather try to hold out as long as possible with the hope that world sympathy would begin to move to Israel's corner. See *FRUS*, vol. 17, 117:209–11, "Probable Effects of a US-supported UN Resolution Applying Sanctions to Israel," February 19, 1957. See also John Foster Dulles Papers, JFD/DDE Telephone Conversations, box 6, telephone call to Lodge, February 24, 1957.

129. Eban, *Autobiography*, p. 233.

130. As the *Economist* stated on April 6, 1957: "Israel is inevitably a loser in the present state of the cold war. Unlike its Arab neighbors with their oil wells,

pipelines and sites for foreign bases, and in spite of its strategic situation on the Mediterranean and Indian Ocean systems, Israel has not been regarded as a prize in the maneuvers of the great powers. Although the United States gives Israel money and private sympathy in plenty it withholds political support. For the hard fact is that Israel is an obstacle in the way of America's fighting mission against Communism. . . . While America and Russia play their wary musical chairs for the Arab states, Israel cannot hope for much change of attitude from either" (p. 19).

131. John Foster Dulles Papers, Subject Series, box 5, Public Law 85-7, March 9, 1957; Lodge Papers, General Correspondence, box 5b, Lodge to Eisenhower, March 11, 1957.

132. Ben-Gurion had come under severe domestic criticism for agreeing to the withdrawal and obviously felt that a stern protest against Nasser was now in order. See, e.g., NA, SD, 784.00(W)/3-157, Tel Aviv to State Department, March 4, 1957; 784.00(W)/3-857, Tel Aviv to State Department, March 10, 1957. However, the *Economist* lauded Ben-Gurion on March 9, 1957, for being willing "to confront anger at home" and urged Nasser "to begin to lead his country instead of following his extremists."

133. Lodge Papers, General Correspondence, box 5, "Notes on Statements made by Secretary Dulles to Lodge over the Telephone, March 6, 1956"; EL, AW, International Series, box 12, Paris to State Department, No. 4744, March 15, 1957; box 29, State Department to Cairo, No. 3030, March 13, 1957; State Department to Tel Aviv, No. 883, March 16, 1957; Eban, *Autobiography*, pp. 256–57; John Foster Dulles Papers, JFD/DDE, Telephone Conversations, box 6, telephone call to Lodge, March 18, 1957; telephone call from Lodge, March 18, 1957; Personal Papers, State Department Press Release No. 155, concerning meeting between Dulles and Meir, March 18, 1957.

134. John Foster Dulles Papers, JFD/DDE, Telephone Conversations, box 6, telephone call to Hammarskjöld, March 19, 1957; Personal Papers, box 123, Dulles to Hare, March 19, 1957.

135. Ibid., JFD/DDE, Telephone Conversations, box 6, telephone call to Knowland, March 19, 1957; Personal Papers, box 123, Dulles to Hare, March 19, 1957. See also McCloy Papers, SC1/32, McCloy Memorandum of Telephone Call with Dulles, March 25, 1957.

136. When a government sequesters property, it takes legal custody of it. According to the *Financial Times* the total value of British assets in Egypt in November 1956 was £55-£60 million; French assets were estimated at £75 million. The British figure included neither the British ownership interest in the Suez Canal nor the value of the Suez Canal base. See NA, SD, Lot file 69 D 488, box 67, Sethian to Norris, May 20, 1957. The best discussion of the Egyptian action against "foreign" interests is found in Tignor, "Decolonization and Business."

137. According to United Nations diplomat Brian Urquhart the Anglo-French policy was "a maddeningly detailed and critical supervision of UN efforts to clean up the mess they had created, questioning every step with a patronizing self-righteousness that was hard to take seriously" (Urquhart, *A Life in Peace and War*, pp. 134–35).

138. PRO, FO 371/125548, P. Ramsbottom to D. S. Laskey, December 22, 1956.

139. Nasser told Hare in April that the Six Principles no longer applied, that they

"had been [the] product of a Security Council meeting in which the British and French had participated at [a] time when, speaking in terms of [a] peaceful solution, they were planning forceful seizure of [the] canal" (NA, SD, 974.7301/4-1157, Cairo to State Department, No. 3204, April 11, 1957). To McCloy on April 1 Nasser had said that "the Six Principles were reminiscent of the whole conspiracy. . . . He added that one of the six points provided that the Canal must be insulated from Egyptian politics; how could it be!—it went down the middle of the street in Port Said, it was a part of Egypt as much as the Nile" (McCloy Papers, SC1/34, Memorandum of Interview with Nasser, April 1, 1957).

140. The United States contributed $5 million, Canada and Australia, $1 million, and other countries contributed smaller amounts. The British government attempted, with limited success, to have various tasks undertaken by its military expedition counted as payment in kind. The cost of clearance was recouped by levying a surcharge on freight passing through the canal.

141. PRO, T 236/4638, Washington to Foreign Office, No. 2551, December 26, 1956; FO 371/125505, Watson, "Suez Canal: Developments since December 20," January 2, 1957; FO 371/125548, Washington to Foreign Office, No. 28, January 5, 1957.

142. PRO, FO 371/125548, CRO to U.K. High Commissioners, W. No. 28, January 5, 1957; FO 371/125505, Washington to Foreign Office, No. 82, January 16, 1957.

143. See, e.g., B/E, OV 43/15, "Notes of A Discussion with Mr. William Armstrong," January 3, 1957; FRBNY, IMF Files 798.3, Exter Memorandum to Files, February 1, 1957.

144. NA, SD, Lot File 69 D 488, box 67, "United States Blocking Control on Egyptian Assets," October 1957.

145. During the months following the second London Conference of September 1956, SCUA had gradually taken on greater reality. Meetings were held, a Scandinavian administrator hired, money was spent, and documents generated. All that was lacking was a reason for existing.

146. PRO, FO 371/125506, Foreign Office to Washington, No. 322, January 24, 1957; PREM 11/1789, Washington to Foreign Office, No. 156, January 28, 1957; CAB 129/85, "Suez Canal: Memorandum by the Secretary of State for Foreign Affairs," January 29, 1957.

147. EL, AW, NSC Series, box 8, memorandum dated February 8, 1957, of a discussion at the 312th meeting of the National Security Council, February 7, 1957; PRO, FO 371/12505, CRO to High Commissioner in Canada et al., W. No. 191, February 8, 1957. At the end of March, State Department officials told McCloy that while the president believed that Israel should have the right to use the canal, McCloy should be very cautious in discussing the whole issue with Nasser. McCloy himself believed that by forcing Israel to withdraw unilaterally "the West has no cards with which to force Egypt to restore shippers' confidence and reopen the Canal without discrimination" (McCloy Papers, SC1/14, McCloy to Wheeler, March 12, 1957; SC1/31, Conversation with Douglas Dillon and Herman Phleger, March 25, 1957).

148. At the same time Dulles requested that Dillon, who had recently become undersecretary of state, take charge of the negotiations about the canal's future. The secretary of state cautioned Dillon that "while I think it is important to try to preserve unity with the British and French, I think you should remember that they

are not the only users of the Canal and not the only nations concerned and that a great many of our friends would not be as rigid as they are disposed to be." (NA, SD, 974.7301/3-557, Dulles to Dillon, March 5, 1957; 974.7301/3-757, Herter to USUN, No. 159, March 7, 1957).

149. B/E, OV 43/16, Washington to Foreign Office, No. 701, March 19, 1957.

150. PRO, FO 371/125510, Record of Meeting held at the Hotel Matignon, Paris, on Saturday, March 9, 1957; PREM 11/2012, Memorandum to Prime Minister, March 19, 1957.

151. B/E, OV 31/57, "Present Position on EXIM Loan and Waiver," March 19, 1957,

152. PRO, T 236/3925, Washington to Foreign Office, No. 538, March 5, 1957. Simultaneously a comparable amendment to the Canadian loan agreement was executed.

153. They shipped 300,000 barrels of oil to Europe that otherwise would have gone to the American East Coast. See Organization of European Economic Cooperation, *Europe's Need for Oil*, p. 23.

154. PRO, FO 371/120840, OEEC Oil Committee Record of First Joint Session of Oil Committee and OPEC held on December 7, 1956; FO 371/120838, OEEC to Foreign Office, Nos. 854 and 859 Saving, December 8, 1956; Organization of European Economic Cooperation, *Europe's Need for Oil*, p. 29.

155. EL, Seaton Papers, box 1, Remarks of Secretary Fred A. Seaton before the National Petroleum Council, December 14, 1956.

156. Appendix C contains information concerning oil supplies and oil shipments to Europe.

157. See, e.g., PRO, FO 371/120838, OEEC to Foreign Office, No. 856 Saving, December 8, 1956; FO 371/120839, Warner to Eden, December 20, 1956; FO 371/120840, Oil Committee, Record, dated December 27, 1956, of the 83d Session held on the mornings of 18 and 19 December, 1956; FO 371/127217, Ministry of Fuel and Power to Washington, No. 6 Fuel, January 4, 1957.

158. Ibid., FO 371/120840, Foreign Office to Bonn, No. 992 Saving, December 18, 1956.

159. The Texas Railroad Commission had jurisdiction over Texas oil production. The commission allocated each of the 160,000 wells in production a rated allowance, the "allowable rate": the maximum efficient rate of daily production. Each month the commission met and determined the amount of a day's full production to be permitted the following month. In February 1957 the average daily allowable production was 3,554,000 barrels as opposed to 3,314,000 barrels in November 1956. In March 1957 production was again raised, to 3,733,000 barrels/day. Both producers and the federal government abided by the commission's decisions concerning monthly production quotas. Because Texas produced the lion's share of American oil, the determination of the Railroad Commission had a major influence on the amount of American production. See Organization of European Economic Cooperation, *Europe's Need for Oil*, p. 30.

160. Oil restrictions in other countries varied. As of January 1957 most countries had made cuts in consumption from 10 percent to 20 percent for gas/diesel oil and 20 percent for fuel oil; in West Germany and France the cut in fuel oil was between 30 percent and 35 percent. See, e.g., PRO, T 234/80, "Oil Restrictions in Member Countries of OEEC," January 16, 1957, and Memorandum to Chancellor of the

Exchequer, January 23, 1957; T 234/81, Memorandum to Chancellor of the Exchequer concerning Further Cuts in Industrial Fuel Oil Consumption, February 1, 1957; FO 371/125536, Summary Record of Discussions During the Meeting of the Group of Experts, January 31 and February 1, 1957.

161. U.S. Congress, Joint Hearings, 85th Cong., 1st sess., pursuant to S. Res. 57.

162. Ibid.

163. Although oil imports decreased in volume after November 1956, their dollar cost increased significantly. The OEEC later estimated that at the most severe point of the crisis the additional dollar cost was running at $300-$400 million a year. While this amount was significant, it is interesting that it was considerably less than the $500-$1,000 million the British and American governments had estimated would be involved. See Organization of European Economic Cooperation, *Europe's Need for Oil*, p. 42.

164. NA, SD, 974.7301/12-2856, U.S. Intelligence Report, No. 7396, December 28, 1956.

165. The Oil Committee of the OEEC drew optimistic lessons from the Suez crisis as well. In a report prepared in January 1958, the committee lauded the cooperation by member countries and commented with approval on the collaboration between governments and industry. The committee, however, did note that a disruption of oil supplies was likely to occur again and that Europe could not count on the United States to play the role of substitute supplier indefinitely. While the committee advocated such measures as accumulating larger European oil reserves, developing further flexibility in transport, diversification of supply, and joint contingency planning by OEEC members, it pointed out that effective methods to insure against future disruptions, such as large reserves, reserve tankers, and spare production capacity, would be extremely expensive. Not surprisingly the favorable denouement of the crisis in 1956–57 allowed governments to postpone any expensive and unpleasant decisions. Taking this easy route would cost the European countries as well as the United States dearly fifteen years later. See Organization of European Economic Cooperation, *Europe's Need for Oil*, pp. 43–46; PRO, FO 371/120839, Falle, "Oil Price and Sales by United Kingdom Companies," December 12, 1956; NA, SD, 974.7301/3-1157KK, Terrill to Moline, March 11, 1957.

166. In fact a position paper prepared for Macmillan's use during the Bermuda summit concluded that "so far as the level of output goes the economy has withstood the impacts of the Suez crisis remarkably well." See PRO, FO 371/127190, Economic Effects of the Suez Crisis, March 18, 1956; PREM 11/1789, Washington to Foreign Office, No. 435, February 22, 1957; T 236/4642, Foreign Office to Washington, No. 9191, February 26, 1957; T 234/81, "Effects of the Oil Shortage," February 5, 1957, and Macmillan to Minister of Power, March 8, 1957.

167. PRO, PREM 11/1178, Caccia to Macmillan, February 1, 1957; John Foster Dulles Papers, JFD/DDE, G, C & M, box 1, Memorandum of Conversation dated January 30, 1957, concerning meeting among Dulles, Sandys, and Caccia, January 27, 1957; EL, AW, Eisenhower Diaries, box 22, March 1957 Diary.

168. EL, AW, Eisenhower Diaries, box 22, Goodpaster Memorandum for the Record, March 22, 1957.

169. Ibid. Bermuda Conference, March 21, 1957; John Foster Dulles Papers, Personal Papers, box 113, Memorandum of Conversation at the Mid-Ocean Club,

March 20, 1957; PRO, PREM, 11/1838, Minutes of First and Second Plenary Meetings, March 21, 1957.

CHAPTER EIGHT

1. The agreement provided that the company would retain Canal Company assets outside Egypt in the amount of E £70-£74 million ($210-$240 million) and the dues it had collected between 1956 and 1958 (E £5 million or $15 million). Egypt would also pay E £23 million ($69 million) over five years beginning in 1959 for its nationalization of the canal. In return the company would assume the liabilities incurred by the company abroad and renounce all rights to the canal and under the franchise agreement that expired in 1968. See NA, 974.7301/4-2258, Rountree to Dillon, April 22, 1958.

2. France and Egypt came to a settlement of all outstanding issues in August 1958.

3. The revocation of the Egyptian Assets Control Regulations released slightly over $23 million of assets belonging to the National Bank of Egypt and held by the FRBNY. Additionally the FRBNY already held $1.3 million in free assets of the National Bank of Egypt. Apparently the National Bank had about $3 million in deposits at the Guaranty Trust Company of New York and the Riggs National Bank in Washington. The revocation of the blocking regulations also freed slightly over $40 million belonging to the Suez Canal Company and held at J. P. Morgan & Co. and Chase Manhattan Bank. See FRBNY, Egypt C261, Davis to Exter, May 1, 1958.

4. As Sir John Coulson, chargé d'affaires of the British embassy in Washington, told William Rountree, the most equitable manner of dealing with the cost of the canal would be to assign the responsibility to Egypt, but "this was impossible, however, because Egypt would not pay" (NA, SD, 974.7301/8-1357, Memorandum of Conversation, August 13, 1957).

5. On Nasser's actions in November 1956, see, e.g., NA, SD, 841.1474/11-1656, Rountree to Wilkins, "Egyptian Attempt to Gain Control of Funds Held in the U.S. by British and French Banks Operating in Egypt," November 16, 1956; 841.1474/11-1956 HBS, Cairo to State Department, No. 1576, November 19, 1956; DD, 1984-1840, Cairo to State Department, No. 1406, November 8, 1956; B/E, EC 5/357, "Egypt-Working Party," November 21, 1956; OV 31/55, Balfour to Moberly, November 28, 1956; PRO, FO 371/118938, Washington to Foreign Office, No. 6 Remac, November 17, 1956; Foreign Office to Washington, No. 5416, November 17, 1956; Washington to Foreign Office, No. 7 Remac, November 19, 1956, and No. 8 Remac, November 23, 1956; FO 371/120822, Washington to Foreign Office, No. 255 ES, November 17, 1956; FO 371/120834, Figures to Ellis Rees, November 23, 1956; FO 371/118938, Watson to Johnston, November 26, 1956, and Foreign Office to Washington, November 26, 1956; CAB 134/815, DTC (56), "Threatened Expulsion of British Subjects From Egypt," November 27, 1956. On the general subject of Egyptian treatment of foreign business interests, see Tignor, "Decolonization and Business"; Tignor, "Foreign Capital."

6. No doubt French officials correctly perceived the increasing administration contempt for their leaders and policies. Dulles, for one, told Eisenhower on December 3 that "I felt that the era of tripartite meetings had about drawn to a close. I hoped to avoid any such meeting in Paris. I felt it was increasingly difficult to

maintain the illusion that France was one of the great world powers, and that this was increasingly an irritant to countries like Germany and Italy" (John Foster Dulles Papers, JFD/DDE, WHM, box 4, Memorandum of Conversation with the President, December 3, 1956).

7. See, e.g., Maurice Vaisse, "Post-Suez France," in Louis and Owen, *Suez 1956*.

8. That the *Economist* had come to the same realization was reflected in a leading article on December 1, 1956: "This crisis has shown that Britain cannot succeed in any major external adventure on which it embarks alone" (p. 758).

9. PRO, FO 371/120342, Washington to Foreign Office, No. 2359, November 28, 1956, Extract from personal letter from Sir Harold Caccia to Mr. Reilly, November 29, 1956; PREM 11/2189, Caccia to Lloyd, "The Present State of Anglo-American Relations," January 1, 1957; FO 371/126682, Washington to Foreign Office, Nos. 1, 2, and 3, January 1, 1957.

10. PRO, T 236/4190, Eccles to Macmillan, December 3, 1956.

11. EL, AW, NSC Series, box 8, "Discussion at the 299th Meeting of the National Security Council, Thursday, October 4, 1956"; John Foster Dulles Papers, JFD/DDE, WHM, box 4, "Memorandum of Conference with the President, November 20, 1956."

12. While Macmillan spearheaded Britain's 1961 application to join the Common Market, the four-year delay ended any chance of Britain seizing the community's leadership in its formative years.

13. Macmillan's comment seems ironic in light of the American concern with the decline of its power, which surfaced in the late 1980s. The most important study of comparative British and American national decline is Kennedy, *The Rise and Fall of the Great Powers*. Also relevant is Calleo, *Beyond American Hegemony*.

14. See PRO, CAB 129/30, CM 2(57), January 8, 1957.

15. "Stop-go" and "zig-zag" referred to the series of sharp, recurring cycles that characterized the British economy during the three decades after the Second World War. See Chapter 1, n. 36.

16. In mid-November columnist James Reston had predicted that the Suez crisis marked a change in the administration's foreign policy. Reston hazarded that henceforth there would be a greater emphasis on working through the United Nations, a greater independence from Britain and France, and a reorientation toward working with the rising nationalist forces of Africa, Asia, and the Middle East. However, the administration's foreign policies after November 1956 were conspicuous more for their continuity than for any real change. See *New York Times*, November 19, 1956, p. 1.

17. As political scientists have paid more attention to the efficacy of economic sanctions than have historians, most of the literature of the subject comes from that discipline. See, e.g., Baldwin, *Economic Statecraft*; Barber, "Economic Statecraft As a Policy Instrument"; Hufbauer and Schott, "Economic Sanctions and U.S. Foreign Policy"; Lenway, "Between War and Commerce"; Mayall, "The Sanctions Problem"; Miller, "When Sanctions Worked." Interestingly, these writers virtually ignore the Suez crisis, although using it as a case study would support their theories.

18. British officials appreciated the relevance of the Suez crisis to this point; on December 27, 1956, Eden's private secretary wrote to him that "it is true that one of the main lessons of Suez is that economically we are not strong enough to 'go it

alone' in international affairs if we are seen to be opposed by world (including U.S.) opinion" (PRO, PREM 11/1826).

19. By contrast France at the end of 1955 had reserves of $1,900 million with which to run the much smaller franc zone. See NA, RG 56, NAC Document No. 1999, October 10, 1956.

20. PRO, PREM 11/1826, Macmillan to Eden, December 31, 1956.

APPENDIX C

1. This information is derived from information compiled by the British government. See PRO, FO 371/127201, S. Falle, "Middle Eastern Oil, January 23, 1957."

2. Production in Bahrein was quite small and not thought likely to increase, but Bahrein contained an important refinery that produced 10 million tons annually, using basically Saudi Arabian crude oil. The Saudi government cut off supplies to this refinery in the wake of the Suez invasion.

3. C. S. Gulbenkian was the individual whose skill at corporate matchmaking had been responsible for the original "Red Line" Agreement.

4. Jointly owned by nine independent American oil companies.

5. Foreign shares were sequestered in wake of Suez invasion.

APPENDIX D

1. This summary is based on a State Department Memorandum of Conversation held on December 12, 1955, reprinted in *FRUS*, vol. 14, 450:849–51, and the "Aide Mémoire to the Government of Egypt," dated December 16, 1955, in NA, SD, Lot File 62 D 11, box 7.

2. It was this provision that Nasser feared would restrict his ability to purchase more arms.

SELECT BIBLIOGRAPHY
~

MANUSCRIPT SOURCES AND ORAL HISTORY

OFFICIAL ARCHIVES

United States

Dwight D. Eisenhower Presidential Library, Abilene, Kansas
    Dwight D. Eisenhower Oral History Collection
    Dwight D. Eisenhower Papers (White House Central Files)
        Confidential Files
        General Files
        Official Files
    Dwight D. Eisenhower Papers (Ann Whitman File)
        Administrative Series
        Cabinet Series
        Dulles-Herter Series
        Eisenhower Diary Series
        International Series
        International Meeting Series
        Legislative Series
        Name Series
        National Security Council Series
        Ann Whitman Diary
        White House Office: National Security Council Staff
        Executive Secretary's Subject File Series
        Operations Coordinating Board Central File Series
        Operations Coordinating Board Secretariat Series

White House Office: Office of Staff Secretary (L. Arthur Minnich file)
Cabinet Series
Legislative Meeting Series
Private Collections
    Robert Cutler Papers
    Fred A. Seaton Papers
    Walter Bedell Smith Papers
Federal Reserve Bank of New York, New York, New York
    Country Files (C261)
    Exim Bank (790.8)
    International Monetary Fund Files (798.3)
    System Foreign Relations-Staff Group (0961)
Federal Reserve Board, Washington, D.C.
    Miscellaneous Records
National Archives, Washington, D.C.
    General Records of the Department of State (RG 59)
    General Records of the Department of the Treasury (RG 56)
    George M. Humphrey Papers (RG 198)
    Records of the Joint Chiefs of Staff (RG 216)

Great Britain

Public Record Office, Kew
    Cabinet Office (CAB 27, 28, 129, 134)
    Foreign Office (FO 371, 800)
    Prime Minister's Private Office (PREM 11)
    Treasury (T 172, 199, 231, 234, 236)
Bank of England, London
    Exchange Control (EC 5)
    Governor's Files (G 1)
    Overseas Finance (OV 31, 38, 43)

PERSONAL PAPERS

United States

Dean Acheson Papers, Yale University, New Haven, Connecticut
Allen Dulles Papers, Princeton University, Princeton, New Jersey
John Foster Dulles Papers, Princeton University, Princeton, New Jersey
George M. Humphrey Papers, Western Reserve Historical Society, Cleveland, Ohio
Henry Cabot Lodge Papers, Massachusetts Historical Society, Boston, Massachusetts
John J. McCloy Papers, Amherst College, Amherst, Massachusetts
H. Alexander Smith Papers, Princeton University, Princeton, New Jersey

Great Britain

Brendan Bracken Papers, Churchill College, Cambridge University
R. A. Butler Papers, Trinity College, Cambridge University
William Clark Papers, Bodleian Library, Oxford University

Patrick Dean Papers, Bodleian Library, Oxford University
Maurice Hankey Papers, Churchill College, Cambridge University
Per Jacobssen Papers, London School of Economics Library
Donald Logan Papers, Churchill College, Cambridge University
Walter Monckton Papers, Bodleian Library, Oxford University
Philip Noel-Baker Papers, Churchill College, Cambridge University

GOVERNMENT DOCUMENTS AND OFFICIAL PUBLICATIONS

Foreign Relations of the United States, 1955–1957. Vol. 9, *Foreign Economic Policy; Foreign Information Program.* Vol. 10, *Foreign Aid and Economic Defense Policy.* Vol. 14, *Arab-Israeli Dispute 1955.* Vol. 15, *Arab-Israeli Dispute, January 1–July 26, 1956.* Vol. 16, *Suez Crisis, July 26–December 31, 1956.* Vol. 17, *Arab-Israeli Dispute 1957.* Washington, D.C., 1987–90.
Organization of European Economic Cooperation. *Europe's Need for Oil: Implications and Lessons of the Suez Crisis.* Paris, 1958.
U.S. Congress. Foreign Relations of the United States, Joint Hearings before the Subcommittees of the Committee on the Judiciary and the Committee on Interior and Insular Affairs. "Emergency Oil Lift Program and Related Problems." 85th Cong., 1st sess., February–March 1957.
U.S. Senate. Foreign Relations Committee. *Executive Sessions* (Historical Series). Vol. 9. 1957.

DECLASSIFIED DOCUMENTS

Declassified documents used in this work are available through the Freedom of Information Act.

NEWSPAPERS

The Economist
The Financial Times
The New York Times
The Times
The Wall Street Journal

INTERVIEWS WITH AUTHOR

Lucius Battle, Washington, D.C., June 9, 1988.
Raymond Bonham Carter, London, July 3, 1989.
Lord Caccia, London, July 5, 1989.
David Dilks, Leeds, England, March 12, 1986.
C. Douglas Dillon, New York, New York, June 28, 1988.
Lord Sherfield, London, November 17, 1987; May 25, 1989.
Lord Thorneycroft, London, May 23, 1989.
Adam Watson, Charlottesville, Virginia, February 8–9, 1988.
Sir Denis Wright, Haddenham, England, July 4, 1989.

BOOKS, ARTICLES, AND UNPUBLISHED DISSERTATIONS AND PAPERS

AUTOBIOGRAPHIES AND MEMOIRS

Acheson, Dean. *Present at the Creation: My Years at the State Department.* New York, 1969, 1987.
Butler, Mollie. *August and Rab: A Memoir.* London, 1987.
Butler, R. A. *The Art of the Possible: The Memoirs of Lord Butler.* London, 1981.
Clark, William. *From Three Worlds.* London, 1986.
Colville, John. *The Fringes of Power: 10 Downing Street Diaries, 1939–1955.* London, 1985.
Dayan, Moshe. *Story of My Life: An Autobiography.* New York, 1976.
Eban, Abba. *An Autobiography.* New York, 1977.
Eden, Anthony. *Full Circle.* Boston, 1960.
Eisenhower, Dwight D. *The White House Years.* Vol. 1, *Mandate for Change: 1953–1956.* Garden City, N.Y., 1963.
———. *The White House Years, Vol. 2, Waging Peace: 1956–1961.* Garden City, N.Y., 1965.
Fawzi, Mahmoud. *Suez 1956: An Egyptian Perspective.* London, n.d.
Georges-Picot, Jacques. *The Real Suez Crisis: The End of a Great Nineteenth Century Work.* New York, 1975.
Heikal, Mohammed H. *Cutting the Lion's Tail: Suez through Egyptian Eyes.* London, 1986.
Henderson, Nicholas. *Channels and Tunnels: Reflections on Britain and Abroad.* London, 1987.
Lloyd, Selwyn. *Suez: 1956.* London, 1986.
Lodge, Henry Cabot. *As It Was: An Inside View of Politics and Power in the 1950's and 1960's.* New York, 1976.
Macdougall, Donald. *Don and Mandarin: Memoirs of an Economist.* London, 1987.
Macmillan, Harold. *Riding the Storm 1956–1959.* London, 1971.
Meir, Golda. *My Life.* New York, 1975.
Murphy, Robert. *Diplomat among Warriors.* New York, 1964.
Nasser, Gamal Abdel. *Egypt's Liberation: The Philosophy of Revolution.* Washington, 1955.
Nutting, Anthony. *I Saw for Myself: The Aftermath of Suez.* London, 1958.
———. *No End of a Lesson.* New York, 1967.
Pineau, Christian. *1956: Suez.* Paris, 1976.
Sadat, Jehan. *A Woman of Egypt.* New York, 1987.
Schuckburgh, Evelyn. *Descent to Suez: Diaries 1951–1956.* London, 1986.
Urquhart, Brian. *A Life in Peace and War.* New York, 1987.

GENERAL WORKS

Ambrose, Stephen E. *Eisenhower.* Vol. 1, *Soldier, General of the Army, President-Elect: 1890–1953.* New York, 1983, 1985.
———. *Eisenhower.* Vol. 2, *The President: 1953–1968.* New York, 1984, 1985.
———. *Rise to Globalism: American Foreign Policy Since 1938.* 4th ed. New York, 1982.

Anderson, Irvine H. *Aramco, the United States and Saudi Arabia: A Study of the Dynamics of Foreign Oil Policy, 1933–1950*. Princeton, 1981.

Aronson, Geoffrey. *From Sideshow to Center Stage: U.S. Policy Toward Egypt, 1946–1956*. Boulder, 1986.

Baldwin, David. *Economic Statecraft*. Princeton, 1985.

Bamberger, Merry and Serge. *Les Secrets de l'Expedition D'Egypte*. Paris, 1957.

Barber, James. "Economic Statecraft as a Policy Instrument." *International Affairs* 55 (1979): 367–84.

Bill, James. *The Eagle and the Lion: The Tragedy of American-Iranian Relations*. New Haven, 1988.

Blair, John M. *The Control of Oil*. New York, 1976.

Bonin, Hubert. *Suez: Du canal a la finance*. Paris, 1987.

Bowie, Robert R. *Suez 1956: International Crises and the Role of Law*. New York, 1974.

Brands, H. W. *Cold Warriors: Eisenhower's Generation and American Foreign Policy*. New York, 1988.

Brendon, Piers. *Ike: His Life and Times*. New York, 1986.

Bullock, Alan. *Ernest Bevin: Foreign Secretary, 1945–1951*. Oxford, 1985.

Burns, William J. *Economic Aid and American Policy toward Egypt: 1955–1981*. Albany, 1985.

Cairncross, Alec. *Years of Recovery: British Economic Policy, 1945–1951*. London, 1985.

Cairncross, Alec, and Eichengreen, Barry. *Sterling in Decline: The Devaluations of 1931, 1949 and 1967*. Oxford, 1983.

Calleo, David. *Beyond American Hegemony*. New York, 1987.

Campbell, John. *Nye Bevan and the Mirage of British Socialism*. London, 1987.

Carlton, David. *Anthony Eden*. London, 1981, 1986.

———. *Britain & the Suez Crisis*. London, 1988.

Childers, Erskine B. *The Road to Suez: A Study of Western-Arab Relations*. London, 1962.

Colville, John. *The Churchillians*. London, 1981.

Cooper, Artemis. *Cairo in the War, 1939–1945*. London, 1989.

Cooper, Chester L. *The Lion's Last Roar: Suez, 1956*. New York, 1978.

Dimbleby, David, and Reynolds, David. *An Ocean Apart*. London, 1987.

Divine, Robert A. *Eisenhower and the Cold War*. New York, 1981.

Donovan, Robert J. *Conflict and Crisis: The Presidency of Harry S. Truman, 1945–1948*. New York, 1977.

Edmonds, Robin. *Setting the Mould: The United States and Britain, 1945–1950*. New York, 1986.

Eisenhower, David. *Eisenhower at War: 1943–45*. New York, 1986.

Epstein, Leon D. *British Politics in the Suez Crisis*. Chicago, 1964.

Finer, Herman. *Dulles over Suez: The Theory and Practice of His Diplomacy*. Chicago, 1964.

Gaddis, John Lewis. *The Long Peace*. Oxford, 1987.

Gardner, Richard. *Sterling-Dollar Diplomacy*. 2d ed. New York, 1969.

Gilbert, Martin. *Never Despair: Winston S. Churchill, 1945–1965*. London, 1988.

Greenstein, Fred I. *The Hidden Hand Presidency: Eisenhower as Leader*. New York, 1982.

Hahn, Peter. "Containment and Egyptian Nationalism: The Unsuccessful Effort to Establish the Middle East Command, 1950–53." *Diplomatic History* 11 (1987): 23–40.

———. *The United States, Great Britain, and Egypt, 1945–1956: Strategy and Diplomacy in the Early Cold War*. Chapel Hill: University of North Carolina Press, 1991.

Harris, Kenneth. *Atlee*. London, 1982.

Hathaway, Robert M. *Ambiguous Partnership: Britain and America 1944–1947*. New York, 1981.

Hennessy, Peter, and Seldon, Anthony, eds. *Ruling Performance: British Governments from Atlee to Thatcher*. London, 1987.

Hogan, Michael J. *The Marshall Plan: America, Britain and the Reconstruction of Western Europe, 1947–1952*. New York, 1987.

Hoopes, Townsend. *The Devil and John Foster Dulles*. Boston, 1973.

Hopwood, Derek. *Egypt: Politics and Society, 1945–1984*. 2d ed. Boston, 1985.

Horne, Alastair. *A Savage War of Peace: Algeria, 1954–1962*. New York, 1977.

———. *Macmillan, 1894–1956: Volume I of the Official Biography*. London, 1988.

———. *Macmillan, 1957–1986: Volume II of the Official Biography*. London, 1989.

Howard, Anthony. *RAB: The Life of R. A. Butler*. London, 1987.

Hufbauer, Clyde, and Schott, Jeffrey J. "Economic Sanctions and U.S. Foreign Policy." *PS* 18 (1985): 727–35.

Immerman, Richard, H., ed. *John Foster Dulles and the Diplomacy of the Cold War: A Centennial Reappraisal*. Princeton, 1989.

James, Robert Rhodes. *Anthony Eden*. London, 1986.

Kaufman, Burton I. *The Oil Cartel Case: A Documentary Study of Anti-Trust Activity in the Cold War Era*. Westport, Conn., 1978.

———. *Trade and Aid: Eisenhower's Foreign Economic Policy*. Baltimore, 1982.

Kennedy, Paul. *The Rise and Fall of the Great Powers*. New York, 1988.

Kolodziej, Edward. *Making and Marketing Arms: The French Experience and Its Implications for the International System*. Princeton, 1987.

Kunz, Diane B. *The Battle for Britain's Gold Standard in 1931*. London, 1987.

Lacoutre, Jean. *Nasser*. New York, 1973.

Lamb, Richard. *The Failure of the Eden Government*. London, 1987.

Lapping, Brian. *End of Empire*. London, 1985.

Lenway, Stefanie Ann. "Between War and Commerce: Economic Sanctions as a Tool of Statecraft." *International Organization* 42 (1988): 397–426.

Louis, Wm. Roger. *The British Empire in the Middle East, 1945–1951: Arab Nationalism, the United States and Post-War Imperialism*. Oxford, 1984, 1985.

———. *Imperialism at Bay: The United States and the Decolonization of the British Empire, 1941–1945*. Oxford, 1977, 1986.

Louis, Wm. Roger, and Bull, Hedley, eds. *The Special Relationship: Anglo-American Relations since 1945*. Oxford, 1986.

Louis, Wm. Roger, and Owen, Roger, eds. *Suez 1956: The Crisis and Its Consequences*. Oxford, 1989.

Love, Kennett. *Suez: The Twice-Fought War*. New York, 1969.

Mayall, James. "The Sanctions Problem in International Economic Relations." *International Affairs* 70 (1984): 631–42.

Miller, Judith. "When Sanctions Worked." *Foreign Policy* 37 (1979): 118–29.

Milward, Alan S. *The Reconstruction of Western Europe*. Berkeley, 1984.

Monroe, Elizabeth. *Britain's Moment in the Middle East*. 2d ed. Baltimore, 1981.

Morgan, Kenneth O. *Labour in Power: 1945–1951*. Oxford, 1983.

Mosley, Leonard. *Dulles: A Biography of Eleanor, Allen and John Foster Dulles and Their Family Network*. New York, 1978.

Neff, Donald. *Warriors at Suez: Eisenhower Takes America into the Middle East*. New York, 1981.

Nutting, Anthony. *Nasser*. London, 1981.

Painter, David S. *Oil and the American Century: The Political Economy of United States Foreign Oil Policy, 1941–1954*. Baltimore, 1986.

Pelling, Henry. *The Labour Governments: 1945–1951*. London, 1984.

Pogue, Forrest C. *George C. Marshall: Statesman: 1945–1959*. New York, 1987.

Pollard, Sidney. *The Development of the British Economy: Third Edition: 1914–1980*. New York, 1983.

Porter, Bernard. *The Lion's Share: A Short History of British Imperialism, 1850–1983*. 2d ed. London, 1986.

Prussen, Ronald. *John Foster Dulles: The Road to Power*. New York, 1982.

Rioux, Jean-Pierre. *The Fourth Republic: 1944–1958*. Cambridge, 1987.

Robertson, Terrance. *Crisis: The Inside Story of the Suez Conspiracy*. New York, 1965.

Rubin, Barry, *The Arab States and the Palestine Conflict*. Syracuse, 1982.

Safran, Nadav. *Israel: The Embattled Ally*. Harvard, 1978.

Sampson, Anthony. *The Seven Sisters: The Great Oil Companies and the World They Shaped*. New York, 1975, 1976.

Sattin, Anthony. *Lifting the Veil: British Society in Egypt, 1768–1956*. London, 1988.

Seldon, Anthony. *Churchill's Indian Summer: The Conservative Government, 1951–1955*. London, 1981.

Shlaim, Avi. *Collusion across the Jordan: King Abdullah, the Zionist Movement and the Partition of Palestine*. New York, 1988.

Spiegel, Steven L. *The Other Arab-Israeli Conflict: Making America's Middle East Policy from Truman to Reagan*. Chicago, 1985.

Stookey, Robert. *America and the Arab States: An Uneasy Encounter*. New York, 1975.

Taheri, Amir. *The Cauldron: The Middle East Behind the Headlines*. London, 1988.

Teveth, Shabtai. *Ben-Gurion: The Burning Ground, 1880–1948*. New York, 1986.

———. *Moshe Dayan: The Soldier, the Man, the Legend*. Boston, 1973.

Tew, Brian. *The Evolution of the International Monetary System*. 3d ed. London, 1985.

Thomas, Hugh. *Suez*. New York, 1966, 1967.

Thompson, Kenneth W., ed. *Portraits of American Presidents*. Vol. 3, *The Eisenhower Presidency*. New York, 1984.

Thorpe, D. R. *Selwyn Lloyd*. London, 1989.

Tignor, Robert. "Decolonization and Business: The Case of Egypt." *Journal of Modern History* 59 (1987): 479–505.

———. "Foreign Capital, Foreign Communities, and the Egyptian Revolution of 1952." Unpublished.

Troen, S. Ilan, and Shemesh, M., eds. *The Suez-Sinai Crisis, 1956: Retrospective and Reappraisal*. New York, 1990.

Vatikiotis, P. J. *The Modern History of Egypt*. 2d ed. London, 1980.

Watt, D. Cameron. *Succeeding John Bull: America in Britain's Place, 1900–1975*. Cambridge, 1984.

Yungher, Israel. "United States-Israel Relations: 1953–1956." Ph.D. dissertation, University of Pennsylvania, 1985.

INDEX

~

Acheson, Dean, 21, 25, 28
Aldrich, Winthrop, 114, 142, 143, 151
Algeria: importance of in French policy
    to Egypt, 4, 16, 77–78, 81
Allen, George, 76
Alpha, Project, 39–40, 44
Alphand, Hervé, 98, 159
Anderson, Robert, 63–64, 141
Anderson Mission, 63–64
Anglo-American Loan Agreement of
    1945 (U.S. Agreement), 8–12, 52,
    104–5, 136–37, 162, 181
Anglo-Egyptian Treaty (1936), 24, 34
Anglo-Egyptian Treaty (1954), 33–34
Arab(s): and Britain, 14–25, 94, 168,
    191–92; and France, 15–16; opposi-
    tion to and boycott of Israel, 15–17;
    opposition to and invasion of Egypt,
    130, 132
Aswan Dam (High Dam), 40; U.S.–
    British withdrawal of assistance to, 2,
    4, 65–72; financing of, 40–43, 48–57,
    65–72, 75
Attlee, Clement, 7, 22
Australia, 61, 101, 146

Baghdad Pact, 38–39
Bank of England, 14, 41, 89, 127, 131, 132,
    136, 137, 138, 142, 146
Barnes, Roswell, 171–72
Baruch, Bernard, 11
Beeley, Sir Harold, 92, 98
Ben-Gurion, David, 17; reaction to pro-
    posed collusion, 118; and U.S., 120,
    163, 164, 174, 176; and arms purchases
    from France, 176; agrees to cease-fire
    and withdrawal from Egypt, 176–77
Bevin, Ernest, 15
Black, Eugene, 42, 43, 50, 51, 54, 57, 59,
    60, 69, 90, 111, 186
Bolton, Sir George, 89, 100, 136, 146
Britain: decline of influence in Middle
    East, 14–25, 157–59, 173–74, 189–92;
    and Iran, 20–22, 31–33; and proposals
    for settlement of Arab-Israeli dis-
    pute, 39–40; and armed intervention
    against Egypt, 76–77, 81–82, 85–86,
    93–95, 96, 97, 103–8, 109, 114–15, 117–
    19, 123, 128–29, 130, 133; economic
    sanctions against Egypt, 78, 80, 186–
    87; and proposals for international

control of Suez Canal, 83–85, 92, 100, 110–12, 114–15, 178–81; and U.N., 100, 111–12, 114–15, 126, 129, 134, 135–36, 143, 163, 167, 170, 176, 179–81; and misjudgment of American reaction to invasion of Egypt, 103–8, 122, 123–24, 126, 128–29, 133–35, 138–52; and collusion with France and Israel, 117–19, 127–28; and ultimatum to Egypt and Israel, 118, 123; and United Nations Emergency Force (UNEF), 126, 134, 135–36, 145; and Conservative party and Suez crisis, 129, 160–61; and public reaction to Suez crisis, 129–30; and Labour party reaction to Suez crisis, 130; and Soviet threats, 131; and cease-fire, 131–33; and withdrawal, 131–33, 145, 148–52; and clearance of Suez Canal, 166, 178–81; and end of cultural and economic influence in Egypt, 187–88; effect of Suez crisis on, 189–92, 193–94

British economy: and sterling balances, 7, 11, 40–41, 43; weakness of, 7–14, 52, 56, 78, 88–89, 100–103, 112–13, 131–33, 136–39, 143–52, 154, 155, 162, 181, 193–94; importance of Middle East oil to, 20–22, 32, 79–80, 87–89, 101, 127, 137–38, 142, 144–45, 181–83; and reserves of foreign currency, 52, 88, 101, 150, 152, 162; and refusal of U.S. financial support to, 120, 123–24, 127–28, 131–33, 134–52, 193–94; and U.S. support after Egyptian invasion, 148–52, 153–57, 181, 193–94. *See also* Anglo-American Loan Agreement of 1945

Bulganin, Nicolai, 44, 46, 131

Buraimi, 20

Burns, General E. L. M., 136, 176

Butler, R. A. (Baron Butler of Saffron Walden), 14, 52, 133, 142, 149, 150, 151, 161

Byroade, Henry, 40, 44, 59, 60, 62, 69–70, 80, 90

Caccia, Sir Harold (Lord Caccia), 137–38, 139, 155, 158, 159, 174, 183–85, 189

Caffery, Jefferson, 34

Canada: policy on Suez crisis, 89, 126, 129, 136, 147; and nationalization of Suez Canal, 91–92; and financial assistance to Britain, 147; and Israel, 167, 174

Central Intelligence Agency (CIA), 32, 37, 45, 108

Challe, Maurice, 117, 128–29

Churchill, Sir Winston, 9, 25, 34

Cobbold, C. F. (Lord Cobbold), 112, 113, 145–46, 150

Colonialism: anti-colonialism of U.S., 109, 125; invasion of Egypt seen as Anglo-French colonialism, 122, 125

Commonwealth: Britain and, 7, 13, 79, 89, 92, 113, 190, 191; divisions among countries over Suez crisis, 131, 174

Consortium, 40, 41, 42, 49, 50, 51, 52–53, 54

Convention of 1888 (Treaty of Constantinople), 81, 84, 85

Convertibility, 12, 13, 88–89, 101

Coulson, Sir John, 122, 124, 127

Czechoslovakia, arms deal with Egypt. *See* Soviet Union: arms deal with Egypt

Dayan, Moshe, 108, 118, 176

Dean, Arthur, 88, 166

Dean, Sir Patrick, 118

De Gaulle, Charles, 188

Dillon, C. Douglas, 77, 96, 109, 114, 149

Dixon, Sir Pierson, 100, 125, 169, 174

Dulles, Allen, 72, 78, 87, 127, 134

Dulles, John Foster, 27–29, 33, 35, 45, 46; and Aswan Dam, 2, 4, 49, 56, 67–72; and Eden, 29, 33, 39, 47, 56, 60–61, 85–86, 99, 109; and Israel, 31, 165, 168, 169–72, 173, 174, 175, 177, 178; and Baghdad Pact, 38–39; and Soviet arms deal with Egypt, 45–46, 47; and policy in Middle East, 45–46, 47, 61, 63–65, 66, 158; and Macmillan, 46, 85–86, 104–5, 156; and nationalization of Suez Canal, 81, 82, 83–86, 91–92, 100, 108–9, 111–12; and opposition to use of force against Egypt, 81, 82, 83–

84, 93–94, 114; and proposals for international control of Suez Canal, 83–85, 92, 97–100, 112, 178–81; and U.N., 84, 96, 121–26; and invasion of Egypt, 120–26, 139; and creation of UNEF, 126; and illness, 126, 139; and U.S. economic pressure on Britain and France, 127, 149, 151; and relations with Britain and France in aftermath, 156, 178–80, 183–85, 189

Eban, Abba, 30–31, 166, 169, 170, 174, 175, 188
Eden, Sir Anthony (Lord Avon), 4, 9, 47, 91, 131; and Eisenhower, 28, 54, 56, 60–61, 77, 82, 94, 96–97, 114, 123, 129, 133–35, 138, 142–43, 160–62; and Anglo-Egyptian Treaty (1954), 34–35; as foreign secretary, 34–35; and policy toward Egypt, 34–35, 45–46, 47–48, 62–63, 65; character and career, 34–35, 46, 62–63; and Aswan Dam, 45, 54, 56, 65; view of Nasser, 62–63, 65, 97; and nationalization of Suez Canal, 76–78, 79, 85–86, 93–94, 96–97, 98–99, 100; and invasion of Egypt, 123; policy after invasion of Egypt, 123, 128, 133–35, 139; illness and retirement of, 142–43, 160–61. See also Dulles, John Foster: and Eden
Egypt, 17, 90–91; and arms deal with Soviet Union, 1, 43–46; revolution of 1952, 24, 25, 36–38; and Aswan Dam, 38, 40–46, 48–57, 58–60, 65–72, 75; and opposition to Baghdad Pact, 38–39, 62, 63; and management of Suez Canal, 76, 90–91, 98–99, 178–81, 186; and U.N., 100, 111–12, 114–15, 126, 129, 134, 135–36, 143, 167, 170, 176, 177–81; and reaction to invasion, 127–28, 134, 187; and clearance of Suez Canal, 166, 178–81; and return to Gaza, 177–78; and leadership in Arab world, 187–88; and effect of Suez crisis on, 187–88, 192. See also Anglo-Egyptian Treaty (1936); Anglo-Egyptian Treaty (1954)

Egypt Committee of British Cabinet, 79, 130, 135
Egyptian economy: and Aswan Dam, 41–42, 43, 44–45, 58–59, 60, 71–72; and Soviet aid, 43–45, 75; and British measures against, 66, 78, 89, 113, 179, 186–87, 192; and American measures against, 80–81, 89–90, 113, 179, 184–85, 186–87, 192; sequestration of British, French, and Jewish assets, 178, 187–88; normalization of relations with West, 187–88. See also Soviet Union: arms deal with Egypt
Eighteen Power Proposal for international operation of Suez Canal, 92
Eisenhower, Dwight D., 2, 12, 25–27, 65, 68; and Britain, 25–26, 49, 61–62, 183–85; and appointment of John Foster Dulles, 28–29; and appointment of Humphrey, 29; and policy toward Israel, 30–31, 124, 163, 165, 168, 169–71, 172–73, 174, 176; and proposals for Egyptian-Israeli mediation, 39–40, 63–64; and policy of containing Soviet influence in the Middle East, 43–46, 48–51, 54–57, 60, 69–72, 120, 121–22, 126–28, 133–34, 157, 158, 159, 160, 177; and Aswan Dam, 54–55, 56–57, 64–65, 68; and Egypt, 63–65, 108, 110–11, 183–85; and nationalization of Suez Canal, 78–79, 82–83; and presidential election, 82–83, 120–21, 133; and opposition to use of force, 93–94, 97, 110–11; meets with Macmillan, 103–4, 162, 183–85; meets with Mollet, 114, 135, 175–76; and Hungarian crisis, 120, 126; and reaction to Anglo-French-Israeli invasion of Egypt, 120–26, 133–35, 137–38, 143, 144, 145, 151; and U.N., 121–26, 137–38; and policy toward Middle East after invasion, 157, 158, 159, 160; and resignation of Eden as prime minister and appointment of Macmillan, 161–62; and policy on Israeli withdrawal, 163, 165, 168, 169–71, 172–76. See also Eden, Sir Anthony: and Eisenhower

Eisenhower Doctrine, 157, 158, 159, 160, 168, 177
Ellis Rees, Sir Hugh, 141, 144, 181
Elson, Edward, 172
Export-Import Bank (EXIM): and loan to Britain, 102–3, 136, 137, 139, 148, 154, 156, 162, 181

Farouk, King, 24, 36, 37, 75
Fawzi, Mohammed, 40
Federal Reserve Bank of New York, 80, 146
Flemming, Arthur, 87, 99, 102, 124, 141, 182
Foreign Office: and Suez invasion, 119, 129
Foster, Andrew, 76–77
Four Power Proposal for international operation of Suez Canal, 180–81
France, 15–16; and Algerian war, 77–78; and decision to overthrow Nasser, 77–78, 81, 117; and economic sanctions against Egypt, 81; and arms sales to Israel, 91, 108, 118, 163–64, 176; and collusion with Britain and Israel, 112–13, 117–19, 120, 130; and economic position of, 113–14, 192–93; and U.S. economic pressure on, 113–14, 192–93; and invasion of Egypt, 117–19, 130; and ultimatum to Egypt and Israel, 118, 123; accepts U.N. cease-fire, 133; and withdrawal of troops from Egypt, 137–38, 145, 151–52; and Israeli evacuation, 175–76; and end of cultural and economic influence in Egypt, 187–88; effect of Suez crisis on, 188, 192–93. See also Egyptian economy: sequestration of British, French, and Jewish assets

Gaza raid, 44
Glubb, Sir John (Glubb Pasha), 62
Great Britain. See Britain

Hammarskjöld, Dag, 84, 112, 129, 145, 151, 165, 166, 167, 174, 177, 178, 180

Harcourt, Lord, 30, 50, 51, 53, 57, 140, 143, 148, 150, 154, 155
Hare, Raymond, 37, 127–28, 134, 157, 177
Heikal, Mohammed, 75, 111
Hollister, John, 55
Hoover, Herbert, Jr., 29, 50–51, 52, 55, 56–57, 65, 78, 80, 81, 111, 123, 142–43, 145, 148, 149
Humphrey, George, 29, 30, 50, 51, 52, 55, 104–5, 143, 147, 148, 150, 151, 153, 154–55, 156, 170, 171
Hungary: and 1956 uprising, 115, 126
Hussein, Ahmed, 68–69, 70–72, 99, 111
Hussein I (king of Jordan), 62, 108

India, 89, 129
International Bank for Reconstruction and Development (IBRD or World Bank), 42–43, 50, 58–60, 111, 179
International Cooperation Administration (ICA), 55, 90, 113
International Monetary Fund (IMF), 3, 52, 100, 101, 102, 113–14, 136, 137, 140, 141, 148, 154, 155, 156, 162
Iran, 132; and British oil interests in, 20–22; and Anglo-American coup, 31–33; and oil settlement, 33
Iraq: and Britain, 18, 76; and Baghdad Pact, 38–39
Israel, 85, 114–15; and withdrawal of forces from Egypt, 3, 164, 175–77; and Soviet Union, 16–17, 165, 166, 177; and Arab states, 17–18; and U.S. position on, 17–18, 30–31, 165, 168–69, 170, 174–75, 177–80; and Britain, 17–18, 118–19, 164–65; and Baghdad Pact, 38; and Project Alpha, 39–40; and Soviet arms deal with Egypt, 45; and Suez Canal, 85, 180; and France, 91, 108, 117–19, 163–64, 176; and Jordan, 114–15; and invasion of Egypt, 119, 120, 164–65, 166, 167, 168; economic pressure on, 124, 163, 166–67, 170–72, 176–77, 193; accepts U.N. cease-fire, 130; and U.N., 164–65, 167–68, 170–76; position in Middle East after Suez crisis, 188; effect of

Suez crisis on, 188, 193. *See also* Britain: and collusion with France and Israel; France: and arms sales to Israel

Johnson, Lyndon Baines, 168, 172
Johnston Plan, 32
Jordan, 114–15; and Baghdad Pact, 62; and Britain, 62, 115, 123

Kaisouni, Abdul, 53, 57, 59, 60, 79
Keynes, John Maynard (Lord Keynes), 7, 8, 9
Khrushchev, Nikita, 44, 45
Kirkpatrick, Sir Ivone, 4, 50, 98, 129
Knowland, William, 70, 120, 168, 172, 178

Lloyd, Selwyn, 60, 63, 81, 114, 124, 139, 140, 149, 151, 156, 169
Lodge, Henry Cabot, Jr., 30, 96, 111, 124–26, 145, 157, 167, 168, 173, 176
Logan, Donald, 118
London Conference of Maritime Powers: first (Aug. 16–23, 1956), 83–85, 92; second (Sept. 19–22, 1956), 100

McCloy, John J., 90, 111, 179
Macmillan, Harold, 45, 48, 61, 86–87, 194; and Aswan Dam, 48–49; and nationalization of Suez Canal, 85–86, 92, 103–8; and economic measures made necessary by crisis, 100–108, 128, 131–33, 137, 138–39, 144–45, 147, 149, 150–52; and Humphrey, 104–5, 156; policy after Suez invasion, 127, 128, 131–33, 138, 140, 142, 147, 148, 149, 151, 152, 156–57; replaces Eden, 160–62; policy as prime minister, 174, 181, 183–85, 189. *See also* Dulles, John Foster: and Macmillan; Eisenhower, Dwight D.: meets with Macmillan
Makins, Sir Roger (Lord Sherfield): as ambassador to the U.S., 30, 94; and Aswan Dam, 48–49, 50, 53–57, 70–71; and nationalization of Suez Canal, 80, 83, 94; and departure from the U.S., 110; as joint permanent undersecretary of the treasury, 140, 145–46, 148, 150, 155
Marshall Plan, 11
Meir, Golda, 4, 166, 176, 188
Menzies, Sir Robert, 85, 91, 92, 95
Middle East Defense Organization, 18, 23
Middle East Emergency Committee (MEEC), 87–88, 102, 123, 127, 141, 149, 181
Mollet, Guy: view of Nasser, 77–78; and collusion, 114, 117–19; and Britain, 131, 133. *See also* Eisenhower, Dwight D.: meets with Mollet
Mountbatten, Louis (Earl Mountbatten of Burma), 129
Murphy, Sir Robert, 79, 81, 106, 145
Mussadiq, Muhammed, 21, 32

Nasser, Gamal Abdel, 1, 2, 24, 87–88; personality and views, 36–38; and Britain, 37–38, 43–44, 46, 50–57, 59, 62, 63, 65–72, 75–76, 78, 79, 85–86, 91, 96–97, 98–99, 111, 138, 166, 177–81, 183, 186–88; opposition to Baghdad Pact, 38–39, 62, 158; and Israel, 39–40, 44, 64; and U.S., 39–40, 44–45, 46, 50–57, 59, 61, 63, 65–72, 75–76, 78–79, 83, 90, 93–94, 103, 110–11, 113, 166, 177–78, 184–85, 187; and Project Alpha, 40, 44–45; and Soviet arms deal, 44–45; and Soviet Union, 44–45, 75, 127–28; and Aswan Dam, 58, 60, 69, 75; and nationalization of Suez Canal, 75–76; and management of Suez Canal, 75–76, 90–91, 92, 95–96, 98, 99–100, 111, 112, 178–81, 186–87; and Menzies mission, 92, 95–96; and invasion of Egypt, 127–28; and U.N., 130, 145, 177–81; and clearance of Suez Canal, 166; as leading figure in Arab world, 187–88
Neguib, Muhammed, 25, 37
Nicholls, Sir John, 164
Nixon, Richard, 125, 156

Nuri Pasha. *See* Said, Nuri al-
Nutting, Anthony, 129, 161

Oil: and U.S., 18–20, 31–33, 86–88, 102, 123, 127, 141, 149, 181; supply of Middle East oil cut off during Suez crisis, 83, 141, 144–45, 181–83; sterling losses through stoppage of Middle East oil, 88, 101–3, 145–46; U.S. refusal of oil to Britain and France, 124, 127, 130–31, 137, 141–42, 143–52. *See also* British economy: importance of Middle East oil to
Operation Musketeer, 5, 117–19, 123, 129
Organization of European Economic Cooperation (OEEC), 141, 142, 144, 181

Pakistan: and Baghdad Pact, 38
Palestine: British policy in, 10, 16–18; U.S. policy in, 16–18; as unresolved issue, 17–18
Palestinian refugee problem, 39–40, 43–45, 63–64, 158
Parliament: and Anglo-Egyptian settlement, 32, 63; and Suez crisis, 130
Pearson, Lester (Mike), 126, 167
Pineau, Christian, 77, 81, 118, 128–29, 156, 175–76
Project Alpha. *See* Alpha, Project

Roosevelt, Kermit (Kim), 37, 45
Rountree, William, 76, 87, 119
Rowan, Sir (Thomas) Leslie, 56, 102–3, 140, 156

Sadat, Anwar, 29
Sadat, Jehan, 24, 37–38
Said, Nuri al- (Nuri Pasha), 76
Saudi Arabia: and U.S., 19–20, 132, 137, 168; and Suez crisis, 132, 137, 168
Schuckburgh, Sir Evelyn, 45, 66, 74–75
Sèvres: Anglo-French-Israeli meeting at, 112–13, 118–19; protocol, 118–19
Sinai peninsula: Israeli attack on, 119; Israeli evacuation of, 176–77
Smith, H. Alexander, 168, 173

Smith, Walter Bedell, 140
Soviet Union: arms deal with Egypt, 44–46; and Aswan Dam, 75; and nationalization of Suez Canal, 84–85; and Hungary, 115; and U.N., 126, 134; and invasion of Egypt, 128, 138; and threats to Britain and France, 131; and Middle East, 134, 158. *See also* Israel: and Soviet Union; Nasser, Gamal Abdel: and Soviet Union
Sterling, position of. *See* British economy
Sterling area, 3, 7, 13, 14, 89, 136, 193–94
Suez Canal, 23; zone, 23, 33–35, 68; importance to Britain of, 73–75, 79–80, 178–81; Egyptian nationalization of, 75, 90–91; Egyptian management of, 76, 90, 98–99, 178–82, 186–87; proposals for international control of, 83–85, 92, 97–100, 110–11, 112, 178–81; Israeli rights of passage through, 85, 180; and U.N., 100, 111–12, 114–15, 178–81; Six Principles to govern settlement of Canal nationalization, 111–12, 114–15, 179, 180; blocking of, 128, 130; clearance of, 166, 178–81, 186; effect of Suez crisis on, 191–92
Suez Canal base, 23, 33–35, 47, 68, 118
Suez Canal base accord. *See* Anglo-Egyptian Treaty (1954)
Suez Canal Company, 23–24, 73–76, 99, 186; pilots, 99; settlement of claims by, 186
Suez Canal Users' Association (SCUA), 97–100, 112, 180
"Suez Group" in British parliament, 35, 46, 62, 85
Syria: Anglo-French policy toward, 15–16

Thorneycroft, Peter (Lord Thorneycroft), 53
Trevelyan, Sir Humphrey, 54, 59, 65, 66
Tripartite Declaration (1950), 17, 119, 120
Truman, Harry S., 7, 8, 16
Turkey: and Baghdad Pact, 38

United Nations: and U.S., 84, 100, 126, 129, 134, 135–36, 143, 163–72, 177–81; and Six Principles, 111–12, 114–15, 179, 180; resolutions after invasion of Egypt, 121, 124–27, 129, 134, 145, 149, 151; resolutions concerning Israeli withdrawal, 166, 167–68, 169, 170–78; and clearance of Canal, 178–81. *See also* Egypt: and U.N.; Israel: and U.N.

United Nations Emergency Force (UNEF), 126, 129, 135–36, 143, 163, 167, 170, 176

United States: and Aswan Dam, 2, 4, 56–57, 58–61, 65–72; postwar financial position of, 6–14; and Baghdad Pact, 38–39, 158; and attempts to mediate Arab-Israeli conflict, 39–40, 43–45, 63–64, 158; and Project Alpha, 39–40, 44–45; and nationalization of Suez Canal, 78–79, 82, 84, 93–94, 110–11; and public opinion on na-

tionalization, 82; and oil policy after Suez Canal nationalization, 87–88, 102, 123, 127, 141, 149, 157, 180–83; and collusion between Britain, France, and Israel, 119–26; and Hungarian uprising, 121–22; and Soviet threats to Britain and France, 131, 134, 138. *See also* British economy: refusal of U.S. financial support to; Egyptian economy: and American measures against; Israel: economic pressure on; Saudi Arabia: and U.S.; United Nations: and U.S.

U.S. Agreement. *See* Anglo-American Loan Agreement of 1945

Watson, Adam, 74–75

World Bank. *See* International Bank for Reconstruction and Development

Zionism, 16–17, 30–31